SIMPSON

IMPRINT IN HUMANITIES

The humanities endowment
by Sharon Hanley Simpson and
Barclay Simpson honors
MURIEL CARTER HANLEY
whose intellect and sensitivity
have enriched the many lives
that she has touched.

The publisher and the University of California Press Foundation gratefully acknowledge the generous support of the Simpson Imprint in Humanities.

HUMANITARIANISM AND MASS MIGRATION

HUMANITARIANISM AND MASS MIGRATION

Confronting the World Crisis

Edited by

Marcelo M. Suárez-Orozco

UNIVERSITY OF CALIFORNIA PRESS

ROSS INSTITUTE

University of California Press, one of the most distinguished university presses in the United States, enriches lives around the world by advancing scholarship in the humanities, social sciences, and natural sciences. Its activities are supported by the UC Press Foundation and by philanthropic contributions from individuals and institutions. For more information, visit www.ucpress.edu.

University of California Press
Oakland, California

Library of Congress Cataloging-in-Publication Data

Names: Suárez-Orozco, Marcelo M., 1956– editor.
Title: Humanitarianism and mass migration : confronting the world
   crisis / edited by Marcelo M. Suárez-Orozco.
Description: Oakland, California : University of California Press, [2019] |
   Includes bibliographical references and index. |
Identifiers: LCCN 2018033187 (print) | LCCN 2018038138 (ebook) |
   ISBN 9780520969629 (Ebook) | ISBN 9780520297128 (cloth : alk. paper) |
   ISBN 9780520297142 (pbk. : alk. paper)
Subjects: LCSH: Emigration and immigration—History—21st century. |
   Humanitarianism.
Classification: LCC JV6033 (ebook) | LCC JV6033 .H86 2019 (print) |
   DDC 362.89/91252—dc23
LC record available at https://lccn.loc.gov/2018033187

Manufactured in the United States of America

26   25   24   23   22   21   20   19
10   9   8   7   6   5   4   3   2   1

CONTENTS

ILLUSTRATIONS

FIGURES

TABLES

ACKNOWLEDGMENTS

Migration is a shared condition of humanity. Global migratory corridors are connecting, shaping, and re-shaping distant and afar nations the world over. Since the dawn of the millennium we have been witnessing a rise in the numbers of a plurality of types of migrants—voluntary and involuntary, internal and international, authorized and unauthorized, environmental refugees and victims of human trafficking. Today the lives over a billion people are shaped by migration—both the migrants themselves and family members left behind. The movement of human beings has intensified under the ascendancy of climate change, rachitic and collapsing states, war, terror, uncontrolled criminality, and growing global inequality.

While immigration is a normal condition of humanity, it has taken a decidedly dystopic turn. At a time when approximately 20 human beings are forcibly displaced every minute (see www.unhcr.org/en-us/figures-at-a-glance.html), catastrophic migrations pose new risks to millions of migrants and test the institutions of sending, transit, and receiving nations alike.

Concurrently, the xenophobic, nativist viper rears its head seemingly everywhere as immigrants and refugees arrive seeking to make a better life.

This volume originates in the humanist ideal to find oneself "in Another,"[1] in the refugee, in the asylum seeker, in the forcefully displaced, in the Other. I am grateful to Bishop Marcelo Sanchez Sorondo, theologian, philosopher, and Chancellor of the Pontifical Academy of Sciences and the Pontifical Academy of Social Sciences, the Holy See, for instigating our collective work. Acting on the Holy Father Pope Francis's call, Bishop Sorondo gathered a group of international scholars, policy makers, and leaders of global NGOs in the Casina Pio IV at Vatican City in early November 2013 to focus on the horrors of modern slavery and global trafficking in human beings. That work suggested an urgent need to draw the emerging cartography of the new catastrophic migrations of our times and to endeavor to confront the world crisis.

With the generous support of Courtney Sale Ross, education visionary, philanthropist, and founder of the Ross Institute, the W. T. Grant Foundation, the Spencer Foundation, the Wasserman Foundation, and others, we invited leading interdisciplinary researchers, practitioners, and religious leaders to the Luskin Conference Center of the University of California, Los Angeles in January 2017. The original papers presented at the gathering formed the seeds of this book. We are grateful to UCLA Chancellor Gene Block and UCLA Executive Vice Chancellor and Provost Scott Waugh for kindly supporting this work. The following scholars acted as incisive discussants and panel chairs of the various papers presented at the Workshop: Leisy Abrego (UCLA), Craig Calhoun (president, Berggruen Institute, former president, London School of Economics), Patricia Gándara (UCLA), José H. Gomez (Archbishop of Los Angeles), Hiroshi Motomura (UCLA), Marjorie Orellana (UCLA), Hilary Pennington (Ford Foundation), and Roger Waldinger (UCLA). Dr. Jody Hymann (dean, Fielding School of Public Health, UCLA), Jeffrey Sachs (Columbia University), Gonzalo Sánchez-Terán (Fordham University), and Maryanne Wolf (Tufts University, Stanford's Center for Advanced Study in the Behavioral Sciences, and UCLA), also joined us, and our work benefited from their thoughtful interventions during the UCLA Workshop.

Our work together at UCLA unfolded flawlessly due to the kind and rigorous efforts of Laura Lindberg, Leigh Leveen, Amy Lassere, and Leah Wilmore. Alfredo Novoa, PhD student at the UCLA Graduate School of Education and Information Studies, our graduate student research assistant for this project, worked with diligence on many phases of this project. We are happy to acknowledge our debt to Vici Casas for her meticulous editorial work on various iterations of the chapters in the book. Naomi Schneider, the inimitable executive editor of the University of California Press, went into swift action to turn the embryonic and somewhat inchoate ideas exchanged at the UCLA Workshop into a coherent volume. Carola Suárez-Orozco, my forever-*compañera,* generously shared her brilliance, discipline, and kindness during the entirety of the project—from our long walks in the Vatican Gardens, where it started, to the final version you now hold in your hands.

NOTES

1. Paul Ricoeur, *Oneself as Another* (Chicago: University of Chicago Press, 1995).

INTRODUCTION

Catastrophic Migrations

Marcelo M. Suárez-Orozco

Since the dawn of the new millennium, the world has been witnessing a rapid rise in the numbers of migrants in a wide array of categories—voluntary and involuntary, internal and international, authorized and unauthorized, and environmental—as well as victims of human trafficking.[1] All continents are involved in the massive movement of people as areas of immigration, emigration, or transit—and often as all three at once. Yet migration is as old as mankind. As a human adaptation,[2] migration is written in our genome and encoded in our bodies: in our bipedalism, in our stereoscopic vision, in our neocortex. Modern humans are the children of migrations.[3] Migrations are complex, multidetermined, and not easily reduced to deterministic algorithms. Migrations elude simple mechanistic models of causality because they unfold in complex ecologies involving demographic factors, economic variables, political processes, cultural models, social practices, historical relationships, the environment itself, and multiple combinations thereof (McLeman 2014; Forman and Ramanathan, chapter 1, this volume). In the twenty-first century, mass migration is the human face of globalization—the sounds, colors, and aromas of a miniaturized, interconnected, and ever-fragile world. Today "migration is a shared condition of all humanity" (Pontifical Academy of Sciences 2017, 1).

According to the United Nations, in 2017 there were approximately 258 million[4] international migrants—3.4 percent of the world's population (UN Department of Economic and Social Affairs 2017, Key Facts)—and upward of 760 million internal migrants (see Bell and Charles-Edwards 2013). Millions more were kith and kin left behind. The largest *international* corridors of human migration today are in Asia, Europe, and the Americas. The largest chains of *internal* migration occur in Asia: by 2015, China had an estimated 280 million internal migrant workers (*China Labor*

Bulletin 2017), and in India well over 320 million people—more than a quarter of the country's population—were internal migrants between 2007 and 2008 (UNICEF 2016). While in terms of sheer numbers more people are now on the move than ever before, the rate of international migration has remained stable over the last fifty years, with roughly 2.5 to 3.3 percent of the world's population living outside their country of birth.

In the aftermath of World War II, well-worn migration corridors came to connect historically linked countries of origin with specific destinations in new societies.[5] That is the story of Latin American migrations to the United States;[6] Mediterranean, African, and Middle Eastern migrations into Northern Europe; Ukrainian and Uzbek migrations to Russia; and Indian, Bangladeshi, and Filipino migrations into East Asia and the Middle East. As the number of international migrants increased, a new research agenda was drawn. It endeavored to define, measure, theorize, and interpret the myriad of push-and-pull factors behind mass migration—above all the labor markets, demographics, wage differentials, social networks, and cultural models structuring and giving momentum to human movement. In recent decades, researchers have come to depict in broad terms how labor migrations begat family reunification, which in turn begat the rise of the second generation now transforming Europe, North America, and Australia.[7]

While there are as many motivations and pathways for migration as there are migrant families, large-scale migration is not random. It is ignited and then gathers momentum along predictable corridors. At the proximate level, migration is a strategy of the household (Foner 2009; Massey and España 1987). Distinct patterns of kinship, household, and social organization carve the pathways for worldwide migratory journeys. The fundamental unit of migration is the family—variously defined and structured by distinct, culturally coded legislative, economic, reproductive, and symbolic forms. At the distal level, immigration is multiply determined by labor markets, wage differentials, demographic imbalances, technological change, and environmental factors. However, up close it is the family that makes migration work. Immigration typically starts with the family, and family bonds sustain it. Immigration profoundly changes families (Foner 2009; C. Suárez-Orozco and M. Suárez-Orozco 2012). "Love and work," Freud's eternal words on the well-lived life, are useful to think about migration as an adaptation both of and for the family.

But migration for "love and work" tells only part of the story. Historically, the clash of powerful nation-states has been the main driver of the sudden, involuntary, and massive displacement of populations. Two world wars, the wars of colonial liberation,[8] and the Cold War pushed millions to seek shelter in safer lands. During World War I, millions of Russians, Germans, Serbians, Armenians, Belgians, Poles, Latvians, Lithuanians, Ukrainians, Jews, and others were forced from their homes:

In August 1914 the Russian occupation of East Prussia caused around one million Germans to flee their homes. Before long, Germany's occupation of Belgium and northern France, Poland and Lithuania provoked a mass movement of refugees. Austria's invasion of Serbia resulted in a humanitarian catastrophe as soldiers and civilians sought to escape the occupation regime. In the Russian Empire, non-Russian minorities such as Poles, Latvians, Lithuanians, Ukrainians and Jews were disproportionately concentrated in the western borderlands and thus particularly vulnerable when Germany and Austria invaded. In addition, Tsarist military commanders accused these minorities—falsely—of aiding and abetting the enemy and deported them to the Russian interior.

In the Ottoman Empire, meanwhile, Turkish troops uprooted Armenians who had lived side by side with their Turkish and Kurdish neighbors for generations but who were now regarded as the enemy within. As Talat Pasha, a leading official, put it in a coded telegram in April 1915: "The objective that the government expects to achieve by the expelling of the Armenians from the areas in which they live and their transportation to other appointed areas is to ensure that this community will no longer be able to undertake initiatives and actions against the government, and that they will be brought to a state in which they will be unable to pursue their national aspirations related to advocating a government of Armenia." (Gatrell 2014a, 1)

By the war's end, perhaps more than ten million people had been displaced internally or internationally. The refugee crisis was deep and lasting. According to British historian Peter Gatrell, "during the First World War the refugee emerged as a liminal figure who threatened social stability partly by virtue of the sheer number of displaced persons, but also because the refugee was difficult to accommodate within conventional classification such as assigned people to a specific social class. Other kinds of disorder were also at stake. The crisis caught everyone by surprise and limited possibilities for political action that might contribute to further upheaval. The social upheaval did not end with the cessation of hostilities" (2014b, 2).

At the end of World War II, there were more than forty million refugees—then the largest number in recorded history. World War II had other significant indirect, long-term effects on migration's new cartography. The United States' entrance into the war led to the creation of a guest worker program to recruit temporary Mexican braceros to labor in US fields. For more than half a century, that temporary program led to the largest flow of immigrants into the United States in history (Massey et al. 1987). Likewise, the various temporary guest worker programs in Europe immediately following World War II ended up delivering permanent immigrant communities now visible in Berlin, Brussels, Rotterdam, and elsewhere.

Decolonization and the wars of national liberation generated their own routes of massive movement, sending Congolese to Belgium, Pied Noirs to France, and Indonesians to the Netherlands. The end of British India, the partition of the British Raj, and the subsequent independence of India and Pakistan (and then Bangladesh) resulted in the largest population exchange in recorded history. Approximately seven million Hindus and Sikhs from Bangladesh and Pakistan moved to India, and approximately seven million Muslims from India migrated to Pakistan.

The United States–Soviet Cold War and the proxy wars it engendered in Africa, the Americas, and Asia created massive displacements. In Angola (1975–2002), four million were displaced internally, and another half million fled as refugees. At the height of the Cold War, the best predictor of who would arrive as a refugee in the West was someone escaping a Communist regime: from 1975 until 1995 more than two million Southeast Asians fleeing Vietnam, Laos, and Cambodia were settled in the West, the majority in the United States but also some in the European Union, Canada, Australia, and New Zealand. Those fleeing the Soviet Union followed Southeast Asians as the second largest number of refugees arriving in the West, including more than a million in the United States and almost two million in Israel. Likewise, more than a million Cubans fleeing the Castro regime in various waves were favored refugees in the United States.[9] Least favored were the casualties of the proxy wars in Central America. Escaping barbaric but, alas, anticommunist regimes in Guatemala, Nicaragua, and El Salvador, millions of folks arrived in North America in search of refuge. Few became formal refugees, yet over time they came to give birth to the new "recombinant migrations" of the recent era (see Suro, chapter 2, this volume).

After holding for three quarters of a century, the map tracing the great global migration corridors of the post–World War II era has become increasingly blurred. Three disparate formations laid the foundations for an emerging new cartography. First, the dismemberment of the Soviet Union (early 1990s) and the end of the Cold War significantly impacted the acceleration of human migrations. Second, the worldwide economic crisis of 2008[10] and the antigovernment uprisings in North Africa and the Middle East beginning in 2010—the so-called "Arab spring"—signaled yet another turn. Third, President Trump's moves to make good on his campaign promises that elected him—rapidly stepping up deportations of unauthorized immigrants in the United States, building a two-thousand-mile wall along the Mexican border, halting Syrian and other refugees from entering the United States, and forcibly separating thousands of mostly Central American children from their parents at the Southern border—marked a brusque turning point in the global migration landscape. In the same vein, the concurrent rise of nativist, anti-immigrant movements in the European Union and elsewhere marks the beginning of an entirely new cartography of mass migration.

A NEW MAP

Migration is increasingly defined by the slow-motion disintegration of failing states with feeble institutions, war and terror, demographic imbalances, unchecked

	New displacements Jan.–Dec. 2016	Total number of IDPs as of the end of 2016
CONFLICT	6.9 million	40.3 million
DISASTERS	24.2 million	?

FIGURE I.1. Internal displacement by conflict and by disasters in 2016. *Source:* IDMC 2017.

climate change, and cataclysmic environmental disruptions.[11] Symbiotically, these forces are the drivers of what I will call the catastrophic migrations of the twenty-first century.[12]

Catastrophic migrations are placing millions of human beings at grave risk. In the first two decades of the twenty-first century, the world witnessed the largest number of forcibly displaced human beings in history: while precise numbers are both elusive and changing,[13] UN data report that more than sixty-five million people—the equivalent of every man, woman, and child in Lagos, Sao Paulo, Seoul, London, Lima, New York, and Guadalajara—are escaping home into the unknown (UNHCR 2016). The majority of those seeking shelter are internally displaced persons (IDPs), not formal refugees across international borders. In addition, approximately nine in ten international asylum seekers remain in a neighboring country—Asians stay in Asia, Africans in Africa, Americans in the Americas. While migration is a normal condition of humanity, it is increasingly catastrophic:[14] "The majority of new displacements in 2016 took place in environments characterized by a high exposure to natural and human-made hazards, high levels of socioeconomic vulnerability, and low coping capacity of both institutions and infrastructure" (IDMC 2017, 9). By the end of 2016, there were 31.1 million *new* internal displacements due to conflict and violence (6.9 million) and disasters (24.2 million) (see fig. I.1), "the equivalent of one person forced to flee every second" (IDMC 2017, 9).

Indeed, by then "there were 40.3 million people internally displaced by conflict and violence across the world. An unknown number remain displaced as a result of disasters that occurred in and prior to 2016" (IDMC 2017, 10). Internal displacement associated with war and terror continues to grow at a staggering pace: "The

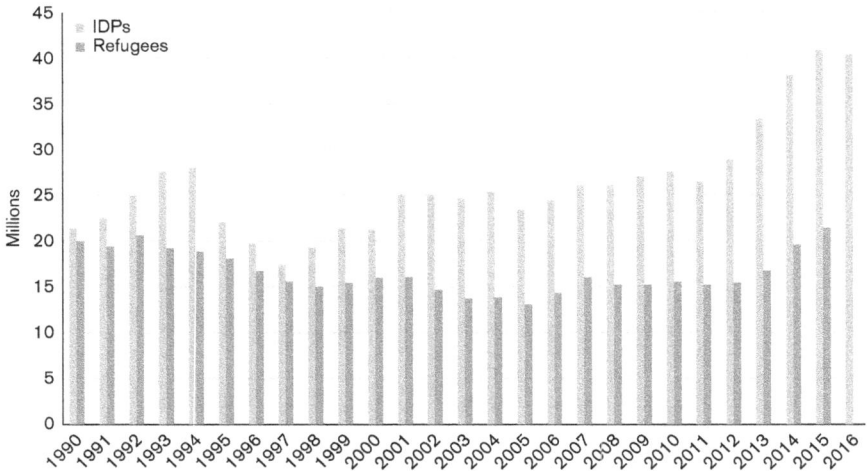

FIGURE I.2. Comparison of the number of internally displaced persons (IDPs) and refugees, 1990 to 2016. *Source:* IDMC 2017 for IDP data, UNHCR 2016 for refugee data (2016 figures not yet available).

number of new internal displacements associated with conflict and violence almost doubled, from 6.9 million in 2016 to 11.8 million in 2017. Syria, the Democratic Republic of the Congo (DRC) and Iraq accounted for more than half of the figure" (IDMC 2018, v). The number of persons internally displaced by war and terror (see fig. I.2) is more than double the number of refugees—today there are 22.5 million refugees under UNHCR terms in the world (UNHCR 2017c, 1).

Environmental Dystopia

Forman and Ramanathan (chapter 1, this volume) argue that unchecked climate change and geophysical hazards increase morbidity and mortality, disrupt production, decrease agricultural yields, decimate livestock, and forcibly displace millions the world over (see also McLeman 2014). In 2017, extreme weather patterns and weather-related hazards—floods and high-intensity cyclones, rising sea levels, but also droughts, hurricanes, heat waves, and forest fires—displaced 18.8 million people in 135 countries. "Of these," the Internal Displacement Monitoring Centre reports, "8.6 million displacements were triggered by floods, and 7.5 million by storms, especially tropical cyclones. The worst-affected countries were China with 4.5 million, the Philippines with 2.5 million, Cuba and the US each with 1.7 million, and India with 1.3 million displacements. In 2017, cyclones displaced millions of people around the world, including Mora which struck Bangladesh in May and hurricane Irma that wreaked havoc in the Atlantic in August" (IDMC 2018, v).

From 2008 to 2016, the IDMC reported 203.4 million displacements, an annual average of 25.4 million (IDMC 2016, 8). By 2017, the majority of new displacements had occurred in "low- and lower-middle-income countries and as a result of large-scale weather events, and predominantly in South and East Asia. While China, the Philippines and India have the highest absolute numbers, small island states suffer disproportionally once population size is taken into account. Slow-onset disasters, existing vulnerabilities and conflict also continue to converge into explosive tipping points for displacement" (IDMC 2017, 10).

Documented displacements due to environmental and weather-related factors took place in 135 countries across all regions of the world. Floods, storms, cyclones, monsoons, hurricanes, earthquakes, volcanic eruptions, wildfires, landslides, and extreme temperatures displaced millions of people in 2017 (see Ramanathan and Forman, chapter 1, this volume). The data over the last couple of years reveal an alarming trend. In 2015, India,[15] China,[16] and Nepal[17] accounted for the largest numbers of people displaced, "with totals of 3.7 million, 3.6 million, and 2.6 million respectively" (IDMC 2016, 15). The Philippines experienced three massive storms, which together displaced two million people.[18] In Myanmar, Cyclone Komen "displaced more than 1.6 million people . . . the fifth highest figure worldwide in absolute terms. . . . Twelve of the country's fourteen states and regions suffered widespread destruction" (15). By 2016, weather-related hazards triggered 24.2 million new displacements . . . [and] 4.5 million displacements were brought on by large-scale geophysical hazards. . . . Over the past eight years, 203.4 million displacements have been recorded, an average of 25.4 million each year" (IDMC 2016, 8—see also Forman and Ramanathan, chapter 1, this volume; McLeman 2014).

Beyond Asia, in 2017, millions were displaced in the Caribbean and in North and Central America by environmental factors.[19] Indeed, the UNHCR predicted that climate change would perhaps become the biggest driver of population displacements, both inside and across national borders. Though there is general consensus that quantitative estimates are presently unreliable, Forman and Ramanathan (chapter 1, this volume) make a plea for an ethical global policy response to the world's emerging climate migration crisis. They argue that we simply cannot await reliable metrics. International cooperation on climate mitigation is more urgent than ever as the United States under President Trump's leadership is moving toward an ever more retrograde agenda on climate issues. Establishing international protocols that outline the rights of climate refugees and the responsibilities of industrialized nations toward them cannot wait.

Jeffrey Sachs (2017) argues that in addition to the physical environment, demography itself is a main driver of today's mass migrations. Africa and the Middle East are a case in point. In the 1950s, Europe had twice the combined populations of the Middle East and all of Africa. So migration to Europe was not a *problématique* of significance—with labor shortages and the need to rebuild after the war, immigration was a solution, not a problem. In an epic reversal, the Middle East and Africa now have twice the population of Europe. Europe now has about 740 million people. The Middle East and Africa combined have about 1.4 billion people. Furthermore, according to UN forecasts, Europe's population will be level because of aging and low fertility rates, whereas the population of the Middle East and Africa combined is on its way to 4 billion people by 2100 (Sachs 2017, 5).[20]

War and Terror

War and terror are pushing millions of human beings from home. Millions of people linger in perpetual limbo in camps far away from the wealthy cities of Asia, Europe, North America, and Australia. The world is experiencing what Sánchez Terán (2017) calls the "forced confinement crisis" of the twenty-first century. Millions have been internally displaced, millions are awaiting asylum, and millions more are living in the shadow of the law as irregular or unauthorized immigrants. The United States, the country with the largest number of immigrants in the world, has an estimated 11.3 million undocumented immigrants and some five million children with at least one undocumented immigrant parent.[21]

In the aftermath of antigovernment uprisings beginning in 2010, the Middle East and North Africa had the largest number of war-and-terror-displaced human beings. Yet by the end of 2016, sub-Saharan Africa led the way with the Democratic Republic of the Congo (DRC) having the greatest number of "new displacements by conflict and violence" (IDMC 2017, 13). Ongoing conflict "in North and South Kivu and an increase in intercommunal clashes in southern and central regions such as Tanganyika, Kasai, Kasai-Oriental, Ituri and Uele caused more than 922,000 new displacements in total during the year. Some people were forced to flee more than once" (13). In Iraq, almost 680,000 new displacements occurred as a result of nine military campaigns. In Yemen, at least 478,000 new displacements took place against the backdrop of a persistently dynamic and volatile security situation (10).

In Syria an estimated 12 million people have fled their homes since 2011 (UNHCR 2017c, 3). In 2017 more than 2.9 million new displacements were recorded in Syria—by far the highest figure in the world (IDMC 2018, 24). By then, more than half of the Syrian population had lived in displacement, either across borders or within their own country. "Now, in the sixth year of war, 13.5 million are in need of humanitarian assistance within the country. Among those escaping the conflict, the majority has sought refuge in neighboring countries or within Syria itself. According to the United Nations High Commissioner for Refugees, 4.8 million have fled to Turkey, Lebanon, Jordan, Egypt, and Iraq, and 6.6 million are internally displaced within Syria. Meanwhile, about one million have requested asylum in Europe. Germany, with more than 300,000 accumulated applications, and Sweden with 100,000 are the EU's top receiving countries" (UNHCR 2017c, 1).

Syrian Arab
Republic ████████████████████████████ 6.6

Iraq ███████████ 3.3

Yemen ███████ 2.5

Pakistan ███ 1.5

Afghanistan ██ 1.2

Turkey █ 1.0

Myanmar █ 0.6

India █ 0.6

Azerbaijan █ 0.6

Bangladesh █ 0.4

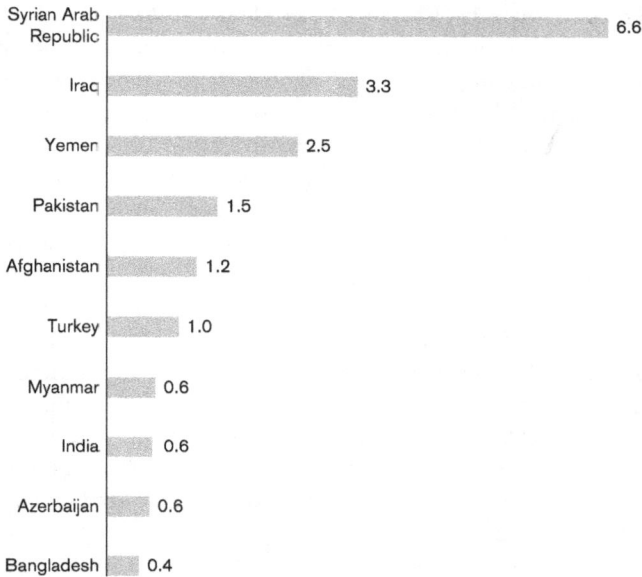

FIGURE I.3. Conflict-related internally displaced persons in Asia by country, 2015 (in millions). More than 19 million people have been internally displaced by conflict in Asia. Source: IDMC 2016.

In 2017, just three countries—Syria,[22] Iraq, and Yemen—accounted for more than half of all internally displaced persons.[23] Likewise, in 2017, more than half of all international refugees under UNHCR mandate originated in four states: Syria (approximately 5.5 million), Afghanistan (2.5 million), South Sudan (1.4 million), and Somalia (900,000).[24] The conflicts in these countries are disparate and incommensurable in nature. Yet they share a chronic, protracted quality. Syria's descent into a Dantesque inferno has been seven years in the making, and there is no end in sight; the Afghanistan conflict has gone on for twice as long. In Somalia, "more than two million Somalis are currently displaced by a conflict that has lasted over two decades. An estimated 1.5 million people are internally displaced in Somalia and nearly 900,000 are refugees in the near region, including some 308,700 in Kenya, 255,600 in Yemen and 246,700 in Ethiopia" (UNHCR 2017b, 7). These conflicts have endured longer than World War I and World War II combined. In each case, environmental dystopia and extreme weather patterns antecede and accentuate the catastrophic movement of people.

Syria continues to represent "the world's largest refugee crisis" (Dunmore 2017, and see fig. I.3). While Syrians are escaping interminable war and terror, in its collapse, Syria also embodies the noxious synergies among the environment, war and terror, and mass human displacement. According to NASA data, Syria's current drought is "the driest on record." NASA scientists found that by "estimating uncertainties using a resampling approach [they could] conclude that there is an 89 percent likelihood that this drought is drier than any comparable period of the last 900 years and a 98 percent likelihood that it is drier than the last 500 years" (Cook et al. 2016, 1). According to UN data, the drought caused "75 percent of Syria's farms to fail and 85 percent of livestock to die between 2006 and 2011. The collapse in crop yields forced as many as 1.5 million Syrians to migrate to urban centers like Homs and Damascus" (Stokes 2016, 2).[25]

The great exodus of the Rohingya from Myanmar into Bangladesh in 2017 gained unprecedented kinetic movement when two-thirds of all Rohingya Muslims, approximately 650,000 human beings, were forcibly displaced in the process of escaping terror at the hands of Myanmar soldiers. "Even in the chaos, it was clear the soldiers were bent on inflicting the most horror and fear possible, boasting that the Rohingya would never see their land again. Hillsides were wrecked; livestock was killed; and entire villages were systematically razed" (*New York Times* 2017).

Long-term conflicts, unchecked climate change, extreme weather patterns, and environmental degradation in Africa are generating massive forced migrations. "Four countries in Africa—Nigeria, the Democratic Republic of the Congo, the Central African Republic, and South Sudan—were among the top ten globally for new violence-induced internal displacements in 2015. . . . In total, more than 12 million people have been internally displaced by conflict and violence within Africa—more than twice the number of African refugees" (UNICEF 2016, 58).

In South Sudan, "some 1.9 million people [have been] displaced internally, while outside the country there are now 1.6 million South Sudanese refugees [who have been] uprooted, mainly in Ethiopia, Sudan, and Uganda" (UNHCR 2017a, 7). Again, the environment looms large: "Drought and environmental degradation, and a food crisis that became a famine because of government neglect and changing regional demographics" were behind the collapse in the Sudan (IDMC 2016, 4). According to the UN, "a famine produced by the vicious combination of fighting and drought is now driving the world's fastest growing refugee crisis. . . . The rate of new displacement is alarming, representing an impossible burden on a region that is significantly poorer [than other African regions] and which is fast running short of resources to cope. Refugees from South Sudan are crossing the borders to the neighboring countries. The majority of them go to Uganda where new arrivals spiked from 2,000 per day to 6,000 per day in February [2017], and currently average more than 2,800 people per day" (UNHCR News Centre 2017a, 8). The UN World Food Program estimates that by 2017, 4.9 million people (40 percent of South Sudan's population) were facing famine (UNHCR News Centre 2017b, 1).

Sudan	3.2
Nigeria	2.1
South Sudan	1.7
Democratic Republic of the Congo	1.5
Somalia	1.2
Libya	0.5
Central African Republic	0.5
Ethiopia	0.5
Kenya	0.3
Côte d'Ivoire	0.3

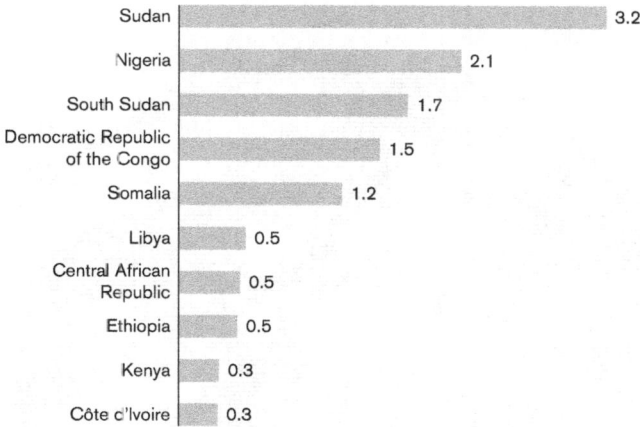

FIGURE I.4. Conflict-related internally displaced persons in Africa by country, 2015 (in millions). There are more than 12 million internally displaced persons in Africa. Source: IDMC 2016, 11.

Famine lurks as a macabre specter:

In all, more than 20 million people in Nigeria, South Sudan, Somalia and Yemen are experiencing famine or are at risk. The regions in which these countries sit, including the Lake Chad basin, Great Lakes, East, Horn of Africa and Yemen together host well over 4 million refugees and asylum seekers. Consecutive harvests have failed, conflict in South Sudan coupled with drought is leading to famine and outflows of refugees, insecurity in Somalia is leading to rising internal displacement, and rates of malnutrition are high, especially among children and lactating mothers. In the Dollo Ado area of southeast Ethiopia for example, acute malnutrition rates among newly arriving Somali refugee children aged between six months and five years are now running at 50–79 percent. (UNHCR News Centre 2017b, 1)

By large margins, African refugees stay on the continent: "Some 86 percent . . . find asylum in other African countries. Five of the largest refugee populations in the world are hosted in Africa, led by Ethiopia, Kenya, and Uganda. . . . The protracted nature of crises in sending countries means that some of these host countries have shouldered responsibilities for more than two decades [see fig. I.4]. Multiple generations of displaced children have been born in some of the longest standing camps" (UNICEF 2016; see also Dryden-Peterson, chapter 10, this volume).

Only small numbers of refugees make it to the high- and middle-income countries (see fig. I.5). Europe is a case in point. By the end of 2015, Europe had approximately one in nine of all refugees under UNHCR's mandate, a total of 1.8 million people.[26] Of these, most were "divided in nearly equal measure among Germany,

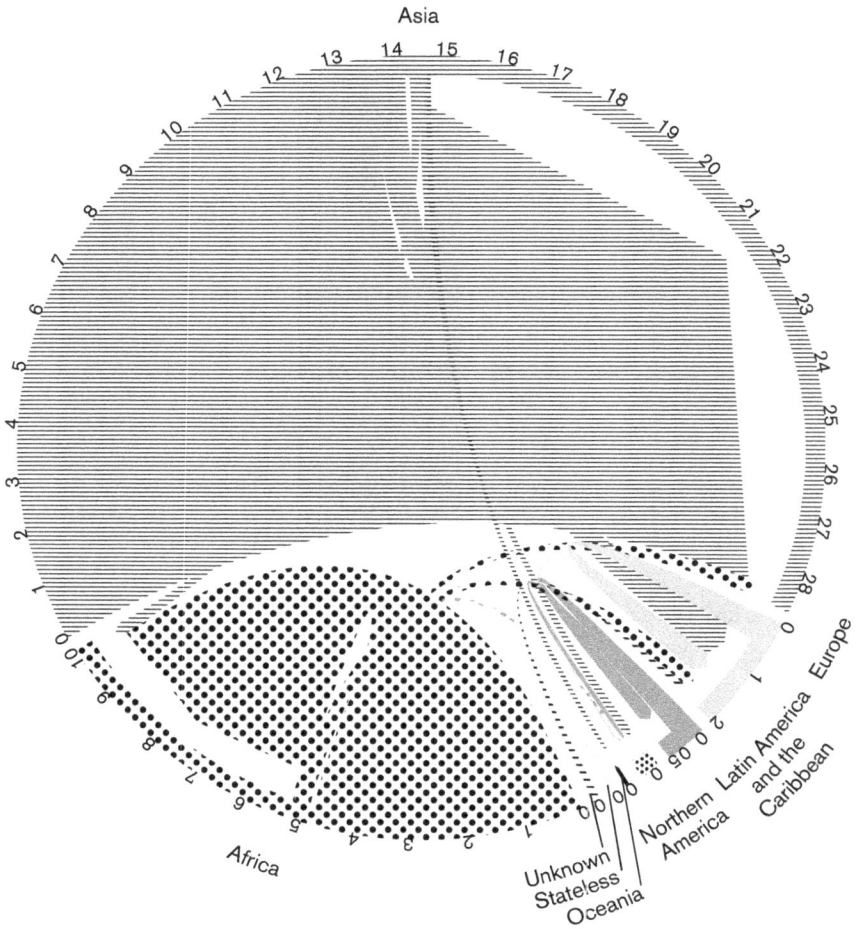

FIGURE I.5. Number of refugees by region of origin and destination, 2015 (in millions). Nine out of ten refugees across the world find asylum within their region of origin.

the Russian Federation and France (17, 17 and 15 percent of refugees in Europe, respectively). In 2015, more than one-third of the refugees living in Germany were from the Syrian Arab Republic, with smaller proportions from Iraq and Afghanistan (38, 17 and 10 percent, respectively). Nearly all of the 315,000 refugees hosted in the Russian Federation by the end of 2015 were from Ukraine. By the end of 2015, Germany had become the world's largest recipient of new individual applications for asylum—receiving more than twice as many as the next closest country" (UNICEF 2016, 92).

In the Americas, a new migration map is also taking form. First, by 2015, Mexican migration to the United States, the largest flow of international migration in U.S. history, was at its lowest in over a quarter of a century. Second, for the first time in recent history, more Mexicans were returning (voluntarily and involuntarily) to their country than were migrating to the United States. According to data analyzed by the Pew Hispanic Center,

> more Mexican immigrants have returned to Mexico from the U.S. than have migrated here since the end of the Great Recession. . . . The same data sources also show the overall flow of Mexican immigrants between the two countries is at its smallest since the 1990s, mostly due to a drop in the number of Mexican immigrants coming to the U.S.
>
> From 2009 to 2014, one million Mexicans and their families (including US–born children) left the U.S. for Mexico, according to data from the 2014 Mexican National Survey of Demographic Dynamics. (ENADID 2014)

Third, as Mexican migration decreases (Gonzalez-Barrera 2015), uncontrolled criminality (Suro, chapter 2, this volume), terror, climate change, and environmental dystopia put Central Americans at the center of the new map. Indeed, the Americas gave the new immigration map a new contour: mass unauthorized immigration,[27] unaccompanied minors, children forcibly separated from their parents at the border,[28] and mass deportations.[29]

The sources of the forced movements of people in Central America have disparate and complex histories, finding their distal origins in the Cold War, inequality, and uncontrolled criminality. The Cold War drastically destabilized Latin America and the Caribbean, setting the stage for multiple cycles of mass forced migrations. Armed with the "doctrine of national security," state terrorism was installed throughout the region. Guatemala came first, with the fall of democratically elected President Jacobo Arbenz in 1954 (Schlesinger and Kinzer 1982). In El Salvador, a key date for the terror and the beginning of the exodus is 1979 and the First Revolutionary Government Board (M. Suárez-Orozco 1989; LaFeber 1993). Protracted conflicts in Nicaragua, the country with a record of US military interventions (LaFeber 1993; M. Suárez-Orozco 1989), likewise sent millions of migrants in search of safe haven. From 1976 to 1996, the Cold War in Central America would leave more than 250,000 dead, more than one million internally displaced, and more than two million seeking shelter, the vast majority in the United States (García 2006).

Honduras and Guatemala are also the countries with the highest levels of inequality in North, Central, and South America. In Honduras, the Gini coefficient[30] ratio was 55.7, making it the tenth most unequal country in the world. Guatemala's index (52.35) placed it as the fourteenth most unequal country.

Honduras has a chilling rate of violence of 90.4 murder deaths per 100,000 inhabitants—the highest per capita in the world.[31] By 2013, more than one thousand children and youth under the age of twenty-three had been murdered in that country. The logic of terror qua migration is not surprising: the vast majority of Honduran children detained at the US southern border originate in San Pedro Sula, first in the ranking of the fifty most violent cities in the world, with a rate of 159 murders per 100,000 inhabitants ("San Pedro Sula" 2012).

According to the *Global Report on Internal Displacement* (IDMC 2016, 45), organized criminal violence associated with drug trafficking, gangs, and extortion has reached "epidemic proportions in Mexico, El Salvador, Guatemala and Honduras." Indeed, the report notes:

> As a result, there were at least a million IDPs in the region as of the end of 2015, up from 848,000 at the end of 2014, many of them driven from cities suffering the highest homicide rates in the world and levels of violence comparable with a war zone. . . .
> There were more than 289,000 IDPs in El Salvador, a country described as the world's most deadly outside a war zone, as of the end of 2015. . . . [In Honduras] a total of 2,138 households were surveyed across 20 municipalities identified as having the highest concentrations of displaced people. Based on an extrapolation of the findings it is estimated that they are home to around 174,000 IDPs, including children born in displacement. Of those surveyed, 67.9 percent said their decision to move was influenced only by violence and insecurity, and without consideration of other factors that usually determine migration, such as employment or living conditions. (IDMC 2016, 45)

In the twenty-first century, catastrophic migrations flow from regions plagued by war and terror, rachitic states, unchecked climate change, extreme weather patterns, environmental dystopia, and rampant criminality. Catastrophic migrations are a subcategory of mass migrations but differ in terms of origins, corridors, and the responses they generate (see Suro, chapter 2, this volume). Catastrophic migrations are putting millions of human beings at grave risk the world over. The failure to respond to the magnitude of suffering is marked by world's largest crisis of confinement in history, leaving millions lingering in interminable limbo, leaving them de facto and de jure with diminishing rights. Syria best embodies the world's crisis of confinement. Syrians can "only move so far. The country's international borders were effectively closed in 2015–2016, leaving hundreds of thousands internally displaced near crossing points into neighboring countries" (IDMC 2017, 4).

Catastrophic migrants seeking shelter outside their countries of birth often face ambivalence, xenophobia, and push-back. Catastrophic migrations are the existential crisis of the twenty-first century.

"CHILDREN ARE A SIGN"

"[Children] are a sign of hope, a sign of life, but also a 'diagnostic' sign, a marker indicating the health of families, society and the entire world. Wherever children are accepted, loved, cared for and protected, the family is healthy, society is more healthy and the world is more human" (Pope Francis 2014). Crying children are the face of the catastrophic migrations of the twenty-first century. Worldwide, one in every two hundred children is a refugee, almost twice the number of a decade ago (UNICEF 2017a, 11). According to UN data, in 2016 there were twenty-eight million children forcibly displaced. Another twenty million children were international migrants. Their total number is now larger than the populations of Canada and Sweden combined. Millions of children are internal migrants. In China alone there were an estimated thirty-five million migrant children in 2010 and a staggering sixty-one million children who were left behind in the countryside as their parents migrated to the coastal cities.

Few of the forcibly displaced children ever make it to the high-income countries. The vast majority of children seeking refuge will remain internally displaced or will settle in a neighboring country. UNICEF (2016) reports that 900,000 children have been forcibly displaced within South Sudan, and more than 13,000 have been reported as "missing" or separated from their families. Jacqueline Bhabha (chapter 3, this volume) notes that of the more than 600,000 South Sudanese refugees currently sheltered in Uganda, some 300,000 are under age 18, and the majority are girls and women.

By 2015, the world had witnessed a record number of unaccompanied or separated children, with 98,400 formal asylum applicants—mainly Afghans, Eritreans, Syrians, and Somalis—lodged in 78 countries. "This was the highest number on record since UNHCR started collecting such data in 2006" (UNHCR 2016, 8). By the end of 2016, a new record had been set, with at least "300,000 unaccompanied and separated children moving across borders . . . registered in 80 countries in 2015–16—a near fivefold increase from 66,000 in 2010–11. The total number of unaccompanied and separated children on the move worldwide is likely much higher" (UNICEF 2017a, 6).

Bhabha (chapter 3, this volume) notes that Europe has witnessed a dramatic increase in the numbers of children and youth, including unaccompanied children, arriving from the Middle East, North and sub-Saharan Africa, and South Asia. More than 30 percent of sea arrivals in Europe since October 2015 have been children; for some nationalities, including Afghans and Eritreans, children constitute the majority of asylum applicants. By 2017, even greater numbers of unaccompanied and separated minors were arriving in Europe via the unforgiving Central Mediterranean Sea passage from North Africa. "Ninety-two percent of children who arrived in Italy in 2016 and the first two months of 2017 were unaccompanied, up from 75 percent in 2015" (UNICEF 2017a, 6).

In 2014, the United States experienced a significant spike in unaccompanied children fleeing Central America (see www.cbp.gov/newsroom/stats/usbp-sw-border-apprehensions), and between 2015 and 2016, in North America 100,000 unaccompanied and separated children were apprehended at the Mexico–US border (UNICEF 2017a, 12).

Thousands of children, the majority of them Central American, were incarcerated with their parents in harsh and punitive US facilities, according to Bhabha, "simply because they [could not] demonstrate a regular immigration status, despite a broad international consensus opposing detention of children for immigration reasons. In Mexico, the United States' de facto immigration buffer zone, detention of child migrants is even more oppressive and pervasive" (chapter 3, Bhabha, this volume). The number of forcibly displaced children and youth arriving in Europe and the United States is but a small proportion of the global total. These children, Bhabha argues, face a "protection deficit."

In the aftermath of World War II, Europe, the United States, and their allies developed policies for refugees based on the assumption that whatever caused them to flee their homes would be resolved eventually. "Civilized nations could promise *'non-refoulement,'* the right not to be returned to a place of violence or persecution, because the promise was only temporary" (M. Suarez-Orozco and Suro 2017, 1). These architectures now are misaligned with the new conditions. Devastated environments in states with weak institutional capacities hold little promise for safe return. Millions are also fleeing existential threats but may not meet the anachronistic standards required for formal refugee status. The twenty-first-century map suggests new forms of migration that do not fit existing policy frameworks. The architectures in place to protect the forcibly displaced, refugees, and asylum seekers are now out of date and out of touch with the current catastrophic kinetics of forced migration. First, most forcibly displaced migrants today linger as internally displaced in their own countries or in camps in neighboring states with weak institutions, often in subhuman conditions with few protections. Indeed, millions of human beings now are "lost in transit" (Crul et al., chapter 13, this volume). Second, protracted conflicts are sending millions fleeing with no expectation of returning. In 2014, in thirty-three conflicts globally, the average length of exile was twenty-five years (Dryden-Peterson, chapter 10, this volume; IDMC 2016). The conflicts in the countries generating the greatest numbers of the forcibly displaced, such as war and terror in Syria, Afghanistan, and Somalia, have endured longer than World War I and World War II.

Third, the architectures in place are generally blind to the developmental needs of children—a topic of grave urgency (C. Suárez-Orozco, chapter 4; Sanchez Sorondo, epilogue; Bhabha, chapter 3, all this volume). Even when temporary protection is possible or desirable, children in flight need more than a safe haven. They need a place to grow up. They need the safety of home. Fourth, the architectures are not aligned with the best evidence and current thinking on physical health, mental health, and trauma (Mollica, chapter 5; Betancourt et al., chapter 6; Yoshikawa et al., chapter 8, all this volume); legal protections (Bhabha, chapter 3, this volume); or education (Noguera, chapter 14; Bokova, chapter 9; Banks, chapter 11; Dryden-Peterson, chapter 10; Léna, chapter 12, all this volume).

In his inaugural address at the conference upon which this volume is based, Jeffrey Sachs articulated a plea for six action items in urgent need of implementation now:

> First, the faster we have widespread economic development so that people can safely and prosperously stay in their own homes and homelands, then [the faster] the pressures of forced mass migration [will be], of course, eliminated.
>
> Second, I believe that it is in Africa's enormous self-interest and in the world's interest to help make sure that every child in Africa, especially the girls right now, have the health and the education they need. . . .
>
> Third, we have to stop the wars. Syria was a war of choice largely by the United States, Turkey, and Saudi Arabia. It led to [over] 10 million people being dislocated. That has had terrible spillover effects on European politics. But it was a war of choice, a so-called regime-change operation, which failed. Similarly, Libya was a war of choice. Iraq was a war of choice. This is one of the great dangers in our world and one of the reasons why we have so many dislocated people.
>
> Fourth, I would emphasize [that] if we do not achieve the Paris Climate Agreement, if we do not successfully stay below 2 degrees Centigrade [in further warming, the planet] will face many disasters, but one of them will be mass forced migration.
>
> Fifth is that even with the tendencies that we have right now, almost all parts of the world, including New York City, need to achieve climate resiliency [that is] built into their regular policymaking. In New York we are still recovering from Storm Sandy in some of the coastal areas of Long Island, for example. So we have to get serious with climate resilience.
>
> And, finally, I would emphasize again that we need to turn the concept of, quote, "Losses and Damages" into a concept of environmental justice and compensation by the rich countries for the damages to the poor countries. Now we have a president [Trump] who wants to blame the poor for America's problems. Of course this is horrendously ignorant and dangerous. We need quite a different approach, which is to say, "Sorry for a lot of the ills we've caused in the world. We're ready to help you to meet those challenges," and that's the approach of justice and the approach that we need to build into any framework for migration as well. (Sachs 2017, 14)

PLAN OF THE BOOK

In the following chapters, we endeavor to identify needs as well as new models to best address the physical and mental health, legal protections, education, and well-being of asylum seekers, refugees, and irregular migrants in varied destinations.

In part 1, "The New Cartography of Mass Migration," we examine the demographic, economic, and environmental processes shaping the new catastrophic migrations. In chapter 1, "Unchecked Climate Change and Mass Migration: A Probabilistic

Case for Urgent Action," Fonna Forman and Veerabhadran Ramanathan of the University of California–San Diego argue that unchecked climate change is creating massive disruptions the world over. A new planetary fever, they contend, is resulting in major climate disruptions such as heat waves, severe storms, floods, and droughts. With unchecked emissions, the warming is likely to exceed 1.5°C by 2030, 2°C by 2050, and perhaps a devastating 4°C by 2100.

Forman and Ramanathan caution social scientists and policy makers that such warming magnitudes and speed of warming are unprecedented when compared with the measured climate changes over the last several thousand years. Any attempts to extrapolate causal links between climate change and migration based on past records to predict future trends are likely to yield unreliable results and may severely underestimate the threats we will face in the coming decades. The authors insist that in the face of uncertainty, an ethical global policy response cannot await reliable metrics. International cooperation on climate mitigation is urgently needed. Establishing international protocols that outline the rights of climate refugees and the responsibilities of industrialized nations toward them cannot wait. We must build a culture of climate resilience.

In 2017, the world witnessed ferocious hurricanes in the Atlantic that devastated entire regions of the Caribbean, including Antigua and Barbuda. According to Prime Minister Gaston Alphonso Browne, after the largest storm ever in the Atlantic Ocean in September 2017, "the island of Barbuda [was] decimated, its entire population left homeless, and its buildings reduced to empty shells" (UN News Centre 2017). The entire island of Puerto Rico was left without power for months. A month earlier (August 2017), devastating monsoons in South Asia killed more than 1,200 people, forced millions from their homes in India, Nepal, and Bangladesh, and shut 1.8 million children out of school.

Climate justice for the global poor, Forman and Ramanathan claim, is as much a battle against what Pope Francis calls "the culture of indifference" as it is about redistributing responsibilities, protections, and reparations.

In chapter 2, "A Migration Becomes an Emergency: The Flight of Women and Children from the Northern Triangle and Its Antecedents," Roberto Suro examines the particulars of the recent catastrophic exodus out of Central America. He identifies a "transmutation" of flows from the same region to the same destinations but sees them as responding to different drivers. Over two generations, Suro traces the Central American flows to the United States that began escaping state terror in earnest in the 1970s and early 1980s to a pattern best characterized as economic and labor migration (during the 1990s and early 2000s), and sees them finally being transformed into a new variant of forced migration, responding to unchecked criminality and inequality in states with rachitic institutional capacities.

In March 2014, more than 5,000 minors and mothers were apprehended at the southern border of the United States. In April the number "went over 6,000. That was just the front edge. In May the number was 12,722 before cresting with 16,330 in June. The great bulk of the increase was made up of Northern Triangle migrants, and the number travelling in family units was almost matched by the number of children apprehended alone. The flow of unaccompanied minors—migrants aged 0 to 17—followed a pattern similar to that of the family units, reaching 10,620 in June, five times what it had been two years earlier. Apprehensions of family members and unaccompanied minors totaled 136,986 in fiscal 2014, accounting for 29 percent of all apprehensions that year." In an act of Herod-like brutality, in 2018 the Trump administration began forcibly separating children from their parents apprehended in the Southern Border.

While earlier waves of migrants from Central America had been escaping state terrorism and then seeking economic opportunity, the newest arrivals were responding to an entirely different set of circumstances. Even with the same origins and destinations, the corridors of mass migration "recombine" in complex and unpredictable ways. The implications of Suro's conceptual work for other well-worn corridors such as the North Africa to Europe route are many and worth considering in careful detail.

In Part II, "Frames on Children and Youth on the Move," we examine mass migrations in light of the experiences of children and youth. Children are on the move in numbers never seen before. UN data suggest that in 2015 there were twenty-eight million children and youth forcibly displaced; another twenty million children were international migrants. Millions more are internal migrants—often encountering the same hardships and threats that international migrant children face.

In chapter 3, "Children on the Move in the Twenty-First Century: Developing a Rights-Based Plan of Action," Jacqueline Bhabha suggests that although children have always migrated, "the protection deficit that accompanies this multifaceted phenomenon, now widely referred to as 'children on the move,' only emerged as a concerted focus of concern relatively recently." Bhabha frames the phenomenon "beyond the current preoccupation with child vulnerability, dependence, and related protection imperatives, critical though that perspective is. A more dynamic and ambitious agenda to complement the focus of current work is needed, one that acknowledges youthful agency and ambition and that places the right to safe and legal child and adolescent mobility at its core." She articulates a coherent set of principles, starting with the "unconditional insistence that all children should be considered as children first and foremost, whatever their migration or nationality status." She reviews policies and principles qua physical health, mental health, and education, among other fields, to ameliorate risk and foster the flourishing of children on the move. As important, she argues that considering the experiences of children and youth on the move should be seen as an opportunity with enormous positive rewards, if well managed, moving forward.

Chapter 4, "A Compassionate Perspective on Immigrant Children and Youth," by Carola Suárez-Orozco, endeavors to "make sense of the experiences of immigrant and refugee children" as they settle in new societies. She introduces conceptual tools to bring clarity to the complexities facing youngsters on the move. First, she proposes an ecological model of immigrant adaptation, anchored in Bronfenbrenner's perspective, "whereby the interrelated contexts of development within which children and youth are embedded shape their opportunities and have important implications for both educational and well-being outcomes." Second, she develops a systematic model of risk and resilience in immigrant and refugee life. Echoing Bhabha's concern, Carola Suárez-Orozco argues that immigrant and refugee children and youth are remarkably resilient, and their agency and assets are a sine qua non to their thriving in new contexts. She reviews the contexts into which immigrants and refugees settle—inter alia, the policy frameworks, economic realities, and xenophobic responses they encounter—and concludes with a plea for "bridging the compassion gap."

In Part III, "Catastrophic Migrant Lives at the Margins," we turn to the triaging of catastrophic migrations. Such migrations in the twenty-first century are delivering millions of human beings into no exit/no entry zones. A "province of liminality" is now the fastest growing region in the new cartography of mass migrations. Millions of internally displaced people are unable to return home and unable to reach a safe country. For them, life is betwixt and between. They linger at the threshold.[32] There are now almost twice as many internally displaced people as there are international refugees with UNHCR protections. Those who do make it across international borders in nine out of ten cases will remain in a neighboring country. The largest "neighboring hosts" include Turkey (hosting 2.9 million forcibly displaced people, including 1.9 million from neighboring Syria); Pakistan (hosting 1.4 million people from neighboring Afghanistan); and Lebanon (hosting 1 million people from neighboring Syria). In addition, there are also "10 million stateless people who have been denied a nationality and access to basic rights such as education, health care, employment, and freedom of movement" (UNHCR 2018a).

In chapter 6, "The New H5 Model: Trauma and Recovery," Richard Mollica of Harvard Medical School argues that "the model of guaranteeing safety and security to refugees used by the United Nations and nongovernmental organizations is outdated. It is obvious to all humanitarian relief players that the current humanitarian assistance model is badly broken and inadequate."

Refugees, as Drosh Marie DeVoe (1981, 88) has long noted, evoke the lasting impression of a needy and helpless victim: "a client in need of assistance. The refugee problem is typically viewed in terms of filling only the immediate requirements of a needy people." Yet refugees are competent agents with the drive, creativity, and inherent capacity to self-heal. They need to be the architects of their healing—indeed, their agency is the sine qua non to healing, according to Mollica.

Theresa Betancourt and her team of collaborators elaborate on the theme of refugee agency in chapter 6, "Addressing Mental Health Disparities in Refugee Children through Family and Community-Based Prevention." They present a culturally relevant intervention in the form of a community-based participatory research (CBPR) process to develop, implement, and evaluate a family intervention aimed at promoting positive caregiver–child relationships, family functioning, and child mental health among refugees resettling in the United States. Their work describes the value of CBPR in such efforts. "Examples are drawn from a process used to develop and evaluate the feasibility and acceptability of a family home visiting intervention . . . among Somali Bantu and Lhotshampa Bhutanese refugees who have resettled in the United States." The tentative results are promising.

In chapter 7, "Surveying the Hard-to-Survey: Refugees and Unaccompanied Minors in Greece," Theoni Stathopoulou, director of the National Centre for Social Research, Athens, turns to the humanitarian crisis that was unfolding in Greece in 2015 with the sudden arrival of more than 850,000 refugees in search of shelter (IOM 2016). Greece, a country badly battered by an enormous economic and social crisis, responded with an extraordinary effort, bringing civil society, state actors, and the international community to relieve and accommodate the new arrivals. The chapter presents the results of *REHEAL,* the first survey conducted by the National Centre for Social Research in refugee camps all over Greece between July and September 2016 with the use of self-completed questionnaires. In addition, Stathopoulou presents the results from a pilot study on unaccompanied minors in Greece conducted in collaboration with the Harvard Program on Refugee Trauma. The chilling findings of this study are central for any understanding of safety and protections needed for the most vulnerable group in this refugee population.

Millions of forcibly displaced children are out of school, and millions more are being schooled on the move. According to a Save the Children 2016 report, "Refugee children are five times less likely to attend school than other children. Currently, 50 percent of primary school-aged refugee children and 75 percent of secondary school-aged children are completely left out of the education system, with none of the safeguards that school environments provide. In 2015 alone, the education of 80 million children was disrupted by humanitarian crises" (Save the Children 2016). Less than one percent of refugees the world over are receiving a college education.

In addition, millions of children and youth are exposed to catastrophic contexts that endanger their safety, health, and well-being. Well-documented risks include both exposure to and direct experiences of violence, including rape, torture, and severe beatings; the loss of loved ones; and violent and protracted family separations. In a recent International Organization for Migration survey, "over three-quarters of 1,600 children aged 14–17 who arrived in Italy via the Central Mediterranean route reported experiences such as being held against their will or being forced to work without pay at some point during their journeys—indications that they may have been trafficked or otherwise exploited. Traffickers and other exploiters thrive especially where state institutions are weak, where organized crime abounds, and also where migrants become stuck and desperate" (UNICEF 2017a, 6).

In chapter 8, "Mitigating the Impact of Forced Displacement and Refugee and Unauthorized Status on Youth: Integrating Developmental Processes with Intervention Research," Hirokazu Yoshikawa, Alice Wuermli, and J. Lawrence Aber of New York University argue that the rights of youth on the move around the world are being violated, with severe consequences for their psychological health and well-being. The authors present a "developmental process-oriented framework for informing the development and evaluation of interventions to mitigate the risks posed by major social and political upheavals, displacement, and refugee and unauthorized status on child and youth development." They examine the best "evidence on the overall risk to child and youth development and learning posed by exposure to these contexts, the emerging evidence on contextual and psychological factors that may exacerbate or mitigate these risks, and the evidence base of rigorous evaluations of interventions from the dyadic to the policy levels that have successfully targeted these factors and mitigated the risks and promoted resilience and healthy development despite adversity."

In Part IV, "The Work of Education in the Transitions of Immigrant and Refugee Youth," we turn to the role of education in migrant and refugee children's transition into new societies. The majority of children in need of refuge today are living lives in limbo within the boundaries of their conflict-ridden nations or settling into precarious conditions in neighboring countries (Dryden-Peterson, chapter 10, this volume). The research by Jacqueline Bhabha and Sarah Dryden-Peterson addresses the "crisis of confinement" (Sánchez Terán 2017, 1), and the near-permanent marginality facing millions of children on the move.

The children and youth who make it to middle- and high-income countries face other realities, challenges, and marginalities. In the United States, Canada, Australia, and most of Europe, the children of refugees and migrants are now the fastest growing sector of the child population. Their education, well-being, and prosperity are imperatives as fundamental conditions of civilization. There are also pragmatic imperatives: Syrian children will be tomorrow's nurses in Germany, police in Sweden, and engineers in Holland. The same is true for Central American children in the United States. Harnessing the resilience, hardiness, and ethic of care in these children is as much a smart policy for a healthy society moving forward as it is a humanitarian imperative.

Education is the Camino Real to socioeconomic mobility, health, citizenship, and engagement. But those growing up in "fragile or conflict-affected countries—migrants, refugees, and displaced persons—are hit hardest." Immigrants and refugees are falling behind: "At a time when educational achievement is a marker of future opportunity, the world remains far off mark, with over 263 million children and adolescents still out of primary and secondary school and close to the same number failing to acquire basic skills after four years in school. Adolescent girls and young women are most vulnerable to exclusion as well as to early marriage, sexual violence, and exploitation" (Bokova, chapter 9, this volume).

Wide-ranging chapter 9, "Empowering Global Citizens for a Just and Peaceful World," by UNESCO's former Director General Irina Bokova, makes a plea for education as a human right and a fundamental instrument for empowerment. She maintains that education "provides women and men with the tools to build resilience and make the most of change. This is especially important in conflict situations, in which learning and going to school can bring a sense of normality and restore hope in the future. Learning provides young minds with confidence when horizons are bleak, making education the best long-term way to break cycles of violence and set communities on the path to peace."

Today's humanitarian crisis is generating intolerance and xenophobia and increasing the risk of immigrant youth's radicalization and gravitation to fundamentalist ideologies. Education's preventive and preemptive role—in particular through the promoting of global citizenship, dialogue, youth engagement in democratic life, intercultural competencies, and digital literacy—is more important today than ever.

In chapter 10, "Inclusion and Membership through Refugee Education? Tensions between Policy and Practice," Sarah Dryden-Peterson of Harvard Graduate School of Education turns to the matter of educating the children of refugees. As she notes, those who do make it into schools are often headed for separate facilities for refugees. Such schools have been the norm in so-called "neighboring host countries," where almost 90 percent of all global refugees are settled. The idea of separate schools is aligned with the notion that refugees are temporary guests soon to return to their countries of origin. Such schools are thus preparing children for their return home.

Yet extended conflicts make the "myth of the return" an ever-distant mirage for millions. As Dryden-Peterson notes, since 2012, global policy has shifted to a new normative ideal to integrate refugees into national education systems. She maintains, "The policy of integration reflects the reality that displacement is protracted, and return to a country of origin is elusive. The practice of integration of refugees reflects a different reality, one often filled with isolation and exclusion." Dryden-Peterson explores the tension between the lofty ideals encoded in the model of integration of refugees into national education systems and the ambiguous belonging enacted in the daily experiences of refugee students in classrooms—a practice that places refugee children "outside of current membership in society."

Mass migrations are generating push-back, nativist anxieties, and anti-immigrant fervor. These reactions are occurring in the United States and in much of

Western Europe, but also in China and throughout Africa and the Middle East. The eminent scholar of education and multiculturalism James A. Banks argues in chapter 11, "Civic Education for Noncitizen and Citizen Students: A Conceptual Framework," that conflicts over diversity and citizenship persist in many forms in many societies marked by ethnic, racial, and religious differences. Banks claims that racial, ethnic, cultural, linguistic, and religious groups are often denied structural inclusion in the nation-state. The children of immigrants and refugees both register and are affected by the increasingly radioactive ethos of reception—how they are viewed in their new societies and the structural barriers that they face (C. Suárez-Orozco 2001; see also chapter 4, this volume). The anomic withdrawal and the cultures of antagonism of the children of stigmatized populations are but an instance of what Banks has called "failed citizenship." The children of refugees, immigrants, and other marked minorities may not make the values and symbols of the nation-state their own. The United States, Western Europe, and other advanced postindustrial societies, as Banks documents, are manufacturing high levels of disconnection, anomie, and social malaise: "*Failed citizenship* exists when individuals or groups who are born within a nation or migrate to it and live within it for an extended period of time do not internalize the values and ethos of the nation-state, feel structurally excluded within it, and have highly ambivalent feelings toward it. Individuals who experience failed citizenship focus primarily on their own needs for political efficacy, group identity, and structural inclusion rather than on the overarching and shared goals of the nation-state. Their allegiance and commitment to the nation-state is eclectic and complex."

Formal education must reclaim its eudemonic, civic, and emancipatory roots if we are to interrupt the life-thwarting momentum threatening millions of youth in marginalized communities. Banks's thoughtful blueprint for an education promoting transformative citizenship should be useful to all educators and policy makers working with immigrant and refugee children.

Pierre Léna of the Académie des Sciences, Paris, notes in chapter 12, "Refugees in Education: What Can Science Education Contribute?," that massive displacements are "putting millions of students in a variety of situations: no schooling for years, poor schooling in precarious environments, and immersion in [new] cultures without the language and necessary bridges with the family culture." Education, he reminds us, thrives with curiosity. Curiosity is the sine qua non for cognitive engagement (C. Suárez-Orozco, M. Suárez-Orozco, and Todorova 2008) and lifelong learning. For Léna, science education, teaching for reasoning and for modeling a rational mind, is the cure for ignorance and the antidote to fundamentalisms and xenophobic intolerance. He argues that with unchecked climate change as a driver of mass migration, climate-change education, with its high science content, is needed on a large scale to implement the difficult objectives of the Paris Agreement. He presents examples from *La main à la pate* ("hands on"), a highly regarded inquiry-based science education program in primary and lower secondary schools implemented throughout the world. This program now reaches children—including those of immigrants and refugees—in fifty countries. He argues that "natural sciences have a character of universality, fostering cognitive development of students, which makes them a precious tool for these displaced children."

In "Lost in Transit: Education for Refugee Children in Sweden, Germany, and Turkey," chapter 13, Maurice Crul and his colleagues compare the ways in which three countries that have received large numbers of refugees are endeavoring to incorporate children into their disparate educational systems. The authors examine in detail the institutional arrangements most likely to shape the school trajectories of refugee children: 1) preschool; 2) entrance into compulsory schooling; 3) the so-called "welcome, submersion, or introduction classes"; 4) second-language instruction; 5) supports for teachers working with refugee students; 6) tracking; and 7) schooling after compulsory school. The programs vary greatly, and the results are varied. While both Germany and Sweden are struggling to provide equitable quality education to new arrivals, the situation in Turkey is bleak. Although Turkish law mandates the schooling of all minors regardless of nationality, about half of all refugee children in Turkey are not being educated in schools. Those who are enrolled in school "are in temporary education centers." The authors suggest which educational institutional arrangements need to be in place to provide equal opportunities for refugee children to succeed in school.

In chapter 14, "From the Crisis of Connection to the Pursuit of Our Common Humanity: The Role of Schools in Responding to the Needs of Immigrant and Refugee Children," Pedro Noguera develops the concept of the *crisis of connection* and reflects upon the flight from humanism and the ethic of care. He maintains:

> Signs of the crisis of connection are particularly evident in the international response to the global refugee crisis. As millions of people are displaced from their homes and forced in many cases to risk their lives as they attempt to flee war, hunger, and violence, a yawning empathy gap acts as a formidable obstruction to the development of humane and creative responses to suffering. . . . The tepid, ineffectual response to the global refugee crisis is reinforced and exacerbated by our acceptance of grotesque inequalities in wealth and access to resources, an imbalance that drives at least some of the refugee crisis and often threatens the quality of life in places where the displaced wait to be settled.

Noguera argues that schools in the United States and elsewhere are unequipped and unprepared to respond adequately to the needs of the new wave of refugees and unaccompanied minors. Although US public schools are mandated to serve all children, including the undocumented and the children of refugees, too many schools and communities are reacting with hostility and resentment. Others are responding with humanity and care. Yet more often than not, these schools respond without guidance, basic supports, training, and resources. Noguera notes the "growing hostility toward immigrants expressed by politicians, civic groups, and the media that erodes public willingness to assist schools in serving the new arrivals. Without a major cultural undertaking to bridge the empathy gap," he observes, "it will be difficult to gather the human and material resources required for the task of educating the largest and most diverse cohort of immigrant and refugee-origin students now making its way through schools the world over."

Chapter 15, "Children of Immigrants in the United States: Barriers and Paths to Integration and Well-Being," by Harvard sociologist of immigration Mary Waters, and chapter 16, "Improving the Education and Social Integration of Immigrants," by Francesca Borgonovi, Mario Piacentini, and Andreas Schleicher of the Organization for Economic Cooperation and Development (OECD), examine the lives and transitions of immigrant children and youth in the United States and the OECD countries.

In the United States, immigration is both history (how the country came to be what it is today) and destiny (the children of immigrants are the fastest-growing sector of the US population). The proportion of today's immigrants is slightly below what it was a century ago. Waters maintains, "First and second generations account for one out of four members of the US population. . . . The successful integration of these immigrants and their children is necessary for the overall success of our society. The well-being of a quarter of our population ought to be one of our highest public policy priorities. As a society that has successfully integrated generations of immigrants and their children throughout its history, the United States ought to be a model for societies around the world who face similar challenges in the age of unprecedented human migration."

Waters examines the integration and well-being among the children of immigrants in the areas of education, socioeconomic outcomes, and mental and physical health. She asks: What policies "facilitate or impede that integration? How does integration affect the well-being of the second generation?" The answers tell a mixed story. She concludes by articulating a new semiotics and ethics of engagement to address the protracted issue of unauthorized immigration in the United States. Waters suggests "that the Catholic Church and other religious organizations have the potential to contribute greatly to the moral underpinnings of the movement that is needed to keep immigrant families together and to strengthen the next generation. The Catholic Church, along with other faith-based organizations, has long been a leader in nongovernmental action in immigrant integration. Faith-based institutions have great potential to also be moral leaders in the kinds of policy changes that are urgently needed in the United States going forward" (Waters, chapter 15, this volume).

In chapter 16, "Improving the Education and Social Integration of Immigrants," Francesca Borgonovi, Mario Piacentini, and Andreas Schleicher of the OECD note that an estimated five million permanent migrants arrived in OECD countries in 2015. The recent wave continues an upward trend in the share of new immigrants in these countries. Since 2000, the immigrant population has grown by more than 30 percent and represents ever more diverse origins. The children of immigrants and refugees are a growing presence in classrooms throughout OECD countries. Education is critical as an end in and of itself, but it also shapes public perception of a country's ability to manage migration well. Schooling shapes the identities and sense of belonging of immigrant children and youth. As important, education will drive their transition to the labor market and to citizenship in new societies.

By 2015, data from the Programme for International Student Assessment (PISA) found that, on average, in OECD countries 12.5 percent of fifteen-year-old students were immigrant-origin (up from 9.4 percent in 2006). The data suggest that children of immigrants have lower levels of academic achievement than other students. However, the authors conclude that the average difference in science performance between immigrant and nonimmigrant students with similar socioeconomic status and familiarity with the test language narrowed between 2006 and 2015.

The lower levels of academic achievement are not surprising. First, testing relies heavily on the academic language of the new country. Language acquisition and academic trajectories are bound together (M. Suárez-Orozco 1989, 1991; C. Suárez-Orozco, M. Suárez-Orozco, and Todorova 2008; Gandara and Contreras 2009). Research in the United States, Canada, Europe, and elsewhere suggests that it takes years for immigrant-origin students to reach academic language parity with native speakers, even under the best teaching and learning conditions. One recurring finding (see Collier 1995; Cummins 2000; Hakuta, Butler, and Witt 2000; National Research Council 1997) is that it takes approximately five to seven years for immigrant language-learners to develop the academic language proficiency required to compete fairly with native speakers in standardized assessment regimes at the center of worldwide education reforms. Another consistent finding suggests that "balanced bilinguals"—that is, youth who continuously develop their home language as they acquire a second academic language—tend to have better educational trajectories over time (Callahan and Gándara 2014).

Second, research suggests that parental socioeconomic status (SES)—including maternal education and paternal occupation—is a powerful predictor of testing outcomes. Children of lower SES immigrant parents are thus at a disadvantage. Research indicates that immigrants are more likely than their native counterparts to encounter poverty in their new societies (Kazemipur and Halli 2001). Poverty is created in part by unique disadvantages that are often associated with immigrant status, such as "language barriers, incompatibility of educational credentials, limited transferability of job skills, unfamiliarity with the market demands, and lack of access to job and educational networks" (Kazemipur and Halli 2001, 1132; see also de Haan and Yaqub 2009).[33]

Third, concentrated disadvantage in immigrant neighborhoods, segregated and inferior immigrant schools, unauthorized immigrant status, and the stresses and trauma of immigration have been empirically linked to lower testing outcomes and academic trajectories. Children raised in disadvantage are also vulnerable to instability of residence as well as to an array of distressors, including difficulty with concentrating and sleeping, anxiety, and depression as well as heightened exposure to delinquency and violence. Concentrated disadvantage has long been recognized as a significant risk factor for poor educational outcomes (Luthar 1999; Weissbourd 1996).

Immigrant poverty and segregation are often compounded by unauthorized status (the United Nations estimates that there are between 30 and 40 million unauthorized migrants worldwide; Papademetriou 2005). The United States has a very large concentration of undocumented immigrants—approximately 11.1 million people (or just about 3.5 percent of the nation's population) were unauthorized, and about 3.9 million kindergarten through twelfth-grade students in US public and private schools in 2014—7.3 percent of the total—were children of unauthorized immigrants, according to Pew Research Center estimates (Passel and Cohn 2016). The number of children who are themselves unauthorized has declined from a peak of 1.6 million in 2005 to about 750,000 a decade later. Research suggests that undocumented youth often arrive after multiple family separations and traumatic border crossings (C. Suárez-Orozco, Yoshikawa, and Tseng 2015). They may continue to experience fear and anxiety about being apprehended, separated again from their parents, and deported (C. Suárez-Orozco and Marks 2016; see also Chaudry et al. 2010; C. Suárez-Orozco, M. Suárez-Orozco, and Todorova 2008). An overview of key research published in the *Harvard Education Review* in 2011 concluded: "The evidence reveals a consistent pattern: the effects of unauthorized status on development across the life span are uniformly negative, with millions of US children and youth at risk of lower educational performance, economic stagnation, blocked mobility and ambiguous belonging. In all, the data suggest an alarming psychological formation" (C. Suárez-Orozco et al. 2011, 461).

Given this powerful undertow, immigrant- and refugee-origin children may be doing better academically than expected. Yet the great influx of refugee-origin children into European OECD countries during the last twelve months is very likely to alter the generally positive picture reported in the PISA data.

CONCLUSIONS

Mass migration and demographic change are, under the best of circumstances, destabilizing and generate disequilibrium. Catastrophic migrations produce multiple additional layers of distress. The forcibly displaced undergo violent separations and carry the wounds of trauma. Millions of human beings are caught in permanent limbo, living in zones of confinement—Stathopoulou's "no-man zones." In these zones "humiliation is re-created in the camp environment when individuals are not allowed to work, grow food, or make money" (Mollica, chapter 5, this volume). Catastrophic migrations assault the structure and coherence of families in their legislative, social, and symbolic functions (Lacan 2006).

The outright rejection of unwanted refugees, asylum seekers, and unauthorized immigrants compounds the trauma they suffer (see C. Suárez-Orozco 2004). In many receiving countries, too, we have identified zones of confinement where de facto and de jure policies are forcing millions of immigrant and refugee families to live in the shadow of the law. In the United States, the country with the largest number of immigrants, millions are separated, millions are deported, millions are incarcerated, and millions more inhabit a subterranean world of illegality (C. Suárez-Orozco, chapter 4, this volume).

Catastrophic migrations and violent family separations disrupt the essential developmental functions necessary for children to establish basic trust, feel secure (Erickson 1950), and have a healthy orientation toward the world and the future. Catastrophic migrations tear children from their families and communities. Furthermore, physical, sexual, and psychological abuse are normative features of forced migrations, especially when they involve human trafficking[34] and the subhuman conditions that prevail in many migrant camps. The camps in Bangladesh are but the most recent example. They were hastily set up for the 650,000 Rohingya refugees, mostly women and children, escaping massacres in Myanmar in late 2017. Once in Bangladesh, the Rohingya encountered rickety camps and "a miasma of untreated trauma, fresh exploitation and apprehension about the future" (*New York Times* 2017, p. 13, see also Stathopoulou, chapter 7, and Mollica, chapter 5, both this volume).

Catastrophic migrations remove children and youth from the proscribed pathways that enable them to reach and master culturally determined developmental milestones in the biological, socioemotional, cognitive, and moral realms required to make the transition to adulthood successfully. Catastrophic migrations are life-thwarting, harming children's physical, psychological, moral, and social well-being by placing them in contexts that are inherently dangerous.

When immigrants and refugees manage to settle in new societies, they bring new kinship systems, cultural sensibilities (including racial, linguistic, and religious), and identities to the forefront. These may misalign with (and even contravene) taken-for-granted cultural schemas and social practices in receiving societies. The world over, immigrants and refugees are arousing suspicion, fear, and xenophobia. Immigration is the frontier pushing against the limits of cosmopolitan tolerance. Immigration intensifies the general crisis of connection and flight from the pursuit of our inherent humanitarian obligations concerning the welfare of others (Noguera, chapter 14, this volume). Reimagining the narrative of belonging, reclaiming the humanitarian call, and recalibrating the institutions of the nation-state are a sine qua non to move beyond the current immigration malaise the world over. In the long term, we must retrain hearts and minds, especially younger ones, for democracy in the context of demographic change and superdiversity. We need to convert a dread of the unfamiliar "Other" into empathy, solidarity, and a democratizing desire for cultural difference. In this book we endeavor to cultivate the humanistic ideal to find oneself "in Another" (Ricoeur 1995) in the refugee, in the asylum seeker, and in the forcibly displaced.

NOTES

Throughout this volume we use the terms *migrants, immigrants, emigrants, asylum seekers, refugees, internally displaced persons, forcibly displaced persons,* and *environmental refugees.* Each term denotes distinct and often disparate circumstances, *seriatim,* context of exit, context of reception, motivations and phenomenology of experience. We find the general definitions of these terms suggested by the International Migration Organization quite useful (www.iom.int/key-migration-terms). The general focus of the volume is on the "catastrophic migrations" of the 21st century. A catastrophe can be defined as a sudden change or upheaval in the order of things, whether physical or social, that affects living beings dramatically and adversely. *Beings,* in this case, are human beings forced to flee. Terror and uncontrolled criminality are now major drivers but, as Pope Francis wisely noted in the encyclical *Laudato Si,* there is also "a tragic rise in the number of migrants seeking to flee from the growing poverty caused by environmental degradation. They are not recognized by international conventions as refugees; they bear the loss of the lives they have left behind, without enjoying any legal protection whatsoever. Sadly, there is widespread indifference to such suffering, which is even now taking place throughout our world. Our lack of response to these tragedies involving our brothers and sisters points to the loss of that sense of responsibility for our fellow men and women upon which all civil society is founded" (Pope Francis 2015).

   1. Human trafficking is not the topic of the current work. It will suffice to say that an estimated thirty million humans are trafficked, representing "all continents and races [and] the world's religions and languages." "Almost every country in the world is affected by trafficking, whether as a country of origin, transit or destination for victims" (UNODC 2012). "Victims of forced labor have been found in nearly every job setting or industry imaginable, including private homes, factories, restaurants, elder care and medical facilities, hotels, housekeeping, child rearing, agriculture, construction and landscaping, food processing, meat-packing, and cleaning services" (US Dept. of State 2013, 30). Many of those trafficked are immigrants.

   2. "When humans first ventured out of Africa . . . they left genetic footprints still visible today. . . . According to the genetic and paleontological record, we only started to leave Africa between 60,000 and 70,000 years ago. What set this [migration] in motion is uncertain, but we think it has something to do with major climatic shifts that were happening around that time—a sudden cooling in the Earth's climate driven by the onset of one of the worst parts of the last Ice Age" (National Geographic, Genographic Project n.d.).

3. "Diverse species have emerged over the course of human evolution, and a suite of adaptations have accumulated over time, including upright walking, the capacity to make tools, enlargement of the brain, prolonged maturation, the emergence of complex mental and social behavior, and dependence on technology to alter the surroundings" (Smithsonian 2016). Indeed, migration is a precursor of modern humans, "the open-country suite of features inferred for *Homo erectus* had evolved together and provided the adaptations for dispersal beyond Africa. These features foreshadowed those of more recent *Homo sapiens* and included large linear bodies, elongated legs, large brain sizes, reduced sexual dimorphism, increased carnivory, and unique life history traits (e.g., extended ontogeny and longevity) as well as toolmaking and increased social cooperation" (Antón, Potts, and Aiello 2014).

4. "These numbers can be problematic because the most widely cited UN figures are cumulative" (Butler 2017).

5. The well-worn migration corridors of the post–World War II era have much older origins—in the age of European exploration, wars of conquest and of empire that began in 1492. War and conquest created the unstable foundations of what would be called the "New World." They destroyed civilizations, induced demographic collapse, and caused massive displacement of indigenous populations and their livelihoods. The expanding European powers systematically linked the Atlantic, Pacific, and Indian Oceans, creating the largest trading systems ever seen in history. The trade routes became the great corridors for global migration during the last five centuries.

6. Latin Americans are the largest immigrant group in the United States. The nation now has approximately four times more immigrants than the second-largest country of immigration (the Russian Federation) does.

7. I subsume under labor migration the categories "sojourners," "target earners," and so-called "guest workers."

8. The colonial struggles of independence in the Americas (in Haiti in 1791), Africa (from the Maghreb to South Africa), and Asia, including the end of the British Raj in India and the subsequent partition of the subcontinent (in 1947), would be punctuated by cycles of "hot wars" such as those in Indochina (1947–54), Algeria (1954–62), and Vietnam (1959–75); "cold wars" such as those in Hungary, Czechoslovakia, and Cuba; and "dirty wars" such as those in Guatemala and El Salvador, resulting in massive movements of people.

9. At the end of the Obama administration (in early 2017), US policy qua Cuban arrivals finally became aligned with the reception of other asylum seekers.

10. The collapse of Lehman Brothers in September 2008 and the ensuing global recession began a significant downturn in patterns of migration—especially irregular, unauthorized migration.

11. According to the *Global Report on Internal Displacement* (IDMC 2016, 8), while there are no figures for the total number of people permanently displaced by disasters, "among a sample of 34 ongoing cases documented in 2015, there were hundreds of thousands of people identified as living in protracted displacement for periods ranging between one and 26 years." For an overview of climate and migration, see also McLeman (2014).

12. Alexander Betts (2010) argues that catastrophic migrations are populated by what he calls "survival migrants" and what Roberto Suro calls "recombinant migrants" (chapter 2, this volume).

13. See "Data on Movements of Refugees and Migrants Are Flawed" (2017).

14. Human beings have always migrated. Migrations have shaped and reshaped the world. Modern humans are the children of immigration. *Homo sapiens sapiens* is the child of *Homo sapiens mobilis*—migration made us human.

15. "In India, the impact of two major flood and storm events were responsible for 81 percent of the displacement, forcing three million people to flee their homes. Heavy rains and flash floods associated with a weak tropical cyclone that tracked across the Bay of Bengal in November displaced 1.8 million in the states of Tamil Nadu and southern Andhra Pradesh. Monsoon flooding associated with Cyclone Komen, which struck neighboring Bangladesh in late July, displaced 1.2 million, mostly in the northern and central states of West Bengal, Odisha, Manipur, Rajasthan and Gujarat" (IDMC 2016, 15).

16. "Three large-scale typhoons and a flood disaster together triggered 75 percent of the displacement in China. Three typhoons, Chan-Hom, Soudelor, and Dujan, struck four eastern provinces between July and September, destroying homes, causing landslides and flooding and, [among] them, displacing more than 2.2 million people. Earlier in the year, heavy rains and flooding in nine southern and eastern provinces forced another 518,000 people to flee their homes in May" (IDMC 2016, 15).

17. "The earthquakes in Nepal in April and May, the thousands of aftershocks that followed and the landslides they triggered left 712,000 homes and much infrastructure damaged or destroyed. The disaster took a heavy toll on the developing nation, affecting almost a third of the population and killing 8,700 people. Many of the 2.6 million who were displaced have been unable to return to their homes, and recovery and reconstruction will take many years to complete" (IDMC 2016, 15).

18. "Typhoon Koppu (local name Lando) was the most severe. It made landfall on Luzon, the country's largest and most populous island, in October, killing 54 people, displacing around 938,000 and causing severe crop damage. Typhoon Melor (local name Nona) forced 743,000 people to flee their homes in the central regions of Bicol Peninsula and Romblan Islands in December, and Typhoon Goni (local name Ineng) displaced more than 318,000 in the north of the country in August" (IDMC 2016, 15).

19. Inequality and unchecked criminality are compounded by manmade environmental malfeasance. The 1969 Honduras–El Salvador war (known in Latin America as the "Soccer War") erupted when approximately 300,000 Salvadorans ran out of cultivable land, spilling over into neighboring Honduras. The enormous concentration of lands in the hands of a few families and the resulting land scarcity for the vast majority of peasants led to the brief war. Durham (1979, 1) argues that "land scarcity, a principal cause of the war, was largely a product of the concentration of landholdings." Deforestation for rare hardwoods and beef production has left an ecological scar as more and more forests are destroyed for export commodities. Between 1990 and 2005, 37.1 percent of the forests of Honduras were consumed. "Worse, since the close of the 1990s, Honduras's rate of forest loss has increased by 9 percent," leaving the country especially vulnerable during hurricane season. Hurricane Mitch hit Central America in 1998, leaving more than 11,000 dead and 8,000 missing and displacing more than 2.5 million Hondurans. Many Hondurans began a massive exodus to a country to which they had not migrated before: the United States. The hurricane left a catastrophic environmental and psychosocial sequel.

Data from the Brown University School of Medicine estimate that out of a total of 3.3 million adults (age fifteen or older) living in Honduras, more than 492,000 have experienced posttraumatic stress disorder due to Hurricane Mitch (Kohn et al. 2005). More recently, as Suro (chapter 2, this volume) notes, "To make a horrific situation worse, Central America experienced the most severe drought in decades during this period with relief agencies counting 3.5 million people in the region as food insecure at mid-decade" (Chishti and Hipsman 2016).

20. Sachs writes, "I believe that it is in Africa's enormous self-interest and in the world's interest to help make sure that every child in Africa, especially the girls right now, have the health and the education they need. That would be followed by a faster voluntary fertility reduction, a demographic transition. . . . If Africa were to reach 5 billion in population or 4 billion in population by 2100, the pressures on survival, well-being, and mass migration would be phenomenally large, indeed tragic" (Sachs 2017, 6).

21. The vast majority of these children, some 4.5 million, are US-born citizens. These children are living in the shadow of the law, in constant fear of deportation and forced family separations. During the term of his presidency, Barack Obama deported more than 2.5 million immigrants. Moving forward, President Trump is making good on his promises to increase deportations and call for the building of a two-thousand-mile wall along the Mexican border.

22. "Of those the Syrian conflict has uprooted, around 6.6 million people have been displaced internally. Away from the media glare and out of reach of humanitarian agencies, many struggle to survive in subhuman conditions" (IDMC 2016, 4).

23. In 2015, Iraq had 3.3 million and Yemen had 2.5 million internally displaced people (IDMC 2016, 4).

24. By 2017, South Sudan had 2.4 million refugees, surpassing Somalia in the number of refugees under UNHRC protection (UNHCR 2018a, 2018b).

25. "The drought 'had displaced Syrians long before the conflict began,' said Francesco Femia, president of the Center for Climate Security. 'And what is frightening is that analysts who study the region completely missed it'" (Stokes 2016).

26. Approximately a quarter of all the 1.8 million refugees in Europe originated in Europe (UNICEF 2016, 92).

27. Approximately two-thirds of the 11.1 million unauthorized immigrants in the United States are Latin Americans. See "Unauthorized Immigrant Population Trends" (2016).

28. Between October 1, 2013, and September 30, 2014, US Customs and Border Protection encountered 67,339 unaccompanied children. The largest number of children (27 percent of the total) came from Honduras, followed by Guatemala (25 percent), El Salvador (24 percent), and Mexico (23 percent) (American Immigration Council 2015).

29. The top nine countries for deportations from the United States are all Latin American nations, led by Mexico. Jamaica is tenth. See "Top 10 Countries of Deportations" (2013).

30. The Gini coefficient is a standard economic measure of income inequality whereby 0 represents perfect equality while an index of 100 implies perfect inequality.

31. St. Louis, Missouri, the most violent city in the United States, has a homicide rate of 59.2 deaths per 100,000 people (Gramlich 2018; see also http://www.city-data.com/crime/crime-St.-Louis-Missouri.html).

32. In 2015, "there were 40.8 million IDPs worldwide as a result of conflict and violence—an increase of 2.8 million on 2014." Internal displacement associated with conflict and violence has been growing since the beginning of the millennium, and the 2015 data represent "the highest figure ever recorded" (IDMC 2016, 5). Today there are 21.3 million refugees under the UNHCR.

33. In affluent countries worldwide, poverty among children of immigrants has increased steadily in recent years, with gaps between the native-born and immigrants ranging from 7 percent in Australia and Germany, to 12 percent in the United States, to between 26 and 28 percent in England and France (Hernandez et al. 2010). In the United States, children of immigrants are more likely than native-born children to live in crowded housing conditions (7 percent versus 2 percent, respectively) and to experience inadequate nutrition (25 percent versus 21 percent, respectively) (Chaudry and Fortuny 2010).

Poverty coexists with a variety of other factors that augment risks, such as single parenthood, residence in violence-ridden neighborhoods, gang activity, and drug trade as well as school environments that are segregated, overcrowded, understaffed, and poorly funded (C. Suárez-Orozco, Yoshikawa, and Tseng 2015). It is also associated with high rates of housing mobility and concurrent school transitions that can be highly disruptive to educational performance (Gándara and Contreras 2009). Segregation matters in immigrant integration. In the United States, immigrant-origin Latino children are the most segregated students in the schools, particularly in the West (Orfield et al. 2014; Orfield and Lee 2005). Immigrants who settle in predominantly minority neighborhoods may have little if any direct, continuous, and intimate contact with peers from the nonimmigrant mainstream population. A pattern of triple segregation—by race, language, and poverty—shapes the lives of many new immigrants in the various countries.

34. "Almost every country in the world is affected by trafficking, whether as a country of origin, transit or destination for victims" (UNODC 2012). Although no precise figures exist, the International Labour Organisation (ILO) (2013) estimated that "980,000 to 1,225,000 children—both boys and girls—are in a forced labor situation as a result of trafficking."

The trafficking in children—internally in countries, across national borders, and across continents—is closely interlinked with the demand for cheap, malleable, and docile labor in sectors and among employment settings where the working conditions and treatment grossly violate the human rights of the children. "These are characterized by environments that are unacceptable (the unconditional worst forms) as well as dangerous to the health and the development of the child (hazardous worst forms). These forms range from bonded labour, camel jockeying, child domestic labour, commercial sexual exploitation and prostitution, drug couriering, and child soldiering to exploitative or slavery-like practices in the informal industrial sector" (ILO 2004, 16).

According to the ILO, "the occupations in which most children are working as forced or slave labourers are in agriculture, drug trafficking, commercial sexual exploitation and as child soldiers [in paramilitary combat units]" (ILO 2013).

REFERENCES

American Immigration Council. 2015. *A Guide to Children Arriving at the Border: Laws, Policies and Responses.* www.americanimmigrationcouncil.org/research/guide-children-arriving-border-laws-policies-and-responses.

Antón, Susan C., Richard Potts, and Leslie C. Aiello. 2014. "Evolution of Early *Homo:* An Integrated Biological Perspective." *Science* 345 (6192). doi:10.1126/science.1236828.

Bell, Martin, and Elin Charles-Edwards. 2013. "Cross-National Comparisons of Internal Migration: An Update on Global Patterns and Trends." United Nations Technical Paper No. 2013/1. www.un.org/en/development/desa/population/publications/pdf/technical/TP2013–1.pdf.

Betts, Alexander. 2010. "Survival Migration: A New Protection Framework." *Global Governance* 16 (3): 361–82.

Butler, Declan. 2017. "What the Numbers Say about Refugees." *Nature: International Weekly Journal of Science* 543. www.nature.com/news/what-the-numbers-say-about-refugees-1.21548.

Callahan, Rebecca M., and Patricia Gándara, eds. 2014. *The Bilingual Advantage: Language, Literacy and the US Labor Market.* Bristol, UK: Multilingual Matters.

Chaudry, Ajay, and Karina Fortuny. 2010. "Children of Immigrants: Economic Well-Being." Urban Institute, no. 4. www.urban.org/sites/default/files/publication/29411/412270-Children-of-Immigrants-Economic-Well-Being.PDF.

China Labor Bulletin. 2017. "Migrant Workers and Their Children." www.clb.org.hk/content/migrant-workers-and-their-children.

Chishti, Muzaffar, and Faye Hipsman. 2016. "Increased Central American Migration to the United States May Prove an Enduring Phenomenon." *Migration Information Source.* February 18, 2016. www.migrationpolicy.org/article/increased-central-american-migration-united-states-may-prove-enduring-phenomenon.

Collier, Virginia P. 1995. "Acquiring a Second Language for School." *Directions in Language and Education* 1 (4): 1–14. https://files.eric.ed.gov/fulltext/ED394301.pdf.

Cook, Benjamin I., Kevin J. Anchukaitis, Ramzi Touchan, David M. Meko, and Edward R. Cook. 2016. "Spatiotemporal Drought Variability in the Mediterranean over the Last 900 Years." *Journal of Geophysical Research* 121 (5): 2060–74. doi:10.1002/2015JD023929.

Cummins, Jim. 2000. *Language, Power, and Pedagogy: Bilingual Children in the Crossfire.* Clevedon, UK: Multilingual Matters.

"Data on Movements of Refugees and Migrants Are Flawed." 2017. *Nature: International Weekly Journal of Science* 543 (7643). www.nature.com/news/data-on-movements-of-refugees-and-migrants-are-flawed-1.21568.

DeVoe, Drosh Marie. 1981. "Framing Refugees as Clients." *International Migration Review* 15 (1/2): 88–94. doi:10.2307/2545327.

Dunmore, Charlie. 2017. "UN Chief Says Aid for Syrian Refugees Is in Global Interest." *United Nations High Commissioner for Refugees.* www.unhcr.org/en-us/news/latest/2017/3/58da5ff64/un-chief-says-aid-syrian-refugees-global-interest.html.

Durham, William H. 1979. *Scarcity and Survival in Central America: Ecological Origins of the Soccer War.* Stanford, CA: Stanford University Press.

ENADID (Instituto Nacional de Estadística y Geografía). 2014. National Survey of Demographic Dynamics 2014. http://en.www.inegi.org.mx/proyectos/enchogares/especiales/enadid/2014/.

Erikson, Erik H. 1950. *Childhood and Society.* New York: Norton.

Foner, Nancy, ed. 2009. *Across Generations: Immigrant Families in America.* New York: New York University Press.

Gándara, Patricia, and Frances Contreras. 2009. *The Latino Education Crisis: The Consequences of Failed Social Policies*. Cambridge, MA: Harvard University Press.

García, Maria C. 2006. *Seeking Refuge: Central American Migration to Mexico, the United States, and Canada*. Berkeley: University of California Press.

Gatrell, Peter. 2014a. "Europe on the Move: Refugees and World War One." *British Library: World War One*. www.bl.uk/world-war-one/articles/refugees-europe-on-the-move#sthash .ZnyN1Nq8.dpuf.

———. 2014b. "Refugees (1914–1918)." In *International Encyclopedia of the First World War*, edited by Ute Daniel, Peter Gatrell, Oliver Janz, Heather Jones, Jennifer Keene, Alan Kramer, and Bill Nasson. Berlin: Freie Universität. doi: 10.15463/ie1418.10134.

Gonzalez-Barrera, Ana. 2015. "More Mexicans Leaving Than Coming to the US." *Pew Research Center Hispanic Trends*. www.pewhispanic.org/2015/11/19/more-mexicans-leaving-than-coming-to-the-u-s/.

Gramlich, John. 2018. "Five Facts about Crime in the U.S." Pew Research Center. www .pewresearch.org/fact-tank/2018/01/30/5-facts-about-crime-in-the-u-s/.

Haan, Arjan de, and Shahin Yaqub. 2009. *Migration and Poverty: Linkages, Knowledge Gaps, and Policy Implications*. Geneva: United Nations Research Institute for Social Development (UNRISD). www.unrisd.org/80256B3C005BCCF9/%28httpPublications%29/82D CDCF510459B36C12575F400474040?OpenDocument.

Hakuta, Kenji, Yuko Goto Butler, and Daria Witt. 2000. "How Long Does It Take English Learners to Attain Proficiency?" *University of California Linguistic Minority Research Institute Policy Report 2000–01*. Stanford, CA: Stanford University. https://web.stanford .edu/~hakuta/Publications/%282000%29%20-%20HOW%20LONG%20DOES%20 IT%20TAKE%20ENGLISH%20LEARNERS%20TO%20ATTAIN%20PR.pdf.

Hernandez, Donald J., Suzanne Macartney, and Victor L. Blanchard. 2010. "Children of Immigrants: Family and Socioeconomic Indicators for Affluent Countries." *Child Indicators Research* 3 (4): 413–37.

IDMC (Internal Displacement Monitoring Centre). 2016. *Global Report on Internal Displacement*. www.internal-displacement.org/globalreport2016/#home2016.

———. 2017. *Global Report on Internal Displacement*. http://www.internal-displacement .org/global-report/grid2017/pdfs/2017-GRID.pdf.

———. 2018. *Global Report on Internal Displacement*. www.internal-displacement.org /global-report/grid2018/downloads/2018-GRID.pdf.

IOM (International Organization for Migration). 2018. *World Migration Report*. Geneva, Switzerland: United Nations. www.iom.int/wmr/world-migration-report-2018.

International Labour Organisation. 2004. *Child Labour: A Textbook for University Students*. Geneva: International Programme on the Elimination of Child Labour. www.ilo.org /ipecinfo/product/viewProduct.do?productId = 174.

———. 2013. *Trafficking in Children*. Geneva: International Programme on the Elimination of Child Labour. www.ilo.org/ipec/areas/Traffickingofchildren/lang--en/index.htm.

Kazemipur, Abdolmohammed, and Shiva S. Halli. 2001. "Immigrants and 'New Poverty': The Case of Canada." *International Migration Review* 35 (4): 1129–56. http://onlinelibrary .wiley.com/doi/10.1111/j.1747-7379.2001.tb00055.x/full.

Kohn, Robert, Itzhak Levav, Irma Donaire, Miguel Machuca, and Rita Tamashiro. 2005. "Psychological and Psychopathological Reactions in Honduras Following Hurricane Mitch: Implications for Service Planning." *Rev Panam Salud Publica* 18 (4/5): 287–95.

Lacan, Jacques. 2006. *Ecrits: The First Complete Edition in English.* Translated by Bruce Fink. New York: Norton.

LaFeber, Walter. 1993. *Inevitable Revolutions: The United States in Central America.* 2nd ed. New York: Norton.

Luthar, Suniya S. 1999. *Poverty and Children's Adjustment.* Thousand Oaks, CA: SAGE.

Massey, Douglas S., Rafael Alarcón, Jorge Durand, and Humberto González. 1987. *Return to Aztlan: The Social Process of International Migration from Western Mexico.* Berkeley: University of California Press.

Massey, Douglas, and Felipe G. Espana. 1987. "The Social Process of International Migration." *Science* 237: 733–38. doi:10.1126/science.237.4816.733.

McLeman, Robert A. 2014. *Climate and Human Migration: Past Experiences, Future Challenges.* Cambridge: Cambridge University Press.

McNicoll, G., and Robert A. McLeman. 2014. "Climate and Human Migration: Past Experiences, Future Challenges." *Population and Development Review* 40: 378–79. doi:10.1111/j.1728-4457.2014.00684.x.

National Geographic, Genographic Project. n.d. "Map of Human Migration." Accessed June 20, 2018. https://genographic.nationalgeographic.com/human-journey/.

National Research Council and Institute of Medicine. 1997. *Improving Schooling for Language-Minority Children: A Research Agenda,* edited by Diane August and Kenji Hakuta. Washington, DC: National Academies Press.

New York Times. 2017. "A Great Migration." December 30, 2017.

Orfield, Gary, Erica Frankenberg, Jongyeon Ee, and John Kuscera. 2014. *Brown at 60: Great Progress, a Long Retreat, and an Uncertain Future.* Los Angeles: Civil Rights Project/Proyecto Derechos Civiles, UCLA. www.civilrightsproject.ucla.edu/research/k-12-education/integration-and-diversity/brown-at-60-great-progress-a-long-retreat-and-an-uncertain-future/Brown-at-60-051814.pdf.

Orfield, Gary, and Chungmei Lee. 2005. *Why Segregation Matters: Poverty and Education Inequality.* Cambridge, MA: Civil Rights Project, Harvard University. www.civilrightsproject.ucla.edu/research/k-12-education/integration-and-diversity/why-segregation-matters-poverty-and-educational-inequality/orfield-why-segregation-matters-2005.pdf.

Papademetriou, Demetrios G. 2005. "The Global Struggle with Illegal Migration: No End in Sight." *Migration Information Source.* www.migrationpolicy.org/article/global-struggle-illegal-migration-no-end-sight.

Passel, Jeffrey S., and D'vera Cohn. 2016. "Children of Unauthorized Immigrants Represent Rising Share of K-12 Students." Pew Research Center. www.pewresearch.org/fact-tank/2016/11/17/children-of-unauthorized-immigrants-represent-rising-share-of-k-12-students/.

Pope Francis. 2014. Homily of Pope Francis: "Pilgrimage to the Holy Land on the Occasion of the Fiftieth Anniversary of the Meeting between Pope Paul VI and Patriarch Athenagoras in Jerusalem." May 25, 2014. https://w2.vatican.va/content/francesco/en/homilies/2014/documents/papa-francesco_20140525_terra-santa-omelia-bethlehem.html.

———. 2015. "Encyclical Letter *Laudato Si'* of the Holy Father Francis on Care for Our Common Home." May 24, 2015. http://w2.vatican.va/content/francesco/en/encyclicals

/documents/papa-francesco_20150524_enciclica-laudato-si.html   francesco_20150524_enciclica-laudato-si.html.

Ricoeur, Paul. 1995. *See Oneself as Another.* Reprint, Chicago: University of Chicago Press.

Sachs, Jeffrey. 2017. "Humanism and the Forced Confinement Crisis." Paper presented at the Workshop on Humanitarianism and Mass Migration, UCLA, Los Angeles, January 18–19, 2017.

Sánchez Terán, Gonzalo. 2017. "Humanism and the Forced Confinement Crisis." Paper presented at the Workshop on Humanitarianism and Mass Migration, UCLA, Los Angeles, January 18–19, 2017.

"San Pedro Sula, la ciudad más violenta del mundo; Juárez, la segunda." 2012. *Seguridad, Justicia y Paz.* www.seguridadjusticiaypaz.org.mx/sala-de-prensa/541-san-pedro-sula-la-ciudad-mas-violenta-del-mundo-juarez-la-segunda.

Save the Children. 2016. "Half of All Refugee Children Are Out of School Leaving Them Exposed to Exploitation and Abuse." May 16, 2016. https://www.savethechildren.org/us/about-us/media-and-news/2016-press-releases/half-of-all-refugee-children-are-out-of-school-leaving-them-expo.

Schlesinger, Stephen, and Stephen Kinzer. 1982. *Bitter Fruit: The Untold Story of the American Coup in Guatemala.* New York: Doubleday.

Smithsonian National Museum of Natural History. 2016. *Climate Effects on Human Evolution.* http://humanorigins.si.edu/research/climate-and-human-evolution/climate-effects-human-evolution.

Stokes, Elaisha. 2016. "The Drought That Preceded Syria's Civil War Was Likely the Worst in 900 Years." *Vice News,* March 3, 2016. https://news.vice.com/article/the-drought-that-preceded-syrias-civil-war-was-likely-the-worst-in-900-years.

Suárez-Orozco, Carola E. 2004. "Formulating Identity in a Globalized World." In *Globalization: Culture and Education in the New Millennium,* edited by Marcelo M. Suárez-Orozco and Desiree Qin-Hilliard, 173–202. Berkeley: University of California Press.

Suárez-Orozco, Carola E., and Amy K. Marks. 2016. "Immigrant Students in the United States: Addressing Their Possibilities and Challenges." In *Global Migration, Diversity, and Civic Education: Improving Policy and Practice,* edited by James A. Banks, Marcelo M. Suárez-Orozco, and Miriam Ben-Peretz, 107–31. New York: Teachers College Press / National Academy of Education.

Suárez-Orozco, Carola E., and Marcelo M. Suárez-Orozco. 2012. "Immigration in the Age of Global Vertigo." *In Arizona Firestorm: Global Immigration Realities, National Media, and Provincial Politics,* edited by Otto Santa Ana and Celeste G. Bustamante, 253–76. Lanham, MD: Rowman and Littlefield.

Suárez-Orozco, Carola E., Marcelo M. Suárez-Orozco, and Irina Todorova. 2008. *Learning a New Land: Immigrant Students in American Society.* Cambridge, MA: Harvard University Press / Belknap Press.

Suárez-Orozco, Carola E., Hirokazu Yoshikawa, Robert T. Teranishi, and Marcelo M. Suárez-Orozco. 2011. "Growing Up in the Shadows: The Developmental Implications of Unauthorized Status." Immigration, Youth, and Education. Special issue, *Harvard Educational Review* 81 (3): 438–73.

Suárez-Orozco, Carola E., Hirokazu Yoshikawa, and Vivian Tseng. 2015. *Intersecting Inequalities: Research to Reduce Inequality for Immigrant-Origin Children and Youth.* New

York: William T. Grant Foundation. www.immigrationresearch-info.org/system/files
/Intersecting_Inequalities_final.pdf.

Suárez-Orozco, Marcelo M. 1989. *Central American Refugees and U.S. High Schools:
A Psychosocial Study of Motivation and Achievement*. Stanford, CA: Stanford University
Press.

———. 1991. "Immigrant Adaptation to Schooling: A Hispanic Case." In *Minority Status
and Schooling: A Comparative Study of Immigrant and Involuntary Minorities*, edited by
Margaret A. Gibson and John U. Ogbu, 37–61. New York: Garland.

Suárez-Orozco, Marcelo M., and Robert Suro. 2017. "Children Are the New Dispossessed."
Medium, January 17, 2017. https://medium.com/@suro_26975/children-are-the-new-
dispossessed-37f54c5ce6ad.

"Top 10 Countries of Deportations = Latin America, Caribbean." 2013. *News Americas*,
December 19, 2013. www.newsamericasnow.com/top-10-countries-of-deportations-
latin-america-caribbean/.

"Unauthorized Immigrant Population Trends for States, Birth Countries, and Regions."
2016. *Pew Research Center Hispanic Trends*. www.pewhispanic.org/interactives/unau-
thorized-trends/.

UN Department of Economic and Social Affairs. 2017. International Migration Report 2017:
Highlights. www.un.org/en/development/desa/population/migration/publications/migra-
tionreport/docs/MigrationReport2017_Highlights.pdf.

UNHCR (United Nations High Commissioner for Refugees). 2016. "Global Trends: Forced
Displacement in 2015." www.unhcr.org/en-us/statistics/unhcrstats/576408cd7/unhcr-
global-trends-2015.html.

———. 2017a. "Situations: South Sudan." data.unhcr.org/SouthSudan/country.php?id = 251.

———. 2017b. "Somalia Situation 2017." www.unhcr.org/591ae0e17.pdf.

———. 2017c. "Syrian Refugees: A Snapshot of the Crisis in the Middle East and Europe."
http://syrianrefugees.eu.

———. 2018a. "Global Trends: Forced Displacement in 2017." www.unhcr.org/global
trends2017/.

———. 2018b. "South Sudan Emergency." http://www.unhcr.org/en-us/south-sudan-
emergency.html.

UNHCR News Centre. 2017a. "Refugee Crisis in South Sudan Now World's Fastest Growing."
www.unhcr.org/en-us/news/latest/2017/3/58cbfa304/refugee-crisis-south-sudan-worlds-
fastest-growing.html.

———. 2017b. "UNHCR Says Death Risk from Starvation in Horn of Africa, Yemen, Nigeria
Growing, Displacement Already Rising." www.unhcr.org/en-us/news/briefing/2017/4
/58ec9d464/unhcr-says-death-risk-starvation-horn-africa-yemen-nigeria-growing-dis-
placement.html.

UNICEF (United Nations Children's Fund). 2016. *Uprooted: The Growing Crisis for Refugee
and Migrant Children*. www.unicef.org/publications/files/Uprooted_growing_crisis_for_
refugee_and_migrant_children.pdf.

———. 2017a. *A Child Is a Child: Protecting Children on the Move from Violence, Abuse, and
Exploitation*. www.unicef.org/publications/index_95956.html.

———. 2017b. *Reaching Children in South Sudan*. www.unicef.org/infobycountry/southsudan_
74635.html.

UN News Centre. 2017. "Hurricane Irma Erased 'Footprints of an Entire Civilization' on Barbuda, Prime Minister Tells UN." September 17, 2017. https://news.un.org/en/story/2017/09/566372-hurricane-irma-erased-footprints-entire-civilization-barbuda-prime-minister.

UNODC (United Nations Office on Drugs and Crime). 2012. *Human Trafficking.* www.unodc.org/unodc/en/human-trafficking/what-is-human-trafficking.html.

US Department of State. 2013. *Trafficking in Persons Report.* www.state.gov/documents/organization/210737.pdf.

Weissbourd, Richard. 1996. *The Vulnerable Child: What Really Hurts America's Children and What We Can Do about It.* Boston: Addison-Wesley.

PART ONE

THE NEW CARTOGRAPHY OF MASS MIGRATION

1
———

UNCHECKED CLIMATE CHANGE AND MASS MIGRATION

A Probabilistic Case for Urgent Action

Fonna Forman and Veerabhadran Ramanathan

Climate migration describes the voluntary and forced movement of people within and across habitats due to changes in climate. Climate change can act as a causal factor of migration or as a threat multiplier. With unchecked emissions of pollutants, global warming is projected to increase to 1.5°Celsius (C) within 15 years, to 2°C within 35 years, and to 4°C by 2100. These projections are central values with a small (less than 5 percent) probability that warming by 2100 can exceed 6°C, with potentially catastrophic impacts on every human being, living and yet unborn (Xu and Ramanathan 2017).

Climate is already changing in perceptible ways through floods, droughts, fires, heat waves, and sea level rise, displacing communities and catalyzing migration. Climate change and associated migratory shifts have also been statistically linked with civil conflict and political unrest. The decades-long drought in Syria, which has led in turn to agricultural failure, dramatic urbanization, and failed government response, is a powerful case in point. Reliable quantitative estimates of future climate migration are yet to be achieved. Reported estimates vary from 25 million to as many as one billion climate change migrants by 2050. Quantitative approaches for projecting mass migration face significant obstacles due to: (1) a wide range of projections for the degree of warming due to uncertainties in climate feedbacks; (2) the lack of a settled definition for climate migration; and (3) the causal complexity of migration due to variability in non-environmental factors such as bioregion, culture, economics, politics, and individual factors. It may take decades to arrive at reliable quantitative estimates. But this creates unacceptable ethical risks.

For this reason, we advocate a probabilistic approach to climate migration that accounts for both central and low probability warming projections as the only ethical response to the unfolding crisis. We conclude that in the absence of drastic mitigating actions, mass migration induced by climate change can become a major threat during the latter half of this century. For the poorest three billion, however, who still depend on thousand-year-old technologies for meeting basic needs such as cooking and obtaining drinking water, forced mass migration will be a reality much sooner. Climate justice demands an urgent global response for the well-being of us all.

CLIMATE CHANGE: HOW SOON AND HOW LARGE?

Climate change has already begun to change our lives through droughts, mega-floods, heat waves, intense hurricanes, glacial melting, forest fires, and other severe weather phenomena. There are also other dramatic changes, such as the melting of the glaciers in Greenland and the west Antarctic, the retreat of the Arctic sea ice, the acidification of the oceans, the disappearance of coral reefs, and rising sea levels.

Massive amounts of data provide compelling, if not convincing, evidence that much of the climate change we are experiencing is caused by the buildup of carbon dioxide and other greenhouse gases produced by human activities. The major human activity warming the climate is the burning of fossil fuels for energy access. Others include deforestation; the release of superwarming pollutants, such as halocarbons (CFCS, HFCs) used for refrigeration and air conditioning; the massive release of the superpollutant methane from the use of natural gas, the growing cattle population, and the dumping of food and other organic waste into landfills; the release of the greenhouse gas nitrous oxide from agriculture; and the release of black carbon (another superwarming pollutant) from diesel combustion and residential biomass burning.

The planet has already warmed by 1°C (from preindustrial temperatures).[1] In about thirteen years, the warming will exceed 1.5°C, largely from the warming pollutants that are already in the air. If current emissions of CO_2 and the superpollutants continue unabated until 2030, the warming is likely to exceed 2°C in another thirty-three years (by 2050). The potential warming of 1.5°C to 2°C during the coming decades is a source of major concern for many reasons, including the following:

· The last time the planet was this warm was about 130,000 years ago. But those earlier warm epochs evolved over thousands of years. Human-induced warming will happen 30 to 100 times faster in a matter of decades from now, raising questions about the ability of ecosystems as well as social systems to adapt.
· The planet undergoes warm (interglacial) to cold (glacial) epochs and is currently in a warm epoch called the Holocene. The last glacial epoch peaked about 20,000 years ago, when the planet was colder by about 5°C. The human-induced warming is occurring on top of the already warm Holocene climate.

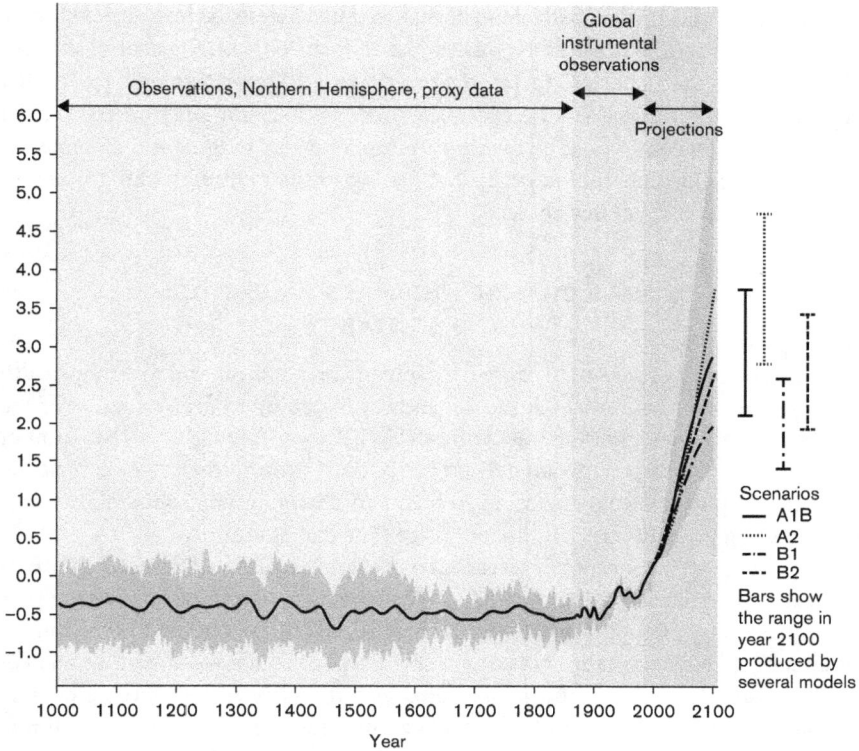

FIGURE 1.1. Variations in Earth's surface temperature: years 1000 to 2100. Deviation in degrees Celsius (in relation to 1990 value). *Source:* UNEP & GRID/Arendal, Vital Climate Graphics update, 2005 (see UNEP 2009, 27).

If the emissions continue unabated until 2050, it is likely that the twenty-first century will witness warming of 4°C or greater by 2100 (see fig. 1.1). These projected warming estimates represent at least a 50 percent probability. In our understanding of the climate system, there is a wide distribution of plausible warming values around the central value of 4°C. For example, there is a 5 percent probability that the warming will be only half as great, an outcome that would be good for society. But the problem is that there is an equal 5 percent probability that the warming could be more than 6°C, an outcome that is likely to be catastrophic for most human beings, rich or poor. In short, there is a one-in-twenty chance that our current fossil fuel use will result in catastrophic consequences for our children and grandchildren. Would we put our children on a plane if the pilot informed us that the aircraft had a one-in-twenty chance of falling from the sky?

It is within this probabilistic context that we must assess the impacts of climate change on migration. It would be misleading to focus only on the central value of about 2°C for 2050 and 4°C for 2100 since there is a 50 percent probability that such warming estimates will be exceeded. Also, by focusing only on the central values, policy makers would be making an implicit value judgment that a one-in-twenty chance of catastrophic events happening to their children and grandchildren is an acceptable policy choice.

CLIMATE CHANGE AND MASS MIGRATION:
WHAT'S AT STAKE?

Climate change is projected to cause widespread and serious harm to public health and the environment on which life depends, threatening to unravel many of the public health advances of the last century (UNEP 2009)(see fig. 1.2). The brunt of the harm will fall disproportionately on the poorest communities, which have the least capacity and fewest resources to adapt to changing environmental conditions, raising urgent issues of climate justice (Forman et al. 2016).

According to the Centre for Research on the Epidemiology of Disasters (CRED) Emergency Events Database (as cited in WMO 2013), 226 million people each year are impacted by natural disasters. In the first decade of the twenty-first century, 1 million people died in natural disasters, 88 percent of which were weather related. In that same decade, 370,000 people died as a direct result of extreme climate conditions, an outcome that amounts to a 20 percent increase over the death rate of the prior decade, primarily as a result of the increased incidence of heat waves (WMO 2013). A Lancet Commission report (2015) concluded that without adequate mitigation and adaptation, climate change poses unacceptable risks to global public health.

United Nations High Commissioner for Refugees (UNHCR) Chief António Guterres predicted in 2009 that climate change would become the largest driver of population displacements, both inside and across national borders. Current estimates of climate migration vary widely, from a low of 25 million to a high of 1 billion migrants by 2050. The most commonly cited estimate is 200 million displaced by 2050 (International Organization for Migration 2008, 11–12; Myers 2005). According to recent estimates, between 2008 and 2014, natural disasters—primarily atmospheric storms and floods—annually displaced an average of 26.4 million individuals (NRC/IDMI 2015, 20). The rate of displacement has more than doubled since 1970, from fewer than 2,000 persons per million to more than 4,000 persons per million in 2014 (NRC/IDMI 2015, 22). These displacements, even if temporary, have a profound impact on individuals' lives, often involving the loss of a home or crops, and particularly harming individuals at the bottom of the

	+1°	+2°	+3°	+4°	+5°
	Global mean annual temperature change relative to 1980–1999				

WATER
Increased water availability in moist tropics and high altitudes →
Decreased water availability and increase in droughts in mid-altitudes and semi-arid low latitudes →

People affected:
0.4 to 1.7 billion ←→   1.0 to 2.0 billion ←→   1.1 to 3.2 billion ←→   Additional people with increased water stress

ECO-SYSTEMS
Increased amphibian extinction →   About 20 to 30% of species at increasingly high risk of extinction →   Major extinctions around the globe →

Increased coral bleaching Most corals bleached   Widespread coral mortality →
Increasing species range shifts and wildfire risk →
Terrestrial biosphere tends toward a net carbon source
~15% of ecosystems affected   ~40% of ecosystems affected →

FOOD
Low latitudes:
Crop productivity decreases for some cereals → All cereals decrease

Mid to high latitudes:
Crop productivity increases for some cereals → Decreases in some regions

COASTS
Increased damage from floods and storms →
About 30% loss of coastal wetlands →
Additional people at risk of coastal flooding each year: 0 to 3 million ←→   2 to 15 million ←→

HEALTH
Increased burden from malnutrition, diarrhoeal, cardio-respiratory, and infectious diseases →
Increased morbidity and mortality from heatwaves, floods, and droughts →
Changed distribution of some disease vectors → Substantial burden on health services

SINGULAR EVENTS
Local retreat of ice in Greenland and West Antarctica → Long term commitment to several meters of sea-level rise due to ice sheet loss → Leading to reconfiguration of coastlines worldwide and inundation of low-lying areas

Ecosystem changes due to weakening of the meridional overturning circulation →
Impacts will vary by extent of adaptation, rate of temperature change, and socio-economic pathway

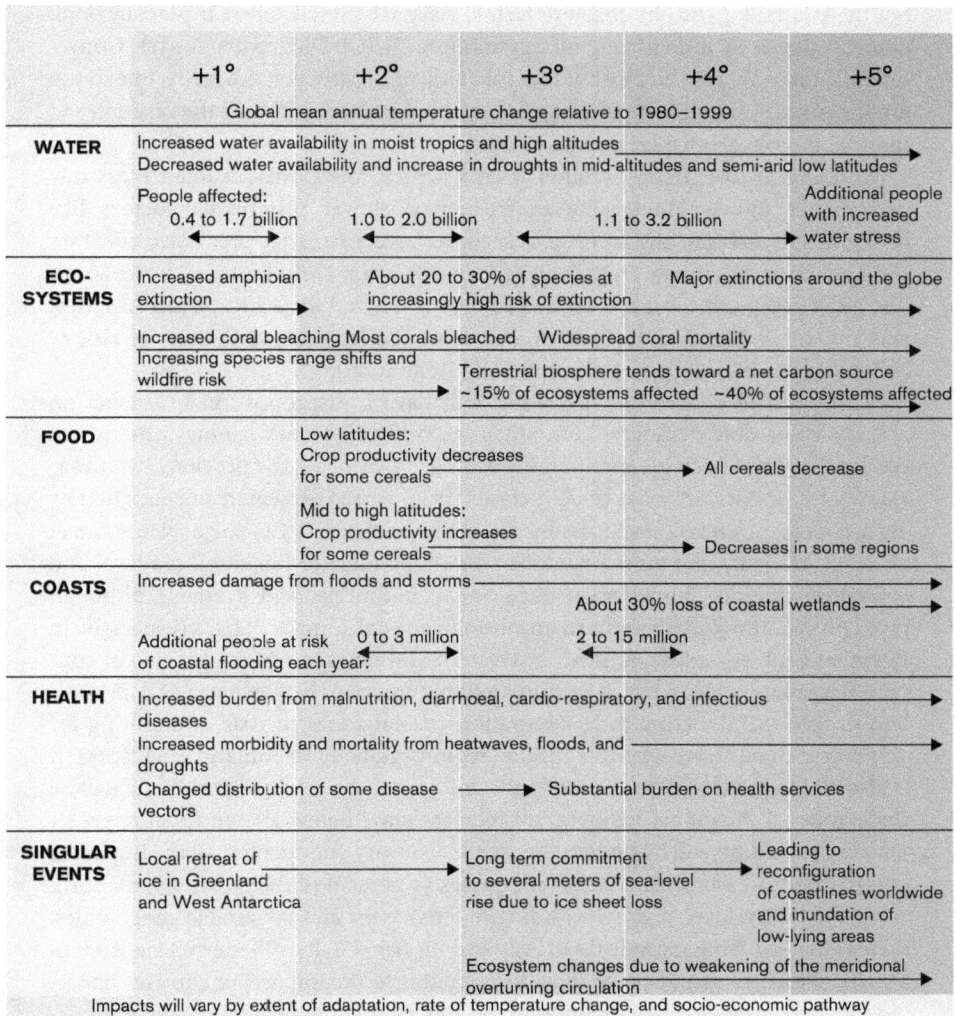

FIGURE 1.2. Impacts associated with global temperature change. *Source:* UNEP 2009. Original color graphics reproduced in black and white.

socioeconomic ladder who lack the resources to adapt to the impacts of a rapidly changing climate.

Climate-related displacement disproportionately impacts Asia and Latin America. Annually, between 2006 and 2014, East Asia had more than 6,000 people per million inhabitants displaced, Latin America had approximately 5,700, and

South Asia had 4,500. In absolute terms, Asia accounted for 82.0 percent of all climate-displaced individuals, or 21.5 million (NRCI/DMI 2015, 30–31). Consequently, not only are the most vulnerable *individuals* impacted heavily, but so too are the more vulnerable *developing countries,* which typically lack the resources to manage large-scale displacements.

In addition to extreme weather events, which often cause sudden mass displacements and are increasing in frequency, slower progressive factors like drought, soil erosion, and forest loss seem to have a stronger predictive effect on the likelihood of climate migration (McLeman 2014; Gutmann and Field 2010). The main geographic impacts are already being felt in Asia, Africa, Latin America, and the small island states, which also have the largest populations at risk of becoming climate refugees (Biermann and Boas 2008).

Rising sea levels around the world will have a disproportionate impact on already vulnerable demographics. Since the mid-nineteenth century, the rate of sea-level rise has been greater than the average rate during the previous two thousand years, and it continues to accelerate (IPCC 2013b). Research suggests that by 2100, average sea levels could rise by one meter or more (IPCC 2013a; Neumann et al. 2015). Globally, the most populous areas vulnerable to increased sea level and coast loss include China, India, Bangladesh, Indonesia, and Vietnam, although rapid population growth and urbanization in coastal zones in Africa (especially in Egypt and sub-Saharan countries in Western and Eastern Africa) are also of concern (Neumann et al. 2015). It is estimated that by 2060, between 729 and 983 million people will be living in low-elevation coastal zones in Asia, accounting for 70 percent of all those who live in such regions globally (Neumann et al. 2015). It is also estimated that approximately 280 million of the world's inhabitants will be underwater if the global temperature increase stays below 2°C and that approximately 630 million will be underwater at 4°C. Seventy-four percent of the impacted population is in Asia (which itself comprises 59 percent of the global population).

At the macro level, regions with fragile ecosystems and vulnerable geographies, such as the low-lying megadeltas in Asia and the Sahel Belt in Western Africa, are in a particularly precarious position and susceptible to the impacts of climate change. On the mesoscale, countries with weak or underfunded bureaucratic and administrative systems are likely to have low adaptive and responsive capacities, leaving their inhabitants exposed to climatic shifts. At the micro level, households and individuals in the Global South are most susceptible to the negative impacts of climate change. Those living in rural areas whose livelihoods are linked with climate-sensitive sectors like agriculture and fishing are most vulnerable and at the highest risk, and they are typically the least capable of making in situ adaptations or exercising out-migration options. The capacity to leave one's home entails certain types of financial and social capital such as education, language skills, and support networks.

HISTORICAL OVERVIEW OF CLIMATE CHANGE AND MIGRATION RESEARCH

Climate-induced migration was identified as an area of concern for scholarly research in the 1990s after the first Intergovernmental Panel on Climate Change report in 1990 contained a section on "Migration and Resettlement."[2] For a long time, catastrophic climate-related events such as hurricanes (or cyclones), flash floods, heat waves, wildfires, and tornadoes typically received the most attention, both from the general public and from academics. While these events are responsible for significant climate-induced migration, slowly progressing but devastating changes to the environment are predicted to play a much larger role in producing population displacement over the next century.

Vulnerability and Adaptation

Migration is presently one in a range of adaptation options people consider when responding to their changing climate and environment (McLeman 2014). For the very poorest, international migration is unlikely since it is increasingly risky and requires an up-front outlay of cash to which many do not have access. Thus, those who are impacted the hardest by climate change are more likely to move regionally or locally. Further, the Intergovernmental Panel on Climate Change (IPCC) in Working Group II's first report noted that "climate change could translate into migration of impoverished people from rural to urban areas ([in] developing countries), from coastal lowlands (particularly densely inhabited delta areas) to inland areas, and possibly across national boundaries" (IPCC 1990, 5–11). The IPCC correctly noted that the majority of migration would be within developing nations, following patterns of urbanization and away from coastal regions.

Additionally, increasing urbanization due to rural dwellers' inability to survive off the land may lead to increased "demand on urban services and increasing political pressure on the state" (Barnett and Adger 2007, 642), a situation that may make macro-level institutions even harder pressed to provide adaptation support for exploding urban populations, exacerbating civil unrest and even revolution, as in the case of Syria (Kelley et al. 2015). However, everything we presently know about vulnerability and adaptation, and about the factors people consider when making decisions about migration, comes from past warming trends, which remained in the range of 0.5°C warming. Although these experiences are instructive, it would be a mistake to assume we can simply extrapolate from them to anticipate future adaptation strategies should warming increase during the coming decades by a catastrophic 2 to 4°C, as probabilities suggest they might. In such a scenario, migration would surely become less of an option for many and more of an imperative for mere survival.

The Impacts of the Securitization and Militarization
of Climate Change and Migration

There has been increased concern about the links among climate migration and immigration, national security, food scarcity, and global instability (Barnett 2003; Brown 2012). T. F. Homer-Dixon (2010) argues that competition for dwindling natural resources such as forests, water, and arable land has the potential to lead to devastating and prolonged violent global conflict, including ethnic conflict, urban instability, and political insurrection. Jon Barnett (2003) warns, however, that these convergences can be exploited by conservative border agendas, among other issues.

THE INTERNATIONAL RESPONSE TO
CLIMATE MIGRATION

A variety of international bodies, including the United Nations Framework Convention on Climate Change, the United Nations Office of the High Commissioner for Refugees, and the IPCC, have considered the matter of climate migration. The IPCC integrates vulnerability variables and adaptation strategies into its approach, recognizing complications in measuring climate-motivated migration. In 2014, the Fifth Assessment Report of the IPCC was released. Working Group II, which focuses on impacts, adaptation, and vulnerability, noted that, while researchers lack reliable quantitative data and have "low confidence in quantitative projections of changes in mobility due to its complex, multi-causal nature" (IPCC 2014, 21), there is nevertheless a high level of agreement that climate change "is projected to increase displacement of people" throughout the twenty-first century, with the highest risks falling on vulnerable rural and urban demographics whose agency is low, especially in low-income developing countries (20). The Paris Agreement, decided upon at the 2015 Conference of the Parties (COP) to the Framework Convention, provides a new global platform for emissions reductions and has legally binding reduction targets for all nations, not just for developed states. However, climate migration remains outside the scope of the Paris Agreement.

Frank Biermann and Ingrid Boas (2008) demand the creation of a global, international protocol outlining the rights of climate refugees and the responsibilities of industrialized nations toward them. They urge the international community to draft a protocol that is framed in "planned and organized voluntary resettlement programs" (15). The Nansen Initiative is a positive step in this direction. Launched in 2012 by Norway and Switzerland, it led to the creation of a Protection Agenda that addresses "the needs of people displaced across borders in the context of disasters and climate change" (Nansen Initiative 2015). It provides effective state practices for managing cross-border disaster displacement and also accounts for measures to manage disaster displacement risks in migrants' countries of origin.

The Platform on Disaster Displacement continues the work of the Nansen Initiative and urges regional, bilateral, and international cooperation, having identified a lack of coordinated effort as a stumbling block to appropriate adaptation responses (Nansen Initiative 2015).

PROPOSAL FOR A NEW MIXED-METHODS APPROACH

This section attempts to weave together research on climate change with social scientific research on migration for a more comprehensive understanding of climate migration and the crisis of climate refugees. We need to think about "climate migration" in terms of the adaptation strategies of more or less vulnerable populations to climate change among a range of options. However, the question remains: to what are we adapting? The range of predictions of average global temperatures increasing by 1.5, 2, or 4°C will require a different adaptation for each temperature. If average global temperatures increase by 4°C or more, the only adaptation pathway for many communities may be migration. Nevertheless, tracing the impact of climate change on migration is not a one-to-one ratio (McLeman 2014, 53–54). Moreover, decisions to migrate usually take place at the individual and/or household level rather than as part of a state-organized population resettlement, making for substantial variation across individuals as well as across regions and populations. In this section, we identify the primary hurdles to developing reliable quantitative estimates of climate migration and discuss two potential approaches to overcoming these hurdles.

Climate research has been the domain of environmental studies, geography, and earth and atmospheric sciences, while migration research has come from sociology, political science, demography studies, and global ethics, drawing on both qualitative and quantitative approaches. Because climate migration is a convergence of sociopolitical factors and environmental conditions, a more rigorous approach to assessing and understanding the future impact of climate on global migratory patterns—which will surely accelerate as the planet continues to warm—requires that we develop a more "integral" methodological approach that merges scientific research with both quantitative and qualitative methods in the social sciences and is charged with an urgent commitment to climate justice. Nevertheless, although we are committed to developing a rigorous metric to refine our understanding over time, and we encourage advancement in scholarship and training along these lines, we also insist that an ethical global policy response to the emerging climate migration crisis cannot wait for reliable metrics.

Diagnosing the Methodological Challenge

There are three principal conceptual hurdles to obtaining reasonable estimates of climate-driven migration. First, as discussed earlier, there is a wide range of projected warming temperatures due to uncertainties in climate feedbacks. So, in other words, each projection will require a different set of adaptations. Therefore, we are swimming in probabilistic waters, scientifically. Studies that use past climate changes to derive the link between climate change and mass migration may not be adequate to assess the likely migration during the twenty-first century because the pace of projected change is drastically faster than the rate of past changes, and the magnitude of the change is also greater.

Second, there is no consensus on what constitutes a climate migrant. Existing definitions and estimates—such as the much-cited and compelling figure of 200 million migrants by 2050—tend to blur essential spatial and temporal categories, so it is unclear, for example, whether migration is a local phenomenon (the most common for those who lack resources and social capital) or an intranational or international one. Similarly, there is often a failure to differentiate short-term movement due to cyclical or seasonal migration from long-term migration. (Gemenne [2011, 546] and Perch-Nielsen et al. [2008] highlight similar methodological issues.) As Crisp (1999, 3) points out, "Any form of enumeration exercise must be based upon a clearly defined unit of measurement if it is to produce reliable, usable and comparable data. In the case of refugee statistics, however, such clarity does not always exist."

Third, the causes of climate migration are complex. Migration is a multicausal phenomenon requiring analysis at a variety of stages and levels involving nonenvironmental factors such as bioregional vulnerability, culture, economics, politics, and a variety of individual factors (Gemenne 2011; McLeman 2014; Perch-Nielsen et al. 2008; Piguet 2010; Warner 2011). Data constraints and insufficient or inaccurate theorization may plague estimation attempts at each stage of analysis.

Migration researchers continue to develop more sophisticated methods to map causality, and two approaches especially are showing some promise in the literature—multilevel modeling and agent-based modeling. Causal maps highlight various chains of influence at each step in the process from climate change to migration. Although the specific processes identified vary depending on the ecosystem effects examined, most process maps outline five interrelated stages (for a clear example, see Perch-Nielsen et al. 2008, 378, 385):

1. climate change (global);
2. ecosystem effects (regional);
3. livelihood effects (individual);
4. adaptive capacity and options (individual decisions influenced by local and state-level social and political resources); and
5. migration options (individual decisions influenced by local and state-level social and political resources).

Note that the temporal sequencing of various adaptations, migration decisions, and livelihood effects can interact in complex ways. Thus, although adaptations may often follow on observed climate changes, preexisting adaptations to potential problems (e.g., building substantial levees in regions prone to riparian floods) may raise the threshold at which ecosystem changes impact individual livelihoods or mitigate livelihood effects in advance (e.g., preexisting crop or flood insurance).

Broadly speaking, it is difficult to identify clearly the type and magnitude of effect that changes at one stage will have on the immediate subsequent stages. Although there are many ways of disaggregating migration patterns, for the purpose of environmental displacement and adaptation, two distinct axes of categorization are important: spatial and temporal. Migration can be categorized along spatial lines in general terms according to the distance that an individual moves from her original residence:

1. short-distance migration (intraurban, intraregional rural, or short-distance rural–urban);
2. long-distance intrastate migration (rural–rural, urban–urban, rural–urban, or urban–rural); and
3. international migration.

Generally speaking, most individuals move short distances before moving longer distances, even when such moves are permanent. For example, a family that has lost property due to river flooding may move first to a new location at a higher elevation in the same locality. However, the exact pattern of migration depends largely on material and social capital. Typically, individuals moving longer distances tend to be more affluent or at least above an affluence threshold (although intense political and civil conflict, as in the case of Syria, can alter this condition). Furthermore, the choice of destination is often influenced by an individual's social networks or social capital. To use a simple example, long-distance rural–urban migration is more likely if an individual has relatives or friends in the destination city and often is influenced by the existence of ethnic enclaves at the destination as well (McLeman 2014, 34).

Migration may also be categorized on temporal lines, depending on the relative permanence of the migration:

1. temporary migration;
2. cyclical migration (seasonal or otherwise); and
3. permanent migration.

These temporal categories, too, are heavily influenced by material and social capital. In general, temporary migration precedes permanent migration, and a majority of temporary migrants return to their original residences (Perch-Nielsen et al. 2008). However, even this regularity is modified by material and social capital.

For example, a year after Hurricane Katrina, although a majority of white migrants had returned to their homes, a majority of black migrants, especially residents of New Orleans's Ninth Ward, had yet to return (McLeman 2014, 98–99). Individuals may also undertake forms of cyclical migration to diversify income streams and mitigate risk of crop loss, or, as in the case of American "snowbirds," affluent individuals may adopt seasonal migration patterns to avoid undesirable seasonal weather conditions. Contrary to recent "securitization" narratives, international migration is particularly unlikely for the poorest individuals, absent countervailing social networks, due to the up-front costs required (IPCC 1990, 5–11).

Potential Solutions—Modeling Complex Causality

Due to the complex nature of causation and vulnerability in determining migration patterns, two approaches are gaining traction in the quantitative literature (see Piguet 2010):

1. Multilevel Modeling / Multivariate event history analysis
   a. *Description:* Analyzes individual survey data on various forms of vulnerability—human capital (e.g., education), social networks capital (e.g., family migrants, migrant communities), physical capital (e.g., money), and natural capital (e.g., land holdings)—and links to local ecological changes (e.g., rainfall) with fixed geolocations (e.g., wet versus dry states).
   b. *Strength:* Incorporates data at both the individual and community levels. Allows for stratified analysis, enabling policy makers to better target potential migration "hot spots" (both sources and destinations) and identify vulnerable groups. Merges individual survey methods with national statistical collection.
   c. *Challenges:* Fine-grained spatial breakdowns of weather patterns are often lacking or limited to state-level data, so the spatial breakdown of the phenomenon may not map onto available spatial hierarchies. Could better account for return migration patterns; often uses survival analysis methods, which have difficulty accounting for return migration.
   d. *Good example studies:* Gray (2009); Gray and Mueller (2012a, 2012b); Gray and Bilsborrow (2013); Henry, Schoumaker, and Beauchemin (2004); Nawrotzki, Riosmena, and Hunter (2013).
2. Agent-Based Modeling:
   a. *Description:* Computer simulation technique allowing simulated responses of individuals and households to climate signals, accounting for heterogeneity in agents' vulnerability (including the various forms of capital discussed above), and social factors such as collective action problems, social learning, and network effects (Patt and Siebenhüner 2005; Piguet 2010).

b. *Strength:* Strong ability to account for heterogeneity among agents as well as social factors. Relies on both individual- and community-level data. Higher predictive power when compared with other methods since it can account for some future adaptations in the system. Can account for return migration.

c. *Challenges:* Depends on the ability to identify rules of behavior in response to stimuli at the subgroup level. Requires excellent data on preexisting responses of heterogeneous subgroups to climate shocks.

d. *Good example studies:* Beine and Parsons (2015); Entwisle et al. (2016); Hassani-Mahmooei and Parris (2012).

HUMAN STORIES

To substantiate the human impact of climate change while climate migration metrics continue to develop in the coming years, we advocate a mixed-methods approach that combines quantitative prediction with compelling qualitative case studies that document the human experience of climate migration, particularly within vulnerable demographics. It may take decades for the numbers to be validated and for causality to be clarified, but we can advance narratives now that illustrate cause and effect with compelling human stories of loss and displacement. Narratives that drill deep into the human experience play an essential role in advancing public awareness of human suffering and motivating collective responses. For example, we can illustrate the disproportionate impact of a catastrophic weather event on a city's most vulnerable demographics through a case study like the African American experience of Hurricane Katrina, or we can communicate the devastation of incremental climate change through a case study of the thirty-year drought still ravaging sub-Saharan Africa, during which millions have perished.

Climate justice is as much a battle of public opinion as it is about redistributing responsibilities, and stories can humanize the impact of climate change better than cold numbers can. We believe that human stories will play an increasingly important role in communicating the harms that climate change is already inflicting on the world's most vulnerable people.

CONCLUSION

Climate change is real, and it is happening now. Data-driven science has provided compelling evidence that most of the observed changes are due to human activities, largely from combustion of coal, oil, and gas. Models that simulate many of the observed changes are projecting a 2°C warming by mid-century and unprecedented warming in the range of 2°C to 4°C toward the latter half of this century. Because of nonlinear feedbacks, there is a small probability (between 5 and 10 percent) that the warming can reach catastrophic levels of much greater than 4°C by 2100. At such levels of warming, mass migration may emerge as a dominant issue of human suffering induced by climate change.

Climate change is here, and its impacts on human health and a variety of indicators of human well-being are well documented.[3] It is also increasingly a factor in human migration. Climate migration research is still in its infancy, and reliable estimates may take far too long to do any good for society. On ethical grounds, we have advocated a probabilistic approach to climate migration in this paper and issued a corresponding call for urgently needed mitigation to slow global warming trends. *When there is insufficient time to quantify an impending crisis, ethics demand an urgent probabilistic response.* When even seemingly small probabilities are combined with the solidity of climate science, with changes in observed environmental phenomena, and with the documented displacement of millions of vulnerable people in recent decades by dramatic catastrophic weather events and slower-moving climate effects, often exacerbated by civil unrest, we have a sufficient ethical basis for swift action to mitigate global warming. We cannot wait for verifiable numbers to catch up with reality.

Climate justice demands a rapid response. The richest one billion people on the planet are responsible for about 50 percent of greenhouse gas emissions, while the poorest three billion, who lack access to affordable fossil fuels, are responsible for about 5 percent (Ramanathan 2014; Dasgupta and Ramanathan 2014). In contrast, the bottom three billion suffer the greatest harms associated with climate change. The susceptibility of the poor to forced climate migration is perhaps the most vivid example of disproportionate harm. Climate justice places an ethical imperative on the most advantaged populations to mitigate harms and improve conditions for the least advantaged. Climate justice demands urgent global intervention to reduce planetary warming, assertion of a global commitment to human rights and the public good, and a broader conception of self-interest that includes the sustainability of human settlements on our planet.

NOTES

We acknowledge University of California–San Diego PhD researchers Sean Morgan (Political Science) and Vanessa Lodermeier (Anthropology) for their assistance during the research and writing of this paper. VR was supported by the Alderson Foundation; FF was supported by the UCSD Center on Global Justice. Our great thanks to Marcelo Suárez-Orozco for his comments.

1. All warming projections here and elsewhere in the text use preindustrial temperatures as the baseline.

2. However, the relationship between environment and climate and migration had previously been discussed, at least in the US context. See Cebula and Vedder (1973), Graves (1980), Knapp and Graves (1989), and Evans (1990).

3. These impacts were discussed at a fall 2017 workshop at the Pontifical Academy of Sciences titled *Health of People, Health of Planet and Our Responsibility: Climate Change, Air Pollution and Health*. Chaired by Veerabhadran Ramanathan, the workshop had some of the leading experts on climate change and public health from around the world as participants, and issued the following declaration: www.pas.va/content/accademia/en/events/2017/health/declaration.html.

REFERENCES

Barnett, Jon. 2003. "Security and Climate Change." *Global Environmental Change* 13 (1): 7–17. doi:10.1016/S0959-3780(02)00080-8.

Barnett, Jon, and W. Neil Adger. 2007. "Climate Change, Human Security, and Violent Conflict." *Climate Change and Conflict* 26 (6): 639–55. doi:10.1016/j.polgeo.2007.03.003.

Beine, Michel, and Christopher Parsons. 2015. "Climatic Factors as Determinants of International Migration." *Scandinavian Journal of Economics* 117 (2): 723–767.

Biermann, Frank, and Ingrid Boas. 2008. "Protecting Climate Refugees: The Case for a Global Protocol." *Environment: Science and Policy for Sustainable Development* 50 (6): 8–17. doi:10.3200/ENVT.50.6.8–17.

Brown, Lester R. 2012. *Full Planet, Empty Plates: The New Geopolitics of Food Scarcity.* New York: Norton.

Crisp, Jeff. 1999. "Who Has Counted the Refugees? UNHCR and the Politics of Numbers." UNHCR Policy Research Unit Working Paper No. 12. June 1999. www.refworld.org/pdfid/4ff58e4b2.pdf.

Dasgupta, Partha, and Veerabhadran Ramanathan. 2014. "Pursuit of the Common Good: Religious Institutions May Mobilize Public Opinion and Action. *Science* 345 (6203). http://dx.doi.org/10.1126/science.1259406.

Entwisle, Barbara, Nathalie E. Williams, Ashton M. Verdery, Ronald R. Rindfuss, Stephen J. Walsh, George P. Malanson, Peter J. Mucha et al. 2016. "Climate Shocks and Migration: An Agent-Based Modeling Approach." *Population and Environment* 38 (1): 47–71.

Evans, Alan W. 1990. "The Assumption of Equilibrium in the Analysis of Migration and Interregional Differences: A Review of Some Recent Research." *Journal of Regional Science,* 30 (4): 515–531.

Forman, Fonna, Gina Solomon, Racel Morello-Forsch, and Keith Pezzoli. 2016. "Bending the Curve and Closing the Gap: Climate Justice and Public Health." *Collabra* 2 (1): 1–17. http://dx.doi.org/10.1525/collabra.67.

Gemenne, François. 2011. "Why the Numbers Don't Add Up: A Review of Estimates and Predictions of People Displaced by Environmental Changes." *Global Environmental Change* 21S: S41–S49.

Gray, Clark L. 2009. "Environment, Land, and Rural Out-Migration in the Southern Ecuadorian Andes." *World Development* 37 (2): 457–468.

Gray, Clark and Richard E. Bilsborrow. 2013. "Environmental Influences on Human Migration in Rural Ecuador." *Demography* 50 (4): 1217–1241.

Gray, Clark L., and Valerie Mueller. 2012a. "Natural Disasters and Population Mobility in Bangladesh." *Proceedings of the National Academy of Sciences* 106 (16): 6000–6005.

———. 2012b. "Drought and Population Mobility in Rural Ethiopia." *World Development* 40 (1): 134–145.

Hassani-Mahmooei, Behrrooz, and Brett W. Parris. 2012. "Climate Change and Internal Migration Patterns in Bangladesh: An Agent-Based Model." *Environment and Development Economics* 17 (6): 763–780.

Henry, Sabine, Bruno Schoumaker, and Cris Beauchemin. 2004. "The Impact of Rainfall on the First Out-Migration: A Multi-level Event-History Analysis in Burkina Faso." *Population and Environment* 25 (5): 423–460.

Homer-Dixon, Thomas F. 2010. *Environment, Scarcity, and Violence.* Princeton, NJ: Princeton University Press.

IOM (International Organization for Migration). 2008. "Migration and Climate Change." IOM Migration Research Series. No. 31. Geneva: International Organization for Migration.

IPCC (Intergovernmental Panel on Climate Change). 1990. *Climate Change: The IPCC Impacts Assessment.* Camberra, Australia: IPCC.

———. 2013a. *Climate Change 2013: The Physical Science Basis: Contribution of Working Group I to the Fifth Assessment Report of the Intergovernmental Panel on Climate Change,* edited by Thomas F. Stocker, Dahe Qin, Gian-Kasper Plattner, Melinda M.B. Tignor, Simon K. Allen, Judith Boschung, Alexander Nauels, Yu Xia, Vincent Bex, and Pauline M. Midgley. Cambridge, UK: Cambridge University Press.

———. 2013b. "Summary for Policymakers." In *Climate Change 2013: The Physical Science Basis: Contribution of Working Group I to the Fifth Assessment Report of the Intergovernmental Panel on Climate Change,* edited by Thomas F. Stocker, Dahe Qin, Gian-Kasper Plattner, Melinda M.B. Tignor, Simon K. Allen, Judith Boschung, Alexander Nauels, Yu Xia, Vincent Bex, and Pauline M. Midgley, 3–29. Cambridge, UK: Cambridge University Press.

———. 2014. "Summary for Policymakers." In *Climate Change 2014: Impacts, Adaptation, and Vulnerability. Part A: Global and Sectoral Aspects. Contribution of Working Group II to the Fifth Assessment Report of the Intergovernmental Panel on Climate Change,* edited by Christopher B. Field, Vicente R. Barros, D.J. Dokken, Katherine J. Mach, Michael D. Mastrandrea, T. Eren Bilir, Monlisa Chatterjee, et al., 1–32. Cambridge: Cambridge University Press.

Kelley, Colin P., Shahrzad Mohtadib, Mark A. Canec, Richard Seagerc, and Yochanan Kushnirc. 2015. "Climate Change in the Fertile Crescent and Implications of the Recent Syrian Drought." *Proceedings of the National Academy of Sciences* 112 (11): 3241–46. www.pnas.org/cgi/doi/10.1073/pnas.1421533112.

Knapp, Thomas A., and Philip E. Graves. 1989. "On the Role of Amenities in Models of Migration and Regional Development." *Journal of Regional Science,* 29 (1): 71–87.

Lancet Commissions. 2015. "Health and Climate Change: Policy Responses to Protect Public Health." *The Lancet* 386: 1861–1914. www.thelancet.com/pdfs/journals/lancet/PIIS0140-6736(15)60854-6.pdf.

McLeman, Robert A. 2014. *Climate and Human Migration: Past Experiences, Future Challenges.* Cambridge, UK: Cambridge University Press. www.cambridge.org/core/books/climate-and-human-migration/0D0D207E8BA3D169452A84FEB7D779CB.

Myers, Norman. 2005. "Environmental Refugees: An Emergent Security Issue." 13th Economic Forum, May 2005, Prague.

Nansen Initiative. 2015. "The Nansen Initiative: Towards a Protection Agenda for People Displaced across Borders in the Context of Disasters and the Effects of Climate Change." www.nanseninitiative.org.

Nawrotzki, Raphael J., Fernando Riosmena, and Lori M. Hunter. 2013. "Do Rainfall Deficits Predict US-Bound Migration from Rural Mexico? Evidence from the Mexican Census." *Population Research and Policy Review* 32: 129–158.

Neumann, Barbara, Athanasios T. Vafeidis, Juliane Zimmermann, and Robert J. Nicholls. 2015. "Future Coastal Population Growth and Exposure to Sea-Level Rise and Coastal Flooding: A Global Assessment." *PloS One* 10 (3): e0118571.

NRC/IDMI (Norwegian Refugee Council and Internal Displacement Monitoring Centre). 2015. *Global Estimates 2015: People Displaced by Disasters.* Geneva: Internal Displacement Monitoring Centre.

Patt, Anthony, and Bernd Siebenhüner. 2005. "Agent Based Modeling and Adaptation to Climate Change." *Die ökonomischen Kosten des Klimawandels und der Klimapolitik* 74: 310–320.

Perch-Nielsen, Sabine L., Michèle B. Bättig, and Dieter Imboden. 2008. "Exploring the Link between Climate Change and Migration." *Climatic Change* 91: 375–398.

Piguet, Etienne. 2010. "Linking Climate Change, Environmental Degradation, and Migration: A Methodological Overview." *WIREs Climate Change* 1 (July/August): 517–524.

Ramanathan, Veerabhadran. 2014. "The Two Worlds Approach for Mitigating Air Pollution and Climate Change." Proceedings of the Pontifical Academy of Sciences and Pontifical Academy of Social Sciences, workshop on Sustainable Humanity, Sustainable Nature, Our Responsibility. Pontifical Academy of the Sciences, Extra Series 41, Vatican City, 2014. http://www.casinapioiv.va/content/dam/accademia/pdf/es41/es41-ramanathan.pdf.

Sen, Amartya. 1981. *Poverty and Famines: An Essay on Entitlement and Deprivation.* Oxford Scholarship Online. Oxford, UK: Oxford University Press.

UNEP (United Nations Environmental Programme). 2009. *Climate in Peril: A Popular Guide to the Latest IPCC Reports.* www.uncclearn.org/sites/default/files/inventory/unep125.pdf.

UNICEF (United Nations Children's Fund). 2015. "Children Will Bear the Brunt of Climate Change." Press release. www.unicef.org/media/media_86347.html.

Warner, Koko. 2011. "Environmental Change and Migration: Methodological Considerations from Ground-Breaking Global Survey." *Population and Environment* 33: 3–27.

WMO (World Meteorological Organization). 2013. *Global Climate 2001–2010: A Decade of Climate Extremes.* https://library.wmo.int/pmb_ged/wmo_1103_en.pdf.

Xu, Yangyang, and Veerabhadran Ramanathan. 2017. "Well Below 2 °C: Mitigation Strategies for Avoiding Dangerous to Catastrophic Climate Changes." *PNAS: Proceedings of the National Academy of Sciences of the United States of America.* http://www.pnas.org/content/pnas/early/2017/09/14/1618481114.full.pdf.

2

___

A MIGRATION BECOMES AN EMERGENCY

The Flight of Women and Children from
the Northern Triangle and Its Antecedents

Roberto Suro

A LONG-STANDING MIGRATION EVOLVES INTO A HUMANITARIAN CRISIS

In 2014, more than 2.8 million people born in El Salvador, Honduras, and Guatemala—the so-called Northern Triangle of Central America—lived in the United States, a population that was the product of migratory streams that were already decades old in some cases. Then, that spring, something extraordinary happened. In May and June, a sudden spike in the number of Central Americans crossing into the United States broke records and overwhelmed immigration facilities. Not only the numbers but also the composition of the flow was anomalous, as it contained a preponderance of women and children, including thousands of young children who entered the United States unaccompanied. Moreover, they made unusual demands, pressing asylum claims based on victimization by criminal gangs. Then, by July, the surge was receding as quickly as it had mounted.

Though it was a relatively small event in terms of its impact on the overall flow of immigrants into the United States and was strikingly short-lived, the 2014 surge of Central Americans had an outsized influence. It prompted a crisis response by the administration of President Barack Obama that included measures that are still in place to deter future flows, and it roiled political debates over immigration in ways that reverberated through the 2016 election. Two subsequent surges in 2015 and 2016, equally sudden but on a lesser scale, further stoked the reaction.

Developing an analysis of the Central American surges and their implications requires understanding them in the context of the long, ongoing migrations that involve the same kinds of people leaving the same places for the same destinations.

Our contention is that the surges, including the extraordinary migration of unaccompanied children, are best characterized as an outgrowth or a mutation of the existing migrations rather than as an aberration or an anomaly. This perspective has important consequences, not only for understanding these movements, but also for explaining their impact on politics and policy.

Those preexisting flows developed out of a variety of circumstances but had settled into labor and family reunification migrations by 2014. The volume of these flows was relatively stable, and they operated through well-established channels that included both legal and unauthorized immigration to the United States. The migration system that facilitated those movements—the kinship networks, smuggling organizations, known routes, and so on—also made the surges possible. Indeed, it is difficult to imagine how thousands of unaccompanied children could be transported clandestinely from Central America to the Rio Grande except via migration channels that had developed over decades and that had already moved many thousands of adults. Equally, the eventual settlement of the great majority of those children into family units in the United States is only conceivable when the children's flight is understood in the context of a long-standing migration that had already created a well-established diaspora.

This perspective in no way minimizes the urgency of the surge, nor does it discount the Central Americans' claims for asylum status. Ample evidence shows that immediate circumstances suddenly rendered migration a life-and-death matter for many of the Central Americans. Nonetheless, their flight to the United States in search of humanitarian protection was undoubtedly made possible by the labor and family reunification migrations that preceded them. We will argue that this combination of old pathways and new migrants is responsible for one of the most significant characteristics of this flow: the volatility so evident in the surges. Another key characteristic is the clandestine, unauthorized quality of this migration and the fact that it takes place across a border fraught with political contention. In our analysis, this too is a product of the evolution of a humanitarian migration out of a long-standing irregular labor migration. These two characteristics—volatility and unlawfulness—have contributed to the negative reactions the Central American children provoked among policy makers and the public.

Although this analysis is focused on the migration channel between the Northern Triangle of Central America and the United States, the conclusions can shed light on similar developments elsewhere. Some flows destined to Western Europe from North Africa and sub-Saharan Africa have mixed aspects of labor, family, and humanitarian migrations, as have flows from Afghanistan and Iraq. While many elements differ from one case to another, understanding a sudden humanitarian flow as an outgrowth of a well-established labor and family reunification migration has important implications for the assessment and management of migrations involving refugees and asylum seekers:

- Migration channels built up over decades by workers and their families can allow a new humanitarian flow to scale up rapidly and overcome numerous obstacles in transit to a protective destination.
- Public opinion in a receiving country may reject a humanitarian response no matter how compelling the case presented by refugees or asylum seekers if they and the modalities of their migration closely resemble an irregular flow that has been the target of control policies.
- The association of a humanitarian emergency with an irregular migration can confound policy responses when the fundamental framework of those policies segregates migrants into discreet categories based on their motives for migrating and the modalities by which they travel.

This line of analysis draws on several recent developments in the study of migration that have broadened our understanding of what constitutes a humanitarian flow. In depicting what he terms "survival migration," for example, Alexander Betts (2010, 361–82) emphasizes the degree to which large numbers of individuals who deserve protection on humanitarian grounds because of violations of their socioeconomic rights often do not fit the standards for refugee or asylum designation based on religious or political persecution. Similarly, research on mixed motives by Nicholas Van Hear (2009) and others emphasizes the blurring of the boundary between voluntary and forced migrations and the consequences of policies aiming at durable solutions to displacement crises. In both cases, humanitarian flows like those of the Central American children are assessed in terms of the aspects they share with substantially economic migrations and the consequences for policy regimes that insist on drawing sharp distinctions between them.

On a theoretical level, an assessment of the interactions among humanitarian and other forms of migration potentially adds to a literature that has focused substantially on the conditions and processes that initiate and sustain migration flows but that has placed less attention on the circumstances that produce changes, particularly sudden changes in the characteristics and volume of migration flows (see, for example, Massey et al. 1993; Castles, Miller, and de Haas 2014).

THE ANTECEDENTS

More than 2.8 million people born in these three countries resided in the United States at the time of the 2014 surge.[1] That number was equivalent to nearly 10 percent of the populations residing in those countries, about the same as the proportion of Mexicans living in the United States. More than half of the Northern Triangle migrants in the United States dated their tenure to 2000 or earlier, according to estimates from the American Community Survey.[2] By any measure, this was already a substantial and well-established migration when the 2014 surge took place.

It was also a migration that had gained entry to the United States through a variety of modalities and that reflected a variety of motives. About 1.5 million of the migrants from the three countries, slightly more than half the total, were unauthorized migrants, according to Pew Research Center estimates (Passel and Cohn 2016). Another 270,000 from El Salvador and Honduras held Temporary Protected Status. Meanwhile, more than 400,000 migrants had been granted legal permanent resident status during the previous decade, and the lion's share of this green card migration—more than 80 percent in 2014—was made up of family reunification migrants (US Department of Homeland Security 2016). Among all migrants who had arrived in the United States from Central America since 2010, the sex ratio was 1.32—nearly a third again as many males as females arriving— compared with a ratio of 0.94 for Asian migrants and 0.99 for European migrants over the same period.[3] Elevated sex ratios typically suggest a labor migration. And, finally, more than 6,000 migrants from the three countries had been granted asylum in the previous decade.

Not surprisingly, this migration developed robust transnational linkages most clearly expressed via remittances. According to World Bank estimates, the three Northern Triangle countries received a combined $12.8 billion in remittances in 2013. That money represented exceptionally large shares of gross domestic product in these small countries—El Salvador: 16.5 percent, Honduras: 15.7 percent, and Guatemala: 10 percent. In Mexico, by contrast, $22 billion in remittances accounted for only 2 percent of GDP (Cohn, Gonzalez-Barrera, and Cuddington 2013).

In sum, by the time of the 2014 surge, a large migration from these three countries was well established, and although the flow was predominantly unauthorized and bore the characteristics of a labor migration, significant numbers of migrants were also entering the country legally through family reunification and humanitarian channels. And the diasporas were contributing significantly to the economic well-being of their communities of origin via remittances.

Finally, each of these three nations had a distinct migration history, with singular characteristics and significant differences among them. A retelling of those histories is beyond the scope of this chapter, but a glance at some of their most salient features shows that prior flows prepared the channels for the migration of children and other humanitarian migrants during the surges since 2014.

Migration to the United States from El Salvador received a major stimulus from a civil war (1980–92) that was one of the last proxy conflicts of the Cold War. However, in contrast to most other migration flows linked to the Cold War—e.g., those from Cuba, Vietnam, the Soviet Union, and Nicaragua—the migrants who fled El Salvador were not explicitly identified with the side backed by the United States. On the contrary, the great majority of Salvadorans who came to the United States pressing humanitarian claims were victims of political violence perpetrated by military and paramilitary forces supported by Washington during the Reagan and

George H. W. Bush administrations. While other Cold War refugees were welcomed with open arms, during the Reagan administration, 97 percent of all Salvadoran asylum claims were denied. That explicit and formal hostility on the part of the immigration system led to the development of self-help organizations, legal aid groups, and alliances with progressive political forces in the United States that remain influential more than a quarter of a century later.

Guatemalan migration was also fed by a civil war (1960–96) that was much longer than El Salvador's and was less ideological and involved less foreign interference but was no less brutal. Guatemalan asylum seekers were also rejected en masse during the Reagan years and were subsequently the subjects of some of the same sorts of complicated litigation and legislation that eventually resolved the status of many Salvadorans. But the Guatemalan migration was distinctive in the degree to which it involved an indigenous population, the Maya, who had suffered what a truth commission later termed "genocidal violence" at the hands of government-supported forces. As such, the Guatemalan migration has been racialized in a manner and to a degree not seen among other Latin American source countries (Jonas 2013).

Honduran migration was jump-started in 1998 by Hurricane Mitch, which displaced nearly a quarter of the population. The number of Hondurans in the United States has nearly tripled since then to about 600,000. Given its relative newness, Honduran migration to the United States did not benefit from the various legalization and adjustment programs of the 1980s and 1990s that put substantial numbers of Salvadorans and Guatemalans on more secure legal footing. As such, more than three-quarters of Hondurans in the United States are believed to be out of status, making them highly vulnerable to immigration enforcement and producing weaker civic integration of them into the United States than that of other Central Americans. Nonetheless, something like a classic irregular labor migration channel developed in the 2000s even as the Great Recession was suppressing other migration flows. In a country with few economic resources that suffers from chronically weak, corrupt, and ineffective governance, migration and remittances have become survival mechanisms for entire communities in the most vulnerable sectors of Honduran society (Reichman 2011).

And there is a fourth country with its own very distinct migration history that has contributed genetic material to the new flows from the Northern Triangle— Mexico. The great majority of unauthorized migrants and asylum seekers from Central America reach the United States by transiting Mexico and crossing the US-Mexico border. The vastly larger and older Mexican migration to the United States created the channels by which Central Americans now travel, especially the smuggling networks that manage the border crossing itself (Donnelly and Hagan 2014, 74–81). Indeed, the Mexican migration can be seen as facilitating the development of the Northern Triangle migrations prior to 2014, and it helped shape both the surge and the reaction that it provoked.

THE NEW MIGRATION

In fiscal year 2012, the US Border Patrol apprehended a monthly average of 926 individuals who were members of family units—at least one child under the age of eighteen with an accompanying adult—making unauthorized entries along the border with Mexico. Apprehensions of unaccompanied minors averaged 2,033 a month that year. Together, these two categories of unusual migrants totaled 35,519 for the year, just 10 percent of all apprehensions on the Southwest border.

The numbers bumped up a bit in the spring and summer of 2013 until monthly apprehensions were running about 50 percent higher than they had been a year earlier. Then, in spring 2014, something unexpected and unprecedented occurred. The number of family unit apprehensions topped 5,000 in March, and in April it went over 6,000. That was just the front edge. In May, the number was 12,722 before cresting at 16,330 in June. The great bulk of the increase was made up of Northern Triangle migrants, and the number traveling in family units was almost matched by the number of children apprehended alone. The flow of unaccompanied minors— migrants 0 to 17 years old—followed a pattern similar to that of the family units, reaching 10,620 in June, five times what it had been two years earlier. Apprehensions of family members and unaccompanied minors totaled 136,986 in fiscal 2014, accounting for 29 percent of all apprehensions that year (Johnson 2016).

The flow of mothers and children dropped off rapidly in the summer of 2014 after the Obama administration stepped up enforcement capabilities on the border and enlisted Mexico to deter Northern Triangle migrants before they reached the United States. A new migratory pattern then developed of ebbs and flows that included similar surges, though with smaller numbers of migrants, in 2015 and 2016.

After the 2014 summer surge, the number of apprehensions of women and children dropped back to the elevated levels seen in late 2013 and early 2014 but far below the summer peaks. Apprehensions of unaccompanied children, for example, fell by 80 percent from June 2014 to a trough in January 2015. The numbers picked up again in late summer and autumn of 2015, hitting levels in November and December of 2015 that were three times higher than the low point. The same pattern repeated in 2016, when apprehensions mounted through the late summer and then hit peaks in November and December that topped any marks set since 2014. In early 2017, the numbers fell back to lows not seen in several years. The pattern for family units was the same. In summary, the flow of mothers and children from the Northern Triangle, as mirrored in apprehensions, developed an extraordinary volatility marked by wide swings in the numbers of migrants, and that volatility has persisted for three years.

While the flows from El Salvador and Guatemala had included large numbers of asylum seekers in the 1980s and 1990s, as noted earlier, the 2014 surge produced unprecedented claims for humanitarian protection. First, there were the extraordinary numbers. An estimated 121,200 asylum claims were filed in the United States in 2014, marking a 44 percent increase (+36,800) from the year before, according to United Nations estimates. And the Northern Triangle drove the phenomenon, with striking increases in asylum applicants: Honduras: +115 percent; Guatemala: +87 percent, and El Salvador: +77 percent (UNHCR 2015a).

Aside from the numbers, the surges marked a difference in the character of the humanitarian flow. Central American asylum seekers of the 1980s and 1990s had been fleeing violence that was indisputably motivated by politics and that was carried out by state actors or organized groups countering the state. In 2014 and thereafter, Central American asylum seekers claimed persecution at the hands of transnational criminal organizations, particularly the Mara Salvatrucha (MS-13) and the 18th Street Gang. These groups are themselves products of the previous Northern Triangle migration and make up another strand of the genetic material of the post-2014 flows. The gangs were founded in the United States by Salvadoran migrants in the 1980s and spread back to the sending communities after US law enforcement authorities utilized large-scale deportations as a crime control measure. Against a backdrop of generally weak and/or corrupt governments, particularly in Guatemala and Honduras, the gangs spread to the rest of the Northern Triangle and eventually became a much bigger presence there than they had been in the United States. Their techniques included the intimidation and extortion of whole communities, the forced recruitment of young men, and systematic violence against women and girls (Seelke 2016).

Although the civil strife experienced in the 1980s and 1990s undoubtedly grew out of some of the same underlying social, economic, political, and cultural conditions as the violence of the 2010s did, it nonetheless represented markedly different phenomena. Gone were the ideological components and the intervention by outside powers that marked the Cold War proxy conflicts of the past, and with them went the national security and diplomatic considerations that once influenced the United States' treatment of Northern Triangle migrants. Instead, a new form of migration has emerged, and the three surges in three years have led some observers to speculate that this new form of migration has become an ongoing and enduring feature of flows from Central America (Chishti and Hipsman 2016).

THE RECOMBINATION

The surges of 2014, 2015, and 2016 were sudden migrations of significant size by groups of individuals whose departure from their home communities was substantially coerced and who sought humanitarian protection in their country of destination. The surges marked a clear departure from the labor and family migrations already well underway but did not supersede or replace them. Rather, this chapter argues for an understanding of the flow of minors and mothers as an outgrowth of those long-standing migrations that, after all, involved the same communities of origin, even the same families, traveling via the same channels to the same destinations. However, the differences in the flows appear to be substantially responsible for the differences in the ways in which the surge migrants were portrayed in the US news media and perceived in US public opinion, and those same differences in the patterns of flow, the characteristics of the migrants, and their motivations for leaving are responsible for the distinctive policy response they provoked.

The challenge, then, is to understand how one kind of migration spawns another. In this case, a stable and steady migration produced one that was volatile. What had primarily been a voluntary labor and family migration generated a coerced humanitarian migration. A movement heavily weighted with working-age males produced an offshoot dominated by women and children. These developments deserve to be assessed for the degree to which they support or challenge the various theories we use to explain migration dynamics, but there are other more compelling and immediate reasons to explore the surges as distinctive migration phenomena.

In 2014, a relatively small labor and family migration set off a humanitarian emergency, a political crisis, and a lasting policy change. If the same dynamics had developed with a much larger migration—for example, the flow from Mexico to the United States—the consequences would have been vastly greater. Although there are numerous examples of humanitarian flows morphing into economic migrations with refugees who make a second move after finding initial protection, this is a different case. Here we have the opposite—an economic migration that produced a surge of humanitarian migrants. In other words, we are familiar with coerced migrants who become voluntary migrants after initial settlements, but we have little experience with a voluntary flow that produces a powerful stream of coerced migrants. Given the size of the Mexican migration to the United States, even a relatively small eruption of asylum seekers would have substantial consequences in the United States.

In seeking to explain how a long-standing and stable migration can suddenly produce a variant that differs so distinctively from previous flows, we have found that the biological concept of *recombination* can serve as analogy. Among the most common applications of the term *recombination* in biology is the process by which DNA molecules are broken and fragments are rejoined in new combinations. This event can happen in nature in processes of cell division, and it can also occur in vitro through processes of cloning in which strands of genetic material from different sources, even from different species, are combined to create genetic sequences not found in the source organisms. This latter process generates what is broadly known as "recombinant DNA" and is used to produce genetically modified organisms (Alberts et al. 2007).

For our purposes, the concept is most useful as an illustration of mechanisms that can produce new creatures—unique and novel entities demanding assessment on their own terms—that are generated from materials that characterized their predecessors. The new creatures are certainly not offspring. This is not a reproductive process in that the new entity differs fundamentally from the parent. Nor is it a form of evolution based on the adaptation of an organism to new circumstances. The existing organism—the long-standing labor and family migration—has continued uninterrupted. Recombination involves a process in which the existing entity is disrupted, broken apart at least temporarily, and pieces of it are put back together again to form something new.

Applied to the migration of Central American minors, the concept of *recombination* yields the portrayal of a migration flow that draws content and characteristics from preceding migrations and yet is an entirely new organism with its own alimentation, behavior, and life cycle. The genetic code came from prior flows that were driven primarily by family reunification, labor market dynamics, or flight from political violence. The new organism combined aspects of all three and made use of the migration channels that had been laid down by them. But the surges of mothers and children involved a newly volatile flow, a different mix of migrants, and a highly distinctive set of motives.

This model gives us access to two aspects of the Central American surges that hold potentially broad significance. First, it points us to the disruption of a well-established and stable migration as the origin of the sudden appearance of a new and highly volatile flow. Secondly, it helps explain why this new kind of migration can have disproportionate impacts on the politics and policy of a receiving society.

In this case, the disruption was violence directed at vulnerable populations, especially women, in the Northern Triangle countries. It served as a major precipitating factor in the surges of 2014 and thereafter, according to numerous accounts (GAO 2015). In El Salvador, the intentional homicide rate was 59 percent higher in 2014 than it was in 2000, according to United Nations data (UNODC 2017). For Guatemala, it was a 26 percent increase, and for Honduras, it was 46 percent. In the years leading up to the new migration, these countries competed for the dubious distinction of being the single most criminally violent country in the world, while all three also consistently ranked among the most dangerous nations for women and girls. A 2015 UNHCR (2015b, foreword) report aptly titled *Women on the Run* described the Central American surge as "unique in its complexity" because of the genderized violence both prompting the migration and then preying on the migrants in transit.

In addition to the violence, the migrants of the surge were also fleeing a sudden worsening of economic conditions in societies that were already among the most impoverished and underdeveloped in the Western Hemisphere. The surges occurred as Central America experienced the most severe drought in decades during this period, with relief agencies counting 3.5 million people in the region as food insecure at mid-decade (Chishti and Hipsman 2016). Simultaneously, the region was struck by the coffee rust fungus that devastated production of the top cash crop for small farmers, causing 300,000 people in Guatemala alone to need food aid in 2014 (Malkin 2014).

Migrants had left these three countries in the past to escape civil wars, political persecution, genocide, and environmental disasters; to find work; and to reunite with their families. In 2014 and during the surges that followed, all of these push factors or their legacies combined with the precipitating effects of violence and collapsing local economies to prompt the flight of women and children. The surge migrants met the criteria of a survival migration as described by Betts (2010). He defines this as "persons outside their country of origin because of an existential threat to which they have no access to a domestic remedy or resolution" (361). Surely the prevalence of violence directed against women and children in the Northern Triangle constituted an existential threat, and no one disputes that the governments of these three countries had failed in their responsibility to protect the safety of their citizens.

Betts advocates the concept of *survival migration* as a way of broadening the definition of migrants deserving humanitarian protection, a matter that has been under debate since the 1990s. The Central American surges renewed debates in the United States about the appropriate criteria for protection (*New York Times* Editorial Board 2016). The 1951 Refugee Convention, which serves as the foundation of US refugee and asylum policies, set the standard as a well-founded fear of individual persecution on ethnic, religious, or political grounds. However, how the standard should be interpreted by governments has been disputed frequently, particularly since the end of the Cold War, which provided much of the moral and political framework for the treaty. On the Convention's fiftieth anniversary in 2001, the United Nations High Commissioner for Refugees (UNHCR) expressed concern that some countries were applying a strict interpretation of the document in order to reject protection seekers who claimed they had suffered persecution by nonstate actors or who were facing generalized rather than individually targeted violence (Feller 2001). According to Betts (2010), survival migrants, no matter how dire their circumstances, might not meet the legal tests if they were strictly applied. Rather than having been persecuted in the traditional sense, these migrants, Betts (2010, 362) notes, have moved "because of serious deprivation of socioeconomic rights related to the underlying political situation" or because of "slow onset environmental displacement." Both conditions apply to the surge migrants from the Northern Triangle, and indeed they challenge the application of the 1951 Convention and the criteria for protection that derive from it.

Aside from its policy applications, the concept of *survival migration* illuminates the ways that multiple factors can be compounded to constitute a form of coercion that obliges people to leave their homes as surely as if they were physically threatened by an agent of the state because of their political beliefs. At a certain threshold, economic deprivation combined with generalized violence and a breakdown of the social order can constitute a life-threatening circumstance for individuals, especially for vulnerable populations like women and children. The Central American surges certainly provide evidence of multiple factors combining to precipitate a sudden migration. Moreover, the surges constitute an extraordinary kind of survival migration that is capable of achieving speed and scale because it grows out of a long-standing labor and family migration. The Central American women and children displayed all the desperate urgency of migrants who have trekked through deserts to escape famine and violence, but they were able to travel well-established routes that carried them to the welcoming embrace of family members.

Following the 2014 surge, the US Government Accountability Office (GAO 2015) conducted a study of the causes of the sudden migration by unaccompanied children from the Northern Triangle in order to better assess policies and programs designed to address those causes. The primary data collection took the form of surveys of officials of the Department of State and other US agencies stationed in those countries who were dealing with prospective migrants. The subsequent report found that the cause most commonly cited by US officials for migration from the region was criminal violence, including extortion and forced conscription at the hands of gangs and drug cartels. However, economic concerns, including livelihoods suddenly lost to the coffee rust fungus as well as the effects of chronic poverty, were also cited by all the officials polled. And the two were seen as deeply intertwined with gang violence that limited economic opportunities and with deep poverty that contributed to the criminality. Just behind concerns about safety and economic survival, the US officials reported family reunification as a driving motive, particularly for children.

The twin concepts of *mixed migrations*—meaning migrations encompassing individuals with a variety of motives—and *mixed motives*—meaning migrants who individually embrace multiple motives—have gained increasing salience as scholars and policy analysts have examined the increasing variety in the forms and types of migration evident around the world (Van Hear 2011). This discourse has relied substantially on the view of migration decisions as falling on a continuum. At one end are proactive choices selected from among multiple options, and at the other are reactive choices that are entirely compelled by circumstance. In one influential formulation of this idea, Anthony Richmond (1994, 61) suggests that between the extremes is "a large proportion of people crossing state boundaries who also combine characteristics, responding to economic, social and political pressures over which they have little control, but exercising a limited degree of choice in the selection of destinations and the timing of their movements."

Numerous migrations in the Middle East, Southwest Asia, and Africa involve people who are forced from their homes by combinations of political, social, and economic factors but who then make choices based on economic and family considerations about where to settle. This blurring of distinctions between forced and voluntary migration exercised an important influence on the development of policy agendas by some European governments and United Nations agencies in the early 2000s that attempted to combine humanitarian protection and the management of labor migrants (Castles and Van Hear 2005). For example, the concept of an *asylum and migration nexus* appeared prominently in UNHCR documents attempting to deal with the rejection of migrants with valid humanitarian claims by governments that perceived an abuse of asylum systems by voluntary economic migrants who would otherwise face sanctions for having crossed borders without permission (Van Hear 2009, 4).

The idea of creating a single policy architecture to deal with migrations that covered the spectrum of voluntary and coerced movements never gained much currency in the United States and has faded substantially in Europe and in United Nations venues. Instead, the rigid logic of the 1951 Refugee Convention, with its sharp juridical distinction between migrants worthy of protection and those who are not, has been substantially reified even as the number of migrants who defy that distinction has exploded since 2010. The Central American surges represent by far the most significant instance of a mixed migration arriving in the United States since the concept gained salience more than a decade earlier. They represent an important variant in the concept of a mixed migration in both how the phenomena are described and how the policy consequences are assessed.

Reflecting on the experience of European governments, Nicholas Van Hear (2009, 17) concludes, "at some point then, forced migration may transmute into economic or livelihood migration, and it is this recognition that forms the basis for the discourse on 'mixed migration.'" Applying the framework of recombination as we have presented it here, the transmutation of the Central American migration went in the opposite direction: an economic migration transmuted into a forced migration. Moreover, it was a very large and well-established economic migration, and it operated substantially through irregular channels that were equally large and well established. This genetic origin shaped the size and character of the migration that then emerged when social and economic conditions precipitated the sudden flight of tens of thousands of women and children seeking protection in the United States. And, in turn, the size and character of the surges conditioned the responses they provoked in American politics and policy. Unlike deracinated refugees who must rely on the kindness of strangers, the Central Americans of the surges had family and friends already in the United States prepared to offer safe havens, and they had highly efficient and very familiar migratory channels for reaching them. Arguably, all these circumstances would have been far different if those women and children had represented an entirely new migration whose origins, mechanisms, and claims for protection derived de novo and unambiguously from circumstances of coercion.

The degree to which the surges represented an outgrowth of the preceding largely voluntary migration is evident in the fact that most of the surge migrants, especially the children, were reuniting with families here. A 2016 US Government Accountability Office report examined the handling of 51,984 unaccompanied children from the Northern Triangle who were apprehended in 2014 by immigration authorities and transferred to the care of the Office of Refugee Resettlement at the Department of Health and Human Services. More than 31,000—60 percent of the total—were released to parents who were already residing in the United States. Another 25 percent were released to siblings or to an aunt or uncle living here. Once grandparents and other relatives are taken into account, fewer than 9 percent were released to nonfamily sponsors, and that group includes 8 percent who went to sponsors identified by relatives as family friends (GAO 2016).

The fact that these children had relatives waiting for them undoubtedly facilitated their migrations, and so too was the situation similar for the children who came with their mothers. And relatives here did much more than provide a destination. According to estimates by the Inter-American Development Bank, remittances to Central America surpassed prerecession levels in 2011 and kept growing robustly up until the time of the surge. During the same period, remittances to Mexico, the Caribbean, and South America were flat and stuck at or below the peaks reached before the downturn (Maldonado and Hayem 2014). While it is impossible, of course, to link the remittance flows directly to the migration surge, extensive research has shown that family members' financing of migration is one of the common uses of such funds. According to the Obama administration's estimates, between 75 and 80 percent of the unaccompanied minors migrating to the United States from the Northern Triangle relied on human smuggling networks (White House 2014). The trip from Central America to the US border costs several thousand dollars in smuggling fees and expenses. It stands to reason that nearly 52,000 children under the age of eighteen did not come up with the funds on their own and that families facing existential threats did not have such money in savings.

Moreover, the women and children of the surges of the past few years have traveled to the United States using the same transit routes, self-help networks, shelters, and smugglers that have facilitated travel by the much larger and ongoing labor and family reunification flows (Villegas 2014). Much of the migration system serving the Central Americans, in turn, is based on the same system that has facilitated the vastly larger and older Mexican labor migration to the United States. The Central Americans must transit through Mexico and must use the same channels that carry Mexicans north. Indeed, the criminal organizations that control much of the irregular human traffic across the US-Mexico border have extended their reach all the way to Central America—especially the drug cartel known as the Zetas, which claims a territory that extends along the shores of the Gulf of Mexico all the way from the Rio Grande to the Yucatan (Martinez 2014). And even as the women and children of the surges were traveling along these routes, so too were other Central Americans and Mexicans whose motives lay at various points across the continuum from forced to voluntary migration.

The women's and children's reliance on smuggling networks established to facilitate a labor migration might not seem exceptional or even noteworthy at first glance, but it helps to highlight one of the distinguishing characteristics of this migration: its volatility. The trip from the Northern Triangle to Texas is about 1,500 miles by land and requires crossing two or three international frontiers as well as jungles, mountains, and deserts. The sudden movement of many tens of thousands of women and children on that route simply would not have been possible as a logistical matter unless the means of transportation were readily available at the onset. The migration channel was an integral element of the preexisting labor migration that then became a critical aspect of the surges. Indeed, the smugglers appear to have played an explicit role in producing the volatility that defined the surges. Following the 2014 surge, US officials reported that "human smugglers have increasingly influenced the rate of migration through more aggressive and misleading marketing approaches" (GAO 2016, 5). While in 2014 and 2015, the surges were in part driven by smugglers' claims that a deadline loomed for a legalization program, in 2016, fear of a crackdown by then President-elect Donald J. Trump helped drive the numbers (Partlow and Miroff 2016).

The recombination meant that a survival migration was able to achieve much greater mass and speed than would have been possible if it were not an outgrowth of a long-standing and very substantial labor and family migration. When it reached the US border, that mass and speed had a substantial impact on the ways in which the women and children were perceived by the media, the public, and policy makers. Those perceptions of the new migration were additionally shaped by one of the key characteristics of the previous migration: its unauthorized nature. This strand of genetic material also deeply colored the ways in which the new migrants were seen. Women and children fleeing hunger and violence were perceived as a sudden and large influx of illegal border crossers.

RECOMBINATION AND RESPONSE

In 2012 and 2013 (fiscal), a total of nearly 90,000 women and children were apprehended on the US southwestern border and barely anybody noticed. There was no significant media coverage, no political rhetoric demanding either acceptance or rejection of these migrants, and no notable change to immigration policy. Nearly 7,000 unaccompanied children were apprehended in May and June of 2013 as the US Senate was in the midst of a debate that resulted in the adoption of the most extensive immigration reform bill in history. The kids hardly merited a mention. However, all of that changed in the late spring of 2014 by virtue of a single new factor: in May and June of that year, the numbers surged, and 21,000 children were apprehended.

As with many other areas of public policy, sudden events in immigration can have an outsized effect. Often the speed of change is more important in determining public responses than the actual dimensions of the event. Even a casual assessment of the news coverage of the surge demonstrates the impact. In 2014, the Associated Press averaged 94 stories a month with a major focus on immigration on its national wire. In June there were 139, and in July, 169. And along with the volume came the characterization of an emergency. In July CNN used the headline "Crisis on the Border" seventy-two times during its prime-time broadcasts. Not surprisingly, the share of respondents listing immigration as the "most important problem" facing the nation surged from 5 percent to 17 percent between June and July 2014 and remained elevated through the fall.[4]

When the surge migrants arrived at the Rio Grande, many Americans saw another wave of newcomers from the South determined to settle in the United States whether they had permission or not. The spectacle of children packed into holding cells at Border Patrol stations and the skyrocketing numbers reported breathlessly in news accounts stoked the impression that the migrants had simply overwhelmed all the barriers and personnel that were supposed to have been put in place to control the border. Rather than understanding the women and children as harbingers of a new kind of migration, many Americans responded with déjà vu and dread. Negative perceptions focused on the characteristics that the surge drew from its antecedents in the long history of irregular migrations in the very same place by the very same kinds of people.

At the beginning of July 2014, President Obama asked Congress for $4 billion in emergency funds to increase both enforcement and humanitarian efforts in response to the surge. Republicans responded with harsh critiques of what they saw as Obama's failure to secure the border and announced plans to amend a 2008 law that they claimed gave Central American children unnecessary legal protections in pressing asylum claims. Protestors in California and Arizona blocked buses carrying children to detention facilities. And amid the rising anxieties, Obama postponed his already promised announcement of executive actions to benefit unauthorized immigrants until after the midterm elections. At Obama's urging, Mexico stepped up enforcement in the region of its southern border, immediately blocking migrants from stowing away on northbound freight trains, a favored mode of transit. With Washington's tangible support and political encouragement, Mexico subsequently adopted a package of policing measures along transit routes known as the *Plan Frontera Sur* that has had two effects. The forced repatriation of Central Americans from Mexico has now exceeded the number removed from the United States, and to avoid apprehension, migrants have been forced into more remote and more dangerous routes and even greater dependency on smuggling networks controlled by the drug cartels, especially the notorious Zetas (Arriola 2016).

Long before the first surge, the long-standing Central American and Mexican migrations had generated a deep and highly negative political discourse about the border in the United States. In 2014, public opinion surveys showed clear majorities of Americans, both Democrats and Republicans, favoring legislation to provide a path to citizenship for unauthorized migrants, but there was equally substantial support for measures to tighten security at the border. And on a key issue in policy debates, Americans were almost evenly split on the question of whether security improvements had to come before any legalization (Pew Research Center 2015).

During the 2016 presidential campaign, the Democratic nominee, Hillary R. Clinton, backed the Obama administration's policies and supported the forced return of child migrants as a deterrent measure that would "send a message" to others considering the trip. She encountered little resistance within her party on this point. Then-presidential candidate Donald Trump made extreme immigration enforcement at the border a hallmark of his ultimately successful campaign.

Meanwhile, as of March 2017, since the first surge some 165,000 unaccompanied children have been released into the custody of sponsors. The great majority are awaiting the dispositions of their cases in hopelessly backlogged immigration courts.

. . .

The surges were warnings.

The United States is unique among the world's prosperous receiving states in that it sits at the terminus of migration channels that are decades old, that allow for continuous transit by land, and that have already carried many millions of unauthorized migrants north in defiance of the government's efforts to shut it down. The surges demonstrated on a small scale what can happen when conditions in the sending communities deteriorate to the point that migration becomes a matter of survival. Tens of thousands of people, including children travelling alone, can move north all at once via large and efficient channels. They travel with the intent not merely to ask for protection but to walk into the country and find safe haven, regardless of how the US government views them. And as they arrive at the Rio Grande, the migrants know that they will be welcomed by family, friends, and compatriots who have traveled those channels before them. They just need to get past the US authorities.

No matter how severe the conditions that precipitated the surges were, worse conditions are coming. As Jeffrey Sachs (2017) tells us, we will soon see much more severe environmental disruptions across Central America, southern Mexico, and northern South America. The vulnerable populations in close proximity to the migration channels are vastly larger than the population that fed the surges. The dynamics of climate change alone foretell with certainty that the United States will face future migrations from its near neighbor countries that will occur suddenly and involve large numbers of people who can readily avail themselves of robust migration channels. And there are many other social, political, and economic factors likely to contribute to the conditions for this unique form of survival migration.

As the surges demonstrated, the United States is ill-equipped to handle such episodes. The 1951 Refugee Convention and other policy frameworks developed in the aftermath of World War II imagined humanitarian migrations as discrete events prompted by specific and temporary dislocations. US immigration policies, like those in other Western democracies, established criteria for humanitarian protection that do not readily encompass migrants fleeing from the kind of generalized social collapse and predation by criminal gangs that pushed many Central Americans from their homes. Over the past two decades, many voices have been raised to argue for a redefinition of those criteria to reflect the realities of forced migration today rather than the politics of the Cold War era. However, merely broadening the criteria will not suffice for the kinds of crises the United States is likely to face on its borders in the years ahead.

The recombinant nature of the surge migration poses more fundamental challenges than other humanitarian flows do. For example, refugees applying for resettlement from a safe haven camp have options even if they are rejected. Typically, they can at least remain where they are. On the other hand, a Central American who has already arrived on American territory before seeking asylum either gains admission or is forcibly repatriated. The zero-sum system either rewards them with a visa for life, or it sends them back to the place they came from, regardless of the depravations awaiting them. Moreover, the surge migrants enter these proceedings at a disadvantage. They are seen as violators who have arrived via illicit channels and must prove their worthiness against a presumption that their claims are false.

Since the last great reform of US immigration laws in 1965, the most common way to be admitted to the United States as an immigrant is through a process that judges individual merit based on humanitarian need, employment, or family relations. The characteristics of the surge migration are exquisitely ill-suited for that sort of individual selection process that is based on narrow categories of fixed criteria. First, the application and adjudication system is not designed for this kind of flow. These migrants arrive suddenly and in large numbers. They include significant shares of unaccompanied children who are incapable of making their way through a complex legal process and may even be unable to provide information about themselves. And second, they present a dizzying mix of motives covering the spectrum from coercion to choice. Over the years, there have been any number of substantial exceptions to the process of individual adjudication that have granted admission to whole categories of people arriving from nearby with claims not easily resolved. Cubans, Haitians, and the Central Americans themselves have benefited from an array of policies that grant various forms of mass adjustments or temporary reprieves on something like an ad hoc basis.

Of course, a substantial long-term effort to find durable solutions to the causes of forced migration should be part of any US policy toward its sending regions. But, given the feeble state of civil authority due to corruption by criminal organizations and the certainty of severe climate disruptions, it seems unlikely that even the best-intentioned and best-funded development plans could fully mitigate the prospects of surge migrations in the future.

When those surges happen, mass grants of admission may become a practical necessity. The alternative might be the creation of camps, either in Mexico or in the southwestern United States, that would rapidly produce a humanitarian crisis that would be twenty-four-hour news for as long as it lasts. Under such circumstances, the rationale for admission to the United States might emerge from the very history that makes this such a difficult form of migration to manage. The surge migrations are the result of past migrations. They are the product of deep relationships between communities of destination and of origin. Those are intimate linkages that bind the United States to Central America and to Mexico, powerful linkages that will be difficult to deter.

But beyond the practical considerations, there is a humanitarian obligation at play here. It is the unique humanitarian obligation that arises between people who are connected by a migration channel. Once this relationship has achieved certain dimensions, it acquires a moral authority of its own. If people at one end of the channel face an existential threat, those at the other end of the channel have an obligation not to let them perish. The channel itself enforces that obligation by bringing the victims, in this case children, to our very doorsteps. Those dimensions have undoubtedly been achieved between the United States and the people who live along the massive channel that runs south through Mexico to Central America. The obligation has been created by the acceptance, sometimes tacit and sometimes grudging but nonetheless real, of millions of migrants who have created homes in the United States for decades. When their relatives and neighbors arrive desperately in need, they cannot be turned away.

NOTES

1. "Place of Birth for the Foreign-Born Population in the United States." *2014 American Community Survey: One-Year Estimates,* table B05006. https://www.census.gov/programs-surveys/acs/technical-documentation/table-and-geography-changes/2014/1-year.html.

2. "Place of Birth by Year of Entry by Citizenship Status for the Foreign-Born Population." *2014 American Community Survey: One-Year Estimates,* table B05007 (see note 1 for link).

3. "Sex by Place of Birth by Year of Entry by Citizenship Status for the Foreign-Born Population." *2014 American Community Survey: One-Year Estimates,* table B05008 (see note 1 for link).

4. Story counts are based on the author's calculations based on electronic archives maintained by LexisNexis.

REFERENCES

Alberts, Bruce, Alexander Johnson, Julian Lewis, Martin Raff, Keith Roberts. 2007. *Molecular Biology of the Cell.* New York: Garland Science.

Arriola, Luis A. 2016. *Mexico's Not-So-Comprehensive Southern Border Plan.* Issue brief. Houston: Baker Institute for Public Policy, Rice University.

Betts, Alexander. 2010. "Survival Migration: A New Protection Framework." *Global Governance* 16 (3): 361–82.

Castles, Stephen, Mark J. Miller, and Hein de Haas. 2014. *Theories of Migration.* 5th ed. London: Guilford.

Castles, Stephen, and Nicholas Van Hear. 2005. *Developing DFID's Policy Approach to Refugees and Internally Displaced Persons.* Report to the Conflict and Humanitarian Affairs Department. Oxford: Refugee Studies Centre.

Chishti, Muzaffar, and Faye Hipsman. 2016. *Increased Central American Migration to the United States May Prove an Enduring Phenomenon.* Washington, DC: Migration Information Source. www.migrationpolicy.org/article/increased-central-american-migration-united-states-may-prove-enduring-phenomenon.

Cohn, D'vera, Ana Gonzalez-Barrera, and Danielle Cuddington. 2013. *Remittances to Latin America Recover—but Not to Mexico.* Washington, DC: Pew Research Center. www.pewhispanic.org/2013/11/15/remittances-to-latin-america-recover-but-not-to-mexico/.

Donnelly, Robert, and Jacqueline M. Hagan. 2014. "The Dangerous Journey: Migrant Smuggling from Mexico and Central America, Asia, and the Caribbean." In *Hidden Lives and Human Rights in the United States: Understanding the Controversies and Tragedies of Undocumented Immigration,* edited by Lois A. Lorentzen, 71–106. Santa Barbara, CA: Praeger.

Feller, Erika. 2001. *Challenges to the 1951 Convention in Its 50th Year: Statement by the Director of the Department of International Protection.* April 24, 2001. www.unhcr.org/en-us/admin/dipstatements/429d74282/challenges-1951-convention-its-50th-anniversary-year-statement-ms-erika.html.

GAO (US Government Accountability Office). 2015. *Information on Migration of Unaccompanied Children from El Salvador, Guatemala, and Honduras.* Report to Congressional Requesters. Report no. GAO-15-362. Washington, DC: GAO.

———. 2016. *Unaccompanied Children: HHS Can Take Further Actions to Monitor Their Care.* Washington, DC: GAO. www.gao.gov/assets/680/675001.pdf.

Johnson, Jeh. 2016. *United States Border Patrol Southwest Family Unit Subject and Unaccompanied Alien Children Apprehensions: Fiscal Year 2016.* US Customs and Border Protection. Department of Homeland Security. www.cbp.gov/newsroom/stats/southwest-border-unaccompanied-children/fy-2016.

Jonas, Susanne. 2013. *Guatemalan Migration in Times of Civil War and Post-War Challenges.* Washington, DC: Migration Information Source. http://www.migrationpolicy.org/article/guatemalan-migration-times-civil-war-and-post-war-challenges.

Maldonado, Rene, and Maria Luisa Hayem. 2014. *Remittances to Latin America and the Caribbean in 2013: Still below Pre-crisis Levels.* Washington, DC: Multilateral Investment Fund, Inter-American Development Bank. http://idbdocs.iadb.org/wsdocs/getDocument .aspx?DOCNUM=38842219.

Malkin, Elizabeth. 2014. "A Coffee Crop Withers." *New York Times,* May 5, 2014. https://nyti .ms/2obhsF2.

Martinez, Oscar. 2014. "How the Zetas Tamed Central America's 'Coyotes.'" *Insight Crime,* May 1, 2014. www.insightcrime.org/news-analysis/how-the-zetas-tamed-central-americas-coyotes.

Massey, Douglas S., Joaquin Arango, Graeme Hugo, Ali Kouaouci, Adela Pellegrino, and J. Edward Taylor. 1993. "Theories of International Migration: A Review and Appraisal." *Population and Development Review* 19 (3): 431–66.

New York Times Editorial Board. 2016. "An Exodus in Our Own Backyard." Editorial, July 4, 2016. https://nyti.ms/2nTWKI4.

Partlow, Joshua, and Nick Miroff. 2016. "Fearing Trump's Wall, Central Americans Rush to Cross the US Border." *Washington Post,* November 18, 2016.

Passel, Jeffrey S., and D'vera Cohn. 2016. *Overall Number of US Unauthorized Immigrants Holds Steady since 2009.* Washington, DC: Pew Research Center.

Pew Research Center. 2014. "Public Divided over Increased Deportation of Unauthorized Immigrants." February 27, 2014. Washington, DC: Pew Research Center. www.people-press.org/2014/02/27/public-divided-over-increased-deportation-of-unauthorized-immigrants/.

Reichman, Daniel. 2011. *The Global Village: Coffee, Migration, and Globalization in Honduras.* Ithaca, NY: Cornell University Press.

Richmond, Anthony. 1994. *Global Apartheid: Refugees, Racism, and the New World Order.* Oxford: Oxford University Press.

Sachs, Jeffrey. 2017. "Economics, Demography, Environment, and Mass Migrations." Paper presented at Humanitarianism and Mass Migrations Conference, UCLA, Los Angeles, January 18–19, 2017.

Seelke, Clare R. 2016. *Gangs in Central America.* Washington, DC: Congressional Research Service. https://fas.org/sgp/crs/row/RL34112.pdf.

UNHCR (United Nations High Commissioner for Refugees). 2015a. *Asylum Trends 2014.* Geneva: UNHCR. www.unhcr.org/551128679.pdf.

———. 2015b. *Women on the Run: Firsthand Accounts of Refugees Fleeing El Salvador, Guatemala, Honduras, and Mexico.* Geneva: UNHCR. www.unhcr.org/5630f24c6 .html.

UNODC (United Nations Office on Drugs and Crime). 2017. Data Portal. Crime and Criminal Justice. *Homicide Counts and Rates (2000–14).* https://data.unodc.org/. Accessed June 26, 2017.

US Customs and Border Protection. 2016. *US Border Patrol, Southwest Border Apprehensions by Sector.* Washington, DC: Department of Homeland Security. www.cbp.gov /newsroom/stats/usbp-sw-border-apprehensions.

———. 2017. *United States Border Patrol: Southwest Family Unit Subject and Unaccompanied Alien Children Apprehensions: Fiscal Year 2016. US Customs and Border Protection Statis-*

tics and Summaries. March 14, 2017. www.cbp.gov/newsroom/stats/southwest-border-unaccompanied-children/fy-2016.

US Department of Homeland Security. 2016. *The 2015 Yearbook of Immigration Statistics.* Washington, DC: US Department of Homeland Security.

Van Hear, Nicholas. 2009. *Managing Mobility for Human Development: The Growing Salience of Mixed Migration.* Human Development Research Paper no. 2009/20. New York: United Nations Human Development Programme.

———. 2011. *Mixed Migration: Policy Challenges.* Oxford: Migration Observatory, University of Oxford.

Villegas, Rodrigo D. 2014. *Central American Migrants and "La Bestia": The Route, Dangers, and Government Responses.* September 10, 2014. Washington, DC: Migration Information Source, Migration Policy Institute.

White House. Office of the Vice President. 2014. "Remarks to the Press with Q&A by Vice President Joe Biden in Guatemala," June 20, 2014.

PART TWO

FRAMES ON CHILDREN AND YOUTH ON THE MOVE

3

CHILDREN ON THE MOVE IN THE TWENTY-FIRST CENTURY

Developing a Rights-Based Plan of Action

Jacqueline Bhabha

Though children have always been significant participants in global migration flows, the protection deficit that accompanies this multifaceted phenomenon, now widely referred to as "children on the move,"[1] only emerged as a concerted focus of concern relatively recently. I describe some elements of this belated but welcome emerging concern and its consequences.

I also suggest that comprehensive engagement with the diverse contemporary phenomenon of children on the move needs to advance beyond the current preoccupation with child vulnerability, dependence, and related protection imperatives, critical though that perspective is. A more dynamic and ambitious agenda to complement the focus of current work is needed, one that acknowledges youthful agency, initiative, and ambition and that places the right to safe and legal child and adolescent mobility at its core.

To be sure, an inclusive and just agenda concerning children on the move in the twenty-first century must include, as a necessary baseline, policies that protect vulnerable children from the pressures that force them into perilous migration in the first place. Such policies entail effective and accessible measures to shield children from the harms of family separation, postconflict trauma, statelessness, discrimination, financial destitution, and sexual exploitation. The absence or failure of such policies in so many regions today has precipitated the large outflows of young people so much in evidence since 2014, outflows that, as Gonzalo Sánchez-Terán (2017) notes, are not evidence of a migration crisis but rather of a migration instinct or opportunity.

A just agenda for contemporary children on the move must also elaborate in detail solutions to current refugee and migration problems not addressed by the existing toolkit of protective measures. We cannot continue to fail the next generation of young people (and several more to follow) with dramatic shortfalls in access to basic rights such as quality education and health care, rights respecting employment, and access to a safe and life-sustaining environment. The solutions needed draw on evolving work in the development context and in the humanitarian domains of harm prevention and risk reduction. They require closer collaboration between the migration and development fields and the design of expanded legal migration options within more flexible mobility regimes.

MAINSTREAMING PROTECTION OF
CHILDREN ON THE MOVE

The urgency of attending to child-specific aspects of migration was not even a minor topic two decades ago, despite the well-known histories of migrant children affected by the ravages of World War II (Zahra 2011) and by the organized exodus from Cuba after the Castro revolution (Torres 2004). This dramatic policy deficit is all the more surprising given the path-breaking 1996 report on the impact of conflict on children produced by UN Special Representative Graça Machel (see https://childrenandarmedconflict.un.org/mandate/the-machel-reports/) and the long-standing pattern of large-scale international labor migration separating parents from their children since the 1960s.

Several accounts have been offered concerning the reasons for this stubborn neglect of the rights of vulnerable children affected, in one way or another, by migration. A common explanation is that migrant children have been neglected because of their invisibility. The claim is that migrant children have been subsumed under the migration claims of related adults (their parents, their guardians) and disregarded as holders of legal entitlements in their own right. A variant of this view is the often-repeated claim that migrant children are widely considered migrants first and foremost, with the entitlements and needs that arise from their status as minors a mere afterthought (if a thought at all). In earlier work, I have rejected this set of views, arguing that it is flawed both as an account of the facts (many child migrant cases have been highly visible) and as an account of the policies implemented (age has often been a factor in decision making, even if it has not generated protective or rights-respecting outcomes).

I have instead argued that a primary reason for the stubborn neglect of the rights of migrant children is the profound ambivalence toward them embedded in the institutional ideology of migration-control regimes and therefore of the officials implementing those regimes. The elements of ambivalence are as follows: On the one hand, there is a protective imperative derived from the human rights and child rights regimes that has been in force for decades, an imperative that prioritizes consideration of "the best interests of the child."[2] On the other hand, there is hostile and exclusionary pressure that feeds the view that child migrants are potential offenders, threats, insubordinates, and even terrorists. The suspicion frequently lurks in the minds of official decision makers at borders, immigration hearings, or holding centers that behind the veneer of fragility and vulnerability lies an incipient gang member, drug dealer, or other miscreant. As a result, policies toward child migrants have been wildly inconsistent, and protection imperatives continue to be routinely neglected (Bhabha 2014; see also Harvard FXB Center for Health and Human Rights 2016).

Fortunately, over the last two decades, there has been a gradual increase in the volume and impact of work addressing lacunae in protection. This work has included impact litigation (especially in the United States) challenging the failure to adequately extend refugee protection to children (Bhabha 2014, 203–37). Effective multistakeholder mobilization highlighting the consequences of migration control policies on fundamental child rights such as family reunification, primary education, and freedom from physical or sexual abuse has grown.[3] As a result, and especially in the past few years, child migration—its features, its consequences, and its ethical and policy implications—has for the first time become a salient aspect of domestic, regional, and international migration discussions and policy making.[4] As Sarah Dryden-Peterson notes in chapter 10 of this volume, this heightened concern for the rights and well-being of children affected by migration also encompasses refugee children and has included more concerted engagement with complex issues arising out of the reality of protracted displacement.

A first warning call to developed states of the urgent political imperative of attending, as a matter of migration policy priority, to child rights aspects of human mobility occurred in the spring and summer of 2014. A tenfold increase in US arrivals of unaccompanied children fleeing acute violence and state disintegration in the so-called "Northern Triangle" countries of Central America—Guatemala, El Salvador, and Honduras (see UNHCR 2014)—prompted then president Obama to speak of a humanitarian emergency. More recently, the dramatic increase in the ratio of children arriving in Europe from Syria and other parts of the Middle East, North and sub-Saharan Africa, and South Asia has taken administrators at the border and further inland by surprise. More than 30 percent of sea arrivals in Europe since October 2015 have been children; for some nationalities, including Afghans and Eritreans, children constitute the majority of asylum applicants (Eurostat 2016; see also UNHCR n. d.). There is inescapable evidence of extensive trauma and other consequences of prolonged exposure to toxic stress among Syrian children (Save the Children UK 2017). And the desperation of unaccompanied children crossing the Mediterranean to reach Western and Northern European countries (Germany, the United Kingdom, and Sweden in particular) has led those trapped in the European Union's southern periphery to resort to dangerous and damaging measures, including routinely selling sex, to generate the funds needed for their onward journey (Harvard FXB Center for Health and Human Rights 2017).

The massive impact in Africa of renewed conflict in South Sudan on this youngest country's children is at least as dramatic as the much more publicized distress migrations just referenced. According to UNICEF, 900,000 children have been internally displaced from their homes since violence broke out at the end of 2013, more than 13,000 have been reported missing or have been separated from their families, and an estimated 16,000 children have been recruited into the country's armed forces (UNICEF n. d.). More than 600,000 South Sudanese refugees, the majority of whom are female, are currently being sheltered in Uganda. Over 60 percent of these extremely vulnerable and destitute refugees are under the age of eighteen (UNICEF n. d.). The combination of the unexpectedly large volume of refugees and their acute protection needs has generated a range of hurried responses, some rights enhancing, many more punitive and exploitative.

ENDURING CHILD PROTECTION DEFICITS

A substantial proportion of all these children forced into distress migration travel alone ("unaccompanied") or without their parents or customary caregivers ("separated")—a particularly frightening and dangerous set of circumstances. The trauma of loss that accompanies departure from home and familiar surroundings is compounded by the insecurities and hazards associated with travel, isolation, and exploitability. In 2015, 88,300 asylum-seekers applying for protection in the European Union (EU) were considered unaccompanied minors (Eurostat 2016), and many more probably were under eighteen but were mired in age dispute procedures (House of Lords 2017).

The protection deficits associated with these large youthful population movements are dramatic. The multiple state agencies charged with managing migration and refugee flows lack the training and protocols, let alone resources, for safely handling the needs of children; their obligation to ensure that the child's best interests are a primary consideration is largely ignored.[5] At the same time, domestic agencies charged with ensuring child welfare have yet to mainstream within their protection mandates the needs of migrant and refugee children.

In the United States, thousands of children are incarcerated with their parents in harsh, punitive circumstances every year simply because they cannot demonstrate a regular immigration status, despite a broad international consensus opposing the detention of children for immigration reasons. In Mexico, the United States' de facto immigration buffer zone, detention of child migrants is even more oppressive and pervasive. Severe overcrowding in primitive facilities affects not only children traveling with their parents (as in the United States) but also unaccompanied or separated children simply because of their immigration status (see Rosenblum 2015).

Other prosperous regions also evidence severe and enduring protection deficits vis-à-vis child migrants. In the EU, which is often considered the leader in rights enforcement for vulnerable minorities, including migrants, child migrants still routinely lack access to effective legal representation and guardianship, to nurturing care and medical attention, and to vigorous policies of social inclusion. The situation in Greece is calamitous, with reports of asylum-seeking children begging or otherwise being exploited on the streets of Athens and accounts of riots within the closed camps as a matter of routine (see Digidiki 2016).

In Australia, draconian exclusion policies have relegated thousands of children to situations of indefinite detention and containment on remote island territories, contributing to despair and mental illness of dramatic proportions (Farrell, Evershed, and Davidson 2016).

SOME POSITIVE RESPONSES

Concern regarding these and other pervasive infringements of child migrants' rights and needs has generated a range of positive responses gradually gaining momentum on the global stage. Two processes are noteworthy.

First, children on the move are now to a growing degree considered the responsibilities of mainstream national child rights constituencies whereas they never had been in the past. At the domestic level, child welfare agencies, increasingly aware of immigrant, refugee, or undocumented children among their populations of concern—whether trafficked, abused, neglected, or simply outside family care—have initiated procedures to encompass these constituencies more robustly in their care protocols. Special trainings, educational programs, mentorship, and community outreach initiatives are some elements of these organizational innovations.[6] More internationally, organizations such as UNICEF, Save the Children, and PLAN International that have traditionally focused on child rights and child protection issues have greatly strengthened their expertise and programming in the area of children on the move (see http://nolostgeneration.org). Work on issues of birth registration, access to education, health care, and social protection now increasingly complement the humanitarian work focused on vaccination, family tracing, and access to a refugee status determination procedure (European Forum 2016). These are important policy developments that directly affect the lives of children affected by migration, whether displaced internally within their own countries, living in neighboring states, or navigating the challenges of relocation or resettlement further afield.

Second, expert and advocacy bodies concerned with questions of migration, refugee protection, and citizenship have begun to incorporate child-specific concerns and competences into their research and policy making. Whereas children were long considered, as indicated at the beginning of this chapter, an undifferentiated population of vulnerable dependents of adult migrants, with claims subordinate to those of the responsible adults and needs and rights derivative from them, more recent work evidences a welcome independent focus on child-specific entitlements and vulnerabilities. As Dryden-Peterson discusses in detail, the United Nations High Commissioner for Refugees (UNHCR), in combination with other agencies, has moved away from its encampment-based approach to refugee protection—an approach that isolated refugee and other children on the move from broader youth constituencies and that confined the services made available to refugee children in limited and low-quality silos—sometimes for decades at a stretch. Instead, in a welcome reversal of policy and practice, both local and international stakeholders now, at least in principle, take responsibility for refugee and other forms of emergency education, acknowledging the importance of mainstreaming schooling, health care, skill training, and other opportunity-creating measures for their populations of concern (Dryden-Peterson 2011, 2016). Though such measures are an improvement over the ghettoized approach that preceded them, mainstreaming refugee children within national educational systems does not ipso facto resolve all problems. As Dryden-Peterson notes in chapter 10 of this volume, the promise of stability that goes with inclusion of refugee children in the national schooling system is often not delivered: stigma, exclusion, and a profound sense of marginalization and danger continue to plague the lives of millions of displaced schoolgoers, even as they gain greater access to more vigorous educational possibilities. These challenges clearly illustrate the complexity of meaningfully delivering children's rights in situations of mass forced migration.

The International Organization for Migration (IOM), a recent entrant to the United Nations (UN) family of agencies, is strengthening its focus and expertise on matters relating to children on the move as part of its broader agenda of promoting legal and safe migration policies, procedures, and practices. Apart from working on the generation of robust tools to enforce and measure this particular migration target encapsulated in the UN's Sustainable Development Goal (SDG) 10.7, IOM is also working more generally to develop rights-based migration management strategies, including measures to prevent trafficking and to enhance the child protection services available to migrant children in the process.[7]

These institutional moves represent a significant achievement, one that merits attention despite the continuing violations of child migrants' rights described at the outset. The fact that the urgent needs of children on the move for protection are finally becoming a central global concern of both child and migration constituencies is encouraging. It is evidence of the multiple drivers that are actively engaged in promoting real social change, including those involved in grassroots advocacy, strategic and impact litigation, and top-down, rights-based reform.

INNOVATIVE APPROACHES TO ADVANCING
CHILD MIGRANT RIGHTS

An example of these multiple stakeholder efforts is the development in June 2016, just before the September 2016 UN Summit meeting on large-scale migration, of a concise set of *Recommended Principles to Guide Actions Concerning Children on the Move and Other Children Affected by Migration* (https://cdn2.sph.harvard.edu /wp-content/uploads/sites/5/2016/06/Principles.pdf). The short compilation of fundamental policies articulates a set of widely agreed-upon principles based in international law that are applicable to children on the move.

The principles open with the unconditional insistence that all children be considered as children first and foremost, no matter what their migration or nationality status might be. This statement is not a cliché. Rather, it is an exacting requirement stating that all parties—be they border patrol guards, police officers, or immigration investigators—ensure the safety and other protection needs of children—from harm and for water, food, medical care, and nurture—prior to investigating their legal status. The insistence on the implementation of established principles at the outset of the encounter between a state and young migrants highlights state parties' obligation to accord the benefit of the doubt to those claiming to be children and the illegitimacy of treating them, as often happens, as illegal adult migrants until proof to the contrary emerges.

Other principles include reference to the imperatives of birth registration (still routinely denied to one-third of the world's children, including many children on the move) (Plan International n. d.), to the provision of health care (including mental-health care so urgently required in the current Syrian context) (Save the Children UK 2017), and to accessible social protection measures in the face of risks of exploitation or abuse (now documented as impinging on up to 50 percent of children on the move in some migration flows). An overarching consideration is the obligation of state actors and other responsible officials to take into account, as a central consideration, the views and wishes of children themselves when making decisions that affect their lives, a fundamental principle still routinely ignored in the overwhelming majority of child-migration procedures (see Harvard FXB Center for Health and Human Rights 2016).

Apart from their content, these principles are significant as an illustration of recent strides in mainstreaming child migrants' rights. Within a few short months of their promulgation, the principles have been widely endorsed by state and non-state actors alike and by worldwide bodies such as the International Committee on the Rights of Migrant Workers and Their Families (for up-to-date details of ratifications and adoptions, see www.terredeshommes.org).

At the September 19, 2016, UN General Assembly meeting on large movements of people, child migrants were featured several times in the discussions. Concerns regarding their treatment and needs were expressed in the *New York Declaration for Refugees and Migrants,* the document that came out of the UN meeting and was signed by 193 UN member states. This declaration commits its signatories to recognizing "the special needs of all people in vulnerable situations who are traveling within large movements of refugees and migrants, including . . . children, especially those who are unaccompanied or separated from their families" (United Nations 2016, paras. 23 and 32; see also paras. 59, 60, and 70).

The *Declaration* reiterates the fundamental principle that "children should not be criminalized or subject to punitive measures because of their migration status or that of their parents" (para. 56). It also articulates an intention to "take steps to address the particular vulnerabilities of women and children during their journey from country of origin to country of arrival. This includes their potential exposure to discrimination and exploitation . . . as well as to sexual, physical and psychological abuse, violence, human trafficking and contemporary forms of slavery" (para. 29). And it specifically addresses the gender-related vulnerabilities that arise in relation to risks of violence, exclusion from appropriate access to health care, and other incidents of migration distress (para. 31). After years on the sidelines, the urgency of the need to attend to child-protection issues related to the current global refugee and migration situation has clearly entered the political and diplomatic mainstream.

BUILDING FLEXIBLE AND COMPREHENSIVE MOBILITY: A CHILD AND YOUTH RIGHTS AGENDA

A protection agenda for children on the move, urgent and essential though it is, is inadequate. It takes as a given the current situation in which very large—indeed, growing—numbers of children, adolescents, and young people are constrained to leave home and embark on hazardous journeys with meager outcome prospects. Many children and young people on the move have spoken candidly about the serious and frightening risks they willingly embrace because the alternatives—conflict, abuse, destitution, hopelessness—are even worse (Vacchiano 2018; see also Bhabha 2015). What is urgently required is a complementary set of strategies that anticipate and prevent such harm by instituting the "safe, legal and regular" migration opportunities for children and young people articulated by SDG 10.7, opportunities that render mobility not the preserve of a small and privileged minority but a widely accessible public good.

The structures needed to generate this mobility for children and young people would underpin a much more equitable and comprehensive mapping of individual aspiration onto social and economic opportunities than the current largely one-way migration options do. Fast-changing work, technology, production, and human resource needs reflect an imperative of human mobility. For this plan to work, though, such human mobility needs to be supported by safe, legal, and flexible migration management structures responsive to the needs and abilities of young people, the most flexible and malleable element of the global working population. As Gonzalo Sánchez-Terán (2017) points out, the scale of climate-related natural disasters alone makes migration opportunity an essential element of our future child-protection toolkit if we want to avoid an even greater "crisis of containment" than the one already in place. Such a process of containment, Sánchez-Terán (2017) rightly argues, constitutes a willful externalization of borders to safeguard social and economic privilege and deny our ineluctable educational and other obligations.

Hard though it is in the present political circumstances to envisage generous and rights-respecting public policies based on inclusion and cosmopolitan humanitarian obligations, these policies nevertheless remain not only just but also wise from the perspective of medium-term global self-interest in productive capacity, international comity, and environmental conservation. Insofar as such revised structures address broad societal needs (production, service, and consumption), they should garner political support. Insofar as the structures guarantee opportunities for material and intellectual development, self-fulfillment, and realization of aspirations to a much wider cohort of young people than currently enjoys such mobility options, they are likely to attract, and to cater legally and safely to, the human capital required by an aging and increasingly skills-based global technological and economic sphere.

From the perspective of children on the move, the relevance of these broad-based considerations is evident. Children on the move, as members of future generations of producers, consumers, and voters, will not acquiesce in being tied to outmoded and manifestly inadequate personal trajectories to individual destinies that deliver disenfranchisement from the global commons. They will not agree to be limited to migration options that subordinate their mobility either (1) to that of related adults (family reunification) or (2) to economic preconditions that are out of reach for the vast majority (e.g., private school fees) or (3) to irregular, exploitative, and potentially life-threatening transport options (e.g., smugglers). This limited menu of options has generated the recent dire unaccompanied minor migration trajectory that so often spells disaster and encourages the search for hazardous alternatives described in the preceding pages of this chapter.

The urgency of these considerations does not just apply to children on the move. It is equally relevant to children and other populations (the vast majority) who do not move. Future generations of currently enfranchised populations, the beneficiaries of hereditary historical inequality—whether in Europe, North America, or elsewhere—will not, as is already evident, be able to sustain their privilege in hermetically sealed nation-states fortified against hostile others. What is called for is a more interdependent, flexible, and permeable vision of collaboration, mobility, and inclusive nurturance.

A FORWARD-LOOKING AND AMBITIOUS AGENDA: INTEGRATING TWENTY-FIRST-CENTURY CHILD MOBILITY WITH THE DEVELOPMENT AGENDA

The starting point is acknowledging that opportunities for self-realization depend on education, skill, and apprenticeship options for children on the move just as they do for children who are not on the move. As past eras have repeatedly shown, historical legacies of wealth and opportunity selfishly guarded against "outsider" intrusion are precarious in the face of pervasive and manifest injustice. The communications revolution and the vastly expanded information supply available to millennials across the globe accelerate the evidence of injustice, not just across proximate boundaries but between far-flung continents.

Youthful long-distance migration flows, there for all to witness, demonstrate the consequences of this revolution. The agenda urgently needed for children on the move in the twenty-first century thus expands from its current focus on humanitarian and child rights norms to incorporate a robust sustainable development agenda. Several targets in the 2030 Sustainable Development Goals (SDGs) articulate key elements of this agenda.

Guaranteeing access to child protection resources, as the UN's *New York Declaration* does, once children have surpassed the horrors of dangerous smuggling routes, of abusive trafficking situations, or of overcrowded and malfunctioning refugee camps, represents a significant child protection stride—and one that is robustly consistent with the strong message of the principles discussed earlier. Several of the SDGs address these child protection principles directly, including SDG 1.3 ("Implement nationally appropriate social protection systems and measures for all"), SDG 3 ("Ensure healthy lives and promote well-being"), and SDG 8.7 ("Take immediate measures to eradicate forced labor, end modern slavery and human trafficking and secure the prohibition and elimination of the worst forms of child labor" (United Nations 2015). But others point to a more ambitious migration agenda, one that promotes mobility and ensures access to safe, regular, and legal migration opportunities.

As already noted, SDG 10.7 establishes this important principle as a central plank of a forward-looking and inclusive development agenda: "Facilitate orderly, safe, regular and responsible migration and mobility of people, including through the implementation of planned and well-managed migration policies" (United Nations 2015). The principle applies with particular force to children and young people since they are the migration constituency with the least access to such opportunities.

Paradoxically, given their needs, ambitions, and capacities, children and young people have to date had exceedingly limited legal migration opportunities. If they do not travel as part of a family unit, or travel to join one, they can only access a legal migration status as humanitarian claimants—as particularly needy refugees, for example. Educational opportunities, skills training or apprenticeship positions, and starter-level employment slots are only available to a privileged minority. These are constituencies who can benefit from regional mobility schemes (e.g., the EU Higher Educational Exchange Program, known as the Erasmus Program) or whose families can afford to pay the high fees levied on international students or trainees. Transforming this discriminatory youth landscape by introducing greatly expanded legal mobility options for young people is an urgent reform priority.

Education in particular lends itself well to such intervention. As other contributors to this volume note with cogent arguments, increasing access to quality secondary and tertiary formal instruction is a critical deliverable for a just and inclusive twenty-first-century global commons. It generates a level playing field for the next generation of workers, inventors, entrepreneurs, and thinkers. These players are an essential redistributive tool for a transnational economy in which manual labor options are rapidly giving way to skilled, technical, specialist service or professional work opportunities as the ticket to income generation.

How is this development relevant to children on the move? Educational opportunity means facilitating access to quality educational institutions well beyond universal compulsory primary education. For this reason, the *New York Declaration* (United Nations 2016) commits its signatories to promoting "tertiary education, skills training and vocational education" for refugee populations. It acknowledges that "in conflict and crisis situations, higher education serves as a powerful driver for change, shelters and protects a critical group of young men and women by maintaining their hopes for the future, fosters inclusion and non-discrimination, and acts as a catalyst for the recovery and rebuilding of post-conflict countries" (para. 82; see also para. 84).

The SDGs also emphasize the importance of educational access and quality across all levels of education.

Higher education is not just crucial for conflict and post-conflict situations. It has a much broader relevance for children on the move, including those escaping from failing social structures, inadequate or unsafe schooling, and bleak work prospects. Without education, income-generating potential is curtailed and rights-respecting and stimulating job options are illusory. Yet during the past decade, the disjuncture between educational supply and demand has increased dramatically, and all the signs indicate that this process will accelerate further. The African continent is home to the largest proportion of children who are out of school at the primary level and beyond; one-third of all out-of-school children of primary school age live in West and Central Africa, and the rate of adolescents who are out of school is nearly double that of primary school children (UNICEF 2015). But it is also the continent with the fastest growing population. As a recent UNESCO (n. d., 26) report notes:

> Between 2000 and 2012, the primary school–age population in sub-Saharan Africa grew from 110 million to 148 million, and the lower secondary school–age population increased from 49 million to 66 million. Sub-Saharan Africa—and this is true for both

Eastern and Southern Africa and West and Central Africa—is the only region that has been confronted with such a rapidly growing population. Countries in this region face a double challenge: not only do they have to provide educational facilities for the children who are out of school today, but they must also accommodate the ever-growing numbers of children who will reach school-going age in the coming years.

It is small wonder that the absence of educational opportunity is a very significant factor affecting many young Africans. As Vacchiano eloquently notes: "In a social environment marked by increased pressure for economic growth and self-improvement, the failure of state institutions to grant effective means of social transmission and reproduction has turned the experience of adolescence into a moment in life marked by a multifarious mix of expectations, desires, sense of duty, frustrations, uncertainties, [and] aspirations" (Vacchiano 2018, 87).

The states' representatives assembled in New York during the summer of 2016 recognized this situation: acknowledging "that the lack of educational opportunities is often a push factor for migration, particularly for young people, we commit to strengthening capacities in countries of origin, including in educational institutions" (United Nations 2016, para. 44). At the same time that sub-Saharan Africa is the place where the fastest acceleration in birth rate is taking place, it contrasts sharply with regions much better endowed with educational opportunities. These are regions such as Europe, North America, or East Asia where ample higher educational provision is not fully utilized given birth rates that are gradually or rapidly declining (see UNESCO 2017).

These considerations are highly relevant to children on the move. Prioritizing quality educational access, not just for primary but also for secondary and tertiary school students, responds to both the protection (child rights) and the mobility (migration rights) mandates that should be central humanitarian concerns. The SDGs recognize this situation. SDG 4b establishes the following target:

By 2020, substantially expand globally the number of scholarships available to developing countries, in particular least developed countries, small island developing states and African countries, for enrollment in higher education, including vocational training and information and communications technology, technical, engineering, and scientific programmes, in developed countries and other developing countries. (United Nations 2015)

What this target envisages is a model of flexible mobility tied to youth development that already exists for some young people. As noted earlier, the Erasmus Program in Europe has for years facilitated the mobility of a generation of European adolescents from east to west, from north to south, and vice versa, generating not only previously unimaginable educational vision and opportunities but also a new form of collective citizenship. The model of flexible educational mobility has also long existed for the privileged elite, who wisely facilitate transnational educational opportunities for their offspring to incentivize learning; the opening up of intellectual, cultural, and personal horizons; and the development of employment-related opportunities. SDG 4b envisions providing a similar opportunity for less privileged millennials—a chance to facilitate legal and safe access to tools that are increasingly essential for personal and familial success. The backers of this goal—UNESCO, United Nations Development Program (UNDP), and UNICEF—envisage a process in which a certain percentage of development aid is consistently earmarked to support educational access across continents.

Again, the UN's *New York Declaration* acknowledges this vital policy obligation. It commits its signatories to considering facilitation of "safe, orderly and regular migration, including . . . circular migration . . . and education-related opportunities. [They] will pay particular attention to . . . transfers of skills and knowledge and the creation of employment opportunities for young people" (United Nations 2016, paras. 57 and 79). These undertakings are timely and welcome. They indicate the growing acknowledgment of a key element for ensuring nondiscriminatory access to mobility and rights.

LOOKING AHEAD FOR CHILDREN ON THE MOVE

The *New York Declaration* commits its signatories to an ambitious educational agenda for emergency situations: "We are determined to ensure that all children are receiving education within a few months of arrival, and we will prioritize budgetary provision to facilitate this, including for host countries as required. We will strive to provide refugee and migrant children with a nurturing environment for the full realization of their rights and capabilities" (United Nations 2016, paras. 32, 81–82).

But insistence on physical access to educational opportunity, at least in the short run, is likely to yield limited results, especially at a time when the scale of distress displacement engulfing young people is so massive. It follows that another element of the educational mobility program is critical, and it is one that is slowly entering academic discussion: the commitment to facilitating global classrooms mediated by technology. This, of course, is an agenda that must concern all educators, including those with no particular interest or expertise in children on the move.[8] It is an agenda that acknowledges the irrationality and injustice of confining education to physical classrooms that benefit a very few and exclude the majority. The parallel with nativist migration policies that for so long have excluded children and young people from legal, safe, and regular access to mobility is clear. Just as resources of social protection, stability, and peace should not be hoarded through highly restrictive and punitive immigration policies that willfully exclude needy outsiders, so also should resources of learning, engagement, and human development not be anachronistically tied to forms of place-confined instruction that belong to a past century. With growing evidence in the commercial and for-profit sectors of the manifold uses of Skype, teleconferencing, and e-information, it is surely time to apply the same techniques to the fundamental challenge of facilitating access to excellence in educational opportunity to those who stand to benefit from it.

Creative use of information technology is one way of addressing the challenge of promoting child and youth mobility, a mobility of access and of ideas. Many others must be generated in the fields of skill development, employment opportunity, and training so that flexible mobility becomes a natural and safe choice for disenfranchised twenty-first-century children on the move as it has long been for other, more privileged constituencies.

NOTES

1. For a concise definition, see OHCHR (2016), note 3.

2. See especially the 1989 UN Convention on the Rights of the Child, article 3 (OHCHR 1989).

3. Among a plethora of reports and publications on this topic, see Chester et al. (2015); "Missing Children in Europe" (2017); IOM Global Migration Data Analysis Center (2016); UNHCR (2014).

4. For a full discussion of these topics, see Bhabha (2014).

5. For an example of dramatic child protection lacunae in migration and refugee management systems, see the March 2017 report on Italy by the UN Special Representative of the Secretary General on Migration and Refugees (Boček 2017).

6. See, for example, the provision of educational access and support to Syrian refugee children provided by the German government or the child welfare support accorded to unaccompanied asylum-seeking children in Sweden (Harvard FXB Center for Health and Human Rights 2016).

7. SDG 10.7 establishes the following target: facilitate the orderly, safe, and responsible migration and mobility of people, including through implementation of planned and well-managed migration policies; see United Nations (2015); IOM (2016).

8. For interesting experiments in information technology (IT)–mediated educational access, see the Borderless Higher Education for Refugees (BHER) project linking York University in Toronto with Dadaab refugee camps in Kenya; KIRON; and new initiatives that use Ed X facilities to make university instruction available through virtual classrooms, such as the work of Sarah Dryden-Peterson (2011, 2016).

REFERENCES

Bhabha, Jacqueline. 2014. *Child Migration and Human Rights in a Global Age.* Princeton, NJ: Princeton University Press.

———. 2016. "When Water Is Safer Than Land: Addressing Distress Migration." *Harvard Magazine* (January–February). http://harvardmagazine.com/2015/12/when-water-is-safer-than-land.

Boček, Tomáš. 2017. *Report of the Fact-Finding Mission to Italy by Ambassador Tomáš Boček, Special Representative of the Secretary General on Migration and Refugees, 16–21 October*

2016. Council of Europe, March 2, 2017. http://unipd-centrodirittiumani.it/public/docs/Report_factfinding_mission_Italy_Tomas_BoceK_mar_2017.pdf.

Chester, Hilary, Nathalie Lumert, and Anne Mullooly. 2015. *Child Victims of Human Trafficking: Outcomes and Service Adaptation within the US Unaccompanied Refugee Minor Programs.* United States Conference of Catholic Bishops. www.usccb.org/about/anti-trafficking-program/upload/URM-Child-Trafficking-Study-2015-Final.pdf.

Digidiki, Vasileia. 2016. "A Harsh New Reality: Transactional Sex among Refugee Minors as a Means of Survival in Greece." *Harvard FXB,* December 17, 2016. https://fxb.harvard.edu/2016/12/17/a-harsh-new-reality-transactional-sex-among-refugee-minors-as-a-means-of-survival-in-greece/.

Dryden-Peterson, Sarah. 2011. "The Politics of Higher Education for Refugees in a Global Movement for Basic Education." *Refugee[0]* 27 (2): 10–[0]18.

Dryden-Peterson, Sarah. 2016. "Refugee Education: The Crossroads of Globalization." *Educational Researcher* 45 (9): 473–82.

European Forum on the Rights of the Child. 2017. *The Protection of Children in Migration.* (Originally published November 24, 2016; revised February 3, 2017). http://ec.europa.eu/newsroom/just/item-detail.cfm?item_id=34456.

Eurostat. 2016. "Almost 90,000 Unaccompanied Minors among Asylum Seekers Registered in the EU in 2015." Press release, May 2, 2016. http://ec.europa.eu/eurostat/documents/2995521/7244677/3-02052016-AP-EN.pdf/.

Farrell, Paul, Nick Evershed, and Helen Davidson. 2016. "The Nauru Files: Cache of 2,000 Leaked Reports Reveal Scale of Abuse of Children in Australian Offshore Detention." *The Guardian,* August 10, 2016. www.theguardian.com/australia-news/2016/aug/10/the-nauru-files-2000-leaked-reports-reveal-scale-of-abuse-of-children-in-australian-offshore-detention.

Harvard FXB Center for Health and Human Rights. [0]2016. *Children on the Move: An Urgent Human Rights and Child Protection Priority.* November 16, 2016. https://cdn2.sph.harvard.edu/wp-content/uploads/sites/5/2016/11/Oak-report2016.pdf.

———. 2017. *Emergency within an Emergency: The Growing Epidemic of Sexual Exploitation and Abuse of Migrant Children in Greece.* https://fxb.harvard.edu/2017/04/17/new-report-emergency-within-an-emergency-exploitation-of-migrant-children-in-greece/.

House of Lords, United Kingdom. European Union Committee. 2017. *Children in Crisis: Unaccompanied Minor Children in the EU,* 15–[0]22. Report of Session 2016–[0]17. www.publications.parliament.uk/pa/ld201617/ldselect/ldeucom/34/34.pdf.

IOM (International Organization for Migration). 2016. "Summit on Refugees and Migrants Begins as IOM Joins the United Nations." September 19, 2016. www.iom.int/news/summit-refugees-and-migrants-begins-iom-joins-united-nations.

IOM (International Organization for Migration) Global Migration Data Analysis Center. 2016. *Children and Unsafe Migration in Europe: Data and Policy: Understanding the Evidence Base,* no. 5, September 2015. https://publications.iom.int/system/files/gmdac_data_briefing_series_issue5.pdf.

"Missing Children in Europe." 2017. In *Lost in Migration: Working Together in Protecting Children from Disappearance.* January 2017. http://lostinmigration.eu/BackgroundNote.pdf.

OHCHR. 1989. *Convention on the Rights of the Child.* Adopted November 20, 1989. www.ohchr.org/EN/ProfessionalInterest/Pages/CRC.aspx.

OHCHR. 2016. *Recommended Principles to Guide Actions Concerning Children on the Move and Other Children Affected by Migration.* Adopted June 2016. www.ohchr.org/Documents /HRBodies/CMW/Recommended-principle_EN.pdf.

Plan International. n.d. "Count Every Child—Birth Registration Initiative." https://plan-international.org/birth-registration/count-every-child-birth-registration.

Rosenblum, Marc R. 2015. "Unaccompanied Child Migration to the United States: The Tension between Protection and Prevention." *Migration Policy Institute,* April 2015. www .migrationpolicy.org/research/unaccompanied-child-migration-united-states-tension-between-protection-and-prevention.

Sánchez-Terán, Gonzalo. 2017. "The Global Forced Migration Crisis and the Education of Children." Paper presented at the Workshop on Humanitarianism and Mass Migration, UCLA, Los Angeles, January 18–19, 2017.

Save the Children UK. 2017. *Invisible Wounds: The Impact of Six Years of War on the Mental Health of Syria's Children.* https://i.stci.uk/sites/default/files/Invisible%20Wounds%20 March%202017.pdf.

Torres, María de los Angeles. 2004. *The Lost Apple: Operation Pedro Pan, Cuban Children in the US, and the Promise of a Better Future.* Boston: Beacon Press.

UNESCO (United Nations Educational, Scientific and Cultural Organization). n.d. *Data for the Sustainable Development Goals.* www.uis.unesco.org/Education/Documents/oosci-global-report-en.pdf.

———. 2017. *Reducing Global Poverty through Universal Primary and Secondary Education.* www.uis.unesco.org/Education/Documents/oosci-global-report-en.pdf.

UNHCR (United Nations High Commissioner for Refugees). n.d. *Figures at a Glance.* www.unhcr.org/figures-at-a-glance.html.

———. 2014. *Children on the Run: Unaccompanied Children Leaving Central America and Mexico and the Need for International Protection.* www.unhcr.org/56fc266f4.html.

UNICEF (United Nations Children's Fund). n.d. *Reaching Children in South Sudan: The Situation of Children in the World's Youngest Country.* www.unicef.org/infobycountry /southsudan_74635.html. Accessed June 21, 2018.

———. 2015. *Fixing the Broken Promise of Education for All: Findings from the Global Initiative on Out-of-School Children.* www.unicef.org/education/files/allinschool.org_wp-content_ uploads_2015_01_Fixing-the-Broken-Promise-of-Education-For-All-full-report.pdf.

United Nations. 2015. *Transforming Our World: The 2030 Agenda for Sustainable Development.* Adopted September 25, 2015. https://sustainabledevelopment.un.org/post2015 /transformingourworld.

———. 2016. *New York Declaration for Refugees and Migrants.* https://refugeesmigrants .un.org/declaration.

Vacchiano, Francesco. 2018. "Desiring Mobility: Children's Migration, Parents' Distress, and Constraints on the Future in North Africa." In *Research Handbook on Child Migration,* edited by Jacqueline Bhabha, Jyothi Kanics, and Daniel Senovilla Hernandez, 82–97. Camberley, Surrey, UK: Edward Elgar Press.

Zahra, Tara. 2011. *The Lost Children: Reconstructing Europe's Families after World War II.* Cambridge, MA: Harvard University Press.

4

A COMPASSIONATE PERSPECTIVE ON IMMIGRANT CHILDREN AND YOUTH

Carola Suárez-Orozco

Most high- and middle-income countries in the world are encountering large and growing numbers of immigrant and refugee-origin children and youth. While there is much immigration trepidation the world over, one area for optimism is the prospect for these youths to rejuvenate countries with aging demographics. For this potential to be realized, countries of immigration will need to find effective ways to help integrate immigrant and refugee-origin children into the fabric of society.

BEYOND THE MONOLITH

The children of immigrants share some common features. Their parents are from a country of origin other than the host country and, as such, bring with them different cultural practices and expectations as well as often bringing another language. The first generation, born abroad, shares in common with the second generation, born in the host country, the fact of having foreign-born parents.

Immigrants do not come as a monolith. Indeed, their children are highly diverse in terms of class, racial, ethnic, religious, and linguistic backgrounds. Beyond that, some are the children of highly educated professional parents, whereas others may have illiterate parents. Some received excellent schooling, whereas others left educational systems that were in shambles. Some escaped political, religious, or ethnic persecution; others are motivated by the promise of better jobs and better educational opportunities. Some are documented migrants, whereas others are unauthorized young migrants: there are perhaps one million undocumented children in the United States today (Yoshikawa, Gonzales, and C. Suárez-Orozco 2017). Some join well-established communities with robust social supports (such as Cubans in

Miami), whereas others move from one migrant camp to another, being forced to change schools frequently. The pathways and outcomes of immigrant youth will vary greatly as a function of both the receiving context in the new society and the resources with which they arrive (M. Suárez-Orozco, C. Suárez-Orozco, and Sattin-Bajaj 2010).

Further, the first generation is much more complex than it is often perceived to be. Rubén G. Rumbaut (2004) has subtly explicated the developmental, accultura-tive, and linguistic implications of arriving prior to entering school (the so-called 1.75 generation), during the elementary school years (the 1.5 generation), or during adolescence and beyond (the 1.25 generation). Arriving at an earlier age, long before puberty, with maximal exposure to the US school system will provide an immi-grant-origin youth with an experience that is much closer to that of a second-generation youth. She will have minimal recollection of her country of origin and is likely to come to speak the host country language with no trace of an accent. Nonetheless, she may share with some of her first-generation peers the burden of not being documented. And she certainly shares the experience with her second-generation peers of having parents who may not readily embrace the new country's norms. Their parents may have strict expectations and child-raising norms attuned to the ways of the old country. She may also have parents who are documented or parents who are not. Alternatively, she may live in a mixed-status family with some members who have documentation and others who do not (therefore living under the shadow of potentially losing a beloved family member at any given moment) (Yoshikawa, C. Suárez-Orozco, and Gonzales 2016). Another characteristic she may share with the second generation is the likelihood that she entered kindergarten without speaking the language of instruction of the new country. Depending upon the social climate of her new country, she may also face a xenophobia[1] reflected in the media, in neighborhood interactions, in school, and even in the leadership at the highest level of government (C. Suárez-Orozco, Abo-Zena, and Marks 2015).

The first generation is particularly complex in its composition. Roughly speak-ing, it can be broken down into two categories that have deep implications for the day-to-day experiences of childhood as well as for longer-term trajectories for "future participation in society" (Dryden-Peterson 2016, 473). The first category, which I term "regularized status," involves the potential for social inclusion. Among these children are those who come with some form of recognized status, including newcomers with any kind of authorization, recognized refugees, or doc-umented longer-term settlers. The second category is composed of immigrants who are living in some form of "liminal status" (Menjívar 2006) with no sense of whether they will be able to stay or will be deported at any given moment. These include those who are outright undocumented, those who are "DACAmented,"[2] asylum seekers, and unaccompanied minors (who have not yet undergone so-called "extreme vetting" (Shear and Cooper 2017) (see fig. 4.1).

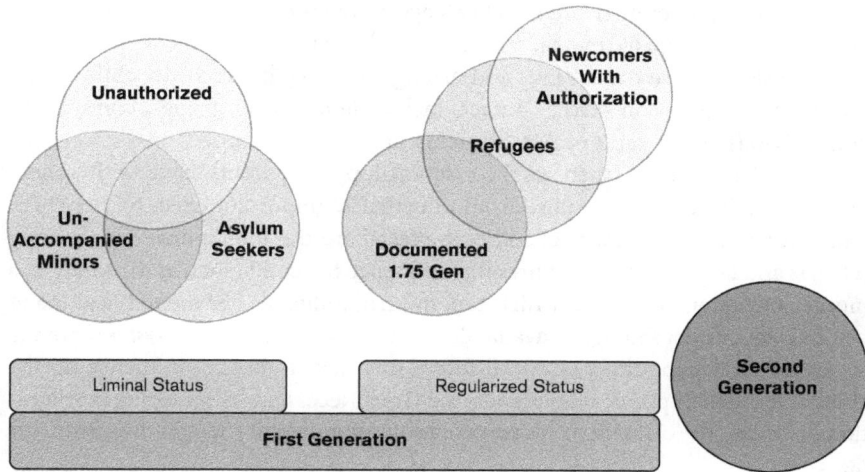

FIGURE 4.1. Children of immigrants.

Immigration status thus adds complexity to social positionality. In complex interactions with socioeconomic status, race, ethnicity, religion, and gender, immigration status will play a role in shaping the kinds of experiences and opportunities children will have in their new societies (García Coll et al. 1996).

MODELS OF UNDERSTANDING

To make sense of the experiences of immigrant and refugee children's and youth's pathways of adaptation, I have developed two complementary conceptual models.

An Ecological Framework

The first model is anchored in a Bronfenbrennerian perspective whereby the interrelated contexts of development within which children and youth are embedded shape their opportunities and have important implications for both educational and well-being outcomes (Bronfenbrenner and Morris 2006; C. Suárez-Orozco, Abo-Zena, and Marks 2015).

As is true for all children, the formative experiences of immigrant children will be shaped by reciprocal interactions between the child and his environment. Outcomes will vary as a function of the child's individual characteristics, her culture, and her environment over the course of time. Each child has his or her own set of characteristics that, when interacting with the environment, will place him or her in varying positions of vulnerability or strength. All children grow within cultural contexts that shape their future selves. For immigrant children, some critical individual characteristics shaping development are the child's age at migration, race and ethnicity, language skills, exposure to trauma, sexual orientation, and temperament.

Microsystems are the settings and arrangements with which the child comes into most intimate and direct contact, such as family, peer groups, community, and religious organizations. Mesosystems are the interconnections among the various microsystems (such as the relationship the parents have with school personnel); these have an indirect but nonetheless important effect on the child. Exosystems, another sphere of indirect effects, are the interconnections among settings and larger social structures that influence the child (such as the safety of a mother's work environment, which can, in turn, influence her mental health and her consequent psychological availability to her child). The *macrosystems* are the larger political, economic, or social forces that have a distinct influence on the child's life (such as political upheavals, the Great Recession, or sweeping immigration policies). The chronosystem represents developmental changes over time (see fig. 4.2).

Risk and Resilience

Immigrant and refugee children and youth are remarkably resilient and bring their own agency and assets to their lives. Further, supports and interventions within the new contexts can reduce the challenges these youth face and promote more positive outcomes (Kia-Keating et al. 2011). Thus, it is important to take into account the social context, family-level variables, and child-level factors when considering outcomes that can either add to risk or serve to buffer it.

Immigrant families and their children arrive in their new lands with distinct social and cultural resources (Perreira, Harris, and Lee 2006). Their high aspirations (Fuligni 2001; Portés and Rumbaut 2006), dual frames of reference (C. Suárez-Orozco and M. Suárez-Orozco 1995), optimism (Kao and Tienda 1995), dedicated hard work, positive attitudes toward school (C. Suárez-Orozco and M. Suárez-Orozco 1995), and ethic of family support for advanced learning (Li 2004) contribute to the fact that some immigrant youth educationally outperform their native-born peers (Perreira, Harris, and Lee 2006). On the other hand, many immigrant youth encounter a myriad of challenges—economic obstacles, xenophobia, language acquisition difficulties, acculturative challenges, family separations, underresourced neighborhoods and schools, and the like—and struggle to gain their bearings in an educational system that may put them on a path of downward trajectory (García-Coll and Marks 2011; Portés and Zhou 1993; C. Suárez-Orozco, M. Suárez-Orozco, and Todorova 2008; C. Suárez-Orozco, Abo-Zena, and Marks 2015).

Refugee and asylum-seeking youth share many of the features of other immigrant youth. In addition, however, most have experienced some form of traumatic

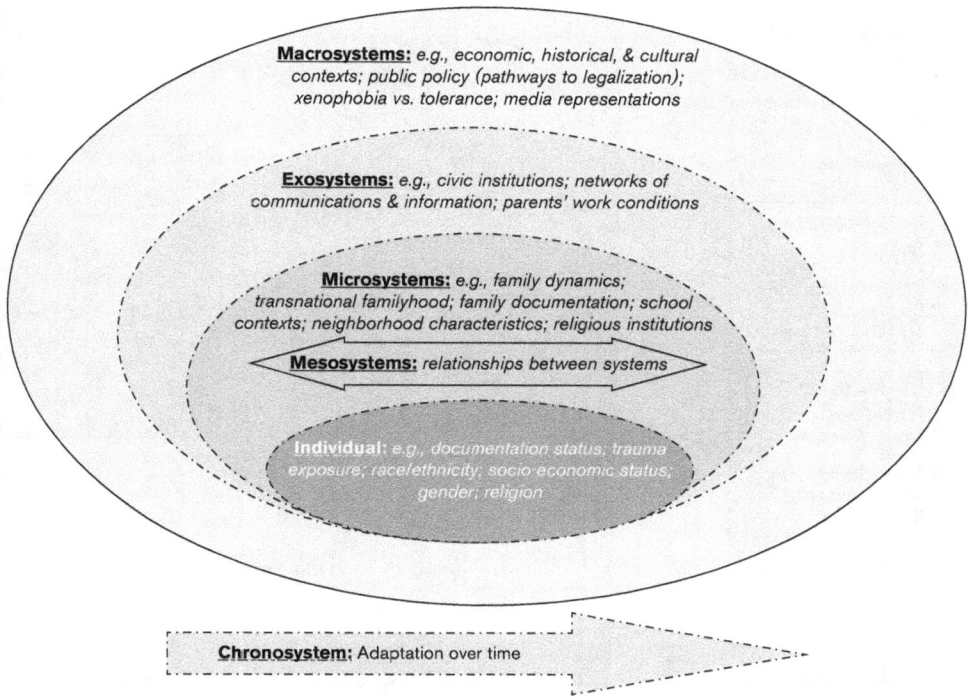

FIGURE 4.2. Ecological model of children of immigrants and refugee children and youth.

event at some point in their journey—either prior to their migration, during the course of their journey, or after arriving at their receiving context (or in some cases at each of these points) (Ehntholt and Yule 2006; Carlson, Cacciatore, and Klimek 2012). Using a stringent criterion, 11 percent of refugee adolescents are estimated to suffer from PTSD; this conservative assessment is double the rate of that of their nonrefugee peers (Ehntholt and Yule 2006). Refugee children and youth also report high levels of depression, anxiety, and bereavement; and comorbidity with PTSD is quite common (Ehntholt and Yule 2006; Stathopoulou, chapter 7, this volume). Not surprisingly, "estimates of psychiatric disorders vary considerably depending upon the type of event(s) experienced, the population studied, and the diagnostic method used" (Ehntholt and Yule 2006, 1198). Further, the number of traumatic events experienced in the country of origin as well as the death of family members is associated with PTSD while the number of current life stressors is more likely to be associated with depression (Ehntholt and Yule 2006). Other psychological difficulties that have been noted in the literature

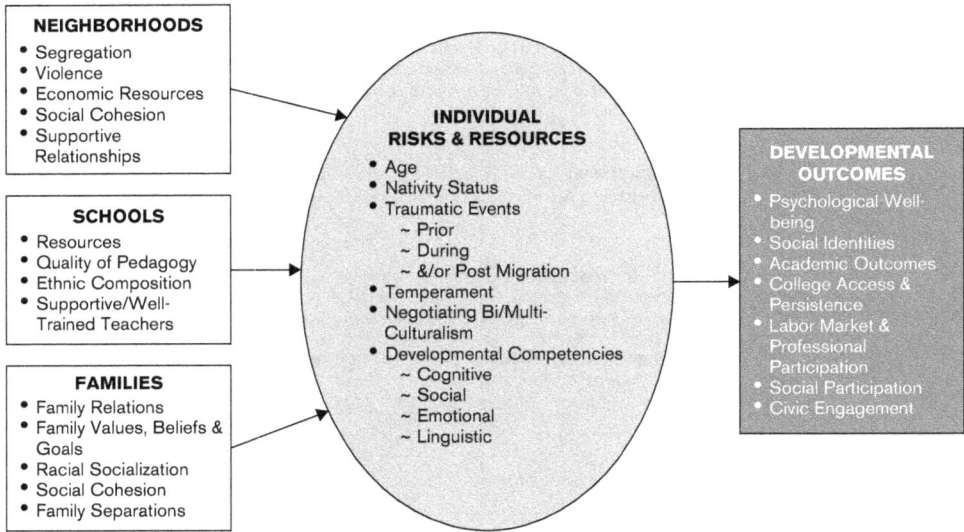

FIGURE 4.3. Risk and resilience model of children of immigrants and refugee children and youth.

include somatic complaints, sleeping difficulties, generalized fears, irritability, impulse control, social withdrawal, constricted affect, and difficulties with concentration (Ehntholt and Yule 2006; Mollica et al. 1997; Thabet, Abed, and Vostanis 2004; see also Mollica, chapter 5, and Betancourt et al., chapter 6, both this volume).

Though not all refugee children and youth respond with emotional difficulties, they are more likely to do so given a higher "dosage" of stress they may have undergone at the various stages of the migration voyage; such difficulties are also affected by the number of losses they have sustained and the degree to which they continue to sustain stressful events in their daily lives (Ehntholt and Yule 2006; Carlson, Cacciatore, and Klimek 2012; Yoshikawa, Wuermli, and Aber, chapter 8, this volume), including perceived social discrimination (Noh et al. 1999). Notably, the presence of supportive relationships serves an important buffering function in refugee children's and youths' resilience (Carlson, Cacciatore, and Klimek 2012) (see fig. 4.3).

THE SOCIAL CONTEXTS OF RECEPTION

The social context into which refugee, migrant, or unaccompanied children settle has significant implications for shaping their short-term adaptation for a variety of outcomes as well as "for their future participation in society" (Dryden-Peterson 2016). Immigration policies and economic opportunities as well as xenophobia matter in affecting the immigrant experience.

Immigration Policies

The myriad of immigration policies that families must navigate as they try to make a home in a new land has significant implications for the short-term and long-term pathways immigrants are able to forge. Over the last decades in the United States, immigration policy has largely focused on security and border controls, with little consideration given to nationwide integration policy for new immigrants (Hansen 2010). Since 1988, when the amnesty provisions of the Immigration Reform and Control Act ended, US immigration policy has restricted pathways out of the shadows for millions of undocumented migrants (Motomura 2008). What in the public imagination is an easily demarcated binary of "legal" versus "illegal" in fact embodies an array of states of liminality masking a deeply broken immigration system (Menjívar 2006). The reality on the ground is that millions of families live with ambiguous documentation, with some family members falling out of legal status, and millions live in families of mixed status in which some members are documented while others are not (Menjívar 2006; Motomura 2008). Furthermore, during the past decade, the United States has become a "deportation nation," deporting four hundred thousand individuals a year (Kanstroom 2007). Concurrently, as attitudes toward undocumented immigrants have grown increasingly harsh, a wave of state and local laws has been enacted targeting undocumented immigrants (Preston 2011). Long backlogs, a Kafkaesque bureaucracy, high rates of denials, and increasing numbers of deportations have cemented growing numbers of transnationally separated and mixed-status families (Yoshikawa, C. Suárez-Orozco, and Gonzales 2016). The new US administration under President Trump has vowed to crank up the deportation machinery, making good on the promise to remove the majority of remaining undocumented immigrants in the country. The new policy will thus tear apart families by deporting parents who are not only the emotional caretakers but also the primary source of economic support for approximately five million US-born citizen children of unauthorized migrants. The implications of these draconian policies for children's well-being are nothing short of barbaric (for a detailed assessment, see Yoshikawa, C. Suárez-Orozco, and Gonzales 2016).

The plight of refugees is likewise rendered inhumane by anachronistic policy frameworks (see Bhabha, chapter 3, this volume). According to Dryden-Peterson (2016), 86 percent of refugees live in neighboring countries with uncertain pathways to move forward. In Europe, in countries like Greece, Sweden, and Germany, millions have applied for asylum, though few are granted refugee status

(Dryden-Peterson 2016; UNHCR 2016). The minuscule numbers of refugees who are admitted to the United States go through years of "extreme vetting" and even after that are subject to vagaries in presidential whims and may be turned away as they attempt to enter the country (Shear and Cooper 2017).

Economic Realities

Securing work is a paramount incentive for immigrants, and the work setting is extremely important in understanding the immigrant experience. It is through work that new arrivals realize substantial benefits secondary to large wage differentials (Hanson 2010). The broader economic context shapes the experience of immigrant family resettlement in a variety of ways: the types of jobs that are available, the stability of employment, and the opportunities to move up the mobility ladder all matter (M. Suárez-Orozco and C. Suárez-Orozco 2013). The stability and quality of jobs, along with parents' status mobility, in turn have implications for immigrant children and youth. The safety of their neighborhoods, the quality of the schools they attend, and how often students change schools are but a few of the variables indirectly linking parents' work with their children's educational experiences and successes (García Coll and Marks 2009). While skilled immigrants who settle in more privileged neighborhoods have been rapidly moving up into the top tiers of the opportunity structure, many others, particularly those with limited skills, have stagnated since the Great Recession (Hanson 2010).

Further, during times of economic downturn, immigrants historically have become a ready target for frustrations. Studies of poll data show that when there is job uncertainty, social attitudes toward immigrants become more negative (Espenshade and Hempstead 1996). Consequently, immigrants have become convenient scapegoats for political manipulation in many national and local contexts.

Xenophobia

In addition to policy and contexts of reception, the social welcome mat profoundly influences the development of immigrant-origin children. Immigrants' identities are shaped by their ethos of reception. The social mirror—the general social and emotional atmosphere and the collective representations of immigrants that new arrivals encounter upon their settlement in the new country—is an important but neglected context of immigration (C. Suárez-Orozco and M. Suárez-Orozco 2001). In the 1980s, a comprehensive look at the experiences of Punjabi immigrants in rural California painted a very troubling picture of the effects of negative social mirroring on academic challenges—from intense peer interactions around race to struggles within the community on how to support (or reject) Punjabi families in schools (Gibson 1988). More recently, and during times of socioeconomic and political anxiety, there is continued evidence that immigrants embody nativists' fear of the unknown. The recent rapid increase in immigration, the terrorist attacks on September 11, 2001, the persistence of unauthorized immigration, and the deep economic recession have aligned to arouse US citizens' unease concerning immigrants of color. Xenophobia has been on the rise, especially as directed toward newer immigrants and toward Muslims (Sirin and Fine 2008) and Latinos (Chavez 2008). There is ample evidence of negative media coverage of immigration (Massey 2010), an increase in hate crimes against immigrants (Leadership Conference on Civil Rights Education Fund 2009), and exclusionary legislation enacted on municipal, state, and federal levels (Carter, Lawrence, and Morse 2011). Furthermore, since new immigrants are predominantly of non-European origin, their children will remain visible minorities for generations, subject to the ongoing racial climate of the nation (García Coll and Magnuson 1997; C. Suárez-Orozco and M. Suárez-Orozco 2001). What, then, are the developmental and educational implications of such a social reception?

Immigrant parents and their children face different tasks when crafting an identity and sense of belonging in the new society (C. Suárez-Orozco and M. Suárez-Orozco 2001). For immigrant parents and latecomer adolescents, a dual frame of reference that brings together "the here and now" and the "there and then" filters the ways in which they view themselves and their new lives. Family roles must be renegotiated. The challenges of providing for the family in a new country, contending with status demotions and promotions, navigating new gendered ideologies and practices, and learning to raise children according to new cultural expectations and standards all become central themes in the creation of these new identities and the development of new social practices. For their children, the work of creating identities will, at different stages of development, involve "fitting in" with peers, struggling with issues of embarrassment about their parents' foreign ways (for example, accents, dress, manners, and ethnic foods), and eventually synthesizing cultural currents from the parental tradition and the norms, values, and worldviews of the new society. Hybridity—the fusion of multiple cultural trends—characterizes second-generation immigrant-origin children's process of creating their new identities (C. Suárez-Orozco and M. Suárez-Orozco 2001). Importantly, these identity processes in turn influence immigrant students' experiences with peers, teachers, and school and influence their sense of academic efficacy, aspirations, and eventual achievement (Marks, Seaboyer, and García Coll 2015).

BRIDGING THE COMPASSION GAP

With heightened xenophobia in the United States, across Europe, and elsewhere, managing the new social anxieties has become a pressing concern. In recent years on both sides of the Atlantic, attitudes toward immigration have gone from mild annoyance to intense concern and apprehension, and, more recently, to near panic. The large sudden inflow of desperate refugees has unsettled many European countries. Growing inequality and economic stagnation, together with the crises of unauthorized immigration and home-grown terrorism, have aligned into a perfect storm. Long-term demographic changes add to these deepening concerns. At a time when nearly all future demographic growth will be via the children of immigrants, both in the United States and throughout Europe, the current malaise over immigration threatens native identities, subverts perceptions of the social contract, puts millions of immigrant-origin children at risk, and is antithetical to fundamental democratic ideals and elemental notions of social justice. It creates an unstable social climate and an unwillingness to invest in the next generation. An understanding of the dynamics behind the compassion gap and how to bridge it is essential for all host societies.

Every society, across history, has stigmatized designated groups, separating "us" from "them" (Link and Phelan 2001). Whenever there are "sharp social groupings[,] the individual is not judged as an individual but as a member of his class" (Boas 1940, 16). In some societies, like the United States, the preoccupation is entangled with issues of documentation status (aka "illegality"), criminality (Waters, chapter 15, this volume), and race. Growing numbers of poor immigrants of color are relegated to spaces where socially constructed phenotypes (Gilman 2000; Bonilla-Silva 2004) come to experience forms of marginalization similar to those experienced by native minorities, like segregation, marginalization, micro- and macro-aggressions, and collective disenfranchisement (Bashi 1998; Omi and Winant 1994). In other countries, racialization is intertwined with religion (Europe and its North African minorities) or historical relations with a country of origin (Koreans in Japan).

Implications for Immigrant-Origin Children and Youth

When large swaths of a society begin loudly and unabashedly to proclaim exclusionary messages toward its immigrants, the actions create a climate of national hatred and xenophobia. Exclusionary messages directed toward immigrant-origin children and youth matter for several reasons. First, they matter because being a member of a disparaged group is linked to negative mental and physical well-being (APA 2012). Second, they create a context of development in which parents and families can be summarily deported and in which even the most basic of services can be denied. This situation contributes to a growing opportunity gap (Yoshikawa, C. Suárez-Orozco, and Gonzales 2016). Third, they send clear signals of who belongs and who does not, undermining the child's sense of social belonging and identity during a formative stage of development. Lastly, this kind of public climate has serious ramifications for our own sense of national unity. At a time of demographic shift, economic stagnation, and social malaise, our society needs to foster cohesive social relations, strengthening the bonds of solidarity between

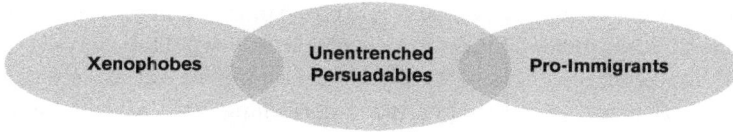

FIGURE 4.4. Relationship of unentrenched persuadables to xenophobes and pro-immigrants.

new and more established citizens (Putnam 2015). As such, we should strive to disrupt narratives of exclusion and division and to nurture practices of inclusion and shared membership in the family of the nation. But how?

Striving to Influence the "Persuadables"

The public mind can be quite fickle—particularly true with those who have not given much thought to a given issue (Howell, Peterson, and West 2009). There are always individuals who are strongly decided one way or another on an issue and are unlikely to shift their opinions through the introduction of rhetoric or popular discourse. Many "persuadables," however, will change their opinions upon exposure to informative public discourse or convincing rhetoric (Howell, Peterson, and West 2009).

The topic of immigration "sits at the edge of [most of the public's] peripheral vision"; it comes in and out of focus (Suro 2009). When in focus, it is blurred at best and is often contentious. In the United States, a survey showed that 51 percent of Americans reported that immigration strengthens the nation, while 41 percent thought that it hurt it (Pew Hispanic Center 2015). In a study conducted in England, the findings of a survey demonstrated that when it came to immigration, a quarter of participants were "Rejectiontionists," another quarter were "Migration Liberals," and the remaining half were in the "Anxious Middle," with an array of views on various aspects of immigration (Katwala, Ballinger, and Rhodes 2014). The question, then, becomes how to reach unentrenched persuadables who may not have reflected much on the topic of immigration because of lack of exposure, information, or deep thought about the issue. How do we reach these persuadables with counternarratives that present a compelling account? (See fig. 4.4.)

How Are Minds Changed?

To change minds and, in turn, behaviors, research by Stanford and Duke professors Chip and Dan Heath (2010) suggests several important strategies. Messages are more likely to "stick" in the minds of audiences when they are understandable and memorable. Providing too much information and complexity in the delivery of the message impedes its delivery. Messages should be clear; in addition, they should be tangible and concrete. Delivering the message in an unexpected manner that takes the audience somewhat by surprise serves to create interest and hold attention. Providing credible information by a convincing and trustworthy expert is also important as the audience must believe the speaker presenting the facts (C. Heath and D. Heath 2010; Cialdini 1984). Using narrative storytelling devices is especially effective. Additionally, drawing upon emotional appeals that make people care, drawing upon self-interest, and appealing to identity are particularly effective (C. Heath and D. Heath 2010). In turn, if the messages stick in people's minds, they will be more likely to change people's behaviors (C. Heath and D. Heath 2010).

When an issue is an especially difficult one, it is important to engage both the emotional and rational sides of people's brains (C. Heath and D. Heath 2010). Nobel Prize winner Daniel Kahneman (2011) speaks of two brains that are often in conflict with one another. He suggests that most people think quickly, allowing their emotional brain to guide them. The intuitive emotional brain tends to be gullible, to suppress ambiguity, and to be overconfident in its assessments. Kahneman (2011) proposes that it is important to slow down and use the more deliberative reasoning brain to assess issues fully when making important decisions.

Relatedly, in order to attempt to "switch" a person's opinions and behaviors under difficult circumstances, it is important to engage both the heart and the mind (C. Heath and D. Heath 2007). The "heart" serves to motivate change. It is essential to provide a narrative that emotionally resonates with the listener and points to *why* change is essential and worthwhile. It is vital for individuals to *feel motivated,* and it is helpful for them to feel they are part of a *collective identity.* To engage the mind, several strategies are effective. These include furnishing what the researchers term "bright spots" that have been effective and can be replicated to provide hope and plans to implement change. Further, they recommend, breaking down the steps toward achieving change into small, concrete units makes the process logical and attainable. Lastly, explaining the whys behind the specific strategies also engages the mind in the process.

It is important to note that all humans have both intuitive and rational minds. Some tend to be swayed more consistently by one approach over another, while others are engaged by the use of different strategies at different times. An effective strategy to change attitudes on a widespread basis therefore should both engage facts and appeal to emotions in order to have the broadest possible reach.

The Empathy Gap

A potential way to break the pattern of stereotyping and prejudice is to minimize the distance across perceived differences. A way to do so is by bridging the so-called "empathy gap" between "others" perceived to be substantively more different than they really are. J. D. Trout, who has written extensively about bridging the empathy gap, defines *empathy* as the capacity to understand the position of others accurately and to "feel this [experience] could happen to me" (2010, 21).

Daniel Goleman (2007) has described three variations of empathy. The first, the *cognitive* form, is the ability to understand another's point of view. This perspective-taking capacity is important for understanding but can be disconnected from an emotional or sympathetic link to the other (as in the case of sociopaths). The *emotional* form of empathy is a kinesthetic attunement to another's emotional world or pain (Goleman 2007). This form of empathy, which is sometimes dubbed the "Dali Llama neurons" (Ramachandran 2000), is inborn in most children across cultures but can be subject to sensory overload or burnout. Lastly, *compassionate empathy* or *empathic concern* is the behavioral form linked to mobilization to *do something* constructive to help (Goleman 2007).

Lamentably, there are a number of obstacles that impede tendencies to feel empathy toward others who differ from us. One cultural obstacle that Trout (2010) describes is the Protestant cultural myth of "free will" and its corollaries: (a) we get what we deserve, and (b) we have the power to overcome all circumstances. In the United States, wealth and poverty are explained by a cultural narrative of rugged individualistic character rather than by one of luck (as it is more likely to be in Europe). Those who are in positions of greater power and privilege typically are less attuned to social pain than those of lower status (Handgraaf et al. 2008). Further, social empathy is state dependent, such that persons tend to be less empathic when they are psychologically aroused to anger (Loewenstein 2000). People are also less readily able to empathize with groups that are significantly different than themselves, whom they have placed in the "them" category (Smith and Mackie 2005; Trout 2010). They are, in addition, more able to empathize with individuals—even if they are members of a disparaged group—than they are with groups (Smith and Mackie 2005).

Psychologically, it is critical that individuals be able to identify with the pain of the suffering of the "other" (Nordgren, Banas, and MacDonald 2011). Typically, people underestimate social pain like ostracism and shame experienced by others. In order for people accurately to assess interpersonal and intrapersonal social pain, they need to have experienced some sort of social discomfort themselves. The actual event of recalling having undergone a previous experience of social pain can act as an empathetic bridge for understanding the experiences of others.

Counternarrative Strategies Aimed at Anti-Immigrant Sentiment

The FrameWorks Institute, an organization specialized in ways to talk about and message complicated social issues, recently did a study of patterns of public thinking about immigrants in the United States (O'Neill, Kendall-Taylor, and Bales 2014). They found that there was a general public unawareness about specificities around the topic of immigration and that immigrants were typically framed as "them" and rarely recognized as part of our shared legacy as a nation of immigrants. Furthermore, the complexity of immigration policy and the politics of gridlock have led to a sense of helplessness and fatalism about resolving these issues.

The institute's recommendation was to boil the message about immigration down to three basic messages. First, focus on humanizing immigrants by reminding people that we are a nation of immigrants. Second, provide counterfactuals about the "economic costs" of immigration, highlighting the significant shared benefits immigrants generate for our country. Lastly, make a moral argument about a broken immigration system that needs to be fixed in order to treat people fairly. Thus, the FrameWorks Institute template for changing the narrative about immigrants incorporates many of the strategies for changing minds discussed previously. Its message is sticky in that it is clear, tangible, and oriented to solutions, and it draws upon appeals to national self-interest. As such, it has potential for a broad reach by both engaging facts and appealing to people's moral intuition and basic sense of fairness.

Arguably, although these strategies may serve to change some of the "persuadable" political minds, in an increasingly divided world in which sectors of the public view their own media and listen to their own sets of "facts," we may need to become more creative in reaching the persuadables. One tool might be active conversations in which we engage in listening tours to hear the other point of view and change minds one at a time by providing real "moving stories" of counternarratives. Placing the focus on children and youth may be an important strategy not only because they can be more relatable and empathy evoking but also because their futures are so inarguably linked to the future of the national well-being. The thoughtful and strategic employment of digital storytelling, blogs, photography, music videos, art, and other media may be particularly effective in opening the hearts and minds of the public.

ECOLOGIES OF CARE

Integration can be defined as "the inclusion of new populations into existing social structures of the immigration country. . . . It concerns primarily the immigrants and their descendants, but is an interactive, mutual process that changes the settlement society as well" (Heckmann and Schnapper 2003, 3). The four key dimensions of integration include (1) structural (access to the labor market and core institutions like schools); (2) cultural (taking on the behaviors, attitudes, and language); (3) social (actively engaging in social relationships); and (4) identification (the feeling of belonging and taking on the new identity) (Heckmann and Schnapper 2003). There is ample evidence that over time, and across generations, new groups typically assimilate, taking on the cultural traits of the host society (Alba and Nee 1997). There is concern, however, that when integration efforts fail and immigrant groups are excluded, there are costs both to the immigrants themselves and to the host society (Alba 2005; Portés and Zhou 1993). Nevertheless, there are many ways in which national, state, and local-level programs as well as community-based initiatives can help facilitate immigrants' adaptation by providing ecologies of care (C. Suárez-Orozco, M. Suárez-Orozco, and Teranishi 2016).

Educational Efforts Oriented toward Parents

Immigrant and refugee parents bring with them a wide range of skills and talents, and their educational backgrounds and linguistic fluency vary as greatly as their geographic and ethnic origins do. Regardless of their personal, professional, or educational backgrounds, many stand to benefit from access to educational opportunities. The concept of *adult education* may be broadly defined and can include instruction aimed at facilitating new language development, courses to strengthen or develop literacy skills in new and/or native languages, and vocational training to help people learn new marketable job skills and competencies or transfer existing skills to different occupational spheres. Providing these kinds of services not only helps the parents but, in turn, also has implications for their children's current and future well-being and is a fundamental part of successful integration programs. Instruction in (1) language competence, (2) literacy, and (3) professional skills is critical to achieving integration. Adult education should be built into all integration efforts since without these opportunities, immigrants may be at risk of exclusion from key sectors of a society and its economy.

Educational Efforts Oriented toward Children and Youth

The successful integration of the children of immigrants into the educational systems of their receiving countries is one of the most important and fundamental challenges of our time. Understanding the specific needs that different immigrant populations face vis-à-vis the educational system is critical in order to determine appropriate interventions. Given the diversity of the immigrant and refugee student populations entering schools in many different countries, it is clear that a one-size-fits-all model will not work. However, a number of key factors have emerged in the cross-national research as demonstrating positive implications for the schooling performance and educational integration of immigrant students (C. Suárez-Orozco et al. 2013). These practices include (1) (short-term) newcomer programs; (2) specialized services for Students with Interrupted Formal Education; (3) (sustained) services focused on new language development; (4) services focused on heritage language development; (5) providing explicit college pathway knowledge; (6) summer academic enrichment programs; (7) facilitating parental involvement (including translation and interpretation services); and (8) advisory groups, after-school academic supports, mentoring and health services, and post-secondary supports.

After-School Activities for Youth

School-based efforts to support immigrant and refugee children and adolescents' adaptation, language acquisition, and overall academic progress are critical to ensuring their successful integration and educational achievement. Students spend only part of their time in school, however, so school-based programs and activities must be complemented and bolstered by additional initiatives to provide immigrant-origin children with academic (Pittman et al. 2004), social, and emotional support (Rhodes 2004) outside of school hours. Given the diverse range of immigrant children's needs and interests, a variety of government agencies and nongovernmental and community organizations may be called upon to provide after-school activities for youth. School–community collaborations in the development of after-school programs represent one way to ensure continuity of instruction and support. Locally sponsored athletic activities, cultural groups, and religious groups constitute another potential avenue. In fact, the realm of possibilities for engaging youth in after-school activities is endless. Recommended areas of intervention include (1) youth academic supports, (2) extracurricular activities, (3) risk behavior prevention, (4) college readiness programs, and (5) youth mentoring.

Improving Perceptions of Immigrants

The immigration process can be a demanding and risky venture, and it often requires considerable energy, commitment, struggle, and sacrifice of those who seek to start a new life in foreign lands. While immigrants and their families shoulder much of the burden of integrating into new societies, the longer-term members of those societies are also implicated in this process. Without their deliberate and thoughtful engagement, which may consist of adapting their own behaviors and expectations and examining their stereotypes about new arrivals, successful integration is not possible. Support for integration cannot be based only upon providing services directly to immigrants learning about how to live in a new society; also needed are programs and activities to support native citizens as they learn about and accept their new neighbors, classmates, colleagues, fellow worshipers, and customers. Disparate countries of immigration have begun experimenting with a wide range of approaches to engage new members in the complex process of immigrant integration; although there is still much to be done, there is also considerable promise in this area. At the same time, however, more needs to be done publicly by all stakeholders—policy makers, opinion leaders, public intellectuals, and the media—to recognize the critical role of the host society in the integration process and the need to support and scale up proven initiatives. As such, facilitating host member understanding and good will remains one of the most underresourced aspects of immigrant integration strategies. Areas of promising intervention include 1) educating local service providers, 2) combating negative stereotypes, and 3) facilitating contact between native residents and newcomers.

Immigrant- and refugee-origin children face considerable challenges as they navigate their new lands, particularly during the transition period. At the same time, it is important to acknowledge, appreciate, and build upon newcomers' resilience, optimism, and energetic work ethic. Concurrently, we must endeavor to lessen and reverse the powerful undertow of xenophobic disparagement threatening to drown the children of immigrants and refugees in nihilism and anomic withdrawal from the new society. Unless we do so, we risk young people's joining gangs, getting involved in crime and long-distance nationalism, or simply sinking into despair. Providing the kinds of ecologies of care outlined in this chapter will go a long way toward helping these children meet their potential and become the kinds of contributing members to their new societies that will serve our future well.

NOTES

1. Defined as "fear or hatred of strangers or foreigners" in *Merriam-Webster's Collegiate Dictionary* (11th ed.).

2. Deferred Action for Childhood Arrivals (DACA) is the policy started by the Obama administration in June 2012. It allows certain undocumented immigrants to the United States—those who entered the country as minors and who fit other eligibility criteria—to receive a renewable two-year period of deferred action from deportation and be eligible for a work permit. However, under the new US administration, DACA youth are at risk of losing their status.

REFERENCES

Alba, Richard. 2005. "Bright vs. Blurred Boundaries: Second-Generation Assimilation and Exclusion in France, Germany, and the United States." *Ethnic and Racial Studies* 28 (1): 20–49.

Alba, Richard, and Victor Nee. 1997. "Rethinking Assimilation Theory for a New Era of Immigration." *International Migration Review* 31 (4): 826–74.

APA (American Psychological Association). 2012. *Dual Pathways to a Better America: Preventing Discrimination and Promoting Diversity.* Washington, DC: APA. www.apa.org /pubs/info/reports/promoting-diversity.aspx.

Bashi, Vilna. 1998. "Racial Categories Matter Because Racial Hierarchies Matter: A Commentary." *Ethnic and Racial Studies* 21 (5): 959–68.

Boas, Franz. 1940. *Race, Language and Culture.* London: Collier-Macmillan.

Bonilla-Silva, Eduardo. 2004. "From Bi-racial to Tri-racial: Towards a New System of Racial Stratification in the USA." *Ethnic and Racial Studies* 27 (6): 931–50.

Bronfenbrenner, Urie, and Pamela Morris. 2006. "The Bioecological Model of Human Development." In *Handbook of Child Psychology,* edited by Richard Lerner and William Damon, 793–828. New York: Wiley.

Carlson, Bonnie E., Joanne Cacciatore, and Barbara Klimek. 2012. "A Risk and Resilience Perspective on Unaccompanied Refugee Minors." *Social Work* 57: 259–69.

Carter, April, Marie Lawrence, and Ann Morse. 2011. *2011 Immigration-Related Laws, Bills, and Resolutions in the States: January 1–March 31, 2011.* Washington, DC: National Conference of State Legislatures. www.ncsl.org/research/immigration/immigration-laws-and-bills-spring-2011.aspx.

Chavez, Leo. 2008. *The Latino Threat: Constructing Immigrants, Citizens, and the Nation.* Palo Alto, CA: Stanford University Press.

Cialdini, Robert B. 1984. *The Psychology of Persuasion.* New York: William Morrow/Quill.

Dryden-Peterson, Sarah. 2016. "Refugee Education: The Crossroads of Globalization." *Educational Researcher* 45 (9): 473–82.

Ehntholt, Kimberly A., and William Yule. 2006. "Practitioner Review: Assessment and Treatment of Refugee Children and Adolescents Who Have Experienced War-Related Trauma." *Journal of Child Psychology and Psychiatry* 47 (12): 1197–1210.

Espenshade, Thomas, and Katherine Hempstead. 1996. "Contemporary American Attitudes toward US Immigration." *International Migration Review* 30 (2): 535–70.

Fuligni, Andrew. 2001. "A Comparative Longitudinal Approach among Children of Immigrant Families." *Harvard Educational Review* 71 (3): 566–78.

García Coll, Cynthia, Keith Crnic, Gontran Lamberty, Barbara Hanna Wasik, Renee Jenkins, Heidie Vazquez Garcia, and Harriet Pipes McAdoo. 1996. "An Integrative Model for the Study of Developmental Competencies in Minority Children." *Child Development* 67 (5): 1891–1914.

García Coll, Cynthia, and Katherine Magnuson. 1997. "The Psychological Experience of Immigration: A Developmental Perspective." In *Immigration and the Family,* edited by Alan Booth, Ann C. Crouter, and Nancy Landale, 91–132. Mahwah, NJ: Lawrence Erlbaum.

García Coll, Cynthia, and Amy K. Marks. 2009. *Immigrant Stories: Ethnicity and Academics in Middle Childhood.* New York: Oxford University Press.

———, eds. 2011. *The Immigrant Paradox in Children and Adolescents: Is Becoming American a Developmental Risk?* Washington, DC: American Psychological Association Press.

Gibson, Margaret. 1988. *Assimilation without Accommodation: Sikh Immigrants in an American High School.* Ithaca, NY: Cornell University Press.

Gilman, Sander L. 2000. "Are Jews White? Or the History of the Nose Job." In *Theories of Racism,* edited by Les Back and John Solomos, 229–37. London: Routledge.

Goleman, Daniel. 2007. *Three Kinds of Empathy: Cognitive, Emotional, Compassionate.* www.danielgoleman.info/three-kinds-of-empathy-cognitive-emotional-compassionate/.

Handgraaf, Michel J. J., Eric Van Dijk, Riël C. Vermunt, Henk A. M. Wilke, and Carston K. W. De Dreu. 2008. "Less Power or Powerless? Egocentric Empathy Gaps and the Irony of Having Little versus No Power in Social Decision Making." *Journal of Personality and Social Psychology* 95 (5): 1136–49.

Hanson, Gordon. H. 2010. *The Economics and Policy of Illegal Immigration in the United States*. Washington, DC: Migration Policy Institute.

Heath, Chip, and Dan Heath. 2007. *Made to Stick: Why Some Ideas Survive and Others Die*. New York: Random House.

―――. 2010. *Switch: How to Change When Change Is Hard*. New York: Broadway Books.

Heckmann, Friedrich, and Dominique Schnapper. 2003. "Introduction." In *The Integration of Immigrants in European Societies: National Differences and Trends of Convergence*, edited by Friedrich Heckmann and Dominique Schnapper, 9–14. Stuttgart, Germany: Lucius and Lucius.

Howell, William G., Paul E. Peterson, and Martin R. West. 2009. "The Persuadable Public." *Education Next* 9 (4). http://educationnext.org/persuadable-public/.

Kahneman, Daniel. 2011. *Thinking, Fast and Slow*. New York: Macmillan.

Kanstroom, Daniel. 2007. *Deportation Nation: Outsiders in American History*. Cambridge, MA: Harvard University Press.

Kao, Grace, and Marta Tienda. 1995. "Optimism and Achievement: The Educational Performance of Immigrant Youth." *Social Science Quarterly* 76 (1): 1–19.

Katwala, Sunder, Steve Ballinger, and Matthew Rhodes. 2014. *How to Talk about Immigration*. London: British Future. www.britishfuture.org/wp-content/uploads/2014/11/How-To-Talk-About-Immigration-FINAL.pdf.

Kia-Keating, Miriam, Erin Dowdy, Melissa L. Morgan, and Gil G. Noam. 2011. "Protecting and Promoting: An Integrative Conceptual Model for Healthy Development of Adolescents." *Journal of Adolescent Health* 48 (3): 220–28.

Leadership Conference on Civil Rights Education Fund. 2009. *Confronting the New Faces of Hate: Hate Crimes in America—2009*. Washington, DC: Leadership Conference on Civil Rights Education Fund. www.protectcivilrights.org/pdf/reports/hatecrimes/lccref_hate_crimes_report.pdf.

Li, Guofang. 2004. "Family Literacy: Learning from an Asian Immigrant Family." In *Multicultural and Multilingual Literacy and Language: Contexts and Practices*, edited by Fenice B. Boyd, Cynthia H. Brock, and Mary Rozendal, 304–21. New York: Guilford Press.

Link, Bruce G., and Jo C. Phelan. 2001. "Conceptualizing Stigma." *Annual Review of Sociology* 27: 363–85.

Loewenstein, George. 2000. "Emotions in Economic Theory and Economic Behavior." *American Economic Review* 90 (2): 426–32.

Marks, Amy K., Lourah Seaboyer, and Cynthia García Coll. 2015. "The Academic Achievement of US Immigrant Children and Adolescents." In *Transitions: The Development of Children of Immigrants*, edited by Carola Suárez-Orozco, Mona Abo-Zena, and Amy K. Marks, 259–75. New York: NYU Press.

Massey, Douglas S. 2010. *New Faces in New Places*. New York: Russell Sage.

Menjívar, Cecilia. 2006. "Liminal Legality: Salvadoran and Guatemalan Immigrants' Lives in the United States." *American Journal of Sociology* 111: 999–1037.

Mollica, Richard F., Charles Poole, Linda Son, Caroline C. Murray, and Svang Tor. 1997. "Effects of War Trauma on Cambodian Refugee Adolescents' Functional Health and Mental Health Status." *Journal of the American Academy of Child and Adolescent Psychiatry* 36 (8): 1098–1106.

Motomura, Hiroshi. 2008. "Immigration outside the Law." *Columbia Law Review* 108 (8): 2037–2097.

Noh, Samuel, Morton Beiser, Violet Kaspar, Feng Zhou, and Joanna Rummens. 1999. "Perceived Racial Discrimination, Depression, and Coping: A Study of Southeast Asian Refugees in Canada." *Journal of Health and Social Behavior* 40 (3): 193–207.

Nordgren, Loran F., Kasia Banas, and Geoff MacDonald. 2011. "Empathy Gaps for Social Pain: Why People Underestimate the Pain of Social Suffering." *Journal of Personality and Social Psychology* 100 (1): 120–28.

Omi, Michael, and Howard Winant. 1994. *Racial Formation in the United States.* New York: Routledge.

O'Neil, Moira, Nathaniel Kendall-Taylor, and Susan N. Bales. 2014. *Finish the Story on Immigration: A FrameWorks Message Memo.* Washington, DC: FrameWorks Institute. www.frameworksinstitute.org/assets/files/domestic_issues/Immigration_mm.pdf.

Perreira, Krista M., Kathleen M. Harris, and Dohoon Lee. 2006. "Making It in America: High School Completion by Immigrant and Native Youth." *Demography* 43: 511–36.

Pew Hispanic Center. 2015. *Modern Immigration Wave Brings 59 Million to US, Driving Population Growth and Change through 2065: Views of Immigration's Impact on US Society Mixed.* www.pewhispanic.org/2015/09/28/modern-immigration-wave-brings-59-million-to-u-s-driving-population-growth-and-change-through-2065/.

Pittman, Karen J., Merita Irby, Nicole Yohalem, and Alicia Wilson-Ahlstrom. 2004. "Blurring the Lines for Learning: The Role of Out-of-School Programs as Complements to Formal Learning." In *After-School Worlds: Creating Social Space for Development and Learning,* edited by Gil G. Noam, 19–41. Vol. 101 of New Directions for Youth Development: Theory and Practice. Hoboken, NJ: Jossey-Bass.

Portés, Alejandro, and Ruben G. Rumbaut. 2006. *Immigrant America: A Portrait.* Berkeley: University of California Press.

Portés, Alejandro, and Minh Zhou. 1993. "The New Second Generation: Segmented Assimilation and Its Variants." *Annals of the American Academy of Political and Social Science* 530 (1): 74–96.

Preston, Julia. 2011. "Immigrants Are Focus of Harsh Bill in Alabama." *New York Times,* June 4, 2011, A10.

Putnam, Robert D. 2015. *Our Kids: The American Dream in Crisis.* New York: Simon and Schuster.

Ramachandran, Vilayanur S. 2000. "Mirror Neurons and Imitation Learning as the Driving Force behind the Great Leap Forward in Human Evolution." *Edge.* www.edge.org/conversation/mirror-neurons-and-imitation-learning-as-the-driving-force-behind-the-great-leap-forward-in-human-evolution.

Rhodes, Jean. 2004. "The Critical Ingredient: Caring Youth–Staff Relationships in After-School Settings." In *After-School Worlds: Creating Social Space for Development and Learning,* edited by Gil G. Noam, 145–161. Vol. 101 of New Directions for Youth Development: Theory and Practice. Hoboken, NJ: Jossey-Bass.

Rumbaut, Ruben G. 2004. "Ages, Life Stages, and Generational Cohorts: Decomposing the Immigrant First and Second Generations in the United States." *International Migration Review* 38 (3): 1160–1205.

Shear, Michael D., and Helene Cooper. 2017. "Trump Bars Refugees and Citizens from Seven Muslim Countries." *New York Times,* January 27, 2017. www.nytimes.com/2017/01/27 /us/politics/trump-syrian-refugees.html.

Sirin, Selcuk R., and Michelle Fine. 2008. *Muslim American Youth: Understanding Hyphenated Identities through Multiple Methods.* New York: NYU Press.

Smith, Eliot R., and Diane M. Mackie. 2005. "Aggression, Hatred, and Other Emotions." In *On the Nature of Prejudice: Fifty Years after Allport,* edited by John F. Dovidio, Peter Glick, and Laurie A. Rudman, 361–76. New York: Blackwell.

Suárez-Orozco, Carola, Mona M. Abo-Zena, and Amy K. Marks, eds. 2015. *Transitions: The Development of Children of Immigrants.* New York: NYU Press.

Suárez-Orozco, Carola, Margary Martin, Mikael Alexandersson, L. Janelle Dance, and Johannes Lunneblad. 2013. "Promising Practices: Preparing Children of Immigrants in New York and Sweden." In *The Children of Immigrants in School: A Comparative Look at Integration in the United States and Western Europe,* edited by Richard D. Alba and Jennifer Holdaway, 204–51. New York: Social Science Research Council and New York University Press, 2016.

Suárez-Orozco, Carola, and Marcelo M. Suárez-Orozco. 1995. *Transformations: Immigration, Family Life, and Achievement Motivation among Latino Adolescents.* Cambridge, MA: Harvard University Press.

———. 2001. *Children of Immigration.* Cambridge, MA: Harvard University Press.

Suárez-Orozco, Carola, Marcelo M. Suárez-Orozco, and Robert Teranishi. 2016. *Pathways to Opportunities: Promising Practices for Immigrant Families, Children, and Youth: A Report for the Ford Foundation.* Los Angeles: Institute for Immigration, Globalization, and Education, UCLA. http://ige.gseis.ucla.edu/PromisingPracticesWhitePaper4.25 .16/.

Suárez-Orozco, Carola, Marcelo M. Suárez-Orozco, and Irina Todorova. 2008. *Learning a New Land: Immigrant Students in American Society.* Cambridge, MA: Harvard University Press.

Suárez-Orozco, Marcelo M., and Carola Suárez-Orozco. 2013. "Taking Perspective: Context, Culture, and History." In *Frameworks and Ethics for Research with Immigrants,* edited by María G. Hernández, Jacqueline Nguyen, Carrie L. Saetermoe, and Carola Suárez-Orozco, 9–23. Vol. 141 of New Directions for Child and Adolescent Development. San Francisco: Jossey-Bass.

Suárez-Orozco, Marcelo M., Carola Suárez-Orozco, and Carolyn Sattin-Bajaj. 2010. "Making Migration Work." *Peabody Journal of Education* 85: 535–51.

Suro, Roberto. 2009. "America's View of Immigration: The Evidence from Public Opinion Surveys." *In Migration, Public Opinion, and Politics: The Transatlantic Council on Migration.* Washington, DC: Migration Policy Institute. www.migrationpolicy.org/research /americas-views-immigration-evidence-public-opinion-surveys.

Thabet, Abdel A.M., Yehia Abed, and Panos Vostanis. 2004. "Comorbidity of PTSD and Depression among Refugee Children during War Conflict." *Journal of Child Psychology and Psychiatry* 45 (3): 533–42.

Trout, John D. 2010. *Why Empathy Matters: The Science and Psychology of Better Judgment.* New York: Penguin.

UNHCR (United Nations High Commissioner for Refugees). 2016. *Global Trends: Forced Displacements in 2015*. Geneva: UNHCR.

Yoshikawa, Hirokazu, Carola Suárez-Orozco, and Roberto G. Gonzalez. 2016. "Unauthorized Status and Youth Development in the United States: Consensus Statement for the Society on Research on Adolescence." *Journal of Research on Adolescence* 27 (1): 4–19. doi:10.1111/jora.1.

PART THREE

CATASTROPHIC MIGRANT LIVES
AT THE MARGINS

5

THE NEW H⁵ MODEL

Trauma and Recovery

Richard F. Mollica

The Workshop on Humanitarianism and Mass Migration at UCLA sponsored by the Pontifical Academies (January 2017) provided a unique opportunity to offer a constructive critique of humanitarian assistance to refugees worldwide. The world is in a historical period as hundreds of millions of citizens worldwide are fleeing their homes. There are now more than sixty-five million refugees worldwide. It is estimated that in five years the world will be facing the care of more than two hundred million refugees. In addition to refugees, hundreds of millions of people live in shantytowns and are urban squatters due to climate change.

The model of guaranteeing safety and security to refugees used by the United Nations and nongovernmental organizations (NGOs) is outdated. It is obvious to all humanitarian relief players that the prevailing humanitarian assistance model is badly broken and insufficient. The currently understood concepts of safety, security, and providing for essential human needs, although extremely necessary, are inadequate. This inadequacy is in part due to the "siloing" of safety/security, humanitarian assistance, health care, mental health care, and economic and cultural development: major barriers exist across each of these critical humanitarian domains. Linkage to mental health and systems of health and mental health care is almost nonexistent.

The safety and protection silo receives the largest amount of attention and money. Ensuring the safety and security of people fleeing dangerous and life-threatening situations, of course, is a major priority. This primary dimension of care easily blends into humanitarian assistance, with concerns for adequate food, water, shelter, and sanitation. The health-care silo has merged with the other two silos, with its focus on the prevention of infectious disease and the medical care of the seriously ill. Concern for the mental health problems of traumatized people, including vulnerable groups such as victims of gender-based violence, the elderly, and children, while highly fashionable, is still rather remote and neglected in policy planning. The focus on the economic and cultural development of refugees is almost nonexistent. Unfortunately, the five silos are rarely integrated, with little planning made for the integration of direct health and mental health services into the mix. A developmental analysis of human development from infancy to adulthood in program planning is limited and lacks an important sensitivity to the core of human beings at different stages of their lives. Humanitarian aid and safety and protection planning for young children may be entirely different from planning for women of child-bearing age, unemployed teenagers, or the elderly. Unfortunately, one size does not fit all traumatized people. For well-known political reasons (that is, the belief that refugees should not have better health care than the local population does), vocational and educational activities are extremely inadequate.

The new H[5] Model is a "bottom-up" model. It does not replace the Harvard Program in Refugee Trauma (HPRT) and World Health Organization (WHO) Global Mental Health Action Plans. This new model begins with the basic assumptions that the principal realities of highly traumatized people are known and that this humanistic knowledge can inform policy planning for traumatized people. In this way, each of the silos can be broken down, and an integration can be made across silos. The refugee camp and/or other environments can be seen, not as internment camps, but as restorative environments. Human beings who have been severely damaged at the sociocultural and physical-emotional levels need environments that can restore their health and wellness.

Restoration of wellness as a concept and policy goal of humanitarian aid can drive the integration of all five silo areas. In addition, the 1948 WHO definition of *health,* "a state of complete physical, mental, and social well-being and not merely the absence of disease of infirmity" (WHO 2006, 1), can be expanded to include a more holistic definition that focuses on an integration of the "body-mind-spirit." The power of this new definition is revealed in the following definition of health: "Health is a personal and social state of balance and well-being in which people feel strong, active, wise, and worthwhile; where their diverse capacities and rhythms are valued; where they may decide and choose, express themselves, and move about freely" (Mollica 2006, 193).

This new concern for a renewal of the healthy body-mind-spirit in traumatized people and communities can help transform as well as integrate the five silos that are now disconnected. The new H[5] Model is based upon cultural and scientific research over the past four decades that has clearly elucidated the major humanistic issues for highly traumatized people throughout the world. The H[5] Model has to be customized for children and adolescents (an effort now in progress), and it needs to be adapted to special cultural and sociopolitical contexts. The new H[5]

Model that follows is an approach that can be adapted, revised, and implemented in many different cultural and sociopolitical settings. It is a bottom-up model that provides highly traumatized refugee families and communities with an active process of restoration and recovery. The plan offers a new approach for reinvigorating the old safety and security model of refugee care.

THE NEW H⁵ MODEL

Recognizing the urgent need to address the humanitarian care of those affected by human violence and aggression, the H⁵ Model focuses specifically on the millions of refugees living in camps worldwide, but it is our hope that it can also be used to serve civilian and mainstream populations suffering from trauma. The H⁵ Model addresses the mental and physical health issues related to trauma suffered by refugees; the relationship between those mental and physical health problems that are prevalent among refugee populations; the potential for trauma to persist in refugee camps; and the need for a new, more comprehensive model of refugee care. This new plan explores five overlapping dimensions essential to trauma recovery by highlighting findings from studies of refugee populations. It presents recommendations for implementing culture- and evidence-based policies and actions for traumatized refugee populations around the world. The H⁵ Model has received widespread acclaim since it is one of the first systems to address from a theoretical perspective the major sources of risk and vulnerability affecting highly traumatized people and communities. Because of its comprehensive and holistic approach to recovery, it is receiving attention from mainstream media and from mental health practitioners engaged in creating a culture of trauma-informed care policies and psychosocial and cultural programs (for the complete model, see Mollica et al. 2005).

A summary of the five overlapping dimensions and the core of the model, the trauma story, follow. This new model for the recovery of traumatized refugee communities worldwide is based upon five dimensions essential to recovery. These are anchored in the centrality of the trauma story. All dimensions of the H⁵ Model are culturally sound and evidence-based (see fig. 5.1).

The Trauma Story

Trauma stories are accounts of distressing and painful personal and social events told by survivor patients. Sharing these stories serves a dual function—not only of healing the survivor but also of teaching and guiding the listener and, by extension, society, in healing and survival. The trauma story has four elements. The primary one is the *factual accounting of events,* or telling what actually happened to the storyteller, that is, presenting the brutal facts. These are usually graphic and detailed presentations of the individual's traumatic life experiences. When such facts are collected from even a few people, they can provide historical documentation of the

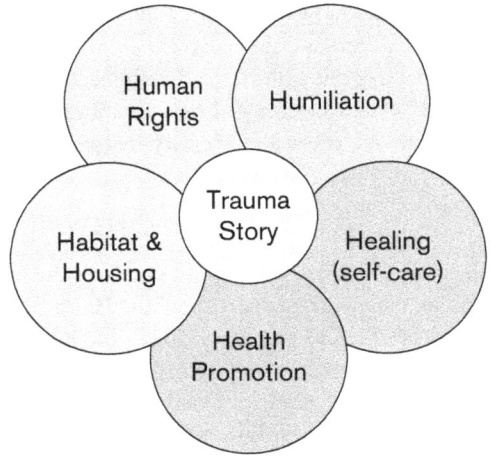

FIGURE 5.1. The five overlapping
dimensions and core elements
of the H⁵ Model.

concrete behavior of perpetrators of crimes against humanity, revealing the intentional, well-orchestrated methods of perpetrators.

In addition to recounting the facts, each trauma story reveals the survivor's
sociocultural history in miniature, depicting the traditions, customs, and values in
which the person's story is embedded. The storyteller cannot avoid revealing the
cultural meaning of trauma. Although men and women in every society perceive
violence as deeply injurious and socially degrading, responses differ by culture.

The trauma story also provides a view into the survivor's spiritual life: his or her
capacity to achieve an *enlightened view of the world* divorced from ugly and distressing emotions. Often the survivor reaches deep insights when reflecting upon
her situation—for example, coming to reject social beliefs or attitudes that say the
person is "bad" for having been involved in a tragic event. These revelations can
prove very liberating. Trauma stories provide unique insights into the narrator's
cultural framework. In every tragic event, there is an opportunity to uncover deep
meaning and gain insights. Some call this "posttraumatic" growth.

The fourth and final element of the trauma story is the *listener–storyteller relationship.* Storytellers are vulnerable to physical and emotional pain when they
retell their stories; therefore, a listener's patience and sensitivity are crucial. The
trauma story does not, in fact, completely exist unless it is told to someone else; the
listener must choose to become part of the story. Under ideal conditions, the storyteller is the teacher, and the listener is the student. The obligation of the listener
is to apply the lessons of survival and healing to his personal and professional life.
By understanding that they are part of a historical process, all who are involved in
the sharing of trauma histories become personally stronger and more resilient.

Repeating the story makes the storyteller feel more comfortable. In effect, having a listener is part of the therapeutic process. In turn, the listener becomes more knowledgeable, not just about the pain of the trauma survivor but also about what the storyteller has accomplished. In particular, the trauma story, in each of its four elements and as a whole, offers an incredible amount of new information on survival and healing, of allowing the survivor to have the motivation and strength to fight for recovery once her tragedy has been shared with another. Survivors must be allowed to tell their stories in their own way, just as listeners must remain enthusiastic and sensitive so that the trauma story can flow without any outside influence. The trauma story can also be told in groups with other people who have faced similar events.

Carefully attending to the four elements of the trauma story lets the storyteller share his deeply private life experiences so that we all might heal from and survive human tragedies. Focusing on these elements provides all people a way to tell and interpret their own stories, not only those of others. Appreciation of the trauma story's scope and depth allows it to play a significant personal and social role in the survivor's recovery from violence's humiliating and disturbing effects.

H1: Human Rights

Human rights violations are embedded in the definition of *refugee*. Providing safety and security is a foundation of refugee care. All human beings faced with the experience of violence want to tell their trauma story to someone else whom they trust. At some point in their refugee camp experience, individuals must have an opportunity to officially tell camp authorities about their violent history and reveal all of the human rights violations, past and present, that they have experienced. While it is not expected that the refugee in an acute crisis will be or should be able to do so, ultimately, as safety and security are established, the individual's traumatic life story must be recorded and acknowledged. Some sense of justice and related human rights violations must be discussed with the refugee and the listener's community.

All violence violates a person's human rights. Usually we reserve the term *human rights violations* to describe actions of extreme violence perpetrated in international and foreign settings. But concern for human rights is equally valid in the American setting. Violence can affect all citizens, whether they are children being sexually abused by a parent or an elderly man being exploited physically and emotionally in a nursing home. Talking about violence in the language of human rights, an important aspect of healing, is often overlooked in therapy. The denial of proper and culturally effective physical and mental health care causes tremendous human suffering and can even lead to death. Stigma attached to the mentally ill and social prejudice and abuse directed at people who differ from those in the mainstream indicate a lack of respect for the human dignity of all living beings. All violated people expect and want justice. The refugee community cannot wait years (a common occurrence) to have their desire for justice addressed by the international community.

H2: Humiliation

Humiliation is closely associated with feelings of shame, embarrassment, disgrace, and depreciation that are common reactions to violent actions. These feelings are often hidden by other intense emotions. Perpetrators intentionally drive victims to a place where all the values and features of *normal* existence have been destroyed. The goal of violent acts, regardless of intensity, is the same—to create an emotional state of humiliation. Every characteristic of the abused person becomes bad or wrong; perpetrators try to introduce into the minds of their victims a sense of their fundamental worthlessness.

Perpetrators of violence use humiliating acts such as rape to create the state of humiliation. Humiliation is a very complex human emotion because it is primarily linked to how people believe the world is viewing them—the sense that others may view the survivor as worthless or deserving of pain. Humiliation leads to a total loss of self-respect and can have major impacts on a refugee's personal and social behavior, being associated with learned helplessness and leading to a lack of self-efficacy. Often, the state of humiliation is re-created in the camp environment when individuals are not allowed to work, grow food, or make money.

The healing and recovery process must consciously attempt to overcome distortions in the refugee's mind that produce feelings of helplessness and worthlessness. The healing response must make clear that violence is wrong, no matter the rationale for it. For healing to move forward, it is important to identify the refugee's feeling of humiliation and its associated emotions. Every traumatized person needs to find that solid ground of original sanity—unblemished by the lies told by aggressors—where her personal power still exists and upon which the healing process can grow.

H3: Healing (Self-Care)

Self-healing is one of the human organism's natural responses to psychological illness and injury. Like the body's response to physical damage, the healing of the emotional wounds inflicted on mind and spirit by severe violence is a natural process. After violence occurs, a self-healing process is immediately activated, transforming through physical and mental responses the damage that has occurred to the psychological and social self. For example, sharing a trauma story can lead to the reduction or elimination of emotional memories that have outlived their adaptive value. Telling the trauma story is only one self-healing pathway that has not traditionally been fully acknowledged. Dreams are now also slowly being appreciated as a major self-healing response in traumatized people.

Self-healing occurs at the psychological level when the mind is able to construct new meaning out of violence. At that point, behaviors are implemented that help the traumatized person cope with emotions of humiliation, anger, and despair. These behaviors can either restore the old life-world of the survivor or, more commonly, create a new one. At the core of the psychological dimension of self-healing is the will to survive and recover. The individual makes a decision to do whatever needs to be done, to not "cave in" to violent acts.

Self-healing involves a social as well as a psychological dimension. Positive social behaviors such as altruism, work, and spirituality enhance neurobiological processes that promote health and reduce the negative consequences of stress. These behaviors and others, such as the use of humor, social support, and physical exercise, help the individual recover psychologically. One of the first steps of a traumatized person's recovery, whether child or adult, is to break his social isolation by acknowledging that the forces of self-healing are at work and will ultimately lead to a good outcome, including the return to normal life. In this regard, helpers are essential because they can use their empathic skills to reinforce this therapeutic optimism in survivors.

H4: Health Promotion

There is emerging evidence that refugees, persons in post-conflict countries, and those impacted by conflict have increased levels of long-term chronic illness attributable to their traumatic experiences and high levels of distress. Research demonstrates that people who experience trauma are more likely to develop chronic illnesses such as ischemic heart disease and diabetes, to have severe social disabilities, and to die younger (Felitti et al. 1998). Trauma survivors have poorer emotional health, smoke more, use alcohol and drugs more, exercise less, and have poorer eating habits that result in obesity and the metabolic syndrome than other populations do. All are risk factors for the development of chronic disease. In other words, trauma generates chronic disease through direct effects and has indirect effects through mental illness (PTSD and depression) and impaired lifestyle. This connection between trauma and poor physical health demands a new emphasis on health promotion.

H5: Habitat

The word *habitat* is used instead of *housing* to connote the total surroundings and/or living environment occupied by refugees, which may not necessarily qualify as a home. The word *habitat* is derived from the Latin *habitare*, which in the ancient world meant the natural environment of a person or the place where an organism dwelled. There was a belief that a reciprocal and positive relationship existed between the physical and natural environment and those organisms which resided and prospered within that environment. The dilapidated tents in which more than half a million Haitians were still living more than three years after the January 12, 2010, earthquake were not just broken-down tents but also a social environment plagued by poverty, chaos, and gender-based violence. After a humanitarian emergency, traumatized people and communities need to enter a healing environment that can initiate the healing process. Unfortunately, the latter concept is still poorly understood by the international humanitarian aid community.

Habitat is a new area of refugee mental health research. Initial studies of refugees' living conditions point to a significant relationship among health problems, mental illness, crowding, lack of privacy, and chronic violence. The H^5 Model understands the overall quality of housing and its relationship to trauma recovery as an important and relevant issue and suggests that new design and building materials can make modern, healthy, and safe housing a cost-effective option.

THE H^5 MODEL APPLIED TO REFUGEE CARE

The following recommendations are based on the H^5 Model.

1. All past and ongoing human rights violations and social justice issues must be openly addressed with the refugee community, immediately documented, closely monitored, and brought to the attention of refugee camp authorities, who can respond to and remedy these violations to the degree to which they are able.

2. Refugee camp policies and programs should be designed to actively enhance self-healing, independence, and self-sufficiency. The humanitarian response must not further degrade refugees or tolerate any form of gender- or age-based violence. Similarly, UN staff and NGOs should never humiliate, degrade, or exploit the vulnerability of the refugees whom they serve. A UN Code of Respect by the United Nations High Commissioner for Refugees (UNHCR) must be written, enforced, and widely disseminated.

3. All refugees should receive an initial needs assessment to determine their self-healing status and then be supported in their recovery by psychosocial programs built on the strengths illuminated by the aforementioned assessment, with psychiatric services readily available for the seriously mentally ill.

4. International aid should implement a universal health promotion program for all refugees that includes diet, exercise, stress reduction, sleep promotion, and other techniques.

5. In order to ensure that the camp meets refugees' cultural and personal needs, refugees should participate in the design, construction, and management of their homes and new living environment. Housing should be safe and well constructed, and adequate lightning (for example, solar powered) should be made available to all women and children. The tents currently used should be replaced by structures built with ecologically sound and inexpensive materials; urban design needs to replace the haphazard, chaotic camp environment. (Mollica 2006, 193)

THE H⁵ MODEL APPLIED TO TRAUMA-INFORMED CARE

The H⁵ Model is extremely relevant and useful for mainstream health and mental health programs. It is consistent with the values and culture of the trauma-informed care (TIC) movement. TIC sets a clear priority that all levels of the health-care and social welfare systems introduce the values and practices of TIC for clients/patients, staff, and administrators. Although the H⁵ Model was initially developed for refugee populations, it certainly can be applied to those communities that have been traumatized by crime, poverty, and catastrophic situations such as 9/11, the Boston Marathon bombings, and Hurricanes Sandy and Katrina.

The H⁵ Model helps us better appreciate the underlying forces necessary for the recovery of those members of the general population who have survived or are coping with domestic violence, childhood sexual abuse, gender-based violence, and the stresses and strains of crime, poverty, family dysfunctionality, and social stigma.

The Trauma Story

The trauma story, again, is the centerpiece of the medical and emotional care of all patients who have experienced or are experiencing violence. The four dimensions of the trauma story described above remain a good approach to understanding the life experiences of traumatized patients living in our mainstream communities. The four elements detailed in the previous section are the brutal facts, the cultural meaning of trauma, revelation ("looking behind the curtain"), and the storyteller–listener relationship.

We must remember that all human beings experience tragedies in their lives. Because of this situation, there is an immediate solidarity between trauma survivor and therapist. Extensive research has revealed the therapeutic power of *deep listening;* that is, patients love being listened to and heard. There are many clinically effective approaches to listening to the trauma story, ranging from a simple acknowledgment of the patient's traumatic narrative to the use of diaries and the systematic reliving of the trauma events through exposure therapy. Due to the potential to trigger a patient's upsetting memories, proper administration of storytelling techniques is necessary; that is, they should only be used after trust has been established. Most patients' recovery is maximized by having an ongoing conversation with a therapist. The moral of the story is that deep listening heals.

Therapists using a holistic approach are familiar with considering the bio-psycho-social and spiritual domains of the patient's suffering. The H⁵ Model overlaps with the latter by offering a broader cultural, wellness-oriented, and sociological approach that integrates into one model all aspects of the trauma survivor's health problems and underlying resiliency. Each of the H⁵ elements is real and forms a platform for understanding the survivor's medical and psychiatric diagnoses such as PTSD and depression. The H⁵ elements encompass the survivor's personal narrative, which helps us to determine the illness and resiliency of each and every survivor within the general population. The H⁵ Model can be easily adapted to a trauma-informed care approach.

H1: Human Rights Violations

All acts of violence are human rights violations. TIC therapists should take a careful look at the United Nations Universal Declaration of Human Rights. This document, codified after World War II by the United Nations, is one of our world's greatest achievements. It is sad that few American doctors and/or their patients have read this work. Acts of domestic violence, for example, are human rights violations. A front-page article in the *Boston Globe* (August 10, 2014) highlighted the hundreds of ways in which people, mainly women and children, are abused. This is not to say that men and the elderly are not frequent victims of domestic violence. This important article, drawing on stories collected from the Boston Police files, reveals that whatever is at hand can become a weapon: "The ways to hurt are infinite when you live with an abuser. Everything is a weapon. In their hands innocent objects like ice-cube trays and checker boards and apples and pillows become ways to inflict suffering to demand submission."

Using culturally validated instruments such as the *Harvard Trauma Questionnaire* (HTQ) over the past three decades, we have been able to document the brutal facts associated with the refugee experience worldwide and with resettled refugees in the United States. Now we need to get this energy into the TIC approach for our local mainstream communities. Psychological experts on the Holocaust have called this "bearing witness." The horrible facts reported in the *Boston Globe* article, for example, need to be brought out in the doctor's office and made public as well. Unfortunately, extensive research reveals that they rarely emerge in our medical and psychological settings or are even acknowledged by medical professionals.

H2: Humiliation

Humiliation is the major instrument of violence used by perpetrators to create the state of experiencing humiliation in all violated persons. Unfortunately, that key emotional state is linked to self-destructive behaviors, self-deprecation, and learned helplessness. Humiliation is hidden behind the more prominent symptoms of somatic complaints, depression, and posttraumatic stress disorder. The state of humiliation needs to be identified and transformed—and can be transformed—as part of the recovery process. This phenomenon also explains why traumatized people are very sensitive to and emotionally distressed by the perceived empathic failure and insensitivity within the health and social service systems.

HPRT's clinical experience after three decades of caring for torture survivors and survivors of mass violence reveals the following.

First, "healing is a shared empathic partnership between two people working together in a community to create a new worldview." This aphorism acknowledges that the humiliated state of the survivor needs to be transformed and that this action can only be accomplished in a "shared" empathic partnership. The survivor and the therapist are *partners,* and each has empathy for the other. While the patient needs the empathic response of the healer, the healer also needs the empathic response of the survivor. Otherwise, how could either of them stand to hear about such unbearable pain and suffering? And although humiliation may have destroyed all that the survivor once believed was good, the survivor and therapist can create a new, and perhaps better, worldview and reality. In its clinic, HPRT has witnessed the latter result thousands of times. It is not a rare experience.

The second acknowledged truth is that "healing can only occur when the patient believes she can become whole again." Some survivors feel so damaged that they believe they can never recover. This phenomenon is called *self-efficacy* in the therapeutic academic literature. In our clinic, we always take this issue up immediately; otherwise, if a patient has no belief in his own self-efficacy, the therapy will fail.

H3: Healing (Self-Care)

The remarkable realization that all people affected by violence have a powerful physical, mental, and social self-healing response is critical to facilitating the patient's healing recovery. In essence, therapists have to recognize the existence of this self-healing response and build upon it. Patient survivors are not passive recipients of medication or talk therapy. They are doing a lot to help themselves over and beyond the brief and important time they spend with a health professional and/or therapist. In fact, in the HPRT clinic we tell all patients that they are our teachers, and we are their students. It is incredible to observe the joy that this statement brings to the most humiliated person when she learns that she is regarded as a *teacher* of the doctor.

The self-healing activities revealed to the therapist are sometimes unbelievable but always profound. Since we have learned through our scientific studies the important self-healing power of (1) work or school, (2) altruism, and (3) spirituality, we examine each of these areas in the survivor's life. If an area is lacking or underdeveloped, we try to find out why, correct and remove the barriers, and work out a prescription to encourage the self-healing activity. Many of our older Cambodian women, for example, have little time for themselves. They are given a prescription to take home to their families and advised to say something like, "The doctor has ordered me to go to the temple on weekends." Usually after seeing the doctor's note, the family agrees to the recommendation.

H4: Health Promotion

The famous Adverse Child Experiences (ACE) study (Felitti et al. 1998) has done more than any other study in America to demonstrate to mainstream US communities the impact of child abuse and past traumatic life experiences on the health and well-being of community members. Many other studies in Canada and the United States have demonstrated the terrible long-term impact of past and current violence on all organ systems but especially the effects of stress-related illnesses such as diabetes, hypertension, heart disease, and the metabolic syndrome. Not surprisingly, depression, posttraumatic stress disorder (PTSD), drug and alcohol abuse, and suicide are also associated with traumatic life events.

HPRT has spent more than a decade developing a culturally valid health promotion curriculum as well as a special diabetes group for Cambodian torture survivors (Berkson et al. 2014). All people who have experienced violence should be in a health promotion activity that includes diet, exercise, meditation, stress reduction, and practical lifestyle changes for dealing with insomnia and symptoms of PTSD such as flashbacks. The data from our refugee studies and from other mainstream population-based studies reveal that health promotion alone can have a dramatic impact on reducing depressive symptoms.

H5: Habitat

Many survivors live not only in psychologically oppressive environments, but also in terrible housing situations. It is not uncommon to find many abused patients and their families living in appalling, filthy conditions; firetraps, overcrowding, and many other adverse living circumstances negatively affect patients. Perpetrators of domestic violence often force their victims to stay in one room or a closet. In one situation reported at HPRT, an elderly Cambodian woman was forced to sleep on a couch in the middle of her landlord's living room. In another situation, a small baby was brought by a Cambodian teenage mother to the crowded house of a boyfriend where a lot of partying and drinking were occurring. The teenage mother and baby slept on the floor, and the baby swallowed a small object there, choking to death. The mother was devastated by this event. Yet it is rare for health professionals and therapists to ask survivors about their living environments. Hopefully, the H^5 Model will help to change this very neglected area of therapy.

THE H^5 MODEL SCALE

A culturally valid scale with known psychometric properties is in its earliest stages of development. However, all therapists can rate a survivor's responses on the following scale as an overview of elements of the H^5 Model (see table 5.1).

First, try to define what *you* mean by each of the responses, since the scale is still being developed. Then, take a look and see how the survivor is doing. This

TABLE 5.1 The H⁵ Model Scale

H⁵ Model Scale	1 (none)	2 (minor)	3 (moderate)	4 (severe)
H.1. Human Rights Violation				
H.2. State of Humiliation				
	1 (very good)	2 (adequate)	3 (poor)	4 (totally inadequate)
H.3. Healing Activities (self) – Altruism – Work – Spirituality				
H.4. Health Promotion				
H.5. Habitat / Housing				

exercise should be very informative, especially regarding those answers on which the survivor is scoring a 3 or 4. This simple assessment may help you guide your treatment approach (Siebens 2005).

Recommendations for Trauma-Informed Care Based on the H⁵ Model

The following recommendations are based on the H⁵ Model:

1. Once trust has been established, try to conduct a trauma story interview by reviewing the four elements of the trauma story. A diary called the *Trauma Story Assessment and Therapy* (TSAT) can be used. It is available at www.lulu .com/shop/richard-f-mollica/trauma-story-assessment-and-therapy-journal- for-field-and-clinic/paperback/product-20342010.html.

2. Having established trust, try to understand the nature and scope of the human rights violation(s) that the survivor experienced. Doing this will help you understand the abuse suffered and enable you to recommend the appropriate medical, psychological, and social supports.

3. Evaluate the survivor's self-healing response. This interview is included in the TSAT diary.

4. All survivors need to be in a health promotion program. Encourage the survivor to enroll in one.

5. Extensively explore the living environment of the survivor. Make doing this a priority.

Hopefully, the H^5 Model will provide professionals with new insights and techniques for assisting the traumatized person in *all* environments. Patients/clients and therapists should add their experience and insights to this working document, especially as the model is adapted to different cultures and ethnic groups.

REFERENCES

Berkson, Sarah Y., Svang Tor, Richard F. Mollica, James Lavelle, and Carol Cosenza. 2014. "An Innovative Model of Culturally Tailored Health Promotion Groups for Cambodian Survivors of Torture." *Torture* 24 (1): 1–16.

Felitti, Vincent J., Robert F. Anda, Dale Nordenberg, David F. Williamson, Alison M. Spitz, Valerie Edwards, Mary P. Koss, and James S. Marks. 1998. "Relationship of Childhood Abuse and Household Dysfunction to Many of the Leading Causes of Death in Adults: The Adverse Childhood Experiences (ACE) Study." *American Journal of Preventive Medicine* 14 (4): 245–58.

Mollica, Richard F. 2000. "Invisible Wounds." *Scientific American* 282 (6): 54–57.

———. 2006. *Healing Invisible Wounds: Paths to Hope and Recovery in a Violent World.* Orlando, FL: Harcourt.

———. 2012. *Trauma Story Assessment and Therapy: Journal for Field and Clinic.* Cambridge, MA: Harvard Program in Refugee Trauma.

Mollica, Richard F., Robert Brooks, Solvig Ekblad, and Laura McDonald. 2015. "The New H^5 Model of Refugee Trauma and Recovery." In *Violence and Mental Health,* edited by Jutta Lindert and Itzhak Levav, 341–78. New York: Springer.

Siebens, Hilary. 2005. "The Domain Management Model: A Tool for Teaching and Management of Older Adults in Emergency Departments." *Academic Emergency Medicine* 12 (2): 162–68.

WHO (World Health Organization). 2006. *The Constitution of the World Health Organization: Basic Documents.* 48th ed. New York: United Nations.

6

ADDRESSING MENTAL HEALTH DISPARITIES IN REFUGEE CHILDREN THROUGH FAMILY AND COMMUNITY-BASED PREVENTION

Theresa S. Betancourt, Rochelle L. Frounfelker,
Jenna M. Berent, Bhuwan Gautam, Saida Abdi,
Abdirahman Abdi, Zahara Haji, Ali Maalim, and Tej Mishra

Significant disparities exist in child mental health among the 3.3 million refugees who have resettled in the United States since 1975 (US Department of State 2017). Many of these refugees have experienced persecution, war-related violence, displacement, and family loss (Toole and Waldman 1993). A growing body of research has shown that resettled refugee families, regardless of ethnicity or national origin, grapple with resettlement and acculturative stressors that pose threats to the emotional, behavioral, and physical health of their children (Derluyn, Mels, and Broekaert 2009; Betancourt et al. 2015; Betancourt et al. 2009; Ellis et al. 2008). Despite this well-documented need, refugee families often face barriers to accessing mental health and other support services due to culturally rooted stigma associated with mental health issues, limited availability of services, and costs of care (Ziaian et al. 2012; Ellis et al. 2010).

To date, development of prevention-oriented mental health interventions for refugees has been limited. Many mental health interventions for refugees take a narrow focus on posttraumatic stress disorder (PTSD), oftentimes with limited community input about needs and preferences. Too often, highly specialized services are developed for a single cultural group despite the rapidly changing dynamics of refugee resettlement. Given the diversity of refugees in the world today, modern intervention models must be flexible and combine core content with both adaptable, deployment-focused components and human resources strategies to best accommodate ever-changing refugee resettlement populations.

Community-based participatory research (CBPR) is a promising approach used to arrive at a mutual understanding of community and family protective resources that can be leveraged in the development of flexible yet culturally appropriate mental health services. Despite the significant challenges of resettlement, refugee populations demonstrate remarkable resilience. Our CBPR work has aimed to identify and build on such strengths and, in working with two diverse refugee communities at once, we have developed and refined a model of the Family Strengthening Intervention for Refugees (FSI-R) that can be flexibly applied and adapted to a range of refugee communities in the future.

COMMUNITY-BASED PARTICIPATORY RESEARCH (CBPR) TO ADDRESS HEALTH DISPARITIES IN REFUGEES

Community-based participatory research (CBPR) approaches have demonstrated promise for addressing health disparities, especially on health topics characterized by stigma or distrust of researchers. In CBPR, the relationship between university investigators and community stakeholders is one of power sharing and two-way, reciprocal learning. In our CBPR work in New England, academic and community stakeholders came together around shared goals and interests and around promoting human capability, building capacity, and facilitating the success of refugee communities.

It is typical in CBPR processes that community members are engaged in all stages of research from selection of focal areas for study to design of the methods, implementation of data collection, and analysis of findings (Wallerstein and Duran 2006). In this manner, community partners are given shared access to the study data and tools, and all team members become representatives of the research.

To date, there has been limited application of CBPR methods in mental health research, particularly with refugees. Notably, research with Somali refugees in the Boston area has indicated how the use of community advisory boards (CABs) proved to be an essential part of strengthening the research focus and also a source of deeper insights into the risk of radicalization of Somali youth. For working more broadly with refugees from a range of backgrounds, CBPR methods are promising, given the stigma around mental health. In order to support healthy integration of refugees into new cultures and contexts, a focus on human capital and family functioning can be a wise investment in ensuring the success of refugee families. In addition, in conducting needs assessments and deciding on action steps, CBPR methods, by emphasizing local context and language (i.e., around mental health problems), can greatly improve community engagement and inform intervention development (Betancourt et al. 2015).

BACKGROUND

Refugee displacement is typically characterized by three phase: preflight, flight, and resettlement (Lustig et al. 2004). Other chapters in this volume, such as those by

Richard Mollica (chapter 5) and Theoni Stathopoulou (chapter 7), portray the many preflight- and flight/displacement-related health and mental health stressors facing refugee families, including high rates of exposure to violence and loss, as well as housing and food insecurity. Upon resettlement, refugee families who have experienced traumatic stress and survived persecution, war, and displacement continue to face resettlement and acculturative stressors as they establish new lives in the United States. Resettlement stressors include socioeconomic disadvantage, low access to health care, and separation from extended family and social networks. In Massachusetts, where our study is based, refugee resettlement is clustered in urban centers marked by concentrated disadvantage (e.g., poverty, overcrowded public housing, low-performing schools, and high exposure to criminal activity/gang violence). Acculturative stressors (e.g., xenophobia, racism, and differences in behavior, values, and attitudes) (Kilpatrick et al. 2003) can have profoundly adverse effects on child mental health (Barenbaum, Ruchkin, and Schwab-Stone 2004; Sabin et al. 2003).

In addition to these contextual hardships, refugee children also face challenges and stressors within their own families. Refugee parents often struggle to find adequate employment, overcome language barriers, and reestablish their self-sufficiency. As a result, children often find themselves forced into new roles to help their parents communicate and navigate a new culture (Renzaho et al. 2011; Scuglik and Alarcon 2005). Shifts in family dynamics contribute to conflict and increased risks for emotional and behavioral problems in children (Beardslee et al. 2003), with potentially negative consequences for parent-child relationships and family functioning. Refugee parents are often challenged to adapt to new cultural norms about child-rearing approaches (Renzaho et al. 2011). A high incidence of mental health problems among refugee adults also negatively affects parenting (Gold 1992) and places families at risk for poor psychosocial outcomes. As a consequence of these many stressors, high levels of mental health disorders in refugee children and adolescents are well documented (Ziaian et al. 2012; Ellis et al. 2010; Kilpatrick et al. 2003; Gold 1992; Geltman et al. 2005; Gersons and Olff 2005; Sack, Him, and Dickason 1999; Fazel and Stein 2002). Research shows high rates of depressive disorders (3–30 percent) and PTSD (19–54 percent) among refugee children (Bronstein and Montgomery 2011), compared with 11 percent for depressive disorders and 5 percent for PTSD among US-born children (Merikangas et al. 2010).

SOMALI BANTU AND LHOTSHAMPA
BHUTANESE REFUGEES

Refugee populations resettled in New England are culturally distinct but share similar refugee experiences and function in a shared societal ecosystem. Between

2011 and 2015, an average of 2,048 refugees arrived annually in Massachusetts, where our study is based; the largest numbers included our two partner refugee communities, the Somali Bantu and the Lhotshampa Bhutanese (Massachusetts Department of Public Health 2016). During this period, 1,316 refugees from Somalia and 1,790 refugees from Bhutan were resettled in Massachusetts (Massachusetts Department of Public Health 2016).

Most Somali Bantu, an ethnic minority, were brought from other parts of Africa in the nineteenth century to serve as slaves in Somalia (Lehman and Eno 2003). In 1991, civil war forced them, along with the Somali majority, from their homes to large camps in Dadaab and Kakuma—nearby Kenyan refugee camps. They have a long history of persecution and limited access to education, and they have been living in some of the most vulnerable parts of the camps for generations (Besteman 2012; Lehman and Eno 2003; Menkhaus 2003). In the United States, Somalis are the largest single African resettlement population in US history. Somali Bantu resettlement started in 2004 across thirty-eight different states. In Boston, resettlement of Somali Bantu families started with a handful of families and ballooned to more than four hundred families in subsequent years.

The Lhotshampa Bhutanese, an ethnic Nepalese minority, had lived in southern Bhutan since the seventeenth century. In the 1990s, the Bhutanese government expelled this population to refugee camps in Nepal, often through acts of violence and attacks on their citizenship rights (Hutt 1996). Following this ethnic cleansing, the Lhotshampas remained for nearly two decades in camps in the eastern part of Nepal (IOM 2008). Large-scale Bhutanese resettlement in the United States began in 2008. Upon resettlement, Lhotshampa Bhutanese refugees have had high rates of suicide, which led the Centers for Disease Control and Prevention (CDC) to sponsor an investigation. At present, the suicide rate among Bhutanese refugees is approaching nearly twice that of the US national average: 24.4 per 100,000 compared with 12.4 per 100,000 (CDC 2013).

To help families better navigate the stressors of resettlement, we began our CBPR project with the intention of helping resettled refugee populations from diverse backgrounds to thrive. Strengths-based preventive models may help address resettlement and acculturative stress by leveraging community resilience in order to address mental health disparities. For refugee children and families, most existing intervention models are initiated only after symptoms become severe. Preventive interventions, in contrast, can help counteract disparities early on by reducing risks for mental health problems and family dysfunction (Kilpatrick et al. 2003; Williams and Berry 1991). Prevention science proposes that these types of interventions anticipate and target family dynamics and stressors known to increase risks for poor mental health, thereby reducing or eliminating undesirable outcomes (Institute of Medicine 1994; Williams and Berry 1991; O'Connell, Boat, and Warner 2009; Bloom 1982). Bolstering resilience across the social ecology can further contribute to prevention (Beardslee and Gladstone 2001; Bronfenbrenner 1979; Lazarus and Folkman 1984); however, little research has investigated indigenous and community-based protective processes and how preventive models might leverage these in interventions for refugees.

It is known that cultural belief systems can greatly influence models of illness and healing (Kleinman, Eisenberg, and Good 1978; see also United Nations 2012). Indeed, many refugee populations may have limited or no experience with Western models of mental health diagnoses and treatment (Muecke 1983; Saadi, Bond, and Percac-Lima 2015; Simmelink et al. 2013) and may hold stigmatizing views of mental health conditions, situations that can present further barriers to seeking and receiving care. Involving community members in the development and implementation of culturally appropriate interventions that engage researchers and community members in more equitable partnerships to address such power differentials has the potential to improve community engagement and facilitate help-seeking. Furthermore, this partnership has demonstrated success in helping refugee communities overcome barriers that they face to accessing both preventive services and necessary mental health treatment for children and families (Leung, Yen, and Minkler 2004; Minkler 2010).

METHODS

Guided by the ecological model of stress adjustment, our CBPR process aimed to illuminate and build on inherent strengths and resources within the refugee communities and at the family and individual levels. Early phases of the project began with qualitative data to investigate community and cultural strengths as the sources of resilience that help families and children do well despite challenges (Luthar and Brown 2007; Luthar, Cicchetti, and Becker 2000; Ungar 2011). Initiation of the project began in 2004, when the team was contacted by a Boston-area resettlement office requesting help with emotional and behavioral problems exhibited by Somali Bantu refugee children in nearby schools.

Follow-up efforts included consulting with Somali Bantu refugee families and local mental health providers and meeting with some of the leaders within the Somali Bantu community. The shared interests in seeing refugee youth thrive and succeed in school and community settings provided a place for coming together around common goals. At the same time, the Chelsea Collaborative, a community-based advocacy organization in the Boston area, had been building the capacity of the leadership within the Somali Bantu refugee mutual assistance organization called the Shanbaro Community Association. This partnership via Shanbaro, an organization created and run by Somali Bantu refugees housed within the Chelsea Collaborative, identified the need to understand more about the emotional and behavioral challenges facing children and youth within the Somali Bantu population. This joint partnership between Harvard University and the two community organizations offered an opportunity to blend mutual goals of gaining greater cross-cultural mental health knowledge and identifying and raising awareness of community service needs.

After many attempts to write grants to fund the work, the partnership successfully completed a needs assessment of the Somali Bantu community in 2012 and was interested in expanding their work to Bhutanese refugees. All parties, including individuals from the Somali Bantu and Bhutanese refugee communities, were included in the grant-writing process to secure additional funding for these purposes. Somali Bantu and Bhutanese community advisory boards provide ongoing project consultation with the research team, ensuring that the project is beneficial both to partners and to the broader refugee communities involved.

The intention of this study is two-fold and reflects the unique and mutual goals of the CBPR partnership: understanding the problems, community strengths, and help-seeking behavior of Somali Bantu and Bhutanese refugees and determining local expressions of emotional and behavioral problems.

PHASE 1: PARTICIPATORY COMMUNITY ASSESSMENT

Hiring and training a local team can help to build community capacity and deepen cultural knowledge that can illuminate important health dynamics via local community-based data collection. In our project, community members have played central roles as CBPR Research Assistants (RAs), interventionists (FSI-R community health workers), and supervisors. Team members who speak the language and understand resettlement and acculturative stressors are better able to engage and communicate with participants and can demonstrate the crucial role that CBPR refugee teams can play in developing and implementing interventions within their communities, given robust training and supervision.

In the early assessment phase of the project, we raised the funds to hire and train local RAs, comprising Somali Bantu and Bhutanese community members who engaged in quantitative and qualitative data collection training in the field and in their communities. Through these steps, we built a strong team of RAs who became well versed in research ethics and in both quantitative and qualitative data collection. RAs include individuals with varying levels of education; several went on to enroll in training for health care and social service professions. In all cases, we endeavored to structure the RA jobs so that they would include strong training and supervision and more compelling pay and professional development than that offered by competing jobs in food services, airport work, beauty salons, or cab driving, which were common alternative jobs that our refugee team members were pursuing.

Free-listing (FL) interview methods were selected as a means of gaining a broad understanding of the problems, strengths, and resources within each of the two refugee communities. The procedure for free-list data collection involved asking three overarching questions, including "What are the problems of Somali Bantu/ Bhutanese children in this community?" Participants were asked to give as complete a list as possible, and interviewers probed, asking for "anything more" until the listing exercise was finished. The RAs then reviewed the list and obtained details, clarity, and contextual information on each free-list item mentioned. Two follow-up questions were asked regarding what people in the community did, if anything, to help each other with such challenges and what people did to get help outside of the immediate refugee community.

The purpose of key informant (KI) interviews was to gather more information about the mental health and behavioral problems that children experience—as identified in the free-list exercise—and to identify cover terms or language in order to effectively discuss mental health syndromes affecting children and adolescents in the two communities. The RAs grouped FL problems related to children's thoughts, feelings, and behaviors together based on a culturally informed understanding of the relationships among these problems. For example, in the Somali Bantu community, behaviors such as "children fighting" and "children not listening to parents" were clustered together. Initial KI interviews asked for more information about these problems, probing for additional problems closely related to these indicators. Once a grouping of symptoms began to emerge, interviewers asked for local terms used to describe the entire cluster of problems/behaviors in children and adolescents. Once a cover term for these behavioral problems had been identified, this term was then used in later KI interviews and further illuminated or refined. In particular, once a cover term was available, such as the conduct problem *aasiwaalidin* in the Somali Bantu community (discussed further below), KI interviewers asked about other ways that a child with *aasiwaalidin* might behave, feel, and think about himself or herself and others.

Refugee team members followed an iterative process when conducting KI interviews. Interviews were followed by a debriefing session with the principal investigator and university-affiliated program managers, after which the interview guide was revised and improved by taking into account the early experiences of interviewers using it in the field. Accordingly, the interviews became increasingly focused on a set of symptoms/indicators and resulting cover terms. As interviews progressed, syndrome/cover terms were validated as participants identified, without any prompting, syndrome indicators previously used at the start of KI interviews, and all results were discussed in collaborative team meetings. RAs tracked the indicators identified for each cover term by every study participant. Once cover terms emerged, interviewers also probed the nature of a problem, its causes, and any gender and age patterns among youth in that particular refugee community.

FL interviews were analyzed using a simple tally of conceptually equivalent (per research team group discussion) problems, resources, and help-seeking behaviors identified by the community; these were then arranged according to rank order of frequency. For the purposes of mental health syndrome development, KI interviews were analyzed by tallying indicators mentioned by study participants. Under a given cover term or syndrome term, conceptually equivalent symptoms/indicators mentioned across interviews were grouped together. For instance, in the Bhutanese community KIs mentioned the indicators "talks filthy words" and "talks using bad words" to describe a child with behavioral problems. The research team decided that these indicators were conceptually equivalent and combined them to create an umbrella indicator—"uses bad language/words"—that encompassed both of these phrases. Indicators endorsed by at least 10 percent of the total KI sample for each refugee community were retained and included in the final list of indicators for each syndrome. The refugee research team and the academic collaborators worked as a group to generate appropriate English translations of syndromes and indicators. Subsequently, results were reviewed with members of the Somali Bantu and Bhutanese refugee communities via "member checks" with CABs. In addition, focus groups among youth were used to validate and clarify syndrome terms and their accompanying symptom descriptions. The full free-list results are available in table 6.3 (Betancourt et al. 2015).

PHASE I: RESULTS

Free-List Exercise from Somali Bantu Refugee Children

Among the Somali Bantu refugee participants interviewed, the most frequently cited problems included not having enough money to pay for rent, food, clothes, and other bills (53 percent), followed by children losing their religious or moral education (40 percent) and children needing assistance with homework (40 percent). Communication was also a frequently identified problem, with parents not able to speak English (35 percent). When asked what helped children with these kinds of problems, support from the Somali Bantu refugee community was frequently mentioned, with 40 percent of participants reporting community support as a major protective factor. Both youth and adults reported that school personnel and parents also helped children with their problems. Twenty percent of participants identified government facilities and welfare services, such as food stamps, as helpful (see table 6.3).

Free-List Exercise from Bhutanese Refugee Children

Among Bhutanese refugee free-list participants, the most frequently cited problems of Bhutanese refugee children were related to language barriers (83 percent), including parents and children being unable to communicate with teachers and other school personnel. Similar to the responses of Somali Bantu refugees, not having enough money for food and rent was a commonly identified problem (38 percent), as was the issue of children traveling to school (26 percent). According to our participants, fighting, loneliness, depression, and fear were the most frequently reported behavioral and emotional issues faced by Bhutanese refugee youth.

As in the responses from Somali Bantu refugees, the Bhutanese refugee community was identified as a major source of support for coping with the challenges mentioned (45 percent), with families, relatives, and friends providing financial help and assisting children with homework. In terms of resources outside of the Bhutanese community, participants frequently mentioned social services and welfare programs (see table 6.3).

Locally Relevant Syndrome Terms for Mental Health Problems in Somali Bantu Refugee Children

Participants identified four domains of mental health problems (see table 6.1).

Aasiwaalidin was a cover term used to capture a set of signs and symptoms (a syndrome) used to describe young people who were disrespectful to their parents and other elders, disobedient, and disinterested in engaging with work or education. They also frequently got into fights or engaged in bullying, became easily angered, and engaged in a range of other rule-breaking and high-risk behaviors.

Wel wel was used to describe children who had anxiety-like problems or were prone to excessive worrying. Children with *wel wel* were thought to exhibit fear about the future and worry about current life stressors. Many of the reported symptoms were found in review to be similar to Western diagnoses of anxiety disorders in children and included inattention, forgetfulness, social withdrawal, weight loss, and somatic complaints.

The syndrome term *dherif* or *isfilit* highlighted symptoms of persistent anger. Children with *dherif* were thought to be defensive, quick to respond with anger, feeling as though they were under pressure or under attack, and easily upset by small issues. While *dherif* explained general anger, *isfilit* characterized people who were always angry and quick to anger and who displayed aggressive behavior.

The term *takoor* was used to describe a problem of persistent sadness. *Takoor* involved sustained low mood, cognitive rumination, and difficulty engaging in social and educational settings.

Locally Relevant Syndrome Terms for Mental Health Problems in Bhutanese Refugee Children

Three main domains of common mental health problems were identified among Bhutanese study participants (see table 6.2).

Badmaas was described as a syndrome similar to *aasiwaalidin* in Somali Bantu culture; it is characterized by conduct-related problems and maladaptive behavior. Participants described a child with *badmaas* as being angry, bullying others, and getting involved in fights. Interviewees identified a *badmaas* child as someone who is arrogant, uses bad language, and disobeys parents, teachers, and elders.

TABLE 6.1 Somali Bantu local mental health syndrome terms and descriptors

Syndrome Term	Descriptor Maay Maay	English
Aasiwaalidin (conduct problems)	Sharaf laawe	Disrespectful
	Edeb laan	Lack of respect (asluup)
	Dherif	Easily angered
	Makoroof	Disagrees/argues/talks back to parents
	Karawai	Does not obey parents
	Dedmekaalmeyay	Does not assist others
	Rabshoole	Has conflict with peers
	Dhega adeeg	Poor follow-through
	Dantiis gorod	Self-centered
	Shaqadiid/Hool beel	Does not like to work/does not engage with education
	Mas'uul dare	Does not take responsibility for actions
	Kerway	"Making trouble"/bullying other children
	Gardaresti	Engages in fighting
	Daroogiste	Engages in negative behaviors (e.g., drinking alcohol, gambling, joining gangs)
Wel Wel (worry)	Was Was	Worries about current and future life stressors
	Absi	Fear
	Fulemimo	Overly scared about things
	Dhug-la'aan	Poor attention
	Damiin	Forgetful
	Siseeg	Poor follow-through
	Tiirman	Engages in quiet, isolative behavior
	Is shuujin	Weight loss
	Mathy dhuury	Headaches
	Indhu-dhuuru	Visual disturbances
Dherif (anger)	Amal	Quick to anger
	Murug	Feel as though they are under pressure
	Amal low	Easily upset by small issues
	Kifle	Defensive (get angry when you joke with them)
	Kerway	"Making trouble"
	Isfilit	Anger without reason
	Hanaang	Anger
Tiire/Takoor (persistent sadness)	Takoor	Sadness
	Ma'abos	Low mood/always unhappy
	Tiire/Joogow maqane	Being absent/your mind is elsewhere/not paying attention
	Shaleen daak	Not comfortable with friends
	Qurb rabshoole	Thinking too much about their problems (rumination)
	Rabshoole	Difficulty getting along with others
	Damiin	Difficulty learning

TABLE 6.2 Bhutanese local mental health syndrome terms and descriptions

Syndrome Term	Descriptor	
	Nepali	English
Badmaas	*Lagu pardarthako sewan*	Using addictive substances (drugs, alcohol, cigarettes)
(conduct	*Lappa kelne*	Fighting (hits others, acts aggressively)
problems)	*Dada-giri/Chot*	Bullying/wounding someone verbally (teases others, pesters, makes fun of others)
	Ghamanda	Arrogant
	Fatah	Scoundrel, delinquent (vandalism, disobedient)
	Aatanka	Causing terror
	Asamajik	Antisocial (does not talk, reacts irritably to others, cannot agree or cooperate with others)
Chinteet	*Chintajanak/chinta*	Worry
(worry)	*Rish*	Anger
	Khulera nabolne	Does not talk openly
	Darr	Afraid
	Badmaas	Bad behavior
	Aatmahatyako soch rakhne	Suicidal thoughts/poses harm to oneself
	Kamjod/Aafailai kamjor thanne	Helplessness/feels helpless
	Haresh	Hopelessness
Dookhit	*Dukhi/dookhit*	Sad
(persistent	*Jharkine/bolna jharko manne*	Irritable
sadness)	*Eklo*	Loneliness
	Ekohorine/tolaune	Fixate (rumination)
	Dherai nabolne	Someone who does not talk much
	Alaggiyeko	Isolated
	Mann dukhne	Mind hurts

Dookhit was used to describe children who were persistently sad and whose "minds hurt." Similar to the Somali Bantu syndrome *takoor*, a child with *dookhit* was someone with persistent feelings of loneliness. To describe children with *dookhit*, community members used phrases such as "their 'heart-mind' may have been hurt," referring to an ethnic Nepali Bhutanese manner of viewing emotional pain.

A child with *chinteet* was identified as someone who worried a lot, feared for the future, and was persistently concerned about things, indicating behaviors similar to the anxiety-related problem of *wel wel* in the Somali Bantu culture.

PHASE II: DEVELOPING A FAMILY-BASED PREVENTIVE INTERVENTION TO PROMOTE CHILD REFUGEE MENTAL HEALTH

From discussions about our qualitative data in both communities, we used CBPR methods to generate community-driven hypotheses about the links between life events and stressors and the emotional and behavioral problems in children and adolescents described in the qualitative data. The FL and KI data were shared in community discussions with both the Bhutanese and Somali Bantu CABs. In discussing problems and syndrome terms, emphasis was given to understanding community and cultural resources that might improve coping and resilience in children and families. Specifically, we endeavored to learn about and bolster—through preventive measures—those resources that support healthy parenting and mitigate the effects of past trauma and acculturative and resettlement stressors. By highlighting community protective processes and strengths as potential "active ingredients" of an intervention model that the team might develop, we aimed to design a preventive intervention that built on local strengths, was a good fit with the culture and context, and addressed issues of engagement, acceptability, and sustainability of services in order to address mental health disparities in refugee children (Ellis et al. 2006).

From reviews of the literature and from our own experiences with a prior initiative for families affected by HIV in Rwanda, we selected the Family-Based Preventive Intervention (FBPI), which is one of the few family-based prevention programs recognized by the National Registry of Effective Programs and Practices. Our collaborator from Boston Children's Hospital, Dr. William Beardslee, developed the FBPI to support healthy parenting in order to prevent depression in the children of depressed caregivers (the leading risk factor for depression in children). It was one of the earliest programs to adopt an ecological approach to chronic family stress and has been adapted to serve a diverse range of cultures (e.g., Finnish, Costa Rican, and Native American communities) (Beardslee 1998). The FBPI was one of the first family-based preventive interventions to demonstrate efficacy in large-scale trials (Beardslee et al. 2003; Beardslee et al. 2007), and it has evidenced sustained effectiveness in low-resource and culturally diverse settings (Podorefsky, McDonald-Dowdell, and Beardslee 2001; Llenera-Quinn et al. 2006), including improved family functioning up to 4.5 years postintervention (Beardslee et al. 1997; Beardslee et al. 2007).

We collaborated with Somali Bantu and Lhotshampa Bhutanese community members to adapt the Family-Based Preventive Intervention (FBPI) to refugees (as FSI-R) and to translate and test the FSI-R scales for assessing child and caregiver relationships, mental health, and family functioning. We also worked with Community Advisory Boards (CABs) and other stakeholders to apply our qualitative findings to FSI-R refinement for serving refugee families. In each refugee community, the CAB was composed of between six and eight individuals identified by their community as knowledgeable about family and children's needs and willing to volunteer their time to advise the project.

CAB members with experience in community issues proved critical for contextualizing qualitative and quantitative findings. In particular, CAB members have reviewed qualitative findings on parent-child relationships, factors contributing to risk and resilience in refugee families, services preferences, and refugee views about seeking help. This feedback was used in making refinements to the FSI-R core intervention components. For instance, additional content was added on positive parenting skills and alternatives to harsh punishment, assistance navigating formal services (e.g., schools, legal aid, housing), and ways to recognize and seek out informal supports (e.g., neighbor relationships). All of these themes arose as key concerns were identified in our needs assessments with both refugee groups. In addition, accessing informal and formal resources was seen as critical to resilient life outcomes in children and families.

Like the original FBPI, the Family Strengthening Intervention for Refugees (FSI-R) involves a series of separate and joint meetings with parents and children to discuss the challenges that families face and the strengths that have helped them make it through challenging times in the past. Sessions with children separate from parents are intended to honor the child's voice and perspective in the family experience. From the perspective of the children and of the caregivers, each family member's experience is woven into a forward-looking "family narrative" that highlights the family story through challenges and successes up to the present time. Compiling the narrative is an opportunity to bring forward unique challenges facing the family from members' own perspectives and also to describe and honor coping strategies that members find productive and that have helped them to face difficult times in the past. The FSI-R also integrates additional psychoeducation content on mental health and promoting resilience along with coaching to enhance parenting skills, which is provided throughout the FSI-R and may be tailored to family needs.

The FSI-R ends with a "family meeting" in which all family members, whenever possible, come together to discuss their shared experiences and goals. Creating and sharing perspectives on the family narrative, especially about facing and overcoming hardships over the course of time, helps to build family connection, confidence, and a sense of self-efficacy. The process of telling the family story allows each person to appreciate the perspectives of other family members; it also builds shared understanding within the family and encourages open communication, cohesion, and problem solving.

We derived the core components of the Family Strengthening Intervention (FSI) from a theoretical framework rooted in the stress-adjustment paradigm and developmental and ecological approaches to understanding the development of children and youth affected by war (see fig. 6.1). We adapted the intervention to address key risk factors that our qualitative data identified as important in the refugee experience, including past family trauma and loss, youth challenges with identity or social isolation, poor family communication or limited time for family connection, stress management or harsh parenting strategies, and difficulties eliciting and navigating formal and informal supports. The core components of the FSI are (1) building parenting skills and improving family communication; (2) developing a "family narrative" to build connectedness and highlight sources of

Holistic intervention

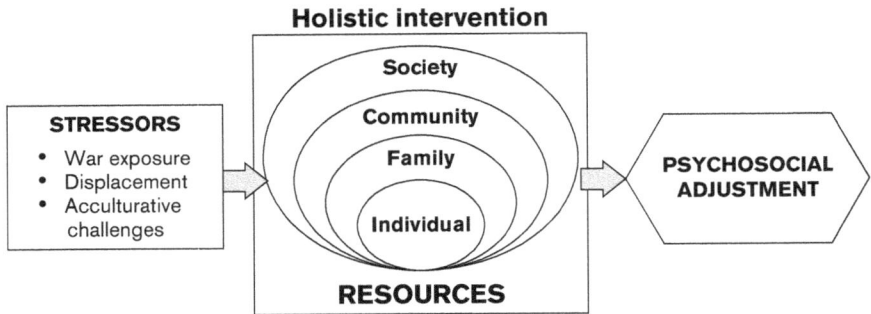

FIGURE 6.1. An ecological view of the stress-adjustment paradigm as applied to refugees resettling in the United States.

resilience for facing challenges; (3) providing psychoeducation on trauma and parenting in the United States; and (4) strengthening problem-solving skills, social support, and navigation of informal and formal community resources (see fig. 6.2). The FSI integrates the core components into nine main modules, including outreach and follow-up sessions. The main modules incorporate culturally relevant language and metaphors (derived from qualitative data) to orient families to the core themes of each module and extensive role-playing to build parenting skills. The number of sessions required to complete the modules has varied according to different families' needs (on average between nine and twelve sessions for the nine main modules). Because the FSI-R is delivered in the home, interventionists can be flexible in the timing of the intervention delivery to respond to family needs and engage all caregivers, including fathers, whenever possible.

In this manner, the FSI-R is intended to build communication and family cohesion, help to illuminate and engage in problem-solving regarding concerns about children, and help families optimistically plan for a promising future together. Drawing from the ecological theory of risk and resilience, the FSI-R aims to diminish the risk of child emotional and behavioral problems by improving family communication and building a more cohesive family identity grounded in family strengths as well as in more successful navigation of formal and informal external resources beyond the family.

The FSI modules are arranged more or less sequentially through a set of content areas deemed as important for promoting parent-child relationships and youth mental health per our formative work. The pre-meeting and module 1 allow the interventionist—for the FSI-R, a health center–affiliated, trained refugee community health worker (CHW)—to begin developing a relationship with the family by introducing the FSI-R goals and preparing parents and children for the delivery format. The home-visitor CHW, also called a "coach," discusses expectations with the

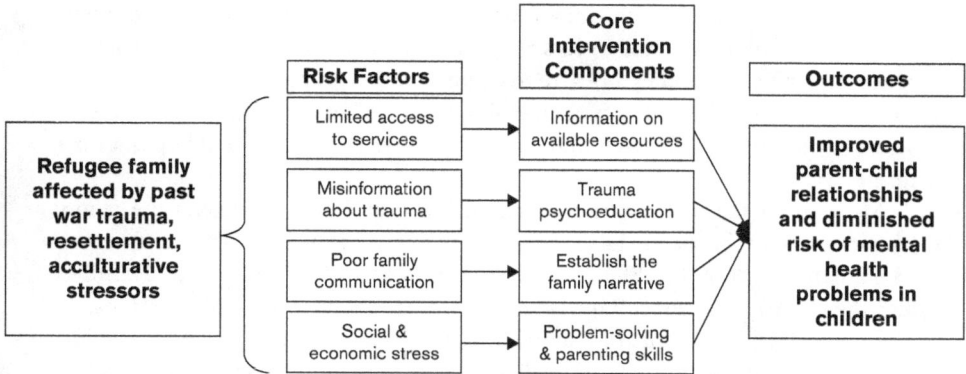

FIGURE 6.2. Conceptual model of the Family Strengthening Intervention for Refugees (FSI-R) resettling in the United States.

family to help illuminate their concerns and their impressions of family strengths. Modules 1 and 2 address basic parenting and communication skills and sharing of the expectations, concerns, and hopes that caregivers have for each of their children.

The family narrative, a very central feature of FSI-R, is also introduced in modules 1 and 2. It covers major life events, including the process of coming to the United States as refugees, from the perspectives of both caregivers and children. In developing the family narrative in modules 1 and 2, milestones are mapped out on paper. This module also includes basic psychoeducation about trauma and its effects on family relationships and functioning. Because the family members select the events in the family narrative, they can choose to include or not include past traumatic events in the story. The CHW is trained to provide strong, supportive listening and to elicit information from family members about what helped them get through difficult times in the past. However, emphasis is not placed on retelling details of the trauma, given the limited skill level of the CHW and the focus on prevention rather than on treatment of traumatic stress reactions via exposure-related therapy. Should such services be indicated, family members can be referred to formal mental health services; such services can continue in complementary fashion with the FSI-R. Given strong links to other health services, referrals can also be made for family members needing a higher level of mental health care for conditions such as depression or posttraumatic stress disorder. The FSI-R does provide trauma psychoeducation, normalization of how past traumatic events can affect one's sense of the world and relationships with others, and support for caregivers who indicate persistent effects of war-related trauma or loss in their lives at the present time.

From the perspective of the child, the family narrative in the FSI-R also offers a unique opportunity. Many refugee children have never heard the story of their family's journey to the United States. This journey often required tremendous resourcefulness as well as loss and adjustment. The FSI-R provides a shared space for refugee families both to recognize their strengths and to problem-solve in a more collective way concerning family challenges that present themselves in the current parent-child relationship, as well as their shared hopes for the future.

Module 3 is the first major meeting with children and establishes the family narrative from their perspective. Children between the ages of seven and seventeen are the target of the FSI-R intervention. However, at the discretion of families and the CHW, younger children can also be included in the child sessions. In module 3, the coach elicits the family narrative from the perspective of the children and emphasizes sources of resilience at the individual, family, and community levels that have helped the family to make it through difficult times. Module 3 may be divided into sessions by age, as needed. Sessions with adolescents can provide a forum to discuss concerns about approaching adulthood, community relationships, risk behaviors, friendships and peer relationships, and even experiences with bullying, racism, and social marginalization. Trauma psychoeducation, when relevant, is also emphasized in this module.

Module 4 is a session with parents that focuses on improving parent-child relationships and parenting skills. Education about the importance of communication with children is provided. Parenting skills are discussed, with an emphasis placed on self-care stress management and alternatives to harsh punishment. As the intervention moves forward and the rapport with a family deepens, role-playing is also used to help caregivers practice skills in communicating in a successful manner with school-aged children in their own language and with their own cultural orientation, with help from the coach who knows the culture and may have navigated such experiences in her or his own life.

Module 5 is focused on helping refugee families navigate the US school system. Many refugee parents know little about the expectations of US schools and teachers, especially when it comes to homework help, the grading system, and expected parental participation, such as parent-teacher meetings.

Module 6 is about promoting health, well-being, and safety, with a strong focus on caregiver stress management and emotion regulation skills. Module 6 also strives to show caregivers how good self-care—including management of illness, mental health, and stress—can help ensure that caregivers stay healthy and functioning, a condition that is fundamental to the broader family's continued success. The module also discusses avoiding problematic use of drugs or alcohol (an issue that is less relevant in the Somali Bantu community given its religious sanctions against such behavior). Given the high rate of suicide among Bhutanese refugees resettling in the United States, there are also psychoeducation tools available in this session for discussion of suicide prevention.

In module 7, with help from the coach, the caregivers work to prepare for the family meeting (module 9). This is an opportunity for the caregivers to revisit the family narrative and discuss concerns, challenges, and sources of resilience in the family. Caregivers identify what they most want to share with their children, with a focus on the unique recognition of the strengths and challenges of each school-aged child in the family and their hopes for each individual child. Applications of child-parent communication skills are discussed and practiced through role-playing in preparation for the session.

Module 8 reconvenes the children and revisits the family narrative. Children brainstorm topics and feelings that they most want their caregivers to know. They also role-play with the CHW to prepare for the family meeting. Both the children and their caregivers can propose ideas and themes that are important to discuss at the family meeting. The CHW then helps the family prepare for how they want to present each topic at the family meeting and may even role-play by bringing up the agenda item to help with preparation.

Module 9 is a family meeting led by the caregivers with support from the CHW. It features facilitated group discussion to articulate family goals and to create an open dialogue about members' shared experience of resettlement in the United States and hopes for the future as a family. The family develops an integrated family narrative by assembling the materials generated during the separate child and caregiver modules. In the family meeting preparation sessions, the children and the caregivers both decide and plan for content that they would like to discuss at the meeting. Discussion focuses on ways in which family members can draw on their unique strengths to face challenges posed by resettlement. Shared family hopes for the future are placed along the integrated family narrative, and participants use problem-solving skills to lay out achievable plans for meeting them. Module 9 also focuses on closure and acknowledging the family's hard work during the FSI-R.

Module 10 is a review session that takes place after completion of the nine modules. Within a month of FSI-R completion, the coach conducts a check-in visit to ask the family to reflect on how they are doing and what skills are being used or maintained, as learned in FSI-R. The CHW will help to troubleshoot persistent issues or difficulties that have arisen since the end of the FSI-R. Following completion of the preventive intervention, families are reminded that they are always welcome to contact the FSI-R team should they need additional information, referrals, or support.

PHASE III: EVALUATING THE FSI-R
AND LESSONS LEARNED

Our FSI-R Pilot Trial was designed to assess feasibility, acceptability, and satisfaction with FSI-R. At the time of this writing, the pilot trial is underway. Initial observations indicate that refugee families view the content of FSI-R as highly applicable to their present situations. Families also report high satisfaction with the sessions. However, several challenges have arisen as well. First, maintaining traditional research boundaries between the refugee assessment team and the refugee intervention team has been exceptionally difficult given the close-knit nature of the community. We have attempted to maintain RAs' being blinded to which families receive the intervention and which the usual treatment, but RAs report that many families freely tell RAs after randomization whether or not they are receiving the intervention. Second, having had their own refugee experiences, the interventionists, as well as the families, have responded emotionally to the sessions' content. However, current interventionists have found culturally appropriate mechanisms for handling difficult emotions during sessions. For example, the Bhutanese staff use breathing exercises, while the Somali Bantu staff use prayer.

The socioeconomic context of refugee families has also led to challenges. In both the Somali Bantu and Bhutanese refugee populations, households comprise several generations living under one roof in often-crowded public housing and other affordable housing arrangements. As a result, finding a private place to engage in interviews as well as in separate family and child sessions has proven particularly challenging. We have also experienced challenges related to scheduling weekly sessions with families due to time constraints. In many refugee households, parents hold more than one job and/or have unaligned work schedules, resulting in limited free time to spend together. Interventionists have to be extremely flexible and strategize with families to find a time to meet. In addition, many refugee families have felt a mismatch between the time commitment required for the assessment battery and the incentives provided. We are working on increasing incentives to better compensate families for their time.

Developing and providing training and supervision to refugee CHWs is an ongoing process. The original family-strengthening intervention was intended to be delivered by master's-level trained clinicians. However, we are committed to hiring individuals from the refugee community as interventionists, with the primary requirement that they be fluent in both their own language and English; most, but not all, have or are pursuing a bachelor's degree. All of our interventionists also have a background in social services such as providing case management to recently resettled refugees. Training and intervention materials are continually being adapted to meet the needs of a less-educated workforce than the original intervention plan intended. For instance, we developed a reduced literacy version of the FSI-R intervention manual to improve comprehension by CHWs. In addition, both initial and booster training sessions have been adapted to include more time spent on understanding and addressing clinical challenges related to the intervention and work with families. On a positive note, refugee CHWs—who have received initial training and ongoing supervision to deliver the FSI-R—report confidence in delivering the FSI-R and are reporting satisfaction with their ability to help the families they are working with in the FSI-R.

The pilot intervention delivery is also supported by weekly group supervision meetings (sixty minutes) that convene FSI-R supervisors and refugee CHWs embedded in refugee-serving social services or mental health agencies in two New England communities. One organization is a large social services agency with a long history of serving diverse refugee groups. The other is a mutual assistance organization started by leaders within the Somali refugee community to serve refugees from Somali and other regions. At each site, there is a clinical supervisor with strong knowledge of local context and options for additional supports as well as referrals. These teams participate in weekly group supervision by phone and in person, depending on their schedules. In addition, the principal investigator, program manager, and site supervisors also participate in "super-supervision" on a bimonthly basis. In supervision sessions, refugee team members report on the intervention's progress as well as on their experiences in delivering the material. Supervision has also been useful for discussing difficult issues arising during home visits (e.g., family conflict) and for identifying challenges in helping families access other services. This format proved to be highly successful in our previous trial of the FSI for families affected by HIV in Rwanda and in our FSI-R pilot work among refugees in the United States.

In terms of fidelity monitoring, we strive to audiotape all family sessions in order to allow FSI-R supervisors to appraise session-by-session fidelity. We tested audiotaping of family sessions in our previous trials and found good acceptability following initial adjustments to the recording equipment. FSI-R fidelity experts review session tapes and code a randomly selected twenty-minute segment for fidelity prior to weekly individual supervision meetings with CHWs, using the FSI-R Fidelity Monitoring Tool. Each FSI-R CHW also completes a weekly Self-Report Fidelity Checklist to self-monitor the level of adherence to the FSI-R core components. Supervisor and self-ratings report on (a) module topics covered, (b) degree of caregiver and child engagement, (c) success in relaying information on parenting, (d) communication skills, (e) navigation of available resources, (f) assessment of the intervention pacing, and (g) appropriate next steps. During weekly meetings, FSI-R supervisors and CHWs review the theory and goals of the FSI-R modules, resolve issues with fidelity as determined by supervisor and self-ratings, and make targeted suggestions to enhance fidelity, including using role-playing to refine skills. We also ask all participants and CHWs to complete a satisfaction questionnaire.

CONCLUSION

CBPR approaches that engage cross-culturally with multiple refugee groups can deepen understanding of common and diverging community needs. Our academic and community partners recognize that interventions designed for single refugee groups have less applicability in light of ever-changing refugee resettlement patterns. We designed our study to bridge informational and cultural gaps, not only between service providers and refugees but also across diverse refugee groups, by including Somali Bantu and Bhutanese refugees. This approach facilitated our prior research on mental health and resilience in these two refugee communities. Cross-group analyses have yielded unprecedented insight into the similarities and differences that exist in the refugee experiences of families resettled in New England and have deepened cohesion and collaboration among partners. Using a CBPR mixed methods approach, we developed and pretested screening and assessment tools for use by a broad range of providers working with refugee communities, and we developed a core intervention that can be feasibly, appropriately, and successfully implemented and evaluated by CBPR methods. It is our intent, as we discovered in adapting this intervention model to the context of families affected by HIV/AIDS in Rwanda (Betancourt et al. 2014), that such a participatory process with strong community engagement and a strengths-based intervention model can help to reduce risks of mental health problems among children and adolescents by improving supports to parenting and the caregiver-child relationship despite known challenges. In this manner, CBPR approaches have the potential to strengthen and expand existing partnerships among refugee groups, service providers, and academic researchers (Israel et al. 1998; Laverack and Wallerstein 2001; Israel et al. 2005; Cornwall and Jewkes 1995). Most importantly, we have built and continue to build capacity within our partner refugee communities by engaging community members as coinvestigators, interventionists, and overall members of our CBPR team.

Our participatory approach to intervention development is informed by the CBPR model outlined by Israel and colleagues (2005). Co-learning among the study investigators, CBPR team, and refugee communities is at the heart of this work, which has been jointly developed by the academic, refugee, and service-provider partners. Our integrated community-research coalition structure and CBPR approach are intended to ensure that the unique and complementary expertise, technical resources, and skills of our academic researchers, refugee community members, and service providers contribute to advancing this important collaboration.

Community-based interventions that address the psychological needs of refugees have rarely included consultation with communities (Williams and Thompson 2011). We developed the refugee adaptation of the evidence-based FSI (the FSI-R) using CBPR and integrated findings from a needs assessment conducted with refugee partners and a participatory review process involving refugee CABs. These efforts documented the psychosocial needs of Somali Bantu and Bhutanese refugees, identified common local terms for mental health syndromes, and identified culturally adapted assessments of youth mental health, parenting, and family functioning (Betancourt et al. 2015). We modified the FSI to address salient topics for refugees, including responsive parenting and strategies for engagement with the US education system, which our pilot data indicate are priorities for refugee parents.

Our CBPR collaboration and project design is intended to build on best practices in both intervention development and mixed methods research (Creswell et al. 2011). We are using CBPR-based qualitative and quantitative research methods to conduct a future randomized controlled trial (RCT) and process evaluation of the FSI-R. A type 2 hybrid effectiveness-implementation study design involves testing a clinical intervention while simultaneously gathering information on intervention delivery via a process evaluation (Curran et al. 2012). This design will allow us to identify strategies for implementing and sustaining high quality FSI-R services and to determine optimal methods for scale up. We will align our type 2 hybrid design with the intervention explanatory sequential mixed methods design (Creswell 2014).

In terms of project conceptualization and design, our community coinvestigators and CABs have been instrumental in project development. Under our planning grant, Somali Bantu CAB and Bhutanese CAB meetings (all audiotaped) have been productive venues for exploring critical issues to advance FSI-R development (e.g., review of FSI-R modules for cultural appropriateness, soliciting ideas for core themes or concepts to integrate into materials). In cases in which we could not reach consensus within or across CABs (e.g., whether or not to include health promotion content), we discussed the issue further to better understand the range of CAB member opinions; CAB members then voted on a final recommendation. CABs revisited unresolved disputes within or across CABs at subsequent meetings until appropriate solutions or compromises were reached. CAB engagement will continue for the duration of our proposed project; CABs will meet monthly, with a semiannual combined Somali Bantu and Bhutanese CAB meeting. CAB members will continue to review and provide feedback on study materials and to advise on methods of ethical and cultural considerations in order to ensure community engagement in research activities throughout the project. We will continue to encourage cooperation and information sharing between Somali Bantu and Bhutanese CAB members in order to enable identification of common strengths and challenges faced by both refugee groups.

The CBPR team of study investigators, refugee RAs, CHWs, and supervisors meet weekly to discuss study processes, CAB feedback, and implementation issues. We developed the *FSI-R Manual,* a succinct and easy-to-use guide with a clear structure that describes the purpose, principles, and implementation of each module and contains detailed delivery instructions to support intervention fidelity by CHWs.

In terms of project dissemination, as discussed earlier, our CABs, RAs, FSI-R CHWs, and agency partners will play key roles in the core implementation activities: recruitment, data collection, and intervention delivery. Somali Bantu and Bhutanese RAs will collect participant data and analyze it under the supervision of academic partners. CABs will review findings and advise on barriers to and facilitators for sustaining the intervention. We will invite all CHWs to participate in key-informant interviews by our trained RAs as part of the FSI-R process evaluation. We will share de-identified data on core barriers and facilitators with CAB meetings and group CHW supervision meetings to problem-solve and refine the FSI-R model and supporting materials for future use. RAs and CAB members will review study results on the effectiveness of the FSI-R in improving parent-child relationships, reducing risk of child mental-health problems, and improving school and social functioning.

In terms of project sustainability, we have designed the CBPR collaboration so that service partners can integrate and sustain the FSI-R as a part of their package of services and share their experiences with other agencies. The FSI-R delivery model is sustainable under provisions of the Affordable Care Act (ACA) and state-level investments in the CHW workforce. Understanding the potential sustainability of the FSI-R model has become increasingly urgent given the political climate influencing refugee resettlement since changes in the current US administration. In particular, President Trump's executive orders on refugees have added additional stress and unease on top of refugees' past traumatic experiences. Many refugees now fear that resettlement may not be a permanent solution and could be undone by the actions of the current administration. Our community partners have reported that the refugee community members are postponing travel plans to see family abroad because they fear not being allowed to reenter the United States or facing false arrest or persecution. Although there are important collaborations between refugee resettlement agencies and community health centers in places like Boston, Springfield, and Chelsea, the support system was already limited and is now being undercut. Refugee resettlement agencies have started to reduce staff due to lowered refugee resettlement numbers and subsequent funding cuts. As a result, there is a great burden on service providers, who are under pressure to close cases due to lack of funding. Our community partners now fear that health disparities are at risk of ballooning among resettled refugees as access to health care providers, social workers, and community support systems is diminishing. In addition, acts of Islamophobia and abject attacks on refugee and migrant populations by ill-informed citizens have spread widely across news and social media venues, further contributing to an environment of fear, pain, and confusion for many resettled refugee families.

Despite these external policy and societal challenges, the value of partnerships among community organizations, refugee stakeholders, and academic institutions could not be more important. Through our work together, we have developed a strong collaborative partnership for this research project. It is our hope that with such commitment, we will be able to work in partnership to address the emerging needs of refugee children and families while simultaneously enabling our community leaders to gain new skills to carry out a shared vision.

TABLE 6.3 Somali Bantu and Bhutanese problems and protective resources

	Youth N (percent)	Adult N (percent)	Total N (percent)
Somali Bantu			
Problem			
Financial problems	10 (50)	11 (55)	21 (53)
Kids losing their religious education; no Madrassa	10 (50)	6 (30)	16 (40)
Trouble with homework	7 (35)	9 (45)	16 (40)
Language difficulties for parents	8 (40)	6 (30)	14 (35)
Problems with housing	7 (35)	7 (35)	14 (35)
Children do not listen to parents, have bad friends	10 (50)	4 (20)	14 (35)
School work difficult; worried will not graduate	5 (25)	7 (35)	12 (30)
Need a job; lack of jobs; do not know how to get a job	5 (25)	5 (25)	10 (25)
Language difficulties for children	4 (20)	6 (30)	10 (25)
Young and old need education/no place to study	1 (5)	8 (40)	9 (23)
No one to watch kids/taking care of children	2 (10)	7 (35)	9 (23)
Protective Resources			
Somali Bantu community organization/other local community organizations	6 (30)	10 (50)	16 (40)
Maay Maay translators	5 (25)	10 (50)	15 (38)
Somali Bantu community support and strength	9 (45)	4 (20)	13 (33)
Teachers/school counselor/principal and parents working together	5 (25)	5 (25)	10 (25)
Friends	1 (5)	9 (45)	10 (25)
Call others in the community with good English skills to translate and help with paperwork	7 (35)	2 (10)	9 (23)
Government benefits/welfare/food stamps/housing subsidies	2 (10)	6 (30)	8 (20)
Hospitals/doctors	3 (15)	4 (20)	7 (18)
After-school tutors and programs to help with homework/ help children learn English	6 (30)	1 (5)	7 (18)
Talk to parents about what is happening and get help	5 (25)	2 (10)	7 (18)
Bhutanese			
Problem			
Language difficulties	15 (75)	20 (91)	35 (83)
Financial problems	6 (30)	10 (45)	16 (38)
Distance to school/no school bus	6 (30)	5 (23)	11 (26)
Difficulty with homework	6 (30)	4 (18)	10 (24)
Bullying/teasing	8 (40)	2 (9)	10 (24)
Lack of friends	3 (15)	6 (27)	9 (21)
Fighting	5 (25)	3 (14)	8 (19)
Loneliness	3 (15)	5 (23)	8 (19)
Fear/Scared	5 (25)	2 (9)	7 (17)
Depressed/Sad	3 (15)	4 (18)	7 (17)

(continued)

TABLE 6.3 *(continued)*

	Youth N (percent)	Adult N (percent)	Total N (percent)
Protective Resources			
Bhutanese community members	9 (45)	10 (45)	19 (45)
Government and resettlement agencies	13 (65)	4 (18)	17 (40)
Parents/family—advise children, help with school work	8 (40)	7 (32)	15 (36)
Refugee/immigrant service organizations	5 (23)	9 (41)	14 (33)
Relatives—financial help/help with homework/mediate conflicts	9 (45)	2 (9)	11 (26)
Friends—play with friends/share problems/help with homework	8 (40)	3 (14)	11 (26)
Teachers—help with studies/language/resolve fights/ encourage	4 (20)	5 (23)	9 (21)
Neighbors—help with homework/financial/give advice	4 (20)	3 (14)	7 (17)
Interpreters	—	5 (23)	5 (12)
Local hospital	4 (20	—	4 (10)

REFERENCES

Barenbaum, Joshua, Vladislav Ruchkin, and Mary Schwab-Stone. 2004. "The Psychological Aspects of Children Exposed to War: Practice and Policy Initiatives." *Journal of Child Psychology and Psychiatry* 45 (1): 41–62.

Beardslee, William R. 1998. "Prevention and the Clinical Encounter." *American Journal of Orthopsychiatry* 68 (4): 521–33.

Beardslee, William R., and Tracy R. G. Gladstone. 2001. "Prevention of Childhood Depression: Recent Findings and Future Prospects." *Biological Psychiatry* 49 (12): 1101–10.

Beardslee, William R., Tracy R. G. Gladstone, Ellen J. Wright, and Andrew B. Cooper. 2003. "A Family-Based Approach to the Prevention of Depressive Symptoms in Children at Risk: Evidence of Parental and Child Change." *Pediatrics* 112 (2): e119–31.

Beardslee, William R., Ellen J. Wright, Tracy R. G. Gladstone, and Peter Forbes. 2007. "Long-Term Effects from a Randomized Trial of Two Public Health Preventive Interventions for Parental Depression." *Journal of Family Psychology* 21 (4): 703–13.

Beardslee, William R., Ellen J. Wright, Patricia Salt, Karen Drezner, Tracy R. G. Gladstone, Eve M. Versage, and Phyllis C. Rothberg. 1997. "Examination of Children's Responses to Two Preventive Intervention Strategies over Time." *Journal of the American Academy of Child and Adolescent Psychiatry* 36 (2): 196–204.

Besteman, Catherine. 2012. "Translating Race across Time and Space: The Creation of Somali Bantu Ethnicity." *Identities* 19: 285–302.

Betancourt, Theresa S., Rochelle Frounfelker, Tej Mishra, Aweis Hussein, and Rita Falzarano. 2015. "Addressing Health Disparities in the Mental Health of Refugee Children and Adolescents through Community-Based Participatory Research: A Study in Two Communities." Supplement, *American Journal of Public Health* 105 (S3): S475–82.

Betancourt, Theresa S. , Lauren C. Ng, Catherine M. Kirk, Morris Munyanah, Christina Mushashi, Charles Ingabire, Sharon Teta, William R. Beardslee, Robert T. Brennan, Ista Zahn, Sara Stulac, Felix R. Cyamatare, Vincent Sezibera. 2014. "Family-Based Prevention of Mental Health Problems in Children Affected by HIV and AIDS: An Open Trial." Suppplement, *AIDS* 28 (3): S359–68.

Betancourt, Theresa S., Liesbeth Speelman, George Onyango, and Paul Bolton. 2009. "A Qualitative Study of Mental Health Problems among Children Displaced by War in Northern Uganda." *Journal of Transcultural Psychiatry* 46 (2): 238–56.

Bloom, Bernard. 1982. "Epilogue." In *New Directions in Prevention among American Indian and Alaska Native Communities,* edited by Spero M. Manson. Portland: Oregon Health Sciences University.

Bronfenbrenner, Urie. 1979. *The Ecology of Human Development: Experiments by Nature and Design.* Cambridge, MA: Harvard University Press.

Bronstein, Israel, and Paul Montgomery. 2011. "Psychological Distress in Refugee Children: A Systematic Review." *Clinical Child Family Psychology Review* 14 (1): 44–56.

CDC (Centers for Disease Control and Prevention). 2013. "Suicide and Suicidal Ideation among Bhutanese Refugees—United States, 2009–2012." *Morbidity and Mortality Weekly Report* 62 (26): 533–36.

Cornwall, Andrea, and Rachel Jewkes. 1995. "What Is Participatory Research?" *Social Science and Medicine* 41 (12): 1667–76.

Creswell, John W. 2014. *A Concise Introduction to Mixed Methods Research.* Thousand Oaks, CA: SAGE.

Creswell, John W., Ann C. Klassen, Vicki L. Plano Clark, and Katherine C. Smith. 2011. *Best Practices for Mixed Methods Research in the Health Sciences.* Bethesda, MD: National Institutes of Health.

Curran, Geoffrey M., Mark Bauer, Brian Mittman, Jeffrey M. Pyne, and Cheryl Stetler. 2012. "Effectiveness-Implementation Hybrid Designs: Combining Elements of Clinical Effectiveness and Implementation Research to Enhance Public Health Impact." *Medical Care* 50 (3): 217–26.

Derluyn, Ilse, Cindy Mels, and Eric Broekaert. 2009. "Mental Health Problems in Separated Refugee Adolescents." *Journal of Adolescent Health* 44 (3): 291–97.

Ellis, B. Heidi, Helen Z. MacDonald, Julie Klunk-Gillis, Alisa K. Lincoln, Lee Strunin, and Howard J. Cabral. 2010. "Discrimination and Mental Health among Somali Refugee Adolescents: The Role of Acculturation and Gender." *American Journal of Orthopsychiatry* 80 (4): 564–75.

Ellis, B. Heidi, Helen Z. MacDonald, Alisa K. Lincoln, and Howard J. Cabral. 2008. "Mental Health of Somali Adolescent Refugees: The Role of Trauma, Stress, and Perceived Discrimination." *Journal of Consulting and Clinical Psychology* 76 (2): 184–93.

Ellis, B. Heidi, Audrey Rubin, Theresa S. Betancourt, and Glenn Saxe. 2006. "Mental Health Interventions for Children Affected by War or Terrorism." In *Violence and Children's Mental Health,* edited by Margaret M. Feerick, 159–87. Baltimore: Brookes.

Fazel, Mina, and Alan Stein. 2002. "The Mental Health of Refugee Children." *Archives of Disease in Childhood* 87: 366–70.

Geltman, Paul L., Wanda Grant-Knight, Supriya D. Mehta, Christine Lloyd-Travaglini, Stuart Lustig, Jeanne M. Landgraf, and Paul H. Wise. 2005. "The 'Lost Boys of Sudan': Functional and Behavioral Health of Unaccompanied Refugee Minors Re-Settled in the United States." *Archives of Pediatric and Adolescent Medicine* 159 (6): 585–91.

Gersons, Berthold P. R., and Miranda Olff. 2005. "Coping with the Aftermath of Trauma." *British Medical Journal* 330: 1038–39.

Gold, Steven J. "Mental Health and Illness in Vietnamese Refugees." 1992. *Western Journal of Medicine* 157 (3): 290–94.

Hutt, Michael. 1996. "Ethnic Nationalism, Refugees, and Bhutan." *Journal of Refugee Studies* 9 (4): 397–419.

IOM (International Organization for Migration). 2008. *Cultural Profile: The Bhutanese Refugees in Nepal: A Tool for Settlement Workers and Sponsors*. Damak, Nepal. www.mnchurches.org/refugee/healing/wp-content/uploads/Microsoft-Word-IOM-Bhutanese-Cultural-Profile-2008.pdf.

Institute of Medicine, Committee on Prevention of Mental Disorders. 1994. *Reducing Risks for Mental Disorders: Frontiers for Preventive Intervention Research*, edited by Robert J. Haggerty and Patricia J. Mrazek. Washington, DC: National Academy Press.

Israel, Barbara A., Edith A. Parker, Zachary Rowe, Alicia Salvatore, Meredith Minkler, Jesus Lopez, Arlene Butz, Adrian Mosley, Lucretia Coats, George Lambert, Paul A. Potito, Barbara Brenner, Maribel Rivera, Harry Romero, Beti Thompson, Gloria Coronady, and Sandy Halstead. 2005. "Community-Based Participatory Research: Lessons Learned from the Centers for Children's Environmental Health and Disease Prevention Research." *Environmental Health Perspectives* 113 (10): 1463–71.

Israel, Barbara A., Amy J. Schulz, Edith A. Parker, and Adam B. Becker. 1998. "Review of Community-Based Research: Assessing Partnership Approaches to Improve Public Health." *Annual Review of Public Health* 19: 173–202.

Kilpatrick, Dean G., Kenneth J. Ruggiero, Ron Acierno, Benjamin E. Saunders, Heidi S. Resnick, and Connie L. Best. 2003. "Violence and Risk of PTSD, Major Depression, Substance Abuse/Dependence, and Comorbidity: Results from the National Survey of Adolescents." *Journal of Consulting and Clinical Psychology* 71 (4): 692–700.

Kleinman, Arthur, Leon Eisenberg, and Byron Good. 1978. "Culture, Illness, and Care: Clinical Lessons from Anthropologic and Cross-Cultural Research." *Annals of Internal Medicine* 88 (2): 251–58.

Laverack, Glenn, and Nina Wallerstein. 2001. "Measuring Community Empowerment: A Fresh Look at Organizational Domains." *Health Promotion International* 16 (2): 179–85.

Lazarus, Richard S., and Susan Folkman. 1984. *Stress, Appraisal and Coping*. New York: Springer.

Lehman, Dan V., and Omar Eno. 2003 *The Somali Bantu: Their History and Culture*. Culture Profile. Washington, DC: Center for Applied Linguistics.

Leung, Margaret W., Irene H. Yen, and Meredith Minkler. 2004. "Community-Based Participatory Research: A Promising Approach for Increasing Epidemiology's Relevance in the Twenty-First Century." *International Journal of Epidemiology* 33 (3): 499–506.

Llenera-Quinn, Roxana, Rachel L. Shapiro, Melinda Bravo, Ane M. Lora, Eugene J. D'Angelo, and William Beardslee. 2006. *Adapted Manual for the Prevention of Depres-*

sion in Families Program, for Use with Latino Families. Boston: Children's Hospital–Boston.

Lustig, Stuart L., Maryam Kia-Keating, Wanda G. Knight, Paul Geltman, Heidi Ellis, J. David Kinzie, Terence Keane, and Glenn N. Saxe. 2004. "Review of Child and Adolescent Refugee Mental Health." *Journal of the American Academy of Child and Adolescent Psychiatry* 43 (1): 24–36.

Luthar, Suniya S., and Pamela J. Brown. 2007. "Maximizing Resilience through Diverse Levels of Inquiry: Prevailing Paradigms, Possibilities, and Priorities for the Future." *Development and Psychopatholgy* 19 (3): 931–55.

Luthar, Suniya S., Dante Cicchetti, and Bronwyn Becker. 2000. "The Construct of Resilience: A Critical Evaluation and Guidelines for Future Work." *Child Development* 71 (3): 543–62.

Massachusetts Department of Public Health. 2016. *Refugee Arrivals in Massachusetts by Country of Origin,* edited by the Division of Global Populations and Infectious Disease Prevention, Bureau of Infectious Disease and Laboratory Sciences. www.mass.gov /eohhs/gov/departments/dph/programs/id/public-health-cdc-refugee-arrivals.html.

Menkhaus, Ken. 2003. "Bantu Ethnic Identities in Somalia." *Annales d'Ethiopie* 19: 323–39.

Merikangas, Kathleen R., Jian-ping He, Marcy Burstein, Sonja A. Swanson, Shelli Avenevoli, Lihong Cui, Corina Benjet, Katholiki Georgiades, and Joel Swendsen. 2010. "Lifetime Prevalence of Mental Disorders in US Adolescents: Results from the National Comorbidity Survey Replication–Adolescent Supplement (NCS-A)." *Journal of the American Academy of Child and Adolescent Psychiatry* 49 (10): 980–89.

Minkler, Meredith. 2010. "Linking Science and Policy through Community-Based Participatory Research to Study and Address Health Disparities." *American Journal of Public Health* Supplement 100 (S1): S81–87.

Muecke, Marjorie A. 1983. "Caring for Southeast Asian Refugee Patients in the USA." *American Journal of Public Health* 73 (4): 431–38.

O'Connell, Mary E., Thomas Boat, and Kenneth E. Warner. 2009. *Preventing Mental, Emotional, and Behavioral Disorders among Young People: Progress and Possibilities.* Washington, DC: National Academy Press.

Podorefsky, Donna L., Marjorie McDonald-Dowdell, and William R. Beardslee. 2001. "Adaptation of Preventive Interventions for a Low-Income, Culturally Diverse Community." *Journal of the American Academy of Child and Adolescent Psychiatry* 40 (8): 879–86.

Renzaho, André M. N., Julie Green, David Mellor, and Boyd Swinburn. 2011. "Parenting, Family Functioning, and Lifestyle in a New Culture: The Case of African Migrants in Melbourne, Victoria, Australia." *Child and Family Social Work* 16 (2): 228–40.

Saadi, Altaf, Barbara E. Bond, and Sanja Percac-Lima. 2015. "Bosnian, Iraqi, and Somali Refugee Women Speak: A Comparative Qualitative Study of Refugee Health Beliefs on Preventive Health and Breast Cancer Screening." *Women's Health Issues* 25 (5): 501–08.

Sabin, Miriam, Barbara Lopes Cardozo, Larry Nackerud, Richard Kaiser, and Luis Varese. 2003. "Factors Associated with Poor Mental Health among Guatemalan Refugees Living in Mexico Twenty Years after Civil Conflict." *Journal of the American Medical Association* 290 (5): 635–42.

Sack, William H., Chanrithy Him, and Dan Dickason. 1999. "Twelve-Year Follow-Up Study of Khmer Youths Who Suffered Massive War Trauma as Children." *Journal of the American Academy of Child and Adolescent Psychiatry* 38 (9): 1173–79.

Scuglik, Deborah L., and Renato D. Alarcon. 2005. "Growing Up Whole: Somali Children and Adolescents in America." *Psychiatry (Edgmont)* 2 (8): 20–31.

Simmelink, Jennifer, Elizabeth Lightfoot, Amano Dube, Jennifer Blevins, and Terry Lum. 2013. "Understanding the Health Beliefs and Practices of East African Refugees." *American Journal of Health Behavior* 37 (2): 155–61.

Toole, Michael J., and Ronald J. Waldman. 1993. "Refugees and Displaced Persons: War, Hunger, and Public Health." *JAMA* 270 (5): 600–05.

Ungar, Michael. 2011. "The Social Ecology of Resilience: Addressing Contextual and Cultural Ambiguity of a Nascent Construct." *American Journal of Orthopsychiatry* 81 (1): 1–17.

United Nations. Sustainable Development Solutions Network. 2012. *World Happiness Report,* edited by John Helliwell, Richard Layard, and Jeffrey Sachs. New York: Earth Institute, Columbia University.

US Department of State. 2017. *Historical Arrivals Broken Down by Region (1975–Present),* edited by the Refugee Processing Center. www.wrapsnet.org/admissions-and-arrivals/.

Wallerstein, Nina B., and Bonnie Duran. 2006. "Using Community-Based Participatory Research to Address Health Disparities." *Health Promotion Practice* 7 (3): 312–23.

Williams, Carolyn L., and John W. Berry. 1991. "Primary Prevention of Acculturative Stress among Refugees: Application of Psychological Theory and Practice." *American Psychologist* 46 (6): 632–41.

Williams, Meagan E., and Sandra C. Thompson. 2011. "The Use of Community-Based Interventions in Reducing Morbidity from the Psychological Impact of Conflict-Related Trauma among Refugee Populations: A Systematic Review of the Literature." *Journal of Immigrant and Minority Health* 13 (4): 780–94.

Ziaian, Tahereh, Helena de Anstiss, Georgia Antoniou, Peter Baghurst, and Michael Sawyer. 2012. "Resilience and Its Association with Depression, Emotional and Behavioral Problems, and Mental Health Service Utilization among Refugee Adolescents Living in South Australia." *International Journal of Population Research.* doi:10.1155/2012/485956.

SURVEYING THE HARD-TO-SURVEY

Refugees and Unaccompanied Minors in Greece

Theoni Stathopoulou

The unprecedented migration flows that Europe has witnessed since the spring of 2015 have become the focus of intense public debate and concern, fueling social and political tensions across European Union (EU) member-states and beyond. During 2015, it is estimated that 856,000 people arrived in Greece (IOM 2016a), a figure indicating that recent migration flows constitute one of the biggest population movements in recent European history.

The EU–Turkey agreement established in March 2016 led to the entrapment of more than sixty thousand refugees, among them a considerable number of unaccompanied minors, within the borders of Greece. Since then, Greece has stopped being a transit country and has become a country of stranded asylum-seekers faced with an extremely long and complicated asylum procedure.

The huge influx of migrants and refugees who entered before the closing of national borders along the migratory corridor has left Greek authorities faced with unprecedented challenges in a context of deep recession, corroded social infrastructure, and limited administrative capacity due to the prolonged economic and social crisis. Additionally, the rise of the radical Right across Greece and the rest of Europe has further complicated the efforts to manage the situation. The question of who is defined as a refugee, and therefore who is entitled to apply for asylum, has become a major political issue.

According to Greek law,

a person seeking international protection is any foreign national or stateless person who declares to any Greek authority, orally or in writing, that he or she is seeking asylum or requests not to be deported because he or she is in fear of persecution because of his or her race, religion, nationality, participation in a particular social group or . . . political beliefs or because he or she is in danger of suffering serious harm in his or her country of origin or country of previous residence, especially because he or she is in danger of facing the death penalty or execution, torture or inhuman or degrading treatment or his or her life or person is in danger because of an international or civil war. (Asylum Service 2017a)

Greece had one of the largest shares in the number of first-time asylum applications in Europe in 2016, four times as high as in 2015, receiving more than four thousand applications per month during 2016 (Eurostat 2017; Asylum Service 2017a). The total number of asylum applications within the EU-28 in 2015 and 2016 (1.3 million) was approximately double the number recorded within the EU-15 during the previous relative peak of 1992 due to the number of applicants from the former Yugoslavia (Eurostat 2017).

Today's mixed migration flows include migrants and trafficked persons who need protection similar to that sought by asylum-seekers and refugees. The massive proportions of people who have embarked on the dangerous journey to Greece have arrived mainly through its sea borders.

According to the International Organization for Migration (IOM 2016b), the cumulative data for arrivals by sea to Greece and Italy recorded 352,471 arrivals in 2016 and 1,011,712 arrivals in 2015, respectively. By the end of 2016, a total of 4,733 others had been reported dead or missing.

Prior to the peak of October 2015, there was an increase of 1,075.3 percent in arrivals by sea to Greece between 2014 and 2015, the top nationalities being those from Syria, Afghanistan, Iraq, and Pakistan (IOM 2016c, UNHCR 2016b). The picture changed after the EU–Turkey agreement, when there was a sharp decrease in arrivals to Greece and an increase in arrivals to Italy of various nationalities from Africa, mostly Nigerians and Eritreans (IOM 2016a).

However, the attempts, in some cases fatal, to reach Europe by sea or land have never stopped. From January to February 2017, 3,037 detected illegal border crossings were reported by Frontex (2017), the top nationalities being from Syria, Pakistan, and Algeria.

For most international, national, and nongovernmental organization (NGO) agencies dealing on the ground with the humanitarian crisis in Greece after the closing down of the Balkan route, the crisis "was neither unexpected nor unpreventable" (Amnesty International 2016, 12). Yet the burden of its management was unequally distributed between Greece and the rest of the European countries.

As UN special rapporteur on the human rights of migrants François Crépeau has stated, "Presenting the current situation as a humanitarian crisis only demonstrates short-sightedness. The real crisis in Europe resides in the lack of political will, resulting from the absence of a common political vision, as to how migration and mobility are part of Europe's present and future" (IRC, NRC, and Oxfam 2017).

The political deficit in the effective handling of the crisis was most apparent in the relocation emergency plan for 160,000 asylum seekers that was provisioned in September 2015 by the European Council to relieve Greece and Italy. A year after the plan was announced, only 11 percent of asylum seekers had been relocated from Greece (UNHCR 2017, 3, UNHCR 2016a). As of March 2017, 26,997 relocation applications had been registered by the Greek Asylum Service, of which 18,241 had been accepted (Asylum Service 2017b). Similarly, the narrative of the "Mediterranean crisis" or "refugee crisis in the Greek islands" obscures the global dimensions of the recent migratory phenomenon.

Greece, traditionally a migrant-sending country, was transformed into a migrant host country during the 1990s after the collapse of former socialist regimes. Massive inflows of migrants, mainly from Central and Eastern Europe, accounted for 75 percent of the foreign population, according to the 2001 census (Cavounidis-Springer 2016). The presence of migrants soon became a topic of public dispute (Stathopoulou 2009) and political exploitation. The rise and parliamentary consolidation of the radical Right party in Greece during the economic crisis was based on an anti-immigrant and anti-tolerance discourse (Stathopoulou and Kostaki 2014; Stathopoulou and Papageorgiou 2016).

ADDRESSING THE NEED TO SURVEY PEOPLE ON THE MOVE: THE REHEAL PROJECT

People on the move are hard to locate and hard to survey. As Tourangeau et al. (2014) point out, "Some segments of the population are hard to sample, some are hard to find, others are hard to persuade to participate in surveys, and still others are hard to interview." The ability to interview this population can add to knowledge about what displaced people themselves think and feel and can sometimes inform policy actors about suitable policies.

The Refugees' Healing (REHEAL)[1] was the first survey to be conducted in the refugee camps in Greece by the National Center of Social Research (EKKE) in Athens. The main goal of the survey was to record refugees' perceptions of living conditions in Greece as well as the self-reported health status, health-care needs, discrimination, and traumatic experiences of the refugee population residing in the camps.

METHODOLOGICAL AND ETHICAL CHALLENGES

The design of the survey had to take into account the dynamic nature of the targeted population (people moving from camp to camp) since refugees are mainly an elusive population. The *survey population* was defined as men and women, designated as refugees and staying at refugee camps across Greece, with the ability to understand one of the following languages: English, Arabic, and Farsi.

Time–location sampling, the use of a specific location to conduct interviews at a specific point of time, was established as the sampling frame (Tourangeau 2014). The designed sample comprised sixty interviews per camp in six camps across Greece: Eleonas, Schisto, and Skaramagas in Attica; Diavata and Veria in Central Macedonia; and Samos camp on the island of Samos in the northeastern Aegean. The achieved sample was 367 respondents.

An interview step of three was used for sample selection. According to this design, after every third lodging in the camp hosting a family, a single person from the family was approached and asked to fill out the questionnaire. The mode of data collection was through the administration of self-completed questionnaires, a choice that, according to literature, facilitates interview privacy in crowded shelters or camps and addresses the difficulties of surveying in emergency situations (Mneimneh et al. 2014, 147).

Although disaster research has shown that traumatized people are willing to be interviewed and that speaking to others can be therapeutic (Brodie et al. 2014, 174), ethical concerns about the vulnerability of the respondents and their potential stress or misunderstanding about the scope of the research are always present (Block et al. 2013; Pennell et al. 2014; Betancourt et al. 2016).

QUESTIONNAIRE DEVELOPMENT

Some of the most significant methodological challenges are to design a culturally informed questionnaire (Harkness et al. 2014; Pennell et al. 2014; Hollifield et al. 2016) and to have the tools and knowledge to adapt it. As Derek Summerfield notes (2005, 104), "One problem is that the cultural worlds in which people are immersed can differ so dramatically that translation of emotional terms needs more than merely finding semantic equivalents." The barriers of language and culture had to be taken into account all the way through the completion of the survey. For example, the coding and quality checks of the questionnaires were made with the help of trained interpreters.[2]

The REHEAL questionnaire was designed in collaboration with the team of Professor T. A. Eikemo at the Norwegian University of Science and Technology (NTNU), and it was translated from English into Arabic and Farsi under the supervision of the EKKE team. It comprised five sections:

· Sociodemographics;
· Staying in another country after leaving your home;
· Arriving in Greece (feelings of safety, living conditions);

- Health issues (health problems before and after fleeing the homeland, Harvard Program in Refugee Trauma questionnaire, sixteen items); and
- Social media usage.

DATA COLLECTION

After the camp residents were registered, self-completed questionnaires were administered, applying the designed interview step. With the assistance of Arabic and Farsi interpreters, the researchers explained the purpose of the survey and gave instructions on how to complete the questionnaires. After half an hour the subjects were revisited, and the questionnaires were collected. In several cases, the respondents asked for clarification or extra time. A second and final visit was made to pick up the remaining questionnaires. There were very few refusals, despite some residents' initial reservations.

CONSTRAINTS

One of the main constraints researchers faced during the preparation of fieldwork was the need to obtain official permission from the Ministry of Interior, General Secretariat for Migration Policy, to enter the camps. The situation in the camps during the summer of 2016 was still very complicated, and the permission was hard to obtain. Camps were overcrowded, and people were trying to organize their daily lives without knowing the actual length of time that they would spend in the place where they were being accommodated. As Greece was not their intended destination, they were very anxious about their relocation, a fact that increased their emotional distress and caused frequent tensions among them.[3]

Another major constraint was that the field operations coincided with the pre-registration exercise, which was launched on June 8, 2016, by the Greek Asylum Service and implemented with the help of the UN Refugee Agency (UNHCR) and the European Asylum Support Office (EASO). Through this large-scale operation, thousands of people were provided with asylum-seeker cards, which allowed them to reside legally in Greece and access health and education services (Asylum Service 2017a).[4] The operation lasted from September 1 to 9, 2016, at most camps; due to this timeframe, the availability of interpreters was extremely limited. In addition, the start of fieldwork originally scheduled for June was postponed due to Ramadan, which was also occurring during the same time period. The wide ethnic variety of the population in the camps also created difficulties during fieldwork. People with different cultural backgrounds and religions or who belonged to ethnic minorities within larger ethnic groups (e.g., various ethnic groups from Afghanistan) had to live together under confining conditions.

INSIGHTS FROM THE FIELD

One of the most valuable sources of information in every survey is the recording of observations during fieldwork. These observations, known as *paradata,* can improve the analytic capacity of the researchers and adjust survey errors (Kreuter 2013). In REHEAL, detailed accounts were recorded in every camp for each day of a visit so as to comprehend the survey setting and responses given.

Fieldwork was impacted by burdensome bureaucratic procedures and an extremely tight time schedule due to the terms of the permission given by the ministry and the availability of interpreters.[5] In some cases the conditions on the ground were difficult, and in certain camps, like Diavata in Northern Greece, the residents were initially reluctant to participate.[6]

The camps visited were overpopulated, with inadequate infrastructure (a poor drainage and sewage system), especially where tents prevailed. Most of the time the camps were situated in a "no-man's land," far from cities and far from shops and local markets, with poor transportation facilities. People stood in long lines waiting for almost everything. The main problem was the lack of privacy, especially for women and children, who did not have a separate space to sleep. Incidents of sexual harassment had also been reported, raising safety concerns.

Shade, vegetation, and common areas were scarce, and the camps had very few playgrounds and sports facilities and lacked activities for adults in general. Consequently, the refugees wandered idly most of the day. Although in each camp there were interpreters available at all times, there were still problems in communication. Despite these shortcomings, the level of medical care and assistance was satisfactory, and needs for food and water were covered. There was a heavy presence of nongovernmental organizations (NGOs) and international humanitarian agencies facilitating everyday life in the camps and organizing various activities for children. The housing conditions were significantly improved from those of the first months of the encampment.

AN OVERVIEW OF THE VISITED CAMPS[7]

Eleonas Camp, Athens (Attica)

Population size as of the date of fieldwork: 2,415 people[8]
Population profile: Families and young males from Syria, Afghanistan, and other countries (Iran, Mali, Senegal, Ethiopia)

Eleonas was the first refugee camp organized in the region of the Attiki, the metropolitan area of Athens. It started receiving refugees in early August 2015. It is located in the midst of the old industrial district of inner-city Athens among factories, warehouses, and transportation companies in an area that appears crowded and noisy during the day but rather deserted at night. A regular bus line connects the camp with the city center.

The camp was built on an open plot that belongs to the Municipality of Athens and had no preexisting infrastructure. It consists of three different sectors that were successively established, two under the auspices of the First Reception Agency (Ministry of Home Affairs) and one run by the Greek army. All sectors have rows of shipping-container living spaces, each with two rooms, one toilet, and two basic kitchenettes. They are supplied with electricity and running water.

The common infrastructure consists of two Rub Hall tents and an outdoor reception space next to the main entrance. During the summer, many residents had to spend most of the day in their air-conditioned containers as there were no common facilities offering protection from high temperatures. Moreover, all common facilities (except for a makeshift volleyball court) and all NGOs are concentrated in the first sector. The camp is walled all along its boundary, while sector 3 is separated from the other two with iron panels. During the time of our visit, one of the walls was removed, possibly by some of the residents to enable internal communication. Security is provided by the police, who operate at the entrances of the camp.

Diavata Camp, Thessaloniki (Central Macedonia)

Population size as of the date of fieldwork: 1,089 people
Population profile: Families from Syria and Afghanistan

Diavata is an old army camp in the industrial area of Thessaloniki. Some of the buildings are in good condition, but these are used for administration and some common purposes (NGO offices, warehouses, and a library run by two residents) while UNHCR tents and prefabricated shelters are used for accommodation. The area is connected to the city by bus, but many residents have to walk a long distance on a dangerous country road to the nearest village due to the infrequent service.

Living conditions in the tents, which had been used for more than six months, were only worsened by the poor common infrastructure (public chemical toilets, few public taps, no kitchen facilities). Residents complained about these conditions and about the quality of the food distributed. Many used makeshift kitchens to prepare their meals, using wood or paper that they collected from the surrounding area as fuel.

Alongside a dense network of NGOs providing various services, traces of a self-help community organization were also evident as well as makeshift outdoor family "rooms," which appeared to be necessary in order to fight the unbearable heat in the tents, and the informal groceries that sold basic goods for everyday cooking and candy for the children.

Veria Camp, Central Macedonia

Population size as of the date of fieldwork: 334 people
Population profile: Families from Syria

Veria is an old army camp about ten kilometers from the city of Veria and three kilometers from the closest village. It is situated in the forest next to the Aliakmon River. The buildings in general are in good condition. The refugees live in quarters similar to those previously described in other camps or in other buildings that are furnished with beds. Families live together, and there have been efforts to ensure privacy. However, sometimes the privacy is achieved by the residents themselves by using blankets and other material. There is plenty of space for outdoor activities. There is also a room for indoor activities close to the administration building. At the time of our visit, it was being used by the doctors of an international NGO. The camp is not connected to the village or the city by regular means of transportation. The main entrance is guarded by the police and army, and it is located rather far from the central residential area of the camp.

Schisto Camp, Attica

Population size as of the date of fieldwork: 950 people
Population profile: Families and young males from Afghanistan

Schisto is a former military camp located in the sparsely populated industrial district on the west side of Piraeus, the largest port of Greece. It is connected to the city center by bus. The refugees live in several types of shelters: UNHCR tents for families, three Rub Hall tents that have been transformed into dormitories, and three preexisting buildings.

Some temporary structures made of wood and synthetic fabric and rough ditches are provided by NGOs to protect residents from the sun and rainfall, respectively. A long plastic cover has been put on the fence to block the view from the outside. The residents themselves have constructed makeshift rooms in front of their tents to increase their living spaces. There is a significant presence of both police officers and army personnel. However, checks at the entrance are quite loose, and refugees from other camps and places of accommodation are allowed to enter, especially for food distribution.

Samos Camp, Northeastern Aegean
Population size as of the date of fieldwork: 500 people

The living arrangements in this camp vary: the majority of refugees live in containers accommodating eight people (usually two families together), in which the conditions are acceptable. However, other refugees live in larger old containers that usually house up to seven families together, with no privacy at all. At the time of our visit, one of these older containers lay empty and destroyed, having been burned during the camp riots that had erupted in June 2016. There are also quite a few tents that have been installed right in front of the containers to accommodate people who want to avoid the congestion in the containers or who have not been assigned a place in one. Despite the occasional incidents of lawbreaking by some refugees or aggression directed against them by native groups, in general, the refugees seem to coexist peacefully with the local population and frequently visit the nearby town of Vathy to do their shopping or just wander around, some even rubbing shoulders with tourists on the beaches. The incoming migration flows have been reduced considerably, although during our visit the Coast Guard and Frontex rescued sixty-two people who had been crossing the borders by boat.

Skaramagas Camp, Attica
Population size as of the date of fieldwork: 3,400 people

The living conditions of the majority of the refugees living in the campsite of Skaramagas, which is run by the Greek navy, are quite acceptable, especially for those living in containers, despite the lack of shade and common spaces where refugees can meet (one was being set up during our visit). However, in several places in the camp, one could see still polluted water on the ground that would be an eventual source of contamination. Incidents of aggressive or even violent behavior by certain refugees directed against members of NGOs working in the camp were reported. Overall, the campsite is isolated at the outskirts of Athens, with difficult access to nearby residential areas and in a landscape with no signs of vegetation.

MAIN FINDINGS

The sampled population was distributed as illustrated in table 7.1. The population surveyed in the selected camps was 63 percent male and 37 percent female and in the age group ranging from 25 to 35. The main countries of origin were Syria (50 percent) and Afghanistan (32 percent).

TABLE 7.1 Sample characteristics of population in Greek refugee camps

	%
Distribution of sample population in the camps	
Eleonas (Athens-Attica)	18
Diavata (Central Macedonia)	22
Veria (Central Macedonia)	12
Schisto (Attica)	18
Skaramagas (Attica)	17
Samos (Northeastern Aegean Sea)	13
Country of origin	
Syria	50
Afganistan	32
Iran	7
Iraq	7
Other*	4
Age group	
<18	6
18–24	14
25–35	37
36–45	25
46–55	12
> 56	6
Gender	
Male	63
Female	37

NOTE: The designed sample was sixty interviews per camp (N=360). The achieved sample was 367 respondents.

*Other countries: Kuwait, Lebanon, Guinea, Israel, Turkey.

The majority of respondents were married (78 percent) with children (80 percent); 23.4 percent had completed at least nine years of schooling, and 68 percent were Sunni Muslims. In their countries of origin, 25.6 percent had been unemployed and 33 percent had primarily worked in industry and/or with machinery; 39.5 percent had first left their homes in 2016. The majority had been in Greece for six or seven months; 16% had previously stayed in a third country (Turkey) for between six and twelve months.

Basic needs were covered in the camps. The majority had adequate food, sleeping and personal hygiene facilities, but only 41 percent of the respondents had been examined by a physician after arriving in Greece. A very low percentage (14 percent) of women and children were able to sleep in separate sections from the men.

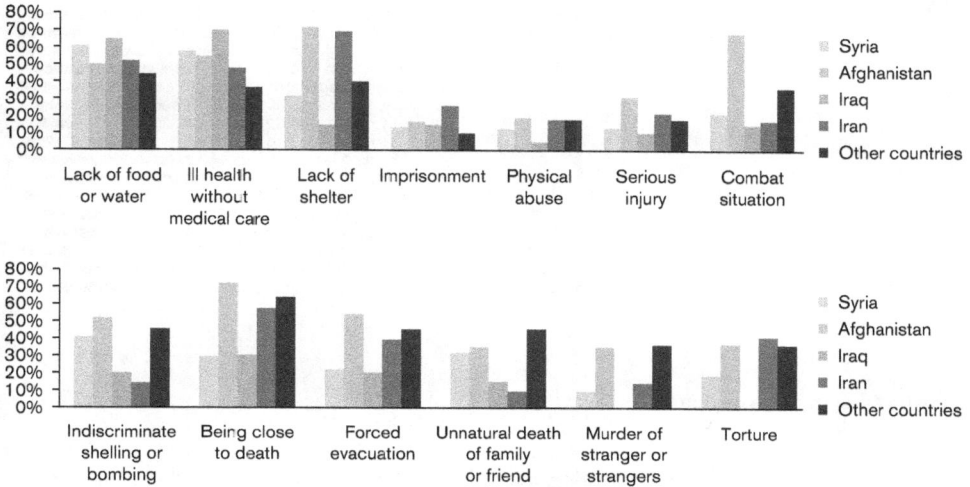

FIGURE 7.1. Traumatic experiences by nationality.

Discrimination is among the predisplacement factors that increase the risk of mental health problems among refugees (Porter and Haslam 2005). The questionnaire included an item on the frequency of discriminative experiences across the different phases of the displacement (before leaving home, while traveling, after arriving in Greece). The data showed that respondents from Iraq and Afghanistan reported being discriminated against all of the time before leaving their home countries. In addition, Afghans had had the most traumatic experiences in comparison with those of other nationalities (see fig. 7.1).

Ill health; lack of food, water, and shelter; and being close to death are the traumatic circumstances that half or more of the population surveyed reported having experienced. Nearly 30 percent of the respondents had witnessed the death of a family member or friend, and 20 percent reported having been tortured. Zachary Steel and colleagues (2009) have found a positive association of torture with mental health disorders across different resettlement settings of the refugee population.

However, traumatic experiences vary substantially according to personal characteristics and culture (Ingleby 2005; Betancourt et al. 2009; Hollifield et al. 2016; Betancourt et al., chapter 6, this volume). As Michael Hollifield and colleagues (2002, 618) have noted, "no empirically developed instruments assess the complete range of trauma experiences in refugees [as] it is difficult to define all relevant events and types of events that influence health status."

To capture the intensity of trauma symptoms, a short sixteen-item version of the forty-item *Harvard Trauma Questionnaire* (HTQ) was included in the respective

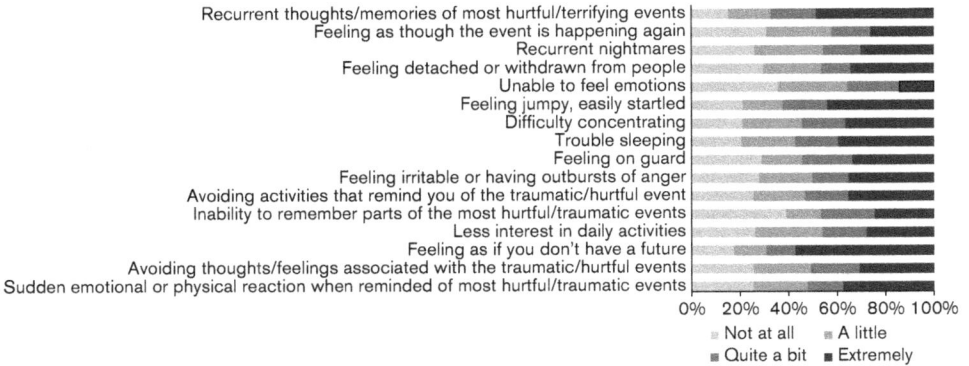

FIGURE 7.2. Trauma symptoms.

section of the REHEAL questionnaire. The initial analysis of the whole data set showed that the item "feeling as if you don't have a future" had the fewest missing values in comparison with the rest. However, figure 7.2 presents the corresponding valid percentages in order to achieve clearer comparisons among the items.

As shown above, more than 60 percent of the respondents were "extremely" bothered by the feeling that they did not have a future. Again, Afghans reported being more desperate about their future than the rest of the nationalities in the sample did.

A good number of refugees rated their health as bad or very bad (37 percent), whereas only 25 percent rated their health as good. As pointed out in the joint policy brief on the situations of displaced persons in Greece (Action Aid 2016, 4), "basic health care services are available to most, but provision of services for more complex conditions is a severe gap, as some have come to Greece with or [have] developed ailments that require care. Similarly, women and children need safe spaces to privately receive care that meets their specific needs."

Questions on social media usage were also included in the survey since mobile phones are the main means of communication among refugees and are also used widely for the facilitation of humanitarian aid. Only a small percentage (17 percent) of the population surveyed had a mobile phone that did not support social media applications. The majority used WhatsApp (26.7 percent) and Facebook (22.3 percent) applications to communicate with relatives in their homelands (55 percent) or in other European countries (52 percent).

REHEAL-UAM: A PILOT SURVEY FOR UNACCOMPANIED MINORS IN GREECE

Refugees' Healing–Unaccompanied Minors (REHEAL-UAM) is a pilot survey for unaccompanied minors in Greece that was conducted alongside the REHEAL survey in collaboration with the Harvard Program in Refugee Trauma. The question-naire was developed by Professor Richard F. Mollica in May 2016 in collaboration with the team from the National Center for Social Research (EKKE) (Greece). The questionnaire has three sections: one on safety and security, one on an adolescent depression scale (Kutcher), and one on child posttraumatic stress disorder (PTSD) (CPSS-V, PTSD). The questionnaire was translated into French and Greek from the original English version.

The interviews were conducted from June 2016 to January 2017 in all shelters for unaccompanied minors (UAM) in Attica (the greater Athens area) that had responded positively to the official request from the National Center for Social Research. Interviews were conducted with the permission of the public prosecutor for the protection of minors in Athens and the responsible authorities in each shelter. At first, the social worker who operated the shelter informed the minors about the purpose of the study and listed the ones who were willing to participate. At the second stage, the minors who had agreed to be interviewed were individu-ally informed by the interviewer about the confidentiality of the study and about their option to discontinue the interview at any time or to skip any question they might find stressful for any reason.

In addition, the interviewers were asked to record their observations about the interview setting (how the interpreters sat, if the responsible person was present, if the door was closed during the interview, other possible interventions, and the willingness of the interviewee to complete the interview). There were no interrup-tions by the authorities running the shelters during the interviews.

OVERVIEW OF THE SITUATION

In May 2016, Eurostat (2016) stated that almost 90,000 unaccompanied minors were among the asylum seekers registered in the EU in 2015. The state agency responsible for accommodating unaccompanied minors (UAMs) in Greece is the National Center for Social Solidarity (EKKA), which is under the auspices of the Ministry of Labor, Social Security, and Social Solidarity. As of November 17, 2016, the estimated number of UAMs, based on referrals to EKKA, was 2,300 (EKKA 2016). The number decreased to 2,000 in 2017. The total number of UAM referrals to EKKA from January 2016 to March 2017 was 6,189, of whom 5,792 were boys, 480 were girls, and 398 were under the age of fourteen (EKKA 2017). Due to exces-sive accommodation needs, a number of UAMs have been detained in closed facil-ities and police stations (Aitima 2016; Anagnostou and Gemi 2015).

As shown in table 7.2, the number of completed interviews in the REHEAL-UAM pilot was forty-four—thirteen females and thirty-one males—living in the shelters of Attica (greater Athens area).[9] The interviews were conducted by the EKKE team in the following shelters: two run by the NGO Praksis, one (Inedivim)

TABLE 7.2 Sample characteristics of unaccompanied minors in Greek shelters

	n	%
Gender		
Male	31	70.5
Female	13	29.5
Age Group		
17–18	16	36.3
15–16	21	47.8
11–14	7	15.9
Nationality		
Syrian	17	38.6
Afghan	11	25.0
Congolese	2	4.5
Indian	1	2.3
Moroccan	1	2.3
Pakistani	7	15.9
Eritrean	1	2.3
Malian	1	2.3
Somali	1	2.3
Iraqi	1	2.3
Palestinian Syrian	1	2.3
Language of Interview		
Arabic	18	40.9
Dari	2	4.5
Kurmanji	2	4.5
Farsi	10	22.7
Urdu	7	15.9
French	3	6.8
English	2	4.5
Total	44	100.0

NOTE: Shelters were run by Praksis, Estia, Inedivim, and Elaia.

by the Ministry of Education, one (Estia) by the NGO Apostoli of the Church of Greece, and one (Elaia) by Doctors of the World. Interviews were conducted in several languages with the aid of certified interpreters provided by the NGO Metadrasi or by the interpreters who worked in each shelter. The majority of the interviewees were male and either fifteen or sixteen years of age, with Syrians being the top nationality.

There were fewer female than male minors in the sample (table 7.2), a situation expected because fleeing their countries of origin was far more dangerous for girls. On the contrary, boys in some cultures (Afghan, Pakistani) are expected

TABLE 7.3 PTSD Symptom Scale (CPSS-5) in unaccompanied minors

PTSD Symptom Severity (score)	n	%
Minimal (0–10)	8	18.2
Mild (11–20)	4	9.1
Moderate (21–40)	21	47.7
Severe (41–60)	9	20.5
Very severe (61–80)	2	4.5
Total	44	100.0
Probable PTSD Diagnosis (> 31)	18	40.9

to assume grown-up responsibilities and protect the family at a very early age. This is the reason that the definition of being a minor (every child under eighteen years of age) in Western cultures is contested. Similarly, age assessment procedures are widely criticized by medical professionals and social workers on the grounds that they arrive at inaccurate estimates of age, noting that certain physical characteristics (dental or bone) can also be affected by other factors such as culture, genetic predisposition, and a person's overall state of health (Doctors of the World 2016).

The initial analysis of the REHEAL-UAM dataset has shown that eighteen of the forty-four minors interviewed were above the cut-off point for post-traumatic stress disorder (PTSD) (Foa et al. 2017), showing scores indicating probable positive diagnosis (table 7.3).

REASONS FOR FLEEING, TRAUMATIC
EXPERIENCES, AND PLANS FOR THE FUTURE:
A MIX OF HOPE AND DESPAIR

The most common reasons given for minors' fleeing their country of origin were the dangerous conditions prevailing in their homelands because of the ongoing war and terrorist attacks by ISIS or the Taliban or family vendettas. Sometimes the family might urge the male minors to flee the country in order to have the opportunity to ask for family reunification (if the minor succeeded in arriving in the destination country). Europe, especially its northern part, was regarded as a secure refuge by most of them. In response to the question of why their parents had sent them away, twenty-six of the forty-four minors replied that it had been too dangerous for them to remain in their home countries. Fear of forced military recruitment and religious oppression were among the reasons reported.

The majority had been victims of violence in their homelands or had witnessed acts of violence such as bomb blasts or the death of a close relative or friend during warfare (thirteen cases). The trip by rubber boat to Greece was frequently reported as terrifying (some boats had been torn apart, and all passengers had fallen into the sea) as well as minors' arrest and detainment after arriving in the country. The long journey across borders under extreme physical conditions and sights that caused emotional distress (such as witnessing dead bodies being eaten by wolves) were among the most traumatic experiences reported.

Some of the minors had witnessed murders in their home countries or while en route to Greece, in Turkey, or at the borders of Syria and Turkey. One of the reasons they said they had witnessed a murder "once or several times" was blood feud. Witnessing the aftermath of a suicide-bomb attack and being severely beaten at the borders of Syria and Turkey were also reported by some as the most traumatic events experienced. For the majority, the traumatic experiences took place between a year or two before the interview. Only nine minors reported that the traumatic event had occurred between three and six years earlier. The less recent traumatic experiences were related to family abuse or local threats in the country of origin (family vendetta).

Northern European countries (Germany, Norway) were mainly reported as the desired destination countries where there were family members or people the underage refugees knew. Most of the minors were either waiting for family reunification or had applied for asylum in Greece. Very few wanted to stay in Greece; they were aware that because of the economic crisis, the possibilities of finding a job were very limited. Some said they had plans to study ("I want to study and live like a human being," a sixteen-year-old boy responded) or start a business. Some minors found waiting in the shelters to be relocated a frustrating and dehumanizing experience.

However, the minors stated that they did feel safe in their current location, although it was clear that they did not equate safety with trust. Twenty-three of the forty-four minors (54.8 percent) said they often trusted people who helped them in Greece, while eight answered that they did not trust anyone. A fifteen-year-old boy responded in this way: "I have lived in war, now I feel safe everywhere. I have nothing to be afraid of."

In a recent illuminating article published in the *New Yorker* titled "The Trauma of Facing Deportation," Rachel Aviv (2017) describes the syndrome of *uppgivenhetssyndrom*, a kind of "willed dying" that leaves refugee children in Sweden unconscious after being informed that their parents will be expelled from the country. According to the article, "the Swedish Board of Health and Welfare advises that a patient will not recover until his family has permission to live in Sweden. A permanent residency permit is considered by far the most effective treatment" (Aviv 2017). Having a proper living environment—habitat—is equally effective and critical toward healing traumatized people (Mollica 2014, 2016). A sense of belonging can cure the rupture of disempowerment caused by forced displacement, the feeling that there is "no future" ahead. Treating refugees as "a human waste" (Bauman 2007, 41) placed "temporally" and "safely" in the fringe of society, in the camps, creates a new precariat (Bauman 2007, 2016; Feldman 2015), reinforcing the sense of disempowerment and neglect as plainly expressed in the words of an Arab boy: "[My] life is going to end[.] I am like a zero."

Nevertheless, trauma has two facets—injury and renewal. In the words of Renos Papadopoulos (2006, 2):

> *Trauma* is a medical term and it refers to an injury or wound. In Greek, *trauma* means wound, injury, and it comes from the verb *titrosko*—to pierce. . . . Recent investigations into the etymology of the word *trauma* . . . show that *titrosko* comes from the verb *teiro,* which means "to rub" and had, in ancient Greek, two connotations: to rub in; and to rub off, to rub away. . . . Then, in so far as the rubbing is of two kinds, we could have two different outcomes: from "rubbing in" an injury or a wound; and from "rubbing off" or "rubbing away," as in cleaning a surface where there [had been] marks previously. . . . With reference to refugees, persons may be either injured (psychologically) to varying degrees of severity as a result of [having been] exposed to violent events ("rubbed in"), or alternatively, they may experience (in addition to the distress) a sense of renewal, rejuvenation and revitalization when the powerful and potentially injurious experiences erase previous values, routines and lifestyles and introduce new meaning to their lives.

However, the new meaning must have a proper "place," both psychological and physical, for the traumatized in order to be fulfilling. A population is characterized as elusive when not linked to one place. The policies enacted so far in Europe do not ensure that displaced people will soon be able to be characterized as a non elusive population.

NOTES

The work presented in this chapter could not have been completed without the contributions of Aliki Mouriki and George Kandylis, researchers at the National Center for Social Research in Athens, and Lydia Avrami, research assistant. I would like to thank the interpreters provided by the NGO Metadrasi and the translators and commentators of the questionnaires in Arabic, Marcel Pirard and Abdelhak Hibou, and in Farsi, Masroor Javid. I also thank the responsible staff in the UAM shelters for their support and cooperation in conducting the REHEAL-UAM study and Professor T. A. Eikemo for co-funding the REHEAL survey.

1. REHEAL was co-funded by the National Centre for Social Research and the Norwegian University of Science and Technology (Professor T. A. Eikemo). It is a project related to MIGHEAL (health inequalities among the migrant population), which was funded by a European Economic Area (EEA) grant. PI: T. Stathopoulou. www.migheal.net.

2. Some respondents from Iran used the Persian calendar when filling in the dates. Dates were properly converted during quality checks of the collected questionnaires.

3. The brief period of encampment does not facilitate the "emotional connection that refugees have to long-term spaces of displacement" (Feldman 2015, 246).

4. Eligible persons were those who had arrived after January 2015 and before March 2016.

5. Fieldwork was conducted during the period September 1–9, 2016, with the exception of the surveying of Eleonas camp (which occurred July 12–13, 2016).

6. Most of the refugees in Diavata had been transferred from Eidomeni, the village on the northern border of Greece where thousands of refugees had been stranded for several months.

7. Observations were collected by George Kandylis and Aliki Mouriki, researchers at the National Center for Social Research and members of the REHEAL team.

8. Information about the population size was provided in situ by the responsible authorities of each camp. The population was not stable in most of the camps.

9. The capacity of shelters in Athens had increased from the nineteen shelters reported in November 2016 to twenty-five shelters reported in April 2017.

REFERENCES

Action Aid, Danish Refugee Council, Jesuit Refugee Service, International Federation of Red Cross and Red Crescent Societies, Norwegian Refugee Council, CARE, Oxfam, International Rescue Committee, Save the Children, and Translators without Borders. 2016. *More Than Six Months Stranded: What Now? A Joint Policy Brief on the Situation for Displaced Persons in Greece.* http://reliefweb.int/sites/reliefweb.int/files/resources /More%20than%20Six%20Months%20Stranded%20-%20What%20Now%20-%20 English%20final.pdf.

Aitima. 2016. *Forgotten: Administratively Detained Irregular Migrants and Asylum Seekers.* With the Support of the European Programme of Integration and Migration. Athens: Aitima. www.aitima.gr/images/pdf/forgotten.pdf.

Amnesty International. 2016. *Trapped in Greece: An Avoidable Refugee Crisis.* Amnesty International. www.amnesty.org/en/documents/eur25/3778/2016/en/.

Anagnostou, Dia, and Eda Gemi. 2015. *Monitoring and Assessing the Integration of Vulnerable Migrants in Greece.* Athens: Hellenic Foundation for European and Foreign Policy. www .eliamep.gr/wp-content/uploads/2015/03/ASSESSNatl.Report.Phase2_.FINAL_.pdf.

Asylum Service, Hellenic Republic, Ministry of Migration Policy. 2017a. *Statistical Data of the Greek Asylum Service.* http://asylo.gov.gr/en/wp-content/uploads/2018/01/Greek_ Asylum_Service_Statistical_Data_EN.pdf.

———. 2017b. *Statistical Data on Relocation Procedures.* http://asylo.gov.gr/en/wp-content /uploads/2018/04/Relocation-procedures-up-to-30-3-2018_en.pdf.

Aviv, Rachel. 2017. "Letter from Sweden: The Trauma of Facing Deportation." *New Yorker,* April 3, 2017. www.newyorker.com/magazine/2017/04/03/the-trauma-of-facing-deportation.

Bauman, Zygmount. 2007. *Liquid Times: Living in an Age of Uncertainty.* Cambridge, UK: Polity Press.

———. 2016. "Behind the World's Crisis of Humanity." Interview with Felicity Barr, *Al Jazeera,* July 23, 2016. www.youtube.com/watch?v=EG63MkQb1r4.

Betancourt, Theresa S., Mary C. Smith Fawzi, Anne Stevenson, Fredrick Kanyanganzi, Catherine Kirk, Lauren Ng, Christina Mushashi, Justin I. Bizimana, William Beardslee, Giuseppe Raviola, Stephanie Smith, Yvonne Kayiteshonga, and Agnes Binagwaho. 2016. "Ethics in Community-Based Research with Vulnerable Children: Perspectives from Rwanda." *Public Library of Science: One* 11 (9): e0157042.

Betancourt, Theresa S., Liesbeth Speelman, Grace Onyango, and Paul Bolton. 2009. "Psychosocial Problems of War-Affected Youth in Northern Uganda: A Qualitative Study." *Transcultural Psychiatry* 46 (2): 238–56. https://dx.doi.org/10.1177%2F1363461509105815.

Block, Karen, Deborah Warr, Lisa Gibbs, and Elisha Riggs. 2013. "Addressing Ethical and Methodological Challenges in Research with Refugee-Background Young People: Reflections from the Field." *Journal of Refugee Studies* 26 (1): 69–87.

Brodie, Mollyan, Claudia Deane, Elizabeth C. Hamel, Melissa Herrmann, and Eran Ben-Porath. 2014. "Interviewing in Disaster-Affected Areas: Lessons Learned from Post-Katrina Surveys of New Orleans Residents." In *Hard-to-Survey Populations,* edited by Roger Tourangeau, Brad Edwards, Timothy P. Johnson, Kirk M. Wolter, and Nancy Bates, 157–80. Cambridge: Cambridge University Press.

Cavounidis-Springer, Jennifer. 2016. *Developments in the Refugee and Migrant Crisis: Greek Economic Outlook.* Athens: Center of Planning and Economic Research. [In Greek].

Doctors of the World. 2016. *Age Assessment for Foreign Unaccompanied Minors.* Athens, Greece: Doctors of the World. https://Mdm. Greece.gr/en.

EKKA (National Center for Social Solidarity). 2016. *Situation Update: Unaccompanied Children in Greece.* November 17, 2016. https://data2.unhcr.org/en/documents/download/53096.

———. 2017. *Situation Update: Unaccompanied Children in Greece.* April 3, 2017. https://data2.unhcr.org/en/documents/download/530962016.

Eurostat. 2016. "Almost 90,000 Unaccompanied Minors among Asylum Seekers Registered in the EU in 2015." Press release. May 2, 2016. http://ec.europa.eu/eurostat/documents/2995521/7244677/3-02052016-AP-EN.pdf.

———. 2017. *Asylum Statistics.* March 13, 2017. http://ec.europa.eu/eurostat/statistics-explained/index.php/Asylum_statistics.

Feldman, Ilana. 2015. "What Is a Camp? Legitimate Refugee Lives in Spaces of Long-Term Displacement." *Geoforum* 66: 244–52.

Foa B. Edna, Anu Asnaani, Yinyin Zang, Sandra Capaldi and Rebecca Yeh. 2017. "Psychometrics of the Child PTSD Symptom Scale for DSM-5 for Trauma-Exposed Children and Adolescents." *Journal of Clinical Child and Adolescent Psychology* 47 (1): 38–46. doi: 10.1080/15374416.2017.1350962.

Frontex. 2017. *Trends and Routes: Eastern Mediterranean Route.* https://frontex.europa.eu/along-eu-borders/migratory-map/.

Harkness, Janet, Mathew Stange, Kristen L. Cibelli, Peter Mohler, and Beth-Ellen Pennell. 2014. "Surveying Cultural and Linguistic Minorities." In *Hard-to-Survey Populations,* edited by Roger Tourangeau, Brad Edwards, Timothy P. Johnson, Kirk M. Wolter, and Nancy Bates, 245–70. Cambridge: Cambridge University Press, 2014.

Hollifield, Michael, Teddy D. Warner, Nityamo Lian, Barry Krakow, Janis H. Jenkins, James Kesler, Jayne Stevenson, and Joseph Westermeyer. "Measuring Trauma and Health Status in Refugees: A Critical Review." 2002. *JAMA* 288 (5): 611–21.

Hollifield, Michael, Eric C. Toolson, Sasha Verbillis-Kolp, Beth Farmer, Junko Yamazaki, Tsegaba Woldehaimanot, and Annette Holland. "Effective Screening for Emotional Distress in Refugees." 2016. *Journal of Nervous and Mental Disease* 204 (4): 247–53.

Ingleby, David, ed. 2005. *Forced Migration and Mental Health: Rethinking the Care of Refugees and Displaced Persons.* Dordrecht, The Netherlands: Springer.

IOM (International Organization for Migration). 2016a. *Mediterranean Update. Migration Flows: Europe: Arrivals and Fatalities.* December 9, 2016. Geneva: IOM.

———. 2016b. *Migration Flows to Europe: The Mediterranean Digest.* December 15, 2016. Geneva: IOM.

———. 2016c. *Mixed Migration Flows in the Mediterranean and Beyond. Analysis: Flow Monitoring Surveys.* Reporting period: January–November 2016. Geneva: IOM.

IRC, NRC, and Oxfam (International Rescue Committee, Norwegian Refugee Council, and Oxfam International). 2017. *The Reality of the EU-Turkey Statement: How Greece Has Become a Testing Ground for Policies That Erode Protection for Refugees.* Joint agency briefing note. March 17, 2017.

Kreuter, Frauke, ed. 2013. *Improving Surveys with Paradata.* New York: Wiley.

Mneimneh, Zeina N., William G. Axinn, Dirgha Ghimire, Kristen L. Cibelli, and Mohammad Salih Al Kaisy. 2014. "Conducting Surveys in Areas of Armed Conflict." In *Hard-to-Survey Populations,* edited by Roger Tourangeau, Brad Edwards, Timothy P. Johnson, Kirk M. Wolter, and Nancy Bates, 134–57. Cambridge: Cambridge University Press.

Mollica, Richard F. 2014. *The New H5 Model: Trauma and Recovery: A Summary.* Cambridge, MA: Harvard Program in Refugee Trauma.

———. 2016. *Healing Invisible Wounds,* 3rd ed. Nashville, TN: Vanderbilt University Press.

Papadopoulos, Renos K. 2006. *Refugees and Psychological Trauma: Psychosocial Perspectives.* www.researchgate.net/publication/252180441_REFUGEES_AND_PSYCHOLOGICAL_TRAUMA_PSYCHOSOCIAL_PERSPECTIVES.

Pennell, Beth-Ellen, Yashwant Deshmukh, Jennifer Kelley, Patty Maher, James Wagner, and Dan Tomlin. 2014. "Disaster Research: Surveying Displaced Populations." In *Hard-to-Survey Populations,* edited by Roger Tourangeau, Brad Edwards, Timothy P. Johnson, Kirk M. Wolter, and Nancy Bates, 111–34. Cambridge: Cambridge University Press.

Porter, Matthew, and Nick Haslam. 2005. "Predisplacement and Postdisplacement Factors Associated with Mental Health of Refugees and Internally Displaced Persons: A Meta-analysis." *JAMA* 294 (5): 602–12.

Stathopoulou, Theoni. 2009. "Immigrants and Immigration in the Greek Daily Press: 2003–2006." In *Aspects of Immigration and Immigration Policies,* edited by Christina Varouxi, Nikos Sarris, and Amalia Frangiskou, 189–221. Athens: National Center for Social Science [in Greek].

Stathopoulou, Theoni, and Anastasia Kostaki. 2014. "Religiosity, Trust, and Tolerance in Times of Recession: The Cases of Spain and Greece." In *The Debt Crisis in the Eurozone: Social Impacts,* edited by Nicholas P. Petropoulos and George O. Tsobanoglou, 251–80. Newcastle-upon-Tyne, UK: Cambridge Scholars.

Stathopoulou, Theoni, and Harris Papageorgiou. 2016. "Radicalized Orthodoxy? Civic Discontent and Religious Identification in Times of Crisis." Paper presented at the 9th International Conference on Social Science Methodology of the International Sociological Association Research Committee 33, September 11–16, 2016, Leicester, UK.

Steel, Zachary, Tien Chey, Derrick Silove, Claire Marnane, Richard A. Bryant, and Mark van Ommeren. 2009. "Association of Torture and Other Potentially Traumatic Events with Mental Health Outcomes among Populations Exposed to Mass Conflict and Displacement: A Systematic Review and Meta-analysis." *JAMA* 302 (5): 537–49.

Summerfield, Derek. 2005. "'My Whole Body Is Sick . . . My Life Is Not Good': A Rwandan Asylum Seeker Attends a Psychiatric Clinic in London." In *Forced Migration and Mental Health: Rethinking the Care of Refugees and Displaced Persons,* edited by David Ingleby, 97–115. Dordrecht, The Netherlands: Springer.

Tourangeau, Roger. 2014. "Defining Hard-to-Survey Populations." In *Hard-to-Survey Populations,* edited by Roger Tourangeau, Brad Edwards, Timothy P. Johnson, Kirk M. Wolter, and Nancy Bates, 3–21. Cambridge: Cambridge University Press.

Tourangeau, Roger, Brad Edwards, Timothy P. Johnson, Kirk M. Wolter, and Nancy Bates, eds. 2014. *Hard-to-Survey Populations.* Cambridge: Cambridge University Press.

UNHCR (UN High Commissioner for Refugees). 2016a. *Greece: Europe Refugee Emergency. Daily Map Indicating Capacity and Occupancy* (governmental figures). October 3, 2016. www.refworld.org/docid/57f397094.html.

———. 2016b. *Questionnaire Findings for Syrians in Greece.* May 2016. http://reliefweb.int/sites/reliefweb.int/files/resources/May2016-Syrians_Final.pdf.

———. 2017. Bureau for Europe. *Desperate Journeys: Refugees and Migrants Entering and Crossing Europe via the Mediterranean and Western Balkans Routes.* www.unhcr.org/news/updates/2017/2/58b449f54/desperate-journeys-refugees-migrants-entering-crossing-europe-via-mediterranean.html.

8

MITIGATING THE IMPACT OF FORCED DISPLACEMENT AND REFUGEE AND UNAUTHORIZED STATUS ON YOUTH

Integrating Developmental Processes with Intervention Research

Hirokazu Yoshikawa, Alice J. Wuermli, and J. Lawrence Aber

As other chapters in this volume show, the flows of forced migration and displacement affecting youth worldwide are unprecedented in their scope and numbers. Over 65 million people, or one in 113 people worldwide, were displaced from their homes for reasons of conflict or persecution in 2015 (UNESCO and UNHCR 2016), the largest number since World War II. Half of the world's 57 million school-aged children who are not in school live in conflict-affected countries, and half of the world's primary-school-aged children who are displaced are not attending primary school (UNESCO and UNHCR 2016). In addition, increasing numbers of youth are being held in conditions that amount to arbitrary detention without access to legal counsel, a rights violation expressly prohibited in Article 9 of the Universal Declaration of Human Rights and the 1966 International Covenant on Civil and Political Rights.

The associated unauthorized status of many refugees and migrants worldwide is also a concern. Much of the social exclusion experienced by refugees in host nations and communities derives from policies that result in lack of authorization, for example, for formal employment; for access to education for their children; and for access to other public services across physical and mental health, social protection, and child protection. Different statuses short of formal asylum or temporary or permanent citizenship status (e.g., completely unauthorized, waiting for determination of status, or detainee or refugee status requiring physical containment in a camp or other locality) also lead to exclusion from learning and developmental supports for children and youth. The legal status contexts of different groups and waves of forced migration and internal displacement vary at the national, within-country, and migrant-group-specific levels and also change rapidly over time (Menjívar 2006; UNESCO and UNHCR 2016).

MITIGATING THE IMPACT ON YOUTH

In this chapter, we present a developmental process-oriented framework for informing the development and evaluation of interventions to mitigate the risks posed by major social and political upheaval, displacement, and refugee and unauthorized status on child and youth development (Dubow et al. 2017; Lundberg and Wuermli 2012; Wuermli et al. 2015).[1] We review evidence on the overall risk to child and youth development and learning posed by exposure to these contexts, the emerging evidence on contextual and psychological factors that may exacerbate or mitigate these risks, and the evidence base of rigorous evaluations of interventions from the dyadic to the policy levels that have successfully targeted these factors and mitigated the risks and promoted resilience and healthy development despite adversity.

THE RISKS OF ARMED CONFLICT, DISPLACEMENT, AND REFUGEE OR UNAUTHORIZED STATUS FOR CHILD AND YOUTH DEVELOPMENT

Both refugee status and unauthorized status are linked to poorer academic, mental health, and behavioral outcomes among children and youth. Refugees can undergo stress and trauma during the preflight, flight, and resettlement phases of their trajectories (Lustig et al. 2004; also see Betancourt et al., chapter 6, this volume). Repeated stress or trauma can also occur in the context of circular migration patterns (repeated crossings of borders, for example). Systematic reviews show higher rates of mental health disorders among refugee youth than among their nonrefugee counterparts (Bronstein and Montgomery 2011), including rates of posttraumatic stress disorder (PTSD), depression, and other emotional and behavioral disorders. For example, evidence indicates that Syrian refugee children show elevated rates of depressive and PTSD symptoms relative to those of population norms (Sirin and Rogers-Sirin 2015). Aside from general disruptions to the lives of refugee children, educational progress is also threatened, and education is often interrupted, partly through exposure to conflict and partly by processes of flight, displacement, and migration (Burde et al. 2016). For instance, the literature on unauthorized status, primarily in the United States, indicates the harmful consequences that this status (whether experienced by children or youth directly or by their parents) produces for early cognitive development, middle-childhood educational achievement and well-being, and adolescent anxiety, depression, school progress, and eventual educational attainment into young adulthood (Bean, Brown, and Bachmeier 2015; Dreby 2015; Gonzales 2015; C. Suárez-Orozco et al. 2011; Yoshikawa, C. Suárez-Orozco, and Gonzales 2017). It is therefore important to better understand the processes underlying adaptive responses and behaviors that lead to worse developmental outcomes.

PROCESSES THAT EXACERBATE OR AMELIORATE
RISKS TO DEVELOPMENT POSED BY ARMED CONFLICT,
FORCED MIGRATION, AND REFUGEE OR
UNDOCUMENTED STATUS

What factors exacerbate or magnify risk processes that link refugee or unauthorized status to problems in well-being and development? What factors may protect against such risk or lead directly to positive outcomes? Understanding the risk-exacerbating or risk-mitigating processes that link a risk factor like refugee and unauthorized status to child and adolescent development can inform interventions (Luthar and Eisenberg 2017; Rutter 1987; Wuermli, Hempel, et al. 2012; Yoshikawa, Whipps, and Rojas 2017; Yoshikawa 1994). That is, if *risk factors* (which amplify the probability of a negative outcome), *protective factors* (which lower the probability of a negative outcome, given exposure to adversity), or *promotive factors* (which are directly targeted at enhancing positive youth outcomes more generally) are causally related to developmental outcomes, then interventions that target these factors, either by mitigating risk or by strengthening protective factors, may be effective strategies to foster resilience (Cicchetti and Rogosch 2009). Figure 8.1 shows how risk and protective factors influence children and youth's adaptive processes in response to significant threats—for instance, undocumented status or armed conflict. The notion that identifying intervention targets that moderate these adaptive processes reduces children and youth's exposure to risk or supports their positive development despite adversity is at the core of developmentally informed prevention and promotion science (Luthar and Eisenberg 2017). Although there is not a large body of literature on these factors specifically looking at populations that are the focus of this chapter, several have received attention, informed by studies looking at other forms of precarious situations (such as community violence, domestic and intimate partner violence, and child maltreatment).

Thinking of these processes within a developmental systems framework (Bronfenbrenner and Morris 2006) facilitates the integration of these bodies of research and enables us to start identifying likely targets for intervention (Cicchetti 2010; Wuermli, Silbereisen, et al. 2012). At the center of this model is the biology of the developing child. Individual differences, for instance in the physiological (e.g., neurological, endocrine) response to a stressful experience (e.g., armed conflict), in part underlie the observed variation in other outcomes later on, including cognitive and socioemotional competencies. However, these phenotypic variations in neuroendocrine responses are not set in stone but instead are malleable, moderated by individual and social factors, and reflected in epigenetic processes.

This dynamic adaptation to the demands of a current situation is crucial for survival. However, such adaptations can have long-term consequences for health and general functioning (Cohen et al. 2012; Miller and Chen 2013). Much of the

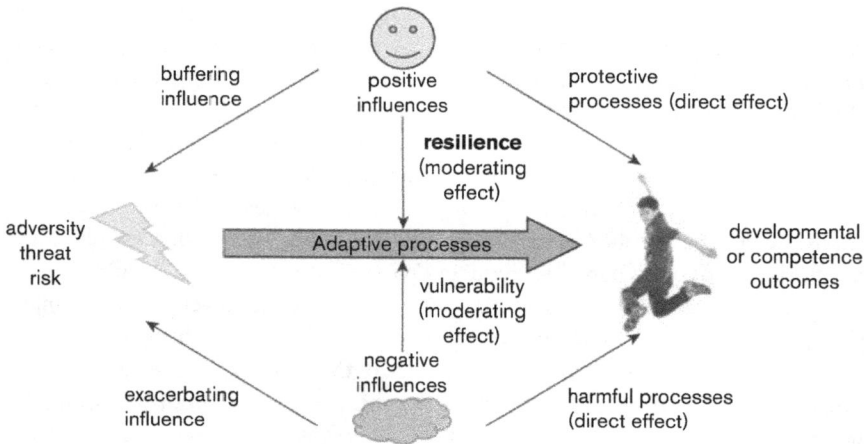

FIGURE 8.1. Risk and resilience in adaptive processes in the face of adversity. *Source:* Adapted from figure 2.3, "Distinction between Resilience and Risk Reduction and Protection," in Aber (2012).

developmental research looking at the neurobiological consequences of experiencing trauma and stress in childhood and how neurobiological processes may be mediating the effects of these experiences on later outcomes has focused on children experiencing maltreatment (i.e., abuse and/or neglect) (Teicher et al. 2003). For example, studies have linked childhood maltreatment–related posttraumatic stress disorder to differences in volumes of the hippocampus and amygdala, areas of the brain centrally involved in stress regulation and cognitive processing (Woon and Hedges 2008). Childhood stress and trauma have also been linked to faster shortening of telomeres, the ends of the gene that ensure proper replication, the shortening of which is associated with disease (e.g., cancer), and generally reflect a person's age (Price et al. 2013). While most of this research is not causal, it is nonetheless very informative, especially when thinking of these factors as parts of multiple interrelated systems.

Of course, genes or telomeres cannot be changed directly and thus cannot be the targets of intervention (though interventions could lead to changes in gene expression or to the halting of accelerated telomere shortening). And thus, although a child may be born with a certain neurobiological predisposition, many other factors play a role in how the child is able to function within a certain context. Individual level factors that have been identified in supporting a child's ability for positive adaptation in the face of adversity include intelligence and general self-regulatory capacity (Masten 2009). Aside from the fact that even these individual-level competencies (e.g., IQ, regulatory capacity) do not develop in a vacuum and are not solely determined by genetics, factors in the child's proximal and distal environments can provide profound sources of resilience (Masten 2009). In some instances these processes could be as proximal as a relationship with a caregiver, teacher, or peer. For example, maternal warmth seems to dampen the negative long-term consequences of early life socioeconomic adversity (Chen et al. 2011). In other cases, more proximal sources of risk or resilience could be mediating or moderating more distal processes. For instance, welfare policies, and as such residence status, determine families' access to support programs and resources that could lessen their economic hardship, reducing parents' stress, and as a result improve parenting, parent–child relationships, and ultimately, child development (Conger, Conger, and Martin 2010; Duncan, Magnuson, and Votruba-Drzal 2014).

It is significant to note that the importance of these factors, processes, and relationships varies depending on the age of the child. The most important protective factor for an infant might be immediate caregivers, their mental and physical health and well-being, and their ability to be responsive and sensitive to the baby's needs. The adolescent may be more directly affected by armed conflict and very much aware of her own or her parents' undocumented status, presenting a host of additional risks to her development. In what follows, we discuss factors that have been identified as risk or protective (and promotive) factors with regard to children and youth who have experienced or are experiencing armed conflict, displacement and forced migration, and refugee or undocumented status.

RISK FACTORS AND PROCESSES

First, the degree of exposure to conflict among migrant or displaced youth has well-known direct impacts on mental health, including depression and other mental health and self-regulatory challenges (Dubow et al. 2009; Panter-Brick et al. 2011). In addition, contexts of armed conflict are also associated with direct experiences of violence, including sexual violence against women perpetrated by combatants and increases in intimate partner violence (Hossain, Zimmerman, and Watts 2014). And when youth themselves report engaging in war and violent activities, the consequences appear even more severe (Betancourt, Borisova, et al. 2010).

Second, experiencing postconflict discrimination in the host community is linked to elevated mental health symptoms. For example, in a sample of reintegrating Sierra Leonean youth who had been recruited into the country's combating armed forces, experiencing community stigma was associated with higher internalizing symptoms (Betancourt et al. 2015; Noh et al. 1999). Paradoxically, discrimination in school contexts has increased as a result of greater integration of refugee children and youth into host-country education systems (Dryden-Peterson, chapter 10, this volume).

Third, parental or caregiver stress and mental health symptoms predict poorer child and youth mental health outcomes. Parental stress can stem from a range of factors, including war, financial hardship, and natural disasters. Increases in parent anxiety and depression, for example, predicted elevated internalizing symptoms in youth from Sierra Leone (Betancourt et al. 2015). Such forms of parents' mental health and stress are also associated with greater intrafamily conflict, including intimate partner violence, and can lead to psychological and physical maltreatment of their children (Taylor et al. 2009). Parent-reported earthquake-related stressors predicted lower literacy and executive function skills of young children in Chilean families affected by the 2010 earthquake (Gomez and Yoshikawa 2017). However, in the United States direct comparisons of authorized and unauthorized parents' mental health, parenting stress, and parenting practices (e.g., early cognitive stimulation) have not found differences in children's outcomes (Brabeck, Sibley, and Lykes 2016a; Yoshikawa 2011).

Fourth, the timing and duration of exposure to these contextual stressors—community conflict, experiences of discrimination, family mental health and conflict—matter for developmental outcomes. Enduring or chronic stress, for example, experienced across preflight, flight, and resettlement phases can represent a "developmental cascade" of risk processes operating through neurobiological mechanisms associated with the stress response, with long-term implications for health, development, and learning (Cohen et al. 2012; McEwen et al. 2012; Crul et al., chapter 13, this volume). There is also convincing evidence of how cumulative risk, or prolonged and/or multiple risks, affects development and learning more severely (Appleyard et al. 2005) and that there are more sensitive periods in development during which adversity can have more severe effects, namely, early childhood (Shonkoff et al. 2012) and adolescence (Fuhrmann, Knoll, and Blakemore 2015).

Finally, at the policy level it appears that harsher immigration enforcement and exclusion are linked to higher levels of more proximal risk. A recent causal study showed, for example, that harsher immigration enforcement at the local level led to higher rates of housing foreclosures among Latino households in the United States (Rugh and Hall 2016). As noted earlier, events threatening the livelihoods of families tend to be very stressful and can lead to major disruptions in family life and relationships, with direct implications for children and youth in the household.

PROTECTIVE AND PROMOTIVE FACTORS IN THE FACE OF ADVERSITY

Among protective and promotive factors are a range of individual (biological, psychological, and cognitive), interpersonal, school, and community factors and processes that can mitigate the effects of exposure to the previously discussed risks factors (Masten and Wright 2010; Obradovic, Burt, and Masten 2006; Sroufe et al.

2005). For example, family acceptance was associated with lower internalizing symptoms among former child soldiers in Sierra Leone (Betancourt et al. 2015) and among Palestinian youth involved in the Intifada (Barber 2001). Social support from peers, peer leaders, and teachers was perceived by Chechen youth as mitigating the stresses of precarious living conditions (Betancourt 2005). Peer support among former child soldiers in Nepal was associated with increased hope and reduced PTSD symptoms and functional impairment (Morley and Kohrt 2013). Interventions that strengthen the social fabric of peer networks can provide sources of resilience that individual adolescents can draw upon.

Social inclusion within school may enhance academic achievement, socioemotional outcomes, and later adult outcomes for immigrant-origin youth in the United States (Crosnoe 2011; Crosnoe and Turley 2011). Structured activities, whether in or out of school, may protect against heightened externalizing and internalizing behaviors, as was found in samples of Palestinian (Loughry et al. 2006), Chechen (Betancourt 2005), and Sierra Leonean youth (Betancourt, Brennan, et al. 2010). Structured out-of-school activities in the study of Palestinian youth included encouragement of cultural traditions and activities with an academic focus. Involvement in religious activities protected Palestinian youth from the association between Intifada involvement and increased antisocial behavior (Barber 2001). Similarly, acceptance at the community level appears to have a protective influence against the association between involvement in armed conflict and mental health outcomes in the areas of PTSD, depression, and functional impairment (Kohrt et al. 2010).

For older youth and young adults, economic and employment opportunities are associated with more positive outcomes for former child soldiers (Betancourt et al. 2013). However, for female former child soldiers, this association may not occur if sources of employment include sex work (Kohrt et al. 2010).

INTERVENTIONS TO MITIGATE THE RISK POSED BY EXPOSURE TO ARMED CONFLICT AND REFUGEE AND UNAUTHORIZED STATUS

Research is increasing on interventions that address the risks to child and youth development represented by exposure to armed conflict, refugee status, and unauthorized immigrant status. Such intervention research is key in pinpointing directions for policy and humanitarian action. Causal intervention evaluations also shed light on the theories of risk and protection that were outlined earlier. We review the existing evidence base, beginning with more micro-level interventions (psychotherapeutic), then address social-setting-level programs focused on school or care settings, and discuss policy-level interventions. Finally, we explore two areas with relatively little research—family-focused and community-level interventions—in the concluding section on gaps in the evidence base. We focus on evaluation designs with relatively strong causal inference.

INTERVENTIONS AT THE INDIVIDUAL
AND DYADIC LEVELS

Psychotherapeutic intervention. Various approaches to psychotherapy, including cognitive behavioral (CB), narrative exposure (structured recollection, NE), and individual and group based, seem to be effective at reducing mental health symptoms and improving psychosocial functioning. For instance, a systematic review of program evaluations to support refugee youth found that interventions based in CB and NE principles showed evidence of effectiveness in reducing mental health symptoms such as depression, PTSD, and anxiety (Tyrer and Fazel 2014). Group-based psychotherapy has proven successful in reducing depressive and other mental health symptoms among Ugandan adolescents and Bosnian and Nepalese children who have been exposed to conflict (Bolton et al. 2007; Layne et al. 2008; Jordans et al. 2010). In a more recent randomized controlled trial for youth in Sierra Leone, an intervention based on both CB and group-based interpersonal therapy (lasting between ten and twelve sessions) produced immediate improvements in emotional regulation, social support, and prosocial behaviors and reductions in functional impairment as reflected in increases in school enrollment and attendance and in improvements in classroom behavior at follow-up (Betancourt et al. 2014).

INTERVENTIONS AT THE SETTING LEVEL

Education and school-based programs. A variety of educational interventions may protect youth against the risks posed as discussed in this chapter. Most fundamentally, access to education itself in situations when schooling is interrupted or unavailable is linked to higher learning and subsequent schooling outcomes (Burde et al., under review). In areas in which government schools may be the target of violence, community-based schools (e.g., those situated in homes or other community settings) may be effective. An experimental evaluation of the expansion of community schools in Afghanistan noted large increases in school enrollment and academic achievement test scores, with particularly large increases for girls. The gender gap in both access and learning had been substantially narrowed (Burde and Linden 2013).

However, policies that previously focused solely on access have more recently shifted toward access to quality education, following global trends in the evolution of the goals of the *Education for All* Framework for Action (e.g., the most recent UNHCR Education Strategy and the Global Partnership for Education's Fragile States Policy) (Dryden-Peterson 2016). One approach to assuring quality education that meets the needs of refugee and conflict-affected youth is using school-based interventions with attention to socioemotional learning and the effects of trauma and exposure to violence. In the Democratic Republic of the Congo (DRC), a school-randomized evaluation of the International Rescue Committee's "Learning in a Healing Classroom" (LHC) intervention, which encompasses a socioemotional and academic curriculum and teacher training, showed positive impacts on students' reading, arithmetic, and geometry skills in the first year of its implementation. Students perceived their teachers and schools in the LHC condition to be safer and more supportive than others, but a mixed pattern of results was obtained on perceptions of their learning environments as predictable and cooperative (Aber, Torrente, et al. 2016; Aber, Tubbs, et al. 2016).

Another approach to school-based intervention aims to reduce intergroup conflict and increase intergroup understanding while also meeting more general learning goals. Peace education curricula, for example, have aimed to increase intergroup contact and/or build perspective-taking skills. Evaluations of school-based programs have been conducted in Israel, Palestine, Northern Ireland, and other conflict and postconflict contexts. Although attitudes toward outgroups appear to be positively impacted in several evaluations in the short term, longer-run effects are rarely studied and appear more mixed (see Bar-Tal and Rosen [2009] and Burde et al. [2016] for reviews).

Early care and education. For young children, exposure to early care and education may protect against the harmful effects of unauthorized status. In one study, center-based child-care enrollment was substantially lower among children of the unauthorized than with enrollment of children of authorized parents. At the same time, enrollment in center-based care was positively associated with early-childhood cognitive skills for both the authorized and unauthorized (Yoshikawa 2011). In a recent study by Kalina Brabeck and colleagues (2016b), Head Start attendance was found to protect young children against the longitudinal effects of parents' unauthorized status on their middle-childhood academic achievement.

INTERVENTIONS AT THE POLICY LEVEL

Migration policies. It is impossible to cover the full range of migration and migration-related policies in this chapter as they affect displacement and refugee or unauthorized status (for example, we do not discuss variations in humanitarian response such as policies for saving lives at sea or immediate emergency assistance). However, three of the core roles that migration policies address include (a) the definition of citizenship and access to basic services; (b) processes of accessing a pathway to citizenship among those with refugee status or unauthorized status; and (c) processes of exclusion, detention, and deportation. In each area, recent unprecedented waves of cross-national migration have revealed great country-level variation in each of these fundamental areas of policy.

First, definitions of *citizenship* strongly influence access to basic services in a country (e.g., health, social protection, education). Although the global trend among host nations of large populations of refugees is greater integration (e.g., in education) (Dryden-Peterson, chapter 10, this volume), even in countries that do integrate refugee children, this population may be excluded from other areas of protection. For example, access to food subsidies or vouchers provided by governments to refugee populations varies greatly across the Middle East / North Africa (MENA) region (Devereux 2016). For internally displaced populations, requirements of residency-based registration and other paperwork requirements can exclude large proportions of migrants (including the majority worldwide who are rural-to-urban migrants) from basic social protection assistance (Hopkins, Bastagli, and Hagen-Zanker 2016). This situation occurs in China and Vietnam, for example, regarding residency-based registration, which historically has been relatively difficult to change. In India, proof of residency requirements can pose bureaucratic challenges for migrants. For youth who are on the verge of transitioning from school to work, status can present a serious obstacle to accessing decent employment opportunities (Yoshikawa, C. Suárez-Orozco, and Gonzales 2017).

Second, for those with refugee or unauthorized status, accessing a pathway to citizenship can be tortuous and in some cases can result in years of what has been termed "liminal" or indeterminate status (Menjívar 2006). Since the Syrian conflict began to result in large new waves of refugees entering southern European countries, restrictions on refugee populations' mobility have shifted dramatically through both border enforcement policy changes and changes in requirements for paperwork in European countries. Many countries have moved to more restrictive border enforcement and legal-status policies, while some, such as Germany, have moved to expand quotas and provide greater access to newly arrived refugee populations. In the United States, policy developments since 1996 have resulted in increased restrictions on pathways to citizenship for those with unauthorized status (Waters and Pineau 2015; Yoshikawa, C. Suárez-Orozco, and Gonzales 2017).

Third, as migrants await consideration for residency or citizenship, they are often detained for extended periods of time. Detention of minors is restricted in some countries to periods of time that are as short as possible and that ensure access to public services such as education and health care. Indefinite detention without access to a process of consideration for residency or citizenship status is prohibited in international rights conventions. For example, the United States (e.g., with reference to length of detention of some unaccompanied minors from Central American countries) and Australia (e.g., with reference to long-term detention of refugees applying for asylum in inaccessible geographic areas such as Christmas Island or Manus Island in Papua New Guinea) have recently been accused of violating both domestic and international rights guidelines and legislation regarding length of detention and access to due process. Longer asylum waiting periods are causally associated with large reductions in subsequent employment in Europe (Hainmueller, Hangartner, and Lawrence 2016).

Policy solutions have recently been put forward as alternatives to simply expanding refugee quotas and streamlining the asylum process (OECD 2016). These include incorporating refugees under labor migration statutes, student programs to facilitate migration and access to education simultaneously, flexibility in humanitarian visas, and family migration policies (for example, those that facilitate family reunification). Each of these has potential implications for children's and adolescents' development through mechanisms such as increasing school enrollment or access to other services, facilitating family reunification, and addressing risk factors such as parent–child separation.

Policy solutions to the exclusion of refugee, unauthorized, and displaced individuals from rights and services also require accurate identification systems. The Aadhaar biometric identification system in India has thus far registered more than one billion Indian residents, with the goal of a single system identifying access to social protection and other benefits. It was implemented alongside new privacy legislation. The challenges of implementing such unique-identifier-based identification systems in precarious contexts such as those that many refugees face concern access to and use of such data in rapidly shifting policy contexts. Technological advances such as advanced encryption techniques may aid in protecting both individuals' rights and their access to services.

Access to social protection programs (a social safety net) may also protect children against the risks of social exclusion wrought by unauthorized status (Brabeck et al. 2016b). In this study, citizen children of unauthorized parents could potentially access programs in the United States such as those that provide early nutritional support (Women, Infants, and Children [WIC]), food stamps, cash welfare, or Medicaid. However, research shows that parents with this status are often reluctant to enroll their children in these antipoverty supports due to paperwork demands and fear of providing information to the government (Yoshikawa 2011). Household-level access to these services in the study by Brabeck and colleagues (2016b) was found to mitigate the risk that parents' unauthorized status represented for early primary grade achievement.

CONCLUSION: GAPS IN THE EVIDENCE BASE AND FUTURE DIRECTIONS

The fields of humanitarian aid and refugee and migration policy, we have argued, benefit greatly from evaluations showing how programs mitigate the risks of displacement or refugee or unauthorized status and thereby improve youth development. Yet such evaluations are few and far between. Thus, all of the areas in this review require a great deal more research to understand productive targets of intervention, how those targets are related to child and youth development, and the circumstances under which interventions are more rather than less successful. We have called for a process-oriented approach in which specific risk-exacerbating or mitigating processes are measured in research and evaluation and inform program and policy development and improvement.

Conversely, policy approaches such as those that increase access or quality of health, education, or social protection for these children and youth should inform research and evaluation. There is a stunning lack of controlled evaluations, for example, of programs that increase either enrollment or quality of education in contexts of conflict, displacement, and forced migration, with a few exceptions (Aber, Torrente, et al. 2016; Betancourt et al. 2014; Burde and Linden 2013). Similarly, there are only a few causal evaluations in rich countries of the impact of policies related to unauthorized status on any outcome for this population, whether in the area of child and youth development or more generally (Bohn, Lofstrom, and Raphael 2014; Hainmueller, Hangartner, and Lawrence 2016; Rugh and Hall 2016). In each of these emergent literatures, there are even fewer studies that identify the conditions under which programs are more rather than less successful (but see Burde [2014]; Burde, Middleton, and Wahl [2015]; and Wolf et al. [2015]). Quality of implementation of programs is rarely evaluated, for example. Filling these gaps in evidence through future research can inform efforts to scale up interventions found to be successful in efficacy trials.

Beyond these general comments, a few areas of intervention appear to be particularly understudied. These include family-focused programs and community-level norm-changing programs.

Family-focused interventions. It is striking that the primary approaches for supporting child and youth development for those exposed to refugee status, conflict, or unauthorized status have been therapeutic in nature or school (or preschool) based. These approaches focus on services directly provided to children and youth. However, data on the protective role of family processes such as family acceptance (Barber 2001) and the exacerbating role of parent stress, anxiety, and depression (Betancourt et al. 2015) suggest that family-focused interventions may help. Principles from successful family-focused interventions suggest that some may operate through both encouragement of positive parenting practices and changes in attitudes. Relatively few interventions of services for parents exposed to conflict, unauthorized migration, or displacement have been evaluated. Ragnhild Dybdahl (2001) evaluated a five-month intervention of psychosocial support for mothers affected by war in Bosnia and Herzegovina using an experimental design. Reductions in mothers' mental health symptoms and improvements in children's weight gain and psychosocial functioning were observed. Katie Murphy and colleagues (2017) review other recent evaluations and provide a framework to guide the design of such interventions.

Community-level interventions. In addition, community-level stigma against refugee, migrant, and displaced youth could be powerfully countered through norm-changing interventions. Media interventions are one such strategy. Bilali, Vollhardt, and Rarick (2015) evaluated the impact of a radio drama that depicted diverse opinions in a nonconflictual way across ethnic groups in Burundi and portrayed members of different groups interacting cooperatively. Elizabeth Paluck (2009) evaluated a similar program in Rwanda. Quasi-experimental evaluations of these programs demonstrated positive effects on a variety of intergroup attitudes, trust, and cooperation and showed reductions in in-group superiority and competitive victimhood.

In the United States, "welcome policy" efforts at the city or county level have aimed to change both local policy and community norms against unauthorized migration and newcomers in general. Welcoming America is a national network of communities, cities, and counties that have explicitly built the welcoming of immigrants into the implementation of their policies, local media campaigns, and work of local nongovernmental organizations (NGOs). More than seventy cities and counties have joined this movement, including a mix of cities across different policy contexts and immigration concentrations—for example, Akron, Memphis, New York City, and Raleigh.

Importantly, these efforts do not limit themselves to media campaigns but instead aim to share leadership in the community between new immigrants and long-time residents. Interactions between these two groups are encouraged to build the social ties that both strengthen the community and reduce the dehumanization of immigrants. In the process, attitudes toward the unauthorized are likely to shift (although there is currently no evaluation evidence to support such shifts in these cities and counties).

In other regions such as Europe, MENA, South Asia, and sub-Saharan Africa, community-level norm-changing interventions to reduce stigma affecting newcomer and refugee children and adults have not to our knowledge been evaluated. Community-level interventions have been developed to change culturally sanctioned practices such as female genital mutilation and cutting (FGM/C). In the well-known Tostan program, classes on a broad set of rights, problem-solving, health, and hygiene topics were provided to women and men in rural villages in Senegal. These were supplemented by communication efforts in which class participants were encouraged to "adopt" those topics in their social networks to communicate information they had discussed in class. Village-level public discussions about FGM/C, in which disagreements could be aired and debated, took place; ultimately, public commitment announcements occurred in multivillage public meetings. In a quasi-experimental evaluation, this approach at the village level produced changes in attitudes toward FGM/C and reductions in parent-reported cutting of daughters (Diop and Askew 2009).

Concluding note on research methods. Process-oriented research exploring and targeting risk and protective factors for children and youth exposed to refugee status, conflict, or unauthorized status is new to the relevant research and evaluation literatures. Eric Dubow and colleagues (2017) outline the many challenges to research using this perspective in the contexts of large-scale studies in Palestine, the DRC, Sierra Leone, and Northern Ireland. Measurement of the specific stresses, risks, and promotive or protective factors experienced by conflict- and displacement-affected children and youth will likewise need to expand as most "standard" measures of developmental risk and protection do not consider these contexts or mediating processes. To address cultural factors in the development and evaluation of interventions, mixed qualitative/quantitative methods and community-based participatory methods can be helpful. Community-based participatory methods of research, for example, were used extensively to build and ensure stakeholder involvement as well as cultural relevance in Theresa Betancourt and colleagues' Sierra Leone study (chapter 6, this volume). As research to inform programs and policies for youth exposed to conflict, displacement, and unauthorized status increases, the field will benefit from a broad mix of qualitative, mixed qualitative/quantitative, causal, and measurement evidence (Burde 2012; Yoshikawa et al. 2008).

NOTES

We thank the NYU Abu Dhabi Research Institute for support of work on this chapter through its grant to the Global TIES for Children Center at New York University.

1. Note that for space reasons we exclude discussion of the related areas of disaster and associated humanitarian interventions. For reviews of these topics, see Masten and Narayan (2012) and Wethington et al. (2008).

REFERENCES

Aber, J. Lawrence. 2012: In *Children and Youth in Crisis: Protecting and Promoting Human Development in Times of Economic Shocks,* edited by Mattias Lundberg and Alice J. Wuermli. Washington, DC: World Bank.

Aber, J. Lawrence, Carly Tubbs, Catalina Torrente, Peter F. Halpin, Brian Johnston, Leighann Starkey, Anjuli Shivshanker, Jeannie Annan, Edward Seidman, and Sharon Wolf. 2016. "Promoting Children's Learning and Development in Conflict-Affected Countries: Testing Change Process in the Democratic Republic of the Congo." *Development and Psychopathology* 29 (1): 53–67.

Aber, J. Lawrence, Catalina Torrente, Leighann Starkey, Brian Johnston, Edward Seidman, Peter Halpin, Anjuli Shivshanker, Nina Weisenhorn, Jeannie Annan, and Sharon Wolf. 2016. "Impacts after One Year of 'Healing Classroom' on Children's Reading and Math Skills in DRC: Results from a Cluster Randomized Trial." *Journal of Research on Educational Effectiveness* 10 (3): 507–29. doi:10.1080/19345747.2016.1236160.

Appleyard, Karen, Byron Egeland, Manfred H. M. van Dulmen, and L. Alan Sroufe. 2005. "When More Is Not Better: The Role of Cumulative Risk in Child Behavior Outcomes." *Journal of Child Psychology and Psychiatry* 46 (3): 235–45. doi:10.1111/j.1469-7610.2004 .00351.x.

Barber, Brian K. 2001. "Political Violence, Social Integration, and Youth Functioning: Palestinian Youth from the Intifada." *Journal of Community Psychology* 29 (3): 259–80.

Bar-Tal, Daniel, and Yigal Rosen. 2009. "Peace Education in Societies Involved in Intractable Conflicts: Direct and Indirect Models." *Review of Educational Research* 79 (2): 557–75.

Bean, Frank D., Susan K. Brown, and James D. Bachmeier. 2015. *Parents without Papers: The Progress and Pitfalls of Mexican American Integration.* New York: Russell Sage Foundation.

Betancourt, Theresa S. 2005. "Stressors, Supports and the Social Ecology of Displacement: Psychosocial Dimensions of an Emergency Education Program for Chechen Adolescents Displaced in Ingushetia, Russia." *Culture, Medicine, and Psychiatry* 29 (3): 309–40. doi:10.1007/s11013-005-9170-9.

Betancourt, Theresa S., Ivelina Borisova, Timothy P. Williams, Sarah E. Meyers-Ohki, Julia E. Rubin-Smith, Jeannie Annan, and Brandon A. Kohrt. 2013. "Psychosocial Adjustment and Mental Health in Former Child Soldiers: Systematic Review of the Literature and Recommendations for Future Research." *Journal of Child Psychology and Psychiatry* 54 (1): 17–36. doi:10.1111/j.1469-7610.2012.02620.x.

Betancourt, Theresa S., Robert T. Brennan, Julia Rubin-Smith, Garrett M. Fitzmaurice, and Stephen E. Gilman. 2010. "Sierra Leone's Former Child Soldiers: A Longitudinal Study of Risk, Protective Factors, and Mental Health." *Journal of the American Academy of Child and Adolescent Psychiatry* 49 (6): 606–15.

Betancourt, Theresa S., Ryan McBain, Elizabeth A. Newnham, Adeyinka M. Akinsulure-Smith, Robert T. Brennan, John R. Weisz, and Nathan B. Hansen. 2014. "A Behavioral Intervention for War-Affected Youth in Sierra Leone: A Randomized Controlled Trial." *Journal of the American Academy of Child and Adolescent Psychiatry* 53 (12): 1288–97. doi:10.1016/j.jaac.2014.09.011.

Betancourt, Theresa S., Ryan K. McBain, Elizabeth A. Newnham, and Robert T. Brennan. 2015. "The Intergenerational Impact of War: Longitudinal Relationships between Caregiver and Child Mental Health in Postconflict Sierra Leone." *Journal of Child Psychology and Psychiatry* 56 (10): 1101–07.

Betancourt, Theresa S., Ivelina I. Borisova, Timothy P. Williams, Robert T. Brennan, Theodore H. Whitfield, Marie de la Soudiere, John Williamson, and Stephen E. Gilman. 2010. "Sierra Leone's Former Child Soldiers: A Follow-Up Study of Psychosocial Adjustment and Community Reintegration." *Child Development* 81 (4): 1077–95.

Bilali, Rezarta, Johanna R. Vollhardt, and Jason R. D. Rarick. 2015. "Assessing the Impact of a Media-Based Intervention to Prevent Intergroup Violence and Promote Positive Intergroup Relations in Burundi." *Journal of Community and Applied Social Psychology* 26 (3): 221–35.

Bohn, Sarah, Magnus Lofstrom, and Steven Raphael. 2014. "Did the 2007 Legal Arizona Workers Act Reduce the State's Unauthorized Immigrant Population?" *Review of Economics and Statistics* 96 (2): 258–69.

Bolton, Paul, Judith Bass, Theresa S. Betancourt, Liesbeth Speelman, Grace Onyango, Kathleen F. Clougherty, Richard Neugebauer, Laura Murray, and Helen Verdeli. 2007. "Interventions for Depression Symptoms among Adolescent Survivors of War and Displacement in Northern Uganda: A Randomized Controlled Trial." *JAMA* 298 (5): 519–27. doi:10.1001/jama.298.5.519.

Brabeck, Kalina M., Erin Sibley, and M. Brinton Lykes. 2016a. "Authorized and Unauthorized Immigrant Parents: The Impact of Legal Vulnerability on Family Contexts." *Hispanic Journal of Behavioral Sciences* 38 (1): 3–30.

Brabeck, Kalina M., Erin Sibley, Patricia Taubin, and Angela Murcia. 2016b. "The Influence of Immigrant Parent Legal Status on US-Born Children's Academic Abilities: The Moderating Effects of Social Service Use." *Applied Developmental Science* 20 (4): 237–49.

Bronfenbrenner, Urie, and Pamela A. Morris. 2006. "The Bioecological Model of Human Development." In *Handbook of Child Psychology: Theoretical Models of Human Development,* edited by William Damon and Richard M. Lerner, 793–828. Hoboken, NJ: Wiley.

Bronstein, Israel, and Paul Montgomery. 2011. "Psychological Distress in Refugee Children: A Systematic Review." *Clinical Child and Family Psychology Review* 14 (1): 44–56.

Burde, Dana. 2012. "Assessing Impact and Bridging Methodological Divides: Randomized Trials in Countries Affected by Conflict." *Comparative Education Review* 56 (3): 448–73.

Burde, Dana. 2014. *Schools for Conflict or for Peace in Afghanistan.* New York: Columbia University Press.

Burde, Dana, Amy Kapit, Rachel L. Wahl, Ozen Guven, and Margot I. Skarpeteig. 2016. "Education in Emergencies: A Review of Theory and Research." *Review of Educational Research* 87 (3): 619–58. https://doi.org/10.3102/0034654316671594.

Burde, Dana, and Leigh L. Linden. 2013. "Bringing Education to Afghan Girls: A Randomized Controlled Trial of Village-Based Schools." *American Economic Journal: Applied Economics* 5 (3): 27–40.

Burde, Dana, Joel A. Middleton, and Rachel Wahl. 2015. "Islamic Studies as Early Childhood Education in Countries Affected by Conflict: The Role of Mosque Schools in Remote Afghan Villages." *International Journal of Educational Development* 41: 70–79.

Chen, Edith, Gregory E. Miller, Michael S. Kobor, and Steve W. Cole. 2011. "Maternal Warmth Buffers the Effects of Low Early-Life Socioeconomic Status on Proinflammatory Signaling in Adulthood." *Molecular Psychiatry* 16 (7): 729–37. doi:10.1038/mp.2010.53.

Cicchetti, Dante. 2010. "Resilience under Conditions of Extreme Stress: A Multilevel Perspective." *World Psychiatry* 9 (3): 145–54.

Cicchetti, Dante, and Fred A. Rogosch. 2009. "Adaptive Coping under Conditions of Extreme Stress: Multilevel Influences on the Determinants of Resilience in Maltreated Children." *New Directions in Child and Adolescent Development* 2009 (124): 47–59. doi:10.1002/cd.242.

Cohen, Sheldon, Denise Janicki-Deverts, William J. Doyle, Gregory E. Miller, Ellen Frank, Bruce S. Rabin, and Ronald B. Turner. 2012. "Chronic Stress, Glucocorticoid Receptor Resistance, Inflammation, and Disease Risk." *Proceedings of the National Academies of Science of the United States of America* 109 (16): 5995–99. doi:10.1073/pnas.1118355109.

Conger, Rand D., Katherine J. Conger, and Monica J. Martin. 2010. "Socioeconomic Status, Family Processes, and Individual Development." *Journal of Marriage and Family* 72: 685–704.

Crosnoe, Robert. 2011. *Fitting In, Standing Out: Navigating the Social Challenges of High School to Get an Education.* Cambridge: Cambridge University Press.

Crosnoe, Robert, and Ruth N. Lopez Turley. 2011. "K-12 Educational Outcomes of Immigrant Youth." *The Future of Children* 21 (1): 129–52.

Devereux, Stephen. 2016. "Social Protection and Safety Nets in the Middle East and North Africa." Research Report, vol. 2015, no. 80. Brighton, UK: Institute of Development Studies.

Diop, Nafissatou J., and Ian Askew. 2009. "The Effectiveness of a Community-Based Education Program on Abandoning Female Genital Mutilation/Cutting in Senegal." *Studies in Family Planning* 40 (4): 307–18.

Dreby, Joanna. 2015. *Everyday Illegal: When Policies Undermine Immigrant Families.* Berkeley: University of California Press.

Dryden-Peterson, Sarah. 2016. "Policies for Education in Conflict and Post-Conflict Reconstruction." In *Handbook of Global Education Policy,* edited by Karen Mundy, Andy Green, Bob Longard, and Antoni Verger, 189–205. West Sussex, UK: Wiley Blackwell.

Dubow, Eric F., J. Lawrence Aber, Theresa S. Betancourt, E. Mark Cummings, and L. Rowell Huesmann. 2017. "Conducting Longitudinal, Process-Oriented Research with Conflict-Affected Youth: Solving the Inevitable Challenges." *Development and Psychopathology* 29 (1): 85–92.

Dubow, Eric F., Paul Boxer, L. Rowell Huesmann, Khalil Shikaki, Simha Landau, Shira Dvir Gvirsman, and Jeremy Ginges. 2009. "Exposure to Conflict and Violence across Contexts: Relations to Adjustment among Palestinian Children." *Journal of Clinical Child and Adolescent Psychology* 39 (1): 103–16.

Duncan, Greg J., Katherine Magnuson, and Elizabeth Votruba-Drzal. 2014. "Boosting Family Income to Promote Child Development." *Future of Children* 24 (1): 99–120.

Dybdahl, Ragnhild. 2001. "Children and Mothers in War: An Outcome Study of a Psychosocial Intervention Program." *Child Development* 72 (4): 1214–30.

Fuhrmann, Delia, Lisa J. Knoll, and Sarah-Jayne Blakemore. 2015. "Adolescence as a Sensitive Period of Brain Development." *Trends in Cognitive Science* 19 (10): 558–66. doi:10.1016/j.tics.2015.07.008.

Gomez, Celia J., and Hirokazu Yoshikawa. 2017. "Earthquake Effects: Estimating the Relationship between Exposure to the 2010 Chilean Earthquake and Preschool Children's Early Cognitive and Executive Function Skills." *Early Childhood Research Quarterly* 38: 127–36.

Gonzales, Roberto G. 2015. *Lives in Limbo: Undocumented and Coming of Age in America.* Berkeley: University of California Press.

Hainmueller, Jens, Dominik Hangartner, and Duncan Lawrence. 2016. "When Lives Are Put on Hold: Lengthy Asylum Processes Decrease Employment among Refugees." *Science Advances* 2 (8). doi:10.1126/sciadv.1600432.

Hopkins, Emma, Francesca Bastagli, and Jessica Hagen-Zanker. 2016. "Internal Migrants and Social Protection: A Review of Eligibility and Take-Up." Oversees Development Institute (ODI) working paper.

Hossain, Mazeda, Cathy Zimmerman, and Charlotte Watts. 2014. "Preventing Violence against Women and Girls in Conflict." *Lancet* 383 (9934): 2021–22.

Jordans, Mark J., Ivan H. Komproe, Wietse A. Tol, Brandon A. Kohrt, Nagendra P. Luitel, Robert D. Macy, and Joop T. de Jong. 2010. "Evaluation of a Classroom-Based Psychosocial Intervention in Conflict-Affected Nepal: A Cluster Randomized Controlled Trial." *Journal of Child Psychology and Psychiatry* 51 (7): 818–26. doi:10.1111/j.1469–7610.2010 .02209.x.

Kohrt, Brandon A., Mark J. Jordans, Wietse A. Tol, Em Perera, Rohit Karki, Suraj Koirala, and Nawaraj Upadhaya. 2010. "Social Ecology of Child Soldiers: Child, Family, and Community Determinants of Mental Health, Psychosocial Well-Being, and Reintegration in Nepal." *Transcultural Psychiatry* 47 (5): 727–53. doi:10.1177/1363461510381290.

Layne, Christopher M., William R. Saltzman, Landon Poppleton, Gary M. Burlingame, Alma Pašalić, Elvira Duraković, Mirjana Mušić, Nihada Ćampara, Nermin Dapo, and Berina Arslanagić. 2008. "Effectiveness of a School-Based Group Psychotherapy Program for War-Exposed Adolescents: A Randomized Controlled Trial." *Journal of the American Academy of Child and Adolescent Psychiatry* 47 (9): 1048–62.

Loughry, Maryanne, Alastair Ager, Eirini Flouri, Vivian Khamis, Abdel Hamid Afana, and Samir Qouta. 2006. "The Impact of Structured Activities among Palestinian Children in a Time of Conflict." *Journal of Child Psychology and Psychiatry* 47 (12): 1211–18.

Lundberg, Mattias, and Alice J. Wuermli, eds. 2012. *Children and Youth in Crisis: Protecting and Promoting Human Development in Times of Economic Shocks.* Directions in Development. Washington, DC: World Bank.

Lustig, Stuart L., Maryam Kia-Keating, Wanda G. Knight, Paul Geltman, Heidi Ellis, J. David Kinzie, Terence Keane, and Glenn N. Saxe. 2004. "Review of Child and Adolescent Refugee Mental Health." *Journal of the American Academy of Child and Adolescent Psychiatry* 43 (1): 24–36.

Luthar, Suniya S., and Nancy Eisenberg. 2017. "Resilient Adaptation among At-Risk Children: Harnessing Science toward Maximizing Salutary Environments." *Child Development* 88 (2): 337–49.

Masten, Ann S. 2009. "Ordinary Magic: Lessons from Research on Resilience in Human Development." *Education Canada* 49 (3): 28–32.

Masten, Ann S., and Angela J. Narayan. 2012. "Child Development in the Context of Disaster, War, and Terrorism: Pathways of Risk and Resilience." *Annual Review of Psychology* 63: 227–57.

Masten, Ann S., and Margaret O'Dougherty Wright. 2010. "Resilience over the Lifespan: Developmental Perspectives on Resistance, Recovery, and Transformation." In *Handbook of Adult Resilience,* edited by Ann S. Masten and Margaret O'Dougherty Wright, 213–37. New York: Guilford Press.

McEwen, Bruce S., Lisa Eiland, Richard G. Hunter, and Melinda M. Miller. 2012. "Stress and Anxiety: Structural Plasticity and Epigenetic Regulation as a Consequence of Stress." *Neuropharmacology* 62 (1): 3–12. doi:10.1016/j.neuropharm.2011.07.014.

Menjívar, Cecilia. 2006. "Liminal Legality: Salvadoran and Guatemalan Immigrants' Lives in the United States." *American Journal of Sociology* 111 (4): 999–1037.

Miller, Gregory E., and Edith Chen. 2013. "The Biological Residue of Childhood Poverty." *Child Development Perspectives* 7 (2): 67–73. doi:10.1111/cdep.12021.

Morley, Christopher A., and Brandon A. Kohrt. 2013. "Impact of Peer Support on PTSD, Hope, and Functional Impairment: A Mixed-Methods Study of Child Soldiers in Nepal." *Journal of Aggression, Maltreatment and Trauma* 22 (7): 714–34.

Noh, Samuel, Morton Beiser, Violet Kaspar, Feng Hou, and Joanna Rummens. 1999. "Perceived Racial Discrimination, Depression, and Coping: A Study of Southeast Asian Refugees in Canada." *Journal of Health and Social Behavior* 40 (3): 193–207.

Obradovic, Jelena, Keith B. Burt, and Ann S. Masten. 2006. "Pathways of Adaptation from Adolescence to Young Adulthood: Antecedents and Correlates." *Annals of the New York Academies of Science* 1094: 340–44. doi:10.1196/annals.1376.046.

OECD (Organization for Economic Cooperation and Development). 2016. "Are There Alternative Pathways for Refugees?" *Migration Policy Debates* 12: 1–4.

Paluck, Elizabeth Levy. 2009. "Reducing Intergroup Prejudice and Conflict Using the Media: A Field Experiment in Rwanda." *Journal of Personality and Social Psychology* 96 (3): 574–87.

Panter-Brick, Catherine, Anna Goodman, Wietse Tol, and Mark Eggerman. 2011. "Mental Health and Childhood Adversities: A Longitudinal Study in Kabul, Afghanistan." *Journal of the American Academy of Child and Adolescent Psychiatry* 50 (4): 349–63. doi:10.1016/j.jaac.2010.12.001.

Price, Lawrence H., Hung-Teh Kao, Darcy E. Burgers, Linda L. Carpenter, and Audrey R. Tyrka. 2013. "Telomeres and Early-Life Stress: An Overview." *Biological Psychiatry* 73 (1): 15–23. http://dx.doi.org/10.1016/j.biopsych.2012.06.025.

Rugh, Jacob S., and Matthew Hall. 2016. "Deporting the American Dream: Immigration Enforcement and Latino Foreclosures." *Sociological Science* 3: 1053–76.

Rutter, Michael. 1987. "Psychosocial Resilience and Protective Mechanisms." *American Journal of Orthopsychiatry* 57 (3): 316–31.

Shonkoff, John P., Andrew S. Garner, Committee on Psychosocial Aspects of Child and Family Health, Committee on Early Childhood, Adoption, and Dependent Care, and Section on Developmental and Behavioral Pediatrics, Benjamin S. Siegel, Mary I. Dobbins, Marian F. Earls, Laura McGinn, John Pascoe, and David L. Wood. 2012. "The Lifelong Effects of Early Childhood Adversity and Toxic Stress." *Pediatrics* 129 (1): e232–46. doi:10.1542/peds.2011–2663.

Sirin, Selcuk R., and Lauren Rogers-Sirin. 2015. *The Educational and Mental Health Needs of Syrian Refugee Children*. Washington, DC: Migration Policy Institute.

Sroufe, L. Alan, Byron Egeland, Elizabeth A. Carlson, and W. Andrew Collins. 2005. *The Development of the Person: The Minnesota Study of Risk and Adaptation from Birth to Adulthood*. New York: Guilford Press.

Suárez-Orozco, Carola, Hirokazu Yoshikawa, Robert Teranishi, and Marcelo M. Suárez-Orozco. 2011. "Growing Up in the Shadows: The Developmental Implications of Unauthorized Status." *Harvard Educational Review* 81 (3): 438–73.

Taylor, Catherine A., Neil B. Guterman, Shawna J. Lee, and Paul J. Rathouz. 2009. "Intimate Partner Violence, Maternal Stress, Nativity, and Risk for Maternal Maltreatment of Young Children." *American Journal of Public Health* 99 (1): 175–83. doi:10.2105/ajph.2007.126722.

Teicher, Martin H., Susan L. Andersen, Ann Polcari, Carl M. Anderson, Carryl P. Navalta, and Dennis M. Kim. 2003. "The Neurobiological Consequences of Early Stress and Childhood Maltreatment." *Neuroscience and Biobehavioral Reviews* 27 (1–2): 33–44.

Tyrer, Rebecca A., and Mina Fazel. 2014. "School and Community-Based Interventions for Refugee and Asylum-Seeking Children: A Systematic Review." *Public Library of Science: One* 9 (2). http://journals.plos.org/plosone/article?id=10.1371/journal.pone.0089359.

UNESCO (United Nations Educational, Scientific, and Cultural Organization) and UNHCR (United Nations High Commissioner for Refugees). 2016. *No More Excuses: Provide Education to All Forcibly Displaced People.* Paris: UNESCO; New York: UNHCR.

Waters, Mary C., and Marisa G. Pineau, eds. 2015. *The Integration of Immigrants into American Society.* Washington, DC: National Academies Press.

Wessells, Michael G., Katie M. Murphy, Katherine Rodrigues, Jaime Costigan, and Jeannie Annan. 2017. "Raising Children in Conflict." *Peace and Conflict: Journal of Peace Psychology* 23 (1): 46–57.

Wethington, Holly R., Robert A. Hahn, Dawna S. Fuqua-Whitley, Theresa Ann Sipe, Alex E. Crosby, Robert L. Johnson, Akiva M. Liberman, Eve Mościcki, LeShawndra N. Price, and Farris K. Tuma. 2008. "The Effectiveness of Interventions to Reduce Psychological Harm from Traumatic Events among Children and Adolescents: A Systematic Review." *American Journal of Preventive Medicine* 35 (3): 287–313.

Wolf, Sharon, Catalina Torrente, Paul Frisoli, Nina Weisenhorn, Anjuli Shivshanker, Jeannie Annan, and J. Lawrence Aber. 2015. "Preliminary Impacts of the 'Learning to Read in a Healing Classroom' Intervention on Teacher Well-Being in the Democratic Republic of the Congo." *Teaching and Teacher Education* 52: 24–36. http://dx.doi.org/10.1016/j.tate.2015.08.002.

Woon, Fu L., and Dawson W. Hedges. 2008. "Hippocampal and Amygdala Volumes in Children and Adults with Childhood Maltreatment-Related Posttraumatic Stress Disorder: A Meta-Analysis." *Hippocampus* 18 (8): 729–36. doi:10.1002/hipo.20437.

Wuermli, Alice J., Kevin Hempel, J. Lawrence Aber, and Mattias Lundberg. 2012. "Policies to Protect and Promote Young People's Development during Crisis." In *Children and Youth in Crisis: Protecting and Promoting Human Development in Times of Economic Shocks,* edited by Mattias Lundberg and Alice J. Wuermli, 229–77. Washington, DC: World Bank.

Wuermli, Alice J., Rainer K. Silbereisen, Mattias Lundberg, Michèle Lamont, Jere Behrman, and J. Lawrence Aber. 2012. "A Conceptual Framework." In *Children and Youth in Crisis: Protecting and Promoting Human Development in Times of Economic Shocks,* edited by Mattias Lundberg and Alice J. Wuermli, 29–101. Washington, DC: World Bank.

Wuermli, Alice J., Carly C. Tubbs, Anne C. Petersen, and J. Lawrence Aber. 2015. "Children and Youth in Low- and Middle-Income Countries: Toward An Integrated Developmental and Intervention Science." *Child Development Perspectives* 9 (1): 61–66. doi:10.1111/cdep.12108.

Yoshikawa, Hirokazu. 1994. "Prevention as Cumulative Protection: Effects of Early Family Support and Education on Chronic Delinquency and Its Risks." *Psychological Bulletin* 115 (1): 28–54.

Yoshikawa, Hirokazu. 2011. *Immigrants Raising Citizens: Undocumented Parents and Their Children.* New York: Russell Sage Foundation.

Yoshikawa, Hirokazu, Carola Suárez-Orozco, and Roberto G. Gonzales. 2017. "Unauthorized Status and Youth Development in the United States: Consensus Statement of the Society for Research on Adolescence." *Journal of Research on Adolescence* 27 (1): 4–19.

Yoshikawa, Hirokazu, Thomas S. Weisner, Ariel Kalil, and Niobe Way. 2008. "Mixing Qualitative and Quantitative Research in Developmental Science: Uses and Methodological Choices." *Developmental Psychology* 44 (2): 344–54.

Yoshikawa, Hirokazu, Mackenzie D. M. Whipps, and Natalia M. Rojas. 2017. "Commentary: New Directions in Developmentally Informed Intervention Research for Vulnerable Populations." *Child Development* 88 (2): 459–65.

PART FOUR

THE WORK OF EDUCATION IN THE TRANSITIONS OF IMMIGRANT AND REFUGEE YOUTH

9

EMPOWERING GLOBAL CITIZENS FOR A JUST AND PEACEFUL WORLD

Irina Bokova

We live in extraordinary times when globalization is transforming societies and creating vast new opportunities for exchange. The revolution in information and communication technology has connected women and men and societies as never before, promoting new forms of dialogue and understanding across borders and opening new possibilities for cooperation and innovation.

At the same time, the world faces ever steeper challenges. We see the deepening of inequalities and the rise of new forms of conflicts. Violence and poverty have led many people to leave their homes in search of work or education. Conflicts in Syria and Iraq are causing humanitarian tragedies and creating the world's worst refugee crisis since World War II. On a constant basis over the past years, the world has borne witness to the unfolding tragedy of large movements of women and men in ways that have challenged the shared values of humanity and our capacity to live together in ever more diverse societies.

Moving forward requires new ways of thinking and acting in order to respect and defend the human rights and dignity of every woman and man. This goal stands at the heart of all of UNESCO's work—to empower every woman and man with skills and opportunities to strengthen a culture of peace. This is the importance of UNESCO's action for advancing new forms of education for global citizenship. Today more than ever, we need deeper global solidarity to nurture respect for all and to promote the values of inclusion, dialogue, and mutual understanding.

A CRISIS OF GLOBAL SOLIDARITY

Migration is not a new phenomenon—it is part of the history of humanity and has contributed to the cultural, economic, scientific, and technological wealth of the world as we know it today. Women and men cross borders because they have no other choice, crossing to flee from war, conflict, and persecution or to search for better living conditions. Today, human mobility has moved to the heart of heated political debates, amplified by the unprecedented numbers of displaced populations in the last years. According to the United Nations, there were 244 million international migrants in 2015—more than a 40 percent increase over the number in 2000. Some 65 million international migrants were forcibly displaced, and more than 20 million are refugees, of whom approximately half are children. In 2015, more than 1 million persons arrived on European soil by sea; 3,771 others lost their lives during the journey.

This migration is a global phenomenon affecting regions across the world and throwing a shadow over their development. At the same time, this tragic situation is being exploited by some to spread hatred of "Others" and to reject diversity as a weakness of societies in the name of mythologized pasts.

In this process of stigmatization, men and women are no longer seen as individuals but instead are perceived as a destabilizing "flow." However, behind the face of every migrant and refugee, there is a story—often a story of tragedy, always one of hardship. Many migrants and refugees are children and young people who have lived through harrowing experiences, separation, and loss. By leaving their countries of origin, many of them have left their rights as national citizens, but not their rights as human beings, in abeyance. This is the reason why I am convinced that we must seize the migrant and refugee crisis as an opportunity to strengthen the humanity we all share and the dignity to which we all aspire. We must raise awareness in every society about the benefits of migration for well-being, innovation, and development, and we must fight against all forms of racism and discrimination. Doing so means recognizing the role of migrants and refugees in deepening cultural diversity and in strengthening the ties of a single humanity bound together by human rights and global solidarity.

This message was sent at the World Humanitarian Summit in Istanbul in May 2016 and at the first-ever United Nations High-Level Summit for Refugees and Migrants held in September 2016. The Summit resulted in the signing of the *New York Declaration,* whereby 193 member states agreed on a single plan to address large movements of refugees and migrants "in a humane, sensitive, compassionate and people-centered manner" (United Nations 2016). This resolution was adopted by the General Assembly on September 19, 2016.

The call for global solidarity is essential at a time when identities are being pushed to the front line of conflicts and when "living together" has become an ever more indispensable condition for stability and peace. We see this need clearly in responding to the challenge of violent extremism and the use of the barbaric attacks perpetrated in many parts of the world—in Paris, in Brussels, in Istanbul, in Tunisia, in Indonesia—as pretexts for new discrimination. New forms of conflicts are tearing at the fabric of societies, and this development calls for ever sharper work to prevent and resist the propaganda of hatred and false assumptions about "Others." In this context, we must redouble our efforts to ensure that forcibly displaced persons and refugees—especially young women and men exposed to conflict situations—do not become easy targets for radicalization.

In responding to violent extremism, measures to halt financing, stop foreign terrorists, and push back violence are essential—but they are not enough. We need a far greater focus on prevention in order to place young women and men at the front of all action and to bolster their role in building lasting peace in their communities and beyond. This process must start on the benches of schools, through global citizenship education, through media literacy, and through new opportunities for youth engagement. This effort is at the core of UNESCO's contribution to the *United Nations Secretary-General's Plan of Action to Prevent Violent Extremism* and the *UN Global Counter-Terrorism Strategy*.

EDUCATION FOR PEACE

Education is a basic human right, and it is also a force for empowerment. It provides women and men with the tools to build resilience and make the most of change. Education is especially important in conflict situations, in which learning and going to school can bring a sense of normalcy and restore hope in the future. Learning provides young minds with confidence when horizons are bleak, making education the best long-term way to break cycles of violence and set communities on the path to peace.

Fulfilling the right to education is a foundation for stability, security, and shared prosperity. This intention is a key aspect of the new *2030 Agenda for Sustainable Development* adopted by the General Assembly at the UN Summit in September 2015. The new agenda sets out seventeen Sustainable Development Goals that are universal and far-reaching to end poverty and hunger, to combat inequalities, to build peaceful and inclusive societies, to protect human rights and promote gender equality, and to ensure the lasting protection of the planet. One goal in particular—Sustainable Development Goal 4—aims to "ensure inclusive and equitable quality education and promote lifelong learning opportunities for all" (United Nations 2015). This goal is unprecedented in both scope and content. Since the new agenda was shaped by UNESCO, the United Nations agency mandated to cover all aspects of education; the organization has been given a special role to lead work toward achieving the goal.

The accelerating pace of globalization, the mismatch between skills and labor markets, and the growing inequalities within and between countries are spurring global awareness about the centrality of education for social cohesion, inclusive growth, and the prevention of violent extremism. This awareness is essential because education is falling through the cracks. At a time when educational achievement is a marker of future opportunity, the world remains far off mark, with more than 263 million children and adolescents still not attending primary and secondary school and with close to the same number failing to acquire basic skills after four years in school. Adolescent girls and young women are the most vulnerable to exclusion as well as to early marriage, sexual violence, and exploitation.

This situation is exacerbated in fragile or conflict-affected countries where migrants, refugees, and displaced persons are hit hardest. A joint policy paper by UNESCO's Global Education Monitoring Report (GEMR) and the United Nations High Commissioner for Refugees (UNHCR) (2016), *No More Excuses: Provide Education to All Forcibly Displaced People,* reveals that among forcibly displaced persons, half of children of primary school age are out of school, and three-quarters of children of secondary school age do not have access to education. Education is often the first budget line cut by governments facing conflict, and it receives only 2 percent of humanitarian aid. No sector has a smaller share of humanitarian appeals actually funded. The current funding gap of US$2.3 billion for education in conflict and crisis situations represents ten times what education receives from humanitarian aid at present.

This situation cannot be allowed to continue. Education cannot wait until a conflict is over, when buildings are being rebuilt and new resources are available. The world cannot afford to lose entire generations to despair and a future of poverty—especially as poverty has always been a powerful recruiting sergeant for new violence. Education and peace building must be integrated with long-term development and built into all humanitarian action from the outset. This is the goal of the Education Cannot Wait Fund launched at the World Humanitarian Summit in Istanbul in May 2016. This fund aims to raise US$3.85 billion over the next five years in order to reach 13.6 million children whose education has been disrupted by conflict and other humanitarian emergencies.

UNESCO is acting across the board to advance education through skills training, remedial classes, and psychosocial support to children and youth, both those internally displaced and refugees—notably, in Jordan, Iraq, Lebanon, and Syria—in both formal and nonformal settings. In Iraq, we are working to bridge learning gaps and enhance teaching quality for some 20,000 students. In Jordan, we are bolstering the Ministry of Education and some fifty centers across the country, while in Lebanon, we are working to support youth, schools, and teachers. In all of these efforts, we place emphasis on secondary education, vocational skills, mentoring programs, and innovative pedagogies in classrooms in order to support vulnerable youth affected by the crises in host communities.

Education is the single most important long-term investment for planting seeds of peace. There is no stronger transformational force for poverty eradication, sustainable growth, and healthy societies. The *2030 Agenda for Sustainable Devel-*

opment recognizes this fact. Governments across the world must now fulfill their promise, and we must do everything to support them.

EDUCATING GLOBAL CITIZENS

For this effort, we must advocate not just for greater access to education, but also for inclusive, equitable, quality lifelong learning to promote social cohesion and living together. Education must be more than just transmitting information and knowledge. It must empower new forms of global citizenship by promoting new values and behaviors to grasp our responsibilities to each other and to the planet. Global citizenship education was a pillar of the *Global Education First Initiative* launched by former United Nations Secretary-General Ban Ki-moon in 2012 and carried forward by UNESCO. The concept is explicitly recognized in the *2030 Agenda for Sustainable Development* as an enabler to foster the values, knowledge, and skills needed to promote sustainable development.

Global citizenship is not a legal term but rather one that indicates a sense of solidarity with others to share the wealth of diversity as a force of renewal, not one of distrust. Educating global citizens is about empowering young women and men to live in a world under pressure, with human rights and dignity as the starting point for all action. This education must be taught from the earliest age to nurture cultural and linguistic diversity as forces for belonging and innovation.

Taking this effort forward requires educational systems that include new competencies and skills to prepare students for the century ahead. Education in a globalized world is increasingly putting emphasis on the importance of values, attitudes, and communication skills as critical complements to cognitive knowledge and skills. The education community is also paying increasing attention to the relevance of education in understanding and resolving social, political, cultural, and global issues. This relevance includes the role of education in supporting peace, human rights, equity, acceptance of diversity, and sustainable development. A UNESCO review of education curricula conducted in seventy-eight countries between 2000 and 2015 showed that fewer than half included any mention of or training for preparing students to handle a diverse and connected world. However, we can reverse such trends through educational guidelines and support for teacher training and curricula that accept differences and promote cultural literacy across the spectrum of learners.

Doing so is vital to strengthen welcoming societies that promote the inclusion and participation of refugees and migrants and that provide education meeting their needs to enable them to start new lives. By recognizing the diversity of their own cultures and societies and by studying history and the humanities, students can become more open to other cultures and better able to understand that what unites them is stronger than that which makes them different.

These goals underpin all of UNESCO's work to promote education for global citizenship and, beyond this effort, to unite young people around the wealth of humanity's cultural heritage that testifies to the history of our shared humanity. In 2013, UNESCO held the first Forum on Global Citizenship Education in Thailand. This was followed by a second forum in January 2015 in Paris and a third one in Ottawa, Canada, in March 2017, with the aim of organizing such events every two years as laboratories of ideas with all relevant education stakeholders (see box 9.1).

UNESCO is also working to provide education guidelines for human rights education and intercultural dialogue—embodied, for instance, in the 2006 *Guidelines on Intercultural Education* and the 2011 *Guidelines for Educators on Countering Intolerance and Discrimination against Muslims,* led with the Council of Europe and the Organization for Security and Cooperation in Europe. In 2015, we launched the Clearing House on Global Citizenship Education, hosted by the Asia-Pacific Center of Education for International Understanding, under the auspices of UNESCO and with the support of the Mahatma Gandhi Institute of Education for Peace and Sustainable Development. This first UNESCO institute of its kind is based in New Delhi, India.

In 2015, UNESCO published pedagogical guidance on global citizenship education to chart out age-specific topics and learning objectives to transform daily classroom practice. These cover a spectrum of cognitive, socioemotional, and behavioral dimensions. The University of California–Los Angeles hosts the first UNESCO Chair in Global Learning and Global Citizenship Education, held by Professor Carlos Torres. The organization is also deepening cooperation on global citizenship education with such key partners as the King Abdullah Bin Abdulaziz International Center for Interreligious and Intercultural Dialogue and the Asia Society.

All of these efforts are built into UNESCO's work to prevent the rise of violent extremism by nurturing the power of education for peace. The organization is developing policy guidelines to support ministers of education to deliver education programs that strengthen youth resilience to violent extremist messaging and that foster a positive sense of identity and belonging. In 2015, we launched a *Teacher's Guide on Violent Extremism* that can be adapted to different contexts to assist educators across the world. In addition, the UNESCO International Bureau of Education is leading a global dialogue on integrating universally agreed-upon values in national curricula as part of an action to prevent violent extremism. UNESCO is also leading the United Nations system in supporting the teaching of the history of the Holocaust and other genocides as a key strategy to fight against discrimination, anti-Semitism, and xenophobia in societies across the world today.

Another approach consists of UNESCO's work to bolster media and information literacy for young people and to advance intercultural dialogue—for instance, to tackle hate speech and false narratives spread on social media. This is a core goal

BOX 9.1. GLOBAL CITIZENSHIP EDUCATION (GCE)

Goal: Global citizenship education (GCE) aims to empower learners to engage and assume active roles both locally and globally to face and resolve global challenges and ultimately to become proactive contributors to a more just, peaceful, tolerant, inclusive, secure, and sustainable world. GCE is transformative, giving learners the opportunity and competencies to realize their rights and obligations to promote a better world and future. It draws upon learning from other transformative education processes, including human rights education, education for sustainable development, education for international/intercultural understanding, and education for peace.

Delivery: GCE is built on a lifelong learning perspective. It is not only for children and youth but also for adults. It can be delivered in all modes and venues, including formal, nonformal, and informal education. GCE can be presented as an integral part of an existing subject (e.g., civics or citizenship education, social studies, social /environmental studies, or health education) or as an independent subject area.

Competencies: Core competencies of GCE include (1) knowledge and understanding of global issues and trends, and knowledge of and respect for key universal values (e.g., peace and human rights, diversity, justice, democracy, caring, nondiscrimination, and tolerance); (2) cognitive skills for critical, creative, and innovative thinking, problem solving, and decision making; (3) noncognitive skills such as empathy, openness to experiences and other perspectives, interpersonal/communicative skills, and aptitude for networking and interacting with people of different backgrounds and origins; and (4) behavioral capacities to launch and engage in proactive actions.

Enabling/facilitating conditions: A climate that is open to universal values (e.g., human rights and peace) is crucial for the promotion of the goals of GCE. Effective implementation requires policy support and pedagogical guidance. The learning environment should promote links to communities (both local and global) and links for learners to real-life experiences (e.g., community-based humanitarian activities, student foreign-exchange programs, foreign languages, and area/regional studies) as alternative or complementary paths of learning. It is important to reach learners early during their formative early childhood stages of development.

Reflecting the goal of GCE in countries' curricula is one of the most urgent tasks. This effort involves the translation of globally accepted concepts into local contexts. A guiding framework at the global level could help accomplish this task. Some indicators or proxies that capture the competencies required for global citizenship education will also be useful for monitoring/assessing the processes and outcomes of learning.

Transformative education requires transformative pedagogy that (1) encourages learners to analyze real-life issues critically and to identify possible solutions creatively and innovatively; (2) supports learners to critically revisit assumptions, world views, and power relations in mainstream discourses and to consider people/groups who are systematically underrepresented/marginalized; (3) respects differences and diversity; (4) focuses on engagement in action to bring about desired changes; and (5) involves multiple stakeholders, including those outside the learning environment in the community and in the larger circle of the society. Education managers and educators need additional training and support to implement or deliver such pedagogy.

There is a need to support youth-led initiatives. Partnerships with civil society are also needed. Utilization of new information and communication technologies (ICTs) is critical. New approaches may meet with reservation and/or resistance, including hesitation on the issue of promoting universality (e.g., common and collective identity, interest, participation, or duty) while also respecting particularity (e.g., individual rights, self-cultivation). An emerging perspective on GCE calls for the need for stakeholders and actors to be open to different but effective venues and solutions.

of UNESCO's *Integrated Framework of Action: Empowering Youth to Build Peace,* launched at the first International Conference on Youth and the Internet: Fighting Radicalization and Extremism, which was organized by UNESCO in 2015. This meeting was followed by a second International Conference in November 2016 in Quebec, Canada.

UNESCO is also acting on the ground to boost youth engagement in political processes, to promote human rights by increasing youth interaction with the media and their use of ICT-based platforms, and to enhance their economic inclusion. Through the NET-MED Youth Project, supported by the European Union, UNESCO is working to bolster the positive engagement of young women and men in ten countries around the Mediterranean, a region at the heart of the migrant and refugee crisis.

In this context, the efforts to craft new ways of living together on the basis of dialogue, respect, and human rights have placed an increasing focus on cities. In 2015, UNESCO launched an initiative, *Welcoming Cities for Refugees—Promoting Inclusion and Protecting Rights,* with the foundation of UNESCO Goodwill Ambassador Marianna V. Vardinoyannis and in partnership with the European Coalition of Cities against Racism. This is part of the UNESCO International Coalition of Inclusive and Sustainable Cities that was initiated in 2004 to promote inclusive urban development free from all forms of discrimination.

LOOKING FORWARD

Young women and men have never been so connected, widely traveled, or outspoken. At the same time, they are the hardest hit by global turbulence, with impacts that include unemployment, exclusion, and marginalization, and they are shouldering the heaviest burdens of the migration and forced displacement.

The world cannot afford to lose entire generations to despair and hatred. We must provide every young person with the values and skills to face a world of change and to believe in her or his capacity to shape it for the better. This effort calls for new forms of education in order to understand others, to feel empathy, to exchange ideas, to resolve conflicts through dialogue, and to tackle global challenges together. For this task, we must make the most of education to turn global citizenship into a practice that is taken forward every day, everywhere, by assuming responsibilities toward others, by nurturing critical thinking and resilience, and by learning to live together in trust.

How to achieve global solidarity is the core question raised by the current migration and refugee crisis. It goes to the heart of our vision of society and humanity, and we must start to answer it in classrooms everywhere.

REFERENCES

UNESCO–GEMR (United Nations Educational, Scientific, and Cultural Organization–Global Education Monitoring Report) and UNHCR (United Nations High Commissioner for Refugees). 2016. *No More Excuses: Provide Education to All Forcibly Displaced People.* Policy Paper 26. Paris: UNESCO.

United Nations. 2015. *2030 Agenda for Sustainable Development.* UN General Assembly. New York: United Nations.

United Nations. 2016. *New York Declaration.* Resolution adopted by the UN General Assembly, Sept. 19. United Nations High-Level Summit for Refugees and Migrants. New York: United Nations.

10

INCLUSION AND MEMBERSHIP THROUGH REFUGEE EDUCATION?

Tensions between Policy and Practice

Sarah Dryden-Peterson

Aker[1] is one of 21.3 million refugees globally who have been forcibly displaced outside of a country of origin. She fled acute conflict in South Sudan and migrated to Kenya to join her cousin and brother, who had crossed the border earlier to avoid possible recruitment into fighting forces. There was one reason why she kept her hopes up about life in exile: she could go to school. She recalled that in South Sudan, "we do not know the good things of education."[2] In Nairobi, on the other hand, she attended a community-based school that had been started by the Sudanese community in 2002 "to educate their youth to become skilled, capable leaders that can assist in the rebuilding of their homeland of southern Sudan."[3]

Until recently, refugee education had been planned with this quite singular purpose: to prepare students to return to their countries of origin (Dryden-Peterson 2016). Refugee students were isolated, largely in camp settings, and attended refugee-only schools, where they were taught in the language of their country of origin. At present, most refugees' return to a country of origin is increasingly unlikely: in 2014, in thirty-three conflicts globally, the average length of exile was twenty-five years (UNHCR and Global Education Monitoring Report 2016). In addition, refugees are less likely to be isolated; in 2015, more than 60 percent of refugees lived in urban areas (UNHCR 2015), like Aker in Nairobi, amid national populations.

Refugeehood is defined by long-term exile and impacted by social and economic factors, national and global policy directives, and refugees' own personal decision-making. In this context, since 2012, global refugee education policy has focused on integrating refugees into national education systems (Dryden-Peterson 2016). This policy of integration, reflecting the reality that displacement

is protracted and that return to one's country of origin is elusive, focuses prag-
matically on creating stability within contexts of exile. In practice, however, the
process of integrating refugees meets a different reality, one often filled with isolation and exclusion. Drawing on more than a decade of research in multiple refugee
contexts, this chapter explores the tensions between the stability that a model of
integrating refugees into national education systems promises and the precarious
situations that it can create. In particular, I provide three scenarios of how refugees' daily experiences in classrooms place them outside of current membership in
society civically, politically, socially, and culturally.

BACKGROUND: RIGHTS, POLICIES, AND GEOGRAPHIES
OF REFUGEE EDUCATION

Refugees are defined as people who have crossed an international border due to a
well-founded fear of persecution. The Office of the United Nations High Commissioner for Refugees (UNHCR) is the organization mandated with the physical,
political, and social protection of refugees; with the delivery of humanitarian
assistance such as food, shelter, and water; and also with the provision of education. As a constituent body, UNHCR's work on education, as on other issues, is
coordinated with the governments of "host countries," as the states in which refugees reside are called.

Eighty-six percent of the world's refugees—like Aker—live in host countries
that border their conflict-affected countries of origin and are called "neighboring
host countries." These countries are generally characterized by education systems
that are overstretched and political and economic institutions that are fragile
(Dryden-Peterson 2016). In contrast, fewer than one percent of refugees globally
settle in more distant countries, such as those in North America and Europe,
where the numbers of refugees are small and educational resources are greater.
Unlike those in distant resettlement countries, refugees living in exile in neighboring host countries do not have a pathway to citizenship or permanent status within
the nation-state, a situation that, as I have discussed elsewhere (Dryden-Peterson
2016), has important implications in the conceptualization of refugee education.
In addition, as Gonzalo Sánchez-Terán (2017) argues, this geographic distribution
of refugees is usefully framed as a "global confinement crisis." It is not an accident
of migration but rather a situation governed by laws and policies, most notably
those of the European Union and the United States, that forcibly contains refugees
outside of nation-states and that can, through power and money, outsource the
"burden" or "threat" of refugees, including millions of children.

What is new is the movement of larger numbers of displaced people further
from their countries of origin. In 2014, Turkey became the largest refugee-hosting
country worldwide, with 1.59 million refugees (UNHCR 2014). While in 2014,

Germany hosted only 217,000 refugees and Greece 7,300 (UNHCR 2015), by 2015, the German government reported 467,649 asylum applications (German Federal Ministry of the Interior 2016), and almost one million asylum seekers arrived in Greece by sea routes (UNHCR 2016; Stathopoulou, chapter 7, this volume). This increased migration outside of regions of origin complicates a neat neighboring host country/distant resettlement country dichotomy. Yet, importantly, asylum seekers in Europe face extreme limbo vis-à-vis permanent residence, as do refugees in neighboring host countries.

Globally, the right to education for all persons, including refugees who are crisis-affected and have been displaced, has been clearly articulated. In 2010, the United Nations General Assembly passed a resolution specifically on the right to education in emergencies (United Nations 2010). The right to education in crisis has been central to global movements as well, from the original *1990 Education for All Declaration* (World Conference on Education for All 1990) and increasing in prominence at each subsequent World Education Forum (see, for example, World Education Forum 2000, 2015). Limited progress on the education targets of the Millennium Development Goals was particularly evident in crisis contexts, with half of the world's out-of-school children living in these settings (UNESCO 2015). In response, the Sustainable Development Goals identify "refugees and internally displaced persons and migrants" as "vulnerable" and call for the elimination of disparities in access to inclusive and quality education for these populations (United Nations 2015, 7/35). Concurrent has been the development and wide adoption of the *INEE Minimum Standards for Education: Preparedness, Response, Recovery*, a set of normative standards to guide policy and practice for education in crisis settings (INEE 2010).

The right to education for refugees, specifically, is articulated in the *1951 Convention Relating to the Status of Refugees* and its companion *1967 Protocol*, which provide international norms defining who is a refugee, refugee rights, and the legal obligations of the state vis-à-vis refugees. Article 22 of the *1951 Convention* specifies that signatory states "shall accord to refugees the same treatment as is accorded to nationals with respect to elementary education . . . [and] treatment as favourable as possible . . . with respect to education other than elementary education" (UNHCR 2010, 24).

Despite this in-principle commitment to the right to education for refugees, the realization of refugees' right to education varies globally (see also Sánchez-Terán 2017). In 2014, 50 percent of refugees had access to primary school, compared with 93 percent of all children globally (UNHCR and Global Education Monitoring Report 2016; Dryden-Peterson 2015). Within each host country, refugees also usually access education at lower rates: in Pakistan, for example, 43 percent of refugees access primary education as compared with 72 percent of nationals who do (Dryden-Peterson 2015).

In 2012, the Office of the United Nations High Commissioner for Refugees adopted a new education strategy, with the integration of refugees into national education systems as its central organizing principle (UNHCR 2012). This new approach had rapid up-take. In 2011, UNHCR had no formal relationships with national ministries of education. By 2016, UNHCR had formal relationships with national ministries of education in twenty of its twenty-five large education operations, with accompanying access to national schools for refugees and coordination mechanisms between a government and UNHCR (Dryden-Peterson 2016). In some ways, this new policy is an initial step toward what Sánchez-Terán (2017) calls the "responsibility to protect for education." It is a global framework that seeks political commitment to the education of refugees at the nation-state level. Importantly, however, it does not trigger a global commitment to action in the absence of a government that is able or willing to provide this education.

This policy decision was based in the clear reality that displacement is protracted and that educational opportunities for refugees cannot wait for a return to stability. Given this context, multiple rationales guided the new policy approach: structural rationales that education of refugees is of higher quality within a national system due to access to trained teachers and possibilities of certification, economic rationales that education of refugees is less expensive within a preexisting system, and sociocultural rationales related to membership in the society of long-term exile (Dryden-Peterson et al., working paper). This chapter explores the final rationale.

CONCEPTUAL FRAMEWORK: MECHANISMS OF INCLUSION AND MEMBERSHIP

T. H. Marshall ([1950] 2009) identified three aspects of citizenship: civil, related to the rights of individual freedom, such as to justice, property, and speech; political, related to enfranchisement; and social, related to access to social services, including education. Is this typology relevant to the situation of refugees in neighboring host countries, specifically as related to assumptions of status and legitimacy?

In almost all cases, refugees in neighboring host countries do not have access to civil and political citizenship (see, for example, Zetter and Ruaudel 2016; Hovil 2016), with the naturalization of long-staying Burundian refugees in Tanzania in 2014 as the only recent example (Hovil 2016, 51). In this way, the three types of productive citizenship—recognized, participatory, and transformative—that Banks (chapter 11, this volume; see also Banks 2017) describes are a priori out of reach for the vast majority of the world's refugees. As Banks notes, to enact *recognized citizenship,* individuals must be structurally integrated into the nation-state, wherein "the state or nation publicly recognizes an individual or group as a legitimate, legal, and valued member of the polity and provides the individual or group full rights and opportunities to participate." Further, to enact participatory or transformative citizenship, "individuals must be recognized by the state as legal and legitimate citizens" (Banks 2017, 367). Are refugees then destined for *failed citizenship*, in which they "do not"—or are not eligible to—"internalize the values and ethos of the nation-state, feel structurally excluded within it, and have highly ambivalent feeling towards it" (chapter 11, this volume)?

While Banks draws primarily on research on marginalized individuals and groups with legal status in distant resettlement countries, work from settings of conflict, even if not exile, is conceptually valuable for framing the distinct situation of refugees. Drawing on Marc Sommers's (2012) concept of *wait adulthood*, developed through empirical work in Rwanda, Michelle Bellino (2017) argues that in the context of postconflict transition in Guatemala, individuals experience what she calls "wait citizenship." *Wait citizenship* is the idea that productive forms of citizenship are promised, but there is a lack of conditions under which individuals or groups can realize it.

Refugees are typically in a similar holding pattern of promises embedded within the frameworks of human rights and refugee policies, yet they lack the legal status that is prerequisite to any future realization of citizenship rights and privileges. They have the means to attain social citizenship, as Marshall defines it, in the form of their growing participation in national schools as well as the ability to obtain other social services in neighboring host countries. This access to education within national education systems promises a certain degree of inclusion. However, refugees' long-term prospects for using that education civically, politically, economically, and socially are slim, leading some refugee children and families to begin regarding education as "pointless" (Sánchez-Terán 2017). Moreover, recent research in neighboring host countries provides evidence that refugees experience marginalization in schools similar to or greater than that experienced by national ethnic and linguistic minorities (Dryden-Peterson 2015; Mendenhall et al. 2015).

In what ways might education enable membership, even if not citizenship, in nation-states of long-term exile? This question leads to a productive exploration of mechanisms by which education might disrupt the marginalizations that refugee children and young people experience that reduce possibilities of their membership in nation-states of long-term exile. Possible mechanisms would involve inclusion in both the structure and content of education. Research in settings of conflict is broadly relevant to refugee education. Unequal access to education can be a driver of conflict. In 2001 in Nepal, for example, the literacy rate among the ruling Brahmins was 70 percent, compared with only 10 percent among the lower/excluded castes (Novelli and Smith 2011). In Sierra Leone, a public education system that was geographically unequal and divided by class was cited as a cause of conflict, and redressing the inequalities in this system was one of the central demands of the rebel RUF army in building peace after the cessation of conflict (Novelli and Smith 2011). The absence of learning opportunities and the gap between educational accreditation and employment are regularly cited as young people's justifications for joining armed groups (World Bank 2011; Brown 2010; Collier and Hoeffler 2004).

Even when educational access is close to universal, the content of education can exclude. (On the humiliation that refugee children experience, see Mollica, chapter 5, this volume.) What is taught in schools clearly demonstrates to children the power structure of the society in which they live. They may see ethnicity and religion mobilized and politicized through education. For example, in Kosovo in the 1990s, the Serbian government used education as an instrument to assimilate minority Albanians. They eliminated teaching in Albanian and introduced a unified curriculum that included standardized textbooks. Without a way to access learning in their own language or to see an Albanian identity reflected in the schools, many Albanian parents refused to send their children to government schools, instead choosing nonaccredited Albanian schools. This parallel system did not allow Albanian children access to the benefits of certification since it was regarded as illegal by the government (Bush and Saltarelli 2000). In the case of Pakistan, A. H. Nayyar undertook a detailed analysis of the nation's curriculum and textbooks, showing that there was systemic indoctrination against non-Muslims. The Pakistani identity, for example, was restricted to Muslims alone, and "Pakistani nationalism [was] repeatedly defined in a manner that exclude[d] non-Muslim Pakistanis from either being Pakistani nationals or . . . even being good human beings" (Nayyar and Salim 2003, vi). Nayyar argues that the perspectives forwarded by the curriculum encouraged "prejudice, bigotry and discrimination towards fellow citizens" (v), an outcome that limits the possibilities for inclusion and breeds the kind of alienation central to Banks's concept of *failed citizenship* (chapter 11, this volume; see also Banks 2017).

There is a clear consensus in the literature of a relationship between the structures and content of education and the sort of marginalization that leads to conflict (Dixon 2009; Thyne 2006; Shields and Paulson 2014). Theories informed by historical and contemporary case studies suggest that the relationship is bidirectional and likely cyclical. In a now-seminal piece, Kenneth Bush and Diana Saltarelli (2000) defined the "two faces" of education in conflict: one that mitigates conflict, the other that contributes to conflict. The "two faces" have recently evolved into the "multiple faces" of education in conflict. Based on research in Afghanistan, Bosnia-Herzegovina, Cambodia, Liberia, and Sri Lanka, Lynn Davies (2011, 35) proposes a "spectrum of impact" to account for the multiple and intersecting ways that educational actors and institutions can simultaneously contribute to or erode stability. At times actions taken to mitigate harm unintentionally have caused it. For example, when Darfurian refugees living in Chad were presented with the option of taking Chadian examinations and receiving certification, many young people instead elected to reenter Sudan, at great risks to themselves, in order to sit for the Sudanese examination.[4]

The following scenarios explore ways in which the structures and content of education for refugees can contribute to or erode possibilities for the inclusion and membership in society that they intend to create.

SCENARIO 1: STRUCTURES OF EDUCATION

In 2012, UNHCR introduced a new global Education Strategy that focuses on the provision of quality education for refugees (UNHCR 2012). The global strategy includes six objectives and four strategic approaches intended to ensure that all refugee children have access to an education of high quality that provides physical protection and personal capacity development. It frames the overall approach to these goals as "integration of refugee learners within national systems where possible and appropriate and as guided by ongoing consultation with refugees" (UNHCR 2012, 8). While global in nature, this strategy was designed to be adapted to each country in which UNHCR works through local processes of contextualization and prioritization. During two years of research on the process of implementing this strategy, we found that these processes of contextualization at the national, regional, and local levels resulted in different forms of "integration" (Dryden-Peterson et al., working paper).

For example, in the Dadaab camps of Kenya, "integration" means following the Kenyan curriculum in English (the official language of instruction in Kenya) and sitting for the Kenyan Primary and Secondary Completion Exams (KCPE and KCSE). It does not, however, involve interacting with Kenyan national students in class, as schools are de facto segregated—located in isolated refugee camps. In Egypt "integration" is available only for Syrian refugees, not for Somalis, Sudanese, and refugees from other sub-Saharan African countries. Syrian refugee children in Egypt attend national schools, use the national curriculum and language, and, unlike their peers in Kenya, are physically together in school with Egyptian nationals. In Lebanon, Syrians have access to the Lebanese national public schools attended by Lebanese children; however, they are assigned, with some exceptions, to a second shift occurring in the afternoons. Thus, while they are integrated in the same physical space with national students, often with the same teachers, who are now teaching much longer days, the refugee students are temporally segregated from the national students. Each of these situations of "integration" is premised on exclusion.

SCENARIO 2: CONTENT OF EDUCATION

School is a central place in which refugee children try to make sense of conflict, flight, and their new situations. However, the curriculum to which refugee children are exposed can be challenging for them to relate to, especially if it ignores or offers unidimensional perspectives on history and/or conflict. For example, in a Kakuma refugee camp in Kenya, children had a hard time understanding the agrarian revolution in Britain. The teacher explained it as follows: "There were few who had resources . . . a plot of land and workers . . . and they [were] what we call serfdom and landlord." He wrote the words *serfdom* and *landlord* on the board and then underlined them. Pointing with his chalk to *serfdom*, he explained, "They were poor, only given what they were supposed to eat, but the rest was going to the land-owner." This was an era called *feudalism*, he explained. He wrote *feudalism* on the board. "And the poor majority lives like this under the landowner class. . . . There was lots of exploitation."[5] Though the teacher talked about these relevant issues of social class during the historical time period under study, he did not help the students make any connections from it to their own personal or national histories. (See Mollica, chapter 5, this volume, on the purposes of and need for narrative.)

Even when teachers choose not to highlight relevant political and social connections in their classroom teaching, the lived experiences of refugee students can often surface in it. Hadia, a Syrian teacher working at a nonformal school for Syrian refugees in Lebanon, described a situation that unfolded in her classroom.[6] Hadia said, "I once had a drawing period and two boys came to me. One drew the revolutionary flag and the other drew the regime flag, and they started arguing [about] which flag is ours, this or that, expecting me to answer them. I asked both of them if they had a house, and they both replied with a no, so I said, 'What about we find a land where we can build a house . . . and then we argue about the flag.' They agreed and went back to their seats. I thanked God that I was able to solve the incident." While noting that she had "solved" the incident for the moment, Hadia also reflected on how these are not issues that go away or disappear. She worried that there would not be enough space within a formal curriculum to continue to address the deep needs that her students had to talk about these issues.[7]

SCENARIO 3: THE INTERSECTION OF STRUCTURE AND CONTENT: OPPORTUNITIES FOR THE FUTURE

Young refugees describe migration as a process, not a one-time endeavor: migration to a host country such as Kenya or Lebanon; migration within the host country, such as from Dadaab to Nairobi; return to a country of origin, and sometimes a subsequent return to the host country; and the prospect, and sometimes reality, of resettlement to a third country such as the United States or Canada (Stathopoulou, chapter 7, this volume, especially the "Expectations/Plans" section).

New Eastleigh School in Nairobi is a government school that has a sizable population of refugee students, primarily from Somalia.[8] The senior teacher at this school explained some of the reasons for ongoing migration and the consequences for learning, inclusion, and membership. He said:

> [At] the start of the year, we have admitted around three hundred [new pupils]. By
> the end of term one, already a hundred are gone. . . . [Of] these hundred, by the next

year, maybe fifty will come back. They have resurfaced again. [We say:] "Where were you?" "Gone to Kakuma, my grandmother was sick in Somalia, we visited, now we are back again." So we accept them. . . . But you know, we are going to be back academic-wise. Because these pupils will still insist, "I was in [Standard] five." They have [been] gone for [a] couple or two terms. Now when [a pupil] is coming, others have moved to the next class. When you tell him to go . . . there[, they say,] "No! I'm going to join my class." And they remember he has missed one term. But he's not . . . willing to join the other ones who are in [Standard] four when he was in [Standard] five.[9]

Many refugee families are not settled in Nairobi; they are in processes of continual migration, seeking strengthened opportunities for their futures. Since refugees do not have the right to work in Kenya, parents and older students described needing to think about relocating in order to be able to use their education. A Standard 7 teacher at New Eastleigh outlined a common situation at the school in which all of a sudden "almost half of the class is not there." He then realized that they had gone to the Kakuma refugee camp for "interviews" or for the head count, which was a way to verify their continued eligibility for resettlement.[10] The deputy head teacher described what we might conceive of as an in-between place in which the Somali children at New Eastleigh School in Nairobi are living. "When they are needed in the camps, they just go," said the deputy head teacher. After all, the students at this school are here, he explained, because they want to prepare for resettlement. They want to be at a certain level of education and of English "by the time they go to America."[11] During that one year, twenty New Eastleigh students were resettled to the United States. "We lost them," the senior teacher said.[12]

While notions of refugeehood may imply clear and unidirectional migration trajectories, the experiences of students at New Eastleigh School highlight an overlapping of migration categories, as Lesley Bartlett and Ameena Ghaffar-Kucher (2013, 3) have described. Further, these experiences highlight the different forms of "integration" that exist at the intersection of the structures and content of education that are available for refugee students. Given the existing structures and content of education, and the possibilities of using their education upon graduation, refugee students pursued multiple options for their futures, in this case, both in their resettlement to the United States *and* in their education in Kenyan schools. Yet this example also demonstrates how pursuing multiple strategies may entail working at cross-purposes: in order to keep alive the possibility of resettlement, students needed to displace themselves over and over again to the camps and away from processes of learning and integration in Nairobi schools (Dryden-Peterson 2011).

Refugee education policy has shifted markedly over the past five years to the integration of refugee students into national education systems. This approach reflects a clear shift in thinking about the purposes of refugee education (Dryden-

Peterson et al., working paper). Rather than preparing refugee students for a return to their country of origin, refugee education within a national education system assumes some longer-term presence for students in the context of exile. At the same time, refugee children do not have access to the types of citizenship that the structures and content of this education presupposes (Dryden-Peterson 2016). Hannah Arendt (2004, 369) noted, reflecting on the post–World War II European refugee crisis, that rights were "supposed to be independent of all governments," and yet "it turned out that the moment human beings lacked their own government and had to fall back upon their minimum rights, no authority was left to protect them and no institution was willing to guarantee them." In this way, the "loss of *national* rights was identical with the loss of *human* rights" (71, emphasis added) because these rights, although "supposedly *inalienable,* proved to be *unenforceable*" (72, emphasis added).

Protecting the right to education for refugees and fostering inclusion and membership—even in the absence of citizenship—to mitigate the marginalization of refugee young people demand shared global responsibility. In the contexts in which most refugees live, even amid major resource constraints, organizations and governments have worked together to create opportunities, particularly those related to the structures of education. For example, as discussed in the scenarios outlined in this chapter, national ministries of education in Lebanon and Kenya have enabled refugees to access national schools. Yet often in classrooms, refugee children feel isolated and excluded through the content of the education and the ways in which structures and content interact to send messages of exclusion.

Very skilled teachers can counter these marginalizations, even in challenging political environments. On a short visit to Germany, I observed one such teacher in action in a class of new arrivals and long-time residents of Germany. This was at a school that had a long history of serving migrant children, primarily from Turkey, and this particular teacher had more than ten years of experience working with German-language learners and children in economic and legal limbo. This teacher fostered an environment in which her students learned about each other and about their nation-state of exile. She did this through discussion about experiences that students had had and the sense they had made of them, and she helped them to see across diverse perspectives to important commonalities. She tailored instruction to the needs—academic, linguistic, social—of each student, including multiple languages in her classroom through, for example, her own speech and choice of books, which made each student feel a sense of inclusion in the classroom (see also Dryden-Peterson, Adelman, and Nieswandt 2016). Even in conducive political contexts, few teachers have these specific skills, and the most common request we hear from teachers of refugees globally is for training in meeting these needs.

To create conditions in which refugee children and young people can access inclusion and membership in their long-term nation-states of exile, we must invest in teachers more than ever before. Individual nation-states cannot bear the costs of this endeavor alone. We need a shared global responsibility to enable the kind of education for all refugees that does not lead to exclusion and failed citizenship but that acts as a mechanism to harness their many potential contributions to the global community in which we all live.

NOTES

Acknowledgements: For sharing their ideas and helping to shape mine, I am grateful to all of my research participants; to Elizabeth Adelman, Michelle Bellino, Vidur Chopra, and students at the Harvard Graduate School of Education in the course Education in Armed Conflict in 2013 and 2014 and in the Refugee Education Policy Lab in 2015; to the members of the University of Nairobi–International Rescue Committee Education in Emergencies collaborative research project; and to participants at the Workshop on Humanitarianism and Mass Migration, in particular Jacqueline Bhabha and Hiroshi Motomura.

1. Names of all research participants have been changed.

2. Interview by Sarah Dryden-Peterson, Nairobi, Kenya, May 23, 2013. Data cited in this chapter were collected as part of a collaborative research study involving the International Rescue Committee (Mary Mendenhall and Mary Tangelder); faculty members at the University of Nairobi (Caroline Ndirangu, Rosemary Imonje, Daniel Gakunga, Lois Gichuhi, Grace Nyagah, and Ursulla Okoth); and professors from the University of Wisconsin (Lesley Bartlett) and Harvard Graduate School of Education (Sarah Dryden-Peterson).

3. Quotation taken from school website. Author does not cite the website directly to maintain the confidentiality of the school.

4. Skype interview by Rebecca Vaudreuil and Victoria Villalba under the supervision of Sarah Dryden-Peterson, NGO working with UNHCR in Chad, March 28, 2014. Data collected as part of a two-year study of the implementation of the UNHCR Education Strategy, 2012–[0]16.

5. Classroom observation by Michelle Bellino under the supervision of Sarah Dryden-Peterson, Kakuma Refugee Camp, Form 1 Social Studies, June 28, 2014. Data collected as part of a two-year study of the implementation of the UNHCR Education Strategy, 2012–16.

6. This observation and interview data are drawn with permission from the dissertation fieldwork of Elizabeth Adelman, to whom I serve as dissertation advisor. See also Dryden-Peterson and Adelman (2016).

7. Interview by Elizabeth Adelman, October 12, 2015.

8. Data collected as part of the collaborative research study described in note 2. See also Mendenhall et al. 2015.

9. Interview by Sarah Dryden-Peterson and Daniel Gakunga, Nairobi, Kenya, May 28, 2013. Data collected as part of the collaborative research study described in note 2.

10. Interview by Rosemary Imonje, Nairobi, Kenya, May 28, 2013. Data collected as part of the collaborative research study described in note 2.

11. Interview by Sarah Dryden-Peterson and Daniel Gakunga, Nairobi, Kenya, May 28, 2013. Data collected as part of the collaborative research study described in note 2.

12. Interview by Sarah Dryden-Peterson and Daniel Gakunga, Nairobi, Kenya, May 28, 2013. Data collected as part of the collaborative research study described in note 2.

REFERENCES

Arendt, Hannah. 2004. *The Origins of Totalitarianism*. 1st ed. New York: Schocken Books.

Banks, James A. 2017. "Failed Citizenship and Transformative Civic Education." *Educational Researcher* 46 (7): 366–377.

Bartlett, Lesley, and Ameena Ghaffar-Kucher. 2013. *Refugees, Immigrants, and Education in the Global South: Lives in Motion*. New York: Routledge.

Bellino, Michelle J. 2017. *Youth in Postwar Guatemala: Education and Civic Identity in Transition*. New Brunswick, NJ: Rutgers University Press.

Brown, Graham K. 2010. *Education and Violent Conflict: Background Paper for EFA Global Monitoring Report 2011*. Paris: UNESCO. http://unesdoc.unesco.org/images/0019 /001907/190706e.pdf.

Bush, Kenneth D., and Diana Saltarelli. 2000. *The Two Faces of Education in Ethnic Conflict: Towards a Peacebuilding Education for Children*. Florence, Italy: UNICEF, Innocenti Research Centre.

Collier, Paul, and Anke Hoeffler. 2004. "Greed and Grievance in Civil War." *Oxford Economic Papers* 56 (4): 563–95.

Davies, Lynn. 2011. "Can Education Interrupt Fragility? Towards the Resilient and Adaptable State." In *Educating Children in Conflict Zones: Research, Policy, and Practice for Systemic Change: A Tribute to Jackie Kirk*, edited by Karen Mundy and Sarah Dryden-Peterson, 33–48. New York: Teachers College Press.

Dixon, Jeffrey. 2009. "What Causes Civil Wars? Integrating Quantitative Research Findings." *International Studies Review* 11 (4): 707–35.

Dryden-Peterson, Sarah. 2011. "Refugee Children Aspiring toward the Future: Linking Education and Livelihoods." In *Educating Children in Conflict Zones: Research, Policy, and Practice for Systemic Change: A Tribute to Jackie Kirk*, edited by Karen Mundy and Sarah Dryden-Peterson, 85–99. New York: Teachers College Press.

———. 2015. "Refugee Education in Countries of First Asylum: Breaking Open the Black Box of Pre-Resettlement Experiences." *Theory and Research in Education* 14 (2): 1–18.

———. 2016. "Refugee Education: The Crossroads of Globalization." *Educational Researcher* 45 (9): 473–82.

Dryden-Peterson, Sarah, and Elizabeth Adelman. 2016. "Inside Syrian Refugee Schools: Making Room for Refugees in Second Shifts." *Brookings Education Plus Development*. Washington, DC: Brookings Institution. Blog entry, February 17, 2016. www.brookings .edu/blog/education-plus-development/2016/02/17/inside-syrian-refugee-schools-making-room-for-refugees-in-second-shifts/.

Dryden-Peterson, Sarah, Elizabeth Adelman, Michelle Bellino, and Vidur Chopra. Working paper. "The Purposes of Refugee Education: Policy and Practice of Integrating Refugees into National Education Systems."

Dryden-Peterson, Sarah, Elizabeth Adelman, and Martina Nieswandt. 2016. "Inside Syrian Refugee Schools: Syrian Children in Germany." *Brookings Education Plus Development.* Washington, DC: Brookings Institution. Blog entry, May 23, 2016. www.brookings.edu /blog/education-plus-development/2016/05/23/inside-syrian-refugee-schools-syrian-children-in-germany/.

German Federal Ministry of the Interior. 2016. *The Number of Refugees Must Be Substantially Reduced on a Permanent Basis.* Berlin: German Federal Ministry of the Interior. www.bmi.bund.de/SharedDocs/Kurzmeldungen/EN/2016/02/meeting-with-morgan-johansson.html;jsessionid = 6E0305629BBED0BE2752A179EA6451DA.2_cid287.

Hovil, Lucy. 2016. *Refugees, Conflict, and the Search for Belonging.* 1st ed. Cham, NY: Springer International.

INEE (Inter-Agency Network for Education in Emergencies). 2010. *Minimum Standards for Education: Preparedness, Response, Recovery.* New York: INEE.

Marshall, T. H. (1950) 2009. "Citizenship and Social Class." In *Inequality and Society,* edited by Jeff Manza and Michael Sauder, 148–54. New York: Norton.

Mendenhall, Mary, Sarah Dryden-Peterson, Lesley Bartlett, Caroline Ndirangu, Rosemary Imonje, Daniel Gakunga, Loise Gichuhi, et al. 2015. "Quality Education for Refugees in Kenya: Pedagogy in Urban Nairobi and Kakuma Refugee Camp Settings." *Journal on Education in Emergencies* 1 (1): 92–130.

Nayyar, A. H., and Ahmed Salim. 2003. *The Subtle Subversion: The State of Curricula and Textbooks in Pakistan, Urdu, English, Social Studies, and Civics.* Islamabad: Sustainable Development Policy Institute.

Novelli, Mario, and Alan Smith. 2011. *The Role of Education in Peacebuilding: A Synthesis Report of Findings from Lebanon, Nepal, and Sierra Leone.* New York: UNICEF.

Sánchez-Terán, Gonzalo. 2017. "The Global Forced Migration Crisis and the Education of Children." Paper presented at the Workshop on Humanitarianism and Mass Migration, UCLA, Los Angeles, January 18–19, 2017.

Shields, Robin, and Julia Paulson. 2014. "'Development in Reverse'? A Longitudinal Analysis of Armed Conflict, Fragility, and School Enrollment." *Comparative Education* 1 (1): 14–47.

Sommers, Marc. 2012. *Stuck: Rwandan Youth and the Struggle for Adulthood.* Athens: University of Georgia Press; Washington, DC: US Institute of Peace.

Thyne, Clayton. 2006. "ABCs, 123s, and the Golden Rule: The Pacifying Effect of Education on Civil War, 1980–99." *International Studies Quarterly* 50 (4): 733–54.

UNESCO (United Nations Educational, Scientific, and Cultural Organization). 2015. *EFA Global Monitoring Report: Education for All 2000–15: Achievements and Challenges.* Paris: UNESCO.

UNHCR (United Nations High Commissioner for Refugees). 2010. *Convention and Protocol Relating to the Status of Refugees.* Geneva: UNHCR.

———. 2012. *Education Strategy 2012–16.* Geneva: UNHCR.

———. 2014. *UNHCR Global Trends 2013: War's Human Cost.* Geneva: UNHCR.

———. 2015. *UNHCR Statistical Yearbook 2014.* Geneva: UNHCR.

———. 2016. *Global Trends: Forced Displacement in 2015.* Geneva: UNHCR.

UNHCR and Global Education Monitoring Report. 2016. *No More Excuses: Provide Education to All Forcibly Displaced People.* Policy Paper 26. Paris: UNESCO.

United Nations. 2010. *The Right to Education in Emergency Situations.* New York: United Nations General Assembly.

United Nations. 2015. *Transforming Our World: The 2030 Agenda for Sustainable Development: Resolution Adopted by the General Assembly on 25 September 2015.* New York: United Nations.

World Bank. 2011. *World Development Report: Conflict, Security, and Development.* Washington, DC: World Bank.

World Conference on Education for All. 1990. *World Declaration on Education for All.* Jomtien, Thailand: World Conference on Education for All.

World Education Forum. 2000. *Education in Situations of Emergency and Crisis: Issues Paper.* Dakar, Senegal: World Education Forum.

———. 2015. *Incheon Declaration: Education 2030: Towards Inclusive and Equitable Quality Education and Lifelong Learning for All.* Incheon, Republic of Korea: World Education Forum.

Zetter, Roger, and Héloïse Ruaudel. 2016. "Refugees' Right to Work and Access to Labor Markets—An Assessment." KNOMAD Working Paper and Study Series. Washington, DC: Global Knowledge Partnership on Migration and Development (KNOMAD).

11

CIVIC EDUCATION FOR NONCITIZEN AND CITIZEN STUDENTS

A Conceptual Framework

James A. Banks

Most of the papers presented at the workshop that was the genesis for this book—Humanitarianism and Mass Migration—document the massive numbers of refugee, undocumented, and other "children on the move" who attend public and state schools in the United States, in nations in Western Europe, and in other regions of the world (Bhabha, chapter 3, this volume; Bhabha 2014). This chapter formulates a conceptual framework for developing effective civic education courses and programs for students from these groups who are attending public and state schools.

This is an emergent, exploratory, and difficult task because most of the voluminous theorizing and publications on civic education—including my own publications (J. Banks 2007, 2008)—focus on civic education for citizens and are consequently called *citizenship education* (Arthur, Davies, and Hahn 2008; Hahn 1998; Hess and McAvoy 2015; Levinson 2012; Malin et al. 2014; Parker 2003; Westheimer and Kahne 2004). Citizenship education theorists and researchers, probably for a number of complex reasons, have devoted scant attention to the civic education of students who do not have legal status as citizens. Most of my work on civic education, for example, focuses on individuals and groups—such as African Americans and Filipino Americans—who are legal citizens but have been denied full citizenship rights because of their racial, ethnic, cultural, and linguistic characteristics (J. Banks 2007, 2008, 2015).

MULTICULTURAL CITIZENSHIP EDUCATION AND COSMOPOLITAN HUMAN RIGHTS EDUCATION

Will Kymlicka (2017), in his foreword to a book I edited that includes chapters on citizenship education in eighteen different nations (J. Banks 2017a), describes two conceptions of civic education, which he identifies in these chapters: (1) *multicultural citizenship education* and (2) *cosmopolitan human rights education*.[1] Multicultural citizenship education focuses on helping students who are citizens from diverse racial, ethnic, cultural, linguistic, and religious groups attain full citizenship rights within their nation-state without having to give up important aspects of their home and community cultures and languages or experiencing cultural self-alienation. In the past, in most Western nations such as the United States, Canada, and Australia, minoritized students had to experience what Joel Spring (2004) calls "deculturalization" in order to become fully participating citizens in school and in society writ large. Angela Valenzuela (1999) calls this phenomenon "subtractive schooling."

The deculturalization and subtractive schooling process was not limited to minoritized ethnic groups of color. In a seminal article published in the *Harvard Educational Review*, William Greenbaum (1974) described how southern and eastern European immigrants such as Jews and Italians experienced *hope* and *shame* in US society. If they gave up their home and community cultures and languages—such as Yiddish and Italian—and acquired the cultural and linguistic characteristics of the white Anglo mainstream, they were given hope for full structural inclusion and participation in American society. However, if they maintained their cultural characteristics and languages, they experienced shame and structural exclusion. Karen Brodkin (1998) provides a discerning and compelling analysis of how Jews become white and the social and psychological price they have paid for cultural and structural assimilation into American society in her seminal book *How the Jews Become White Folks and What That Says About Race in America*. In an editorial written after the election of Donald Trump, Brodkin (2016) ponders whether Jews will remain white during the Trump era. Attacks and threats on Jewish centers increased significantly after Trump won the 2016 presidential election (Haberman and Chokshi 2017).

Kymlicka (2017) states that cosmopolitan human rights education "focuses on an ethics of respect for human dignity, which is inherently cosmopolitan. Human rights education is applicable regardless of whether people are members of a given society, are staying temporarily, or are even present in the country" (xii). He maintains that the combination of *multicultural citizenship and cosmopolitan human rights education* "represents a compelling ideal" for many theorists who are concerned about attaining full citizenship rights for minoritized students (xii). Kymlicka worries, however, because some citizenship education theorists view national citizenship as increasingly obsolete because of global migration, the weakening of national borders caused by globalization, and the increasing recognition of the influence of supranational bodies such as the European Union and UNESCO. These theorists, he maintains, focus almost exclusively on the human rights dimension of civic education and insufficiently on the multicultural citizenship issues within nation-states. Kymlicka contends that we cannot do without a "politics of *membership* and *belonging* and rely solely on a cosmopolitan ethic of respect for humanity" (xiv). He writes:

> [T]here are both pragmatic and principled objections to pure cosmopolitanism. Pragmatically, if it is difficult to ask national majorities to embrace more inclusive concepts of national memberships, it seems utopian to ask them to stop caring about membership at all. . . . [O]ne of the central tasks [of civic education] is not to transcend or evade the distinction between members and nonmembers, but to think in a critical and ethically responsible way about the diversity of people who belong to society . . . and the diversity of ways in which they legitimately express that belonging. [Multicultural citizenship education] remains an essential part of civic education, alongside calls for more cosmopolitan human rights education. (xv–xvi)

Angela Banks (2017), a legal scholar and immigrant specialist, agrees with Kymlicka "because in many respects the human rights framework does not ensure that noncitizens have all of the rights they will need to be successfully incorporated into their states of residence, such as the right to reside and remain" (personal communication, February 13, 2017). She states that the "fear of deportation presents a significant impediment to the ability of individuals to reach their highest potential in school or within the workforce." Roberto Gonzales (2016), in *Lives in Limbo: Undocumented and Coming of Age in America,* presents powerful stories that illuminate the fear of deportation and its consequences that noncitizens experience. Hirokazu Yoshikawa (2011) details the anxiety and uncertainty experienced by undocumented parents of children who are citizens. In the United States the fear of deportation has increased significantly since Donald Trump was elected president in 2016 (Chozick 2017; Vizguerra 2017).

A FRAMEWORK FOR CIVIC EDUCATION FOR NONCITIZENS

The framework this chapter describes has two major components that are based on Kymlicka's concept: (1) *multicultural citizenship education* (MCCE), which focuses on helping youth who are legal citizens become recognized and participating civic actors in their communities and nation-states, and (2) *human rights cosmopolitan education* (HRCE), which describes ways in which the social studies curriculum can foster human rights for noncitizen youth such as refugees, asylees, and undocumented students. I discuss the human rights and cosmopolitanism conception first because it is the focus of this chapter. I will briefly summarize the multicultural citizenship education concept in the latter part of this chapter because I have discussed that concept comprehensively in a recent article (J. Banks 2017b).

I am conceptualizing human rights cosmopolitan education (HRCE) as the major focus of civic education for noncitizen students and multicultural citizen-

TABLE 11.1 Civic education programs for noncitizen and citizen students

Civic Education Program	Descriptor
Human Rights Cosmopolitan Education	Focuses on helping non-citizen students to internalize human rights and cosmopolitan values by experiencing an education about human rights, through human rights, and for human rights.
	Helps non-citizen students to attain higher stages of cultural identity, e.g., to transition from "Cultural Psychological Capacity" to "Globalism and Global Competency (Cosmopolitanism)."
	Creates a school environment that enables citizens and non-citizens to have equal-status contact and positive interactions.
Multicultural Citizenship Education	Focuses on helping minoritized students who are citizens from diverse racial, ethnic, cultural, linguistic, and religious groups attain full citizenship rights within their nation-state without having to give up important aspects of their home and community cultures and languages or to experience cultural self-alienation.
	Helps structurally excluded minoritized groups to transition from failed citizenship to recognized, participatory, and transformative citizenship by attaining a sense of structural inclusion, political efficacy, and civic action skills.
	Helps minoritized and structurally excluded citizen students to act to make their communities, schools, and nations more just and equal.
	The curriculum fosters civic equality, recognition, understanding, and acceptance of non-citizen students.

ship education (MCCE) as the main focus for citizen students who experience failed citizenship and structural exclusion (see table 11.1). However, these two conceptions of civic education are interrelated. Components of human rights cosmopolitan education should also be included in the education of citizen students so that they will internalize values and perspectives that will facilitate their acceptance and understanding of noncitizen students. Some of the components of MCCE should also be included in the civic education of noncitizens because they need to acquire knowledge about ways in which they can participate in the political system, such as in peaceful protests, even though they are not citizens. Many of the Dreamers—immigrant youth who were brought illegally to the United States by their parents before the age of sixteen and were given certain privileges by DACA (Deferred Action for Childhood Arrivals), the program initiated by President Barack Obama—have participated in peaceful protests. Transformative civic education has pedagogical elements that will benefit both noncitizen and citizen students. Angela Banks (personal communication, February 25, 2017) maintains that noncitizens need to acquire the knowledge and skills necessary to participate in the political system of their resident nations because they are likely to remain in these nations for many years. She writes, "It is more than likely that these noncitizens will spend the majority, if not the remainder, of their lives in the nation-states in which they do not have citizenship status. It is critical that they have opportunities to attain economic, social, and political rights that facilitate their full participation in their states of residence even if they do not have citizenship status. It is also important that they have the opportunity to develop an identity that mirrors that of citizens and to have that identity recognized and accepted."

HUMAN RIGHTS, COSMOPOLITANISM, AND THE EDUCATION OF NONCITIZEN STUDENTS

The human rights component of civic education is grounded in democratic ethics—the human rights tenets that have been codified in documents endorsed and published by supranational organizations such as the United Nations and the European Union, and in the theoretical ideas that have been formulated by political and social scientists such as Seyla Benhabib (2004), Linda Bosniak (2006), Joseph Carens (2013), and Hiroshi Motomura (2006). Citizenship education scholars such as Walter C. Parker (2017), Audrey Osler (2016), and Hugh Starkey (2017) have also formulated important notions about the teaching of human rights and cosmopolitanism. Human rights education is a major recommendation in chapter 9, this volume, by Irina Bokova, former director general of UNESCO, which was presented at the workshop from which this book was developed. A human rights focus is also a major tenet of the "Final Statement of the Workshop on Humanitarianism and Mass Migration" that was issued after the workshop ended (Pontifical Academy of Sciences and Pontifical Academy of Social Sciences 2017): "The workshop participants underscored the fact that education must not focus exclusively on knowledge but must also train the will towards the common good, friendship and charity. It must be a force against the evils of war and terror and the inhumane treatment of the other. This suggests the importance of teaching virtues and values, in particular, social justice [and] solidarity towards one's peers and future generations as well as friendship and *convivencia* [coexistence]" (p. 7).

In his book *The Ethics of Immigration,* John Carens (2013) argues compellingly that the actions of nation-states regarding all individuals and groups, including those who are refugees and those he refers to as "irregular migrants" (undocumented), should be guided by democratic ethics, whether the actions taken by nation-states are morally right or wrong and whether these actions are consistent with democratic principles. He writes, "In this book I am primarily concerned with minimum standards that flow from democratic principles" (8). Carens takes an extreme ethical position when he argues that nations must have open borders in order to be consistent with democratic principles. He maintains "that discretionary control over immigration is incompatible with fundamental democratic principles and that justice requires open borders" (10). However, he acknowledges that his ideas about open borders are unlikely to convince most readers. In addition, Carens argues that irregular migrants are "morally entitled to some important legal rights and that democratic states have a duty to build a firewall between the enforcement of their migration laws and the protection of many of those rights" (14). He maintains that "ultimately there is almost no justification for refusing to admit refugees" and that they "may need only a safe haven at first but are entitled to full membership in a new society eventually if they cannot go home safely" (15).

Other social scientists, such as Seyla Benhabib (2004) and Hiroshi Motomura (2006), have views regarding the rights of noncitizens that are similar to Carens's ideas, although they are not as extreme. Benhabib (2004) believes that noncitizens such as refugees and asylees should be given substantial rights in democratic nation-states. She describes the ways in which international law limits the power of nation-states regarding the treatment of refugees and asylees. Benhabib sets forth a "cosmopolitan theory of justice" that recognizes "the moral claim of refugees and asylees to *first admittance;* a regime of *porous* borders for immigrants; an injunction against denationalization and the loss of citizenship rights; and the vindication of the right of every human being 'to have rights,' that is, to be a *legal person,* entitled to certain inalienable rights, regardless of the status of [her or his] political membership" (3, emphasis in original).

EDUCATION FOR HUMAN RIGHTS AND COSMOPOLITAN CITIZENSHIP

A number of scholars who focus on education, such as Osler (2016), Starkey (2017), Martha Nussbaum (2002a), and Parker (2017), have written thoughtfully about education for human rights and cosmopolitanism. Starkey (2017) uses the phrase "education for cosmopolitan citizenship" to describe his ideas about educating students for citizenship in a global world. His views about citizenship and citizenship education extend beyond the nation-state and focus on the global community. Starkey maintains that "cosmopolitan citizens have a commitment to people rather than governments. They are likely to challenge any actions or discourses of governments that fail to respect, protect, and fulfill human rights." They make "judgments on the basis of the universal standards of human rights" (43). Nussbaum (2002b) also contends that cosmopolitans view themselves as citizens of the world rather than of a nation-state. She states that their "allegiance is to the worldwide community of human beings" (4). Nussbaum contrasts cosmopolitan universalism and internationalism with parochial ethnocentrism and inward-looking patriotism. She points out, however, that "to be a citizen of the world one does not need to give up local identifications, which can be a source of great richness in life" (9).

Osler (2016) has developed a framework for human rights education based in part on the United Nations Declaration on Human Rights Education and Training (cited in Osler, 4) that conceptualizes human rights education as consisting of three components: (1) education *about* human rights, (2) education *through* human rights, and (3) education *for* human rights. Education about human rights involves helping students acquire knowledge about human rights norms, values, and principles. Education *through* human rights is actualized when educators create classrooms and school communities that exemplify the principles of human rights that students internalize by experiencing them. Education *for* human rights occurs when students acquire the knowledge, political efficacy, and skills needed to take action to make human rights a reality in their schools and communities.

Human rights concerns, Osler (2016) points out, are often regarded by school practitioners and other educators in the United States, as well as in other nations in the Global North, as being primarily relevant in the Global South—especially when despotic leaders victimize their own citizens or media workers and other citizens from nations in the Global North. In other words, educators in the Global North often view "human rights" concerns and issues as for "them" and not for us.

One of the original contributions of Osler's (2016) recent book is the broad and inclusive way in which she conceptualizes and theorizes human rights. She conceives of human rights as an issue within all communities, institutions, societies, and nations. She maintains that human rights issues exist for students and teachers in families, local communities, the classroom, and the school in all communities and nations, including Western nations such as Canada, Australia, the United States, and France. Consequently, one of the most salient points she makes is that human rights are not about the Other in distant lands but are about all of us and the everyday lives of students and teachers. Osler provides teachers and students with a well-formulated legal and moral framework that can be used to guide the analysis of human rights issues in classroom discussions and deliberations. She describes how the experiences of people in the Global North are connected to, rather than separate from, the lives of people in Global South nations in Africa, Asia, Latin America, and the Middle East.

THE UNIVERSAL DECLARATION OF HUMAN RIGHTS IN EDUCATION: CHALLENGES AND OPPORTUNITIES

The Universal Declaration of Human Rights (UDHR) was adopted by the United Nations General Assembly on December 10, 1948, in Paris. A consequence of the experiences of World War II, the declaration has been highly influential. It has been translated into more than three hundred languages, has facilitated the spread of the concept of human rights around the world, has helped to shape national constitutions and court decisions, and has stimulated quests for the attainment of human rights among individuals and groups in many different nations (Clapham 2007). The International Covenant on Economic, Social, and Cultural Rights adopted by the UN General Assembly on December 16, 1966, describes specific human rights related to education: "[Each member state] agree[s] that education shall be directed to the full development of the human personality and the sense of its dignity . . . and shall strengthen the respect for human rights and fundamental freedoms. [The states] further agree that education shall enable all persons to participate effectively in a free society, promote understanding, tolerance and friendship among all nations and all racial, ethnic, or religious groups, and further the activities of the United Nations for the maintenance of peace" (UNHCR 1966).

The promise of the UDHR is that it specifies ideals related to human rights and social justice that all nations in multicultural democratic nation-states should endorse and implement. The difficulty with the ideals expressed in UDHR is that it is much easier for nation-states and institutions such as schools to articulate these ideals than to implement them in the classroom and on the schoolyard.

In order for human rights ideals to be implemented in schools and to become meaningful for noncitizen children and youth, they must speak to and address the children's and youth's experiences, personal identities, hopes, struggles, dreams, and possibilities. In other words, in order for students to internalize the concept of human rights, they must have experiences in school as well as in the larger society that validate them as human beings; affirm their ethnic, cultural, racial, and linguistic identities; and empower them as individuals in school and in the larger society. John Dewey (1938) stated that students must experience democracy in order to internalize democratic ideals and behaviors. I am making a similar argument about human rights—that is, students must experience human rights and an education *through* human rights in order to internalize human rights ideals, beliefs, and behaviors.

Rather than affirm the cultural identities of students from diverse groups and create an educational environment in which students can experience human rights, schools in nation-states around the world often marginalize students from minoritized racial, ethnic, cultural, language, and religious groups. In the past, nations have tried to create national unity by forcing racial, cultural, ethnic, linguistic, and religious minorities to give up their community languages and cultures in order to fully participate in the national civic culture. In the United States, Mexican American students were punished for speaking Spanish in school, and Native American youth were forced to attend boarding schools, where their cultures and languages were eradicated (Lomawaima and McCarty 2006). In Australia, Aboriginal children were taken from their families and forced to live on state missions and reserves (Broome 1982), a practice that lasted from 1869 to 1969. These children are called "the stolen generation." Kevin Rudd, the Australian prime minister, issued a formal apology to the stolen generation on February 13, 2008 (Australian Government 2008). In order to embrace the national civic culture, students from diverse groups must feel that it reflects their experiences, hopes, and dreams. Teachers and educational leaders cannot marginalize the cultures of groups and expect them to feel structurally included within the nation and to develop a strong national allegiance.

Although there has been increasing diversity as well as growing recognition of diversity in the United States as well as in other nations around the world since the civil rights and ethnic revitalization movements of the 1960s and 1970s, the assimilationist ideal and concept of citizenship are still robust in most nation-states. My recent book (J. Banks 2017a), *Citizenship Education and Global Migration: Implications for Theory, Research, and Teaching,* includes chapters that describe the extent to which assimilationism, social cohesion, nationalism, and securitization are widespread in eighteen nations around the world. This book's chapters describe the ways that students such as Muslims in Germany and France, indigenous groups in Brazil and Mexico, the Malay in Singapore, and the Uyghurs and Tibetans in China experience marginalization and inequality when they do not attain sufficient levels of cultural and linguistic assimilation into the mainstream cultures of the nation-states in which they reside. This book also details the ways in which securitization strategies are used in schools when teachers interact with students who are members of groups that educators associate with terrorism.

Minoritized groups whose members are legal citizens of their nation-states still experience marginalization and structural exclusion in society and the schools. Research indicates that noncitizen groups—such as refugees, undocumented students, and the children of noncitizen parents—are having similar but more challenging experiences (Noguera, chapter 14, this volume; C. Suárez-Orozco, Yoshikawa, and Tseng 2015; C. Suárez-Orozco, Abo-Zena, and Marks 2015; Yoshikawa 2011). I hypothesize that citizen and noncitizen youth will not be able to internalize concepts of *human rights* and *cosmopolitanism* until they believe that they have attained a minimal level of acceptance, recognition, and civic equality within the nation-states in which they reside (Gutmann 2004). Essential conditions for the internalization of human rights values, attitudes, and behaviors include a sense of perceived social justice, equity, and equality. Students cannot be expected to internalize human rights values and perspectives when their experiences in school contradict justice and equality.

THE STAGES OF CULTURAL IDENTITY AND HUMAN RIGHTS COSMOPOLITAN EDUCATION

Self-acceptance is a prerequisite to valuing outside racial, ethnic, and linguistic groups and to developing human rights values and cosmopolitan attitudes and values. Students from racial, ethnic, cultural, and linguistic minoritized groups who have historically experienced institutionalized discrimination, racism, or other forms of marginalization—such as being refugees, being undocumented, or "living in the shadows" as the children of undocumented parents (C. Suárez-Orozco et al. 2011)—often have a difficult time accepting and valuing their own cultures, languages, and experiences because of the ways in which their languages and cultures are marginalized within the schools and the larger society. These students need to experience a school culture that will help them to attain a reflective understanding and acceptance of their families and communities, and a comprehension of the institutionalized structures that have victimized them (Baldwin 1985). Knowledge about factors that cause victimization and about ways to acquire political efficacy is essential for these students to attain in order to develop human rights and cosmopolitan values and behaviors, acceptance of outside groups, and reflective cultural, national, regional, and global identifications. Individuals and groups must accept themselves before they can reach out to and accept outsiders. Educators should be aware of and sensitive to the stages of cultural identity development that all students—including mainstream students, students of color, and other marginalized groups such as refugees and undocumented students— experience so that they can facilitate these students' cultural identity development and enable them to reach the higher levels of cultural identity.

I have developed a Stages of Cultural Identity Typology (J. Banks 2016) that teachers and psychologists can use when trying to help refugee and undocumented students to internalize human rights and cosmopolitan values, to attain higher stages of cultural identity development, and to develop clarified cultural, national, regional, and global identifications (see figure 11.1). Research indicates that refugee and undocumented students experience many psychological and identity challenges when they arrive in their new nations of residence (Doosje, Loseman, and van den Bos 2013; Lyons-Padilla et al. 2015). The problems that these students experience are intensified when they perceive discrimination and injustice and when they believe that their cultural characteristics—including their behaviors and languages—are being assaulted by public institutions such as schools.

Studies of the factors that cause immigrant youth to become radicalized and to join groups such as ISIS provide important insights into the kinds of educational experiences immigrant youth need to experience in order to attain a sense of efficacy, self-worth, and higher stages of cultural identity development. Sarah Lyons-Padilla and colleagues (2015) found that "marginalized immigrant groups in the United States may be at a greater risk for a feeling of loss of significance, which in turn, may be related to increased support for fundamentalist groups and ideologies" (6–7). A study by Doosje, Loseman, and van den Bos (2013) indicates that the radicalization of Dutch Muslim youth was caused by three major factors: "(a) personal uncertainty, (b) perceived injustice, and (c) perceived group threat" (586). These studies reveal that an effective and empowering educational environment for immigrant and noncitizen youth should provide opportunities for them to develop positive attitudes and feelings toward their cultures and languages as well as validate their cultural experiences and self-perceptions. These kinds of experiences can facilitate immigrant and noncitizen students' attainment of Stage 3 in the typology.

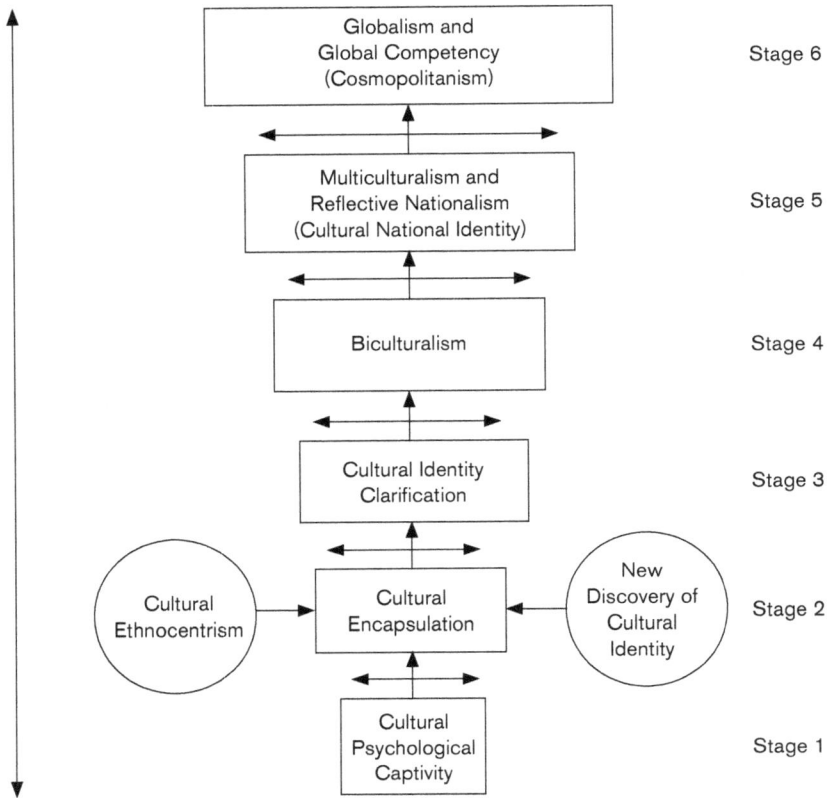

FIGURE 11.1. Stages of Cultural Identity Typology. Copyright © 2016 by James A. Banks.

Students need to reach Stage 3 of this typology, "Cultural Identity Clarification," before they can be expected to embrace other cultural groups, internalize human rights and cosmopolitan values, and attain thoughtful and clarified national and global identifications. The typology is an ideal construct in the Weberian sense and constitutes a set of hypotheses based on existing and emerging theory and research as well as on the author's study of ethnic and cultural behavior (J. Banks 2006).

Max Weber, the German sociologist and political economist, developed the concept of *ideal types,* which are generalized models that can be used to compare observations in society. The Stages of Cultural Identity Typology, like other ideal-type conceptions, does not describe the actual identity development of any particular individual. Rather, it is a framework for thinking about and facilitating the identity development of students who approximate one of the stages. The stages in the typology are not discrete and distinct but rather are overlapping and interrelated. The Stages of Cultural Identity Typology shares some characteristics with the stages of ethnic identity development typologies created by psychologists Janet Helms (1993) and William Cross Jr. (1991).

The divisions between the stages are blurred rather than sharp. Thus, a continuum exists between the stages as well as within them. The culturally encapsulated individual (Stage 2) does not suddenly attain clarification and acceptance of his or her cultural identity (Stage 3). This is a gradual and developmental process. Also, the stages should not be viewed as strictly sequential and linear.

During Stage 1—"Cultural Psychological Captivity"—individuals internalize the negative stereotypes and beliefs about their cultural groups that have been institutionalized within the larger society and may exemplify cultural self-rejection and low self-esteem. Cultural encapsulation, cultural exclusiveness, and the belief that their ethnic group is superior to others, characterize Stage 2—"Cultural Encapsulation." Often individuals within this stage have newly discovered their cultural consciousness and try to limit their participation to their cultural group. They have ambivalent feelings about their cultural group and try to confirm, for themselves, that they are proud of it. In Stage 3—"Ethnic Identity Clarification"—individuals are able to recognize their personal attitudes and cultural identity and to develop clarified positive attitudes toward their cultural group. In this stage, cultural pride is genuine rather than contrived. Individuals within Stage 4—"Biculturalism"— have a healthy sense of their cultural identity and possess the psychological characteristics and knowledge and skills to participate effectively in their own cultural community as well as in another cultural community. They also have a strong desire to function effectively in two cultures.

Stage 5 individuals ("Multiculturalism and Reflective Nationalism") have reflective and positive personal, cultural, and national identifications and positive attitudes toward other racial, cultural, and ethnic groups. At Stage 6—"Globalism and Global Competency"—individuals have reflective national and global identifications. They have the knowledge, skills, and attitudes needed to function effectively in their own cultural community, in other cultures within their nation-state, and in the civic culture of their nation as well as in the global community. Individuals within Stage 6 exemplify *cosmopolitanism,* have internalized human rights values, and have a commitment to all human beings in the world community (Nussbaum 2002b). Amy Gutmann (2004) maintains that the primary commitment of these individuals is to justice, not to any human community.

Strong, positive, and clarified cultural identifications and attachments are a prerequisite for developing cosmopolitan beliefs, attitudes, and behaviors. It is not realistic to expect refugee and undocumented students in Los Angeles to have a robust allegiance to American national values or deep empathy for the problems of African Americans if they feel marginalized and rejected within their own community and school and in the United States. Educators and psychologists must nurture, support, and affirm the identities of students from marginalized cultural, ethnic, language, and religious groups if they expect these students to endorse national and human rights values, become cosmopolitans, and work to make their local communities, the nation, and the world more just and humane.

MULTICULTURAL CITIZENSHIP EDUCATION
FOR CITIZEN STUDENTS

This section focuses on multicultural citizenship education (MCCE), civic education for students who are legal citizens but are denied full citizenship rights and privileges because they are members of racial, ethnic, cultural, linguistic, and religious groups that are marginalized and victimized. These groups experience *failed citizenship* because they are denied full citizenship rights and privileges. A primary goal of the citizenship curriculum for students who are legal citizens but who experience failed citizenship is to create a civic education curriculum and a school learning environment in which these students can acquire a sense of *structural inclusion,* political efficacy, and the knowledge and skills needed to take effective civic action in their schools, communities, and nation-states. In other words, the goal of the civic education curriculum for citizen students is to help them to acquire the knowledge and skills needed to help change their status from failed citizens to *recognized, participatory,* and *transformative* citizens.

I am defining *structural inclusion* as a set of attitudes and beliefs that students have that are characterized by feelings of political efficacy and political empowerment and a sense that they can influence political and economic decisions that affect their lives by participating in the political system. In other words, students who feel structurally included within the civic culture of their nation have political efficacy and believe that their participation in the polity can make a difference. Students who feel structurally included within their nation-state and society also believe that they are an integral part of their nation-state, have clarified national identities, and view themselves as Americans.

Research on immigrant students by scholars such as Thea Abu El-Haj (2007), Sunaina Maira (2004), and Diem Nguyen (2012) indicate that immigrant youth have complex national identities. These researchers found that the immigrant youths in their studies did not define their national identities in terms of their places of residence but felt that they belonged to national communities that transcended the boundaries of the United States. They defined their national identities as Palestinian, Vietnamese, Indian, Pakistani, and Bangladeshi. They also believed that an individual could be Palestinian or Vietnamese and live in many different nation-states. The youth in these studies distinguished between *national identity* and *citizenship*. They viewed themselves as Palestinian, Vietnamese, or Pakistani but also recognized and acknowledged their US citizenship, which they valued for the privileged legal status and other opportunities it provided them. Some of the Vietnamese youth in Nguyen's study said, "I am Vietnamese and a citizen of the United States." These students did not believe that they were "Americans" because to be "American" was to be white and middle-class. Students who are structurally included believe that they are both citizens of the United States and Americans. They also have clarified national identities and political efficacy.

People who are not structurally included within the political and cultural systems of their nation-state are politically alienated, lack political efficacy, and participate at low levels in the political system. They often do not vote because they believe that their votes do not make a difference and that politicians do not care about them. They also have negative views of politicians. In her important study *Democracy Remixed: Black Youth and the Future of Politics*, Cathy Cohen (2010) found that black and Latino youth have a high level of political alienation, which has a negative effect on their political activism and political participation. Writes Cohen, "It is only a feeling of political efficacy that can bolster the positive feelings black youth have about government officials. The belief that one is politically efficacious diminishes negative feelings toward the government" (136).

Students who experience failed citizenship develop weak identities and ambivalent attachments to the nation-state, experience political alienation, and have low levels of political participation. To help practicing educators conceptualize and construct effective citizenship education courses and programs that will facilitate the structural inclusion of marginalized citizen students, I have developed a typology that consists of four categories: (1) failed citizenship, (2) recognized citizenship, (3) participatory citizenship, and (4) transformative citizenship. This typology is a Weberian concept because the four categories approximate but do not describe reality in its total complexity. The categories are useful conceptual tools for thinking about citizenship socialization and citizenship education. Although the four categories can be conceptually distinguished, in reality they overlap and are interrelated in a dynamic way. For example, individuals must be recognized by the state as legal and legitimate citizens before they can become participatory citizens who can take actions to implement existing laws and policies. The aim of civic instruction for marginalized citizen students should be to facilitate their transition from being failed citizens to becoming participatory and transformative citizens. The following are brief descriptions of the four categories in the typology:

Failed citizenship exits when individuals or groups who are born within a nation or migrate to it and live within it for an extended period of time do not internalize the values and ethos of the nation-state, feel structurally excluded within it, and have a highly ambivalent feeling toward it. Individuals who experience failed citizenship focus primarily on their own needs for political efficacy, group identity, and structural inclusion rather than on the overarching and shared goals of the nation-state. Their allegiance and commitment to the nation-state are eclectic and complex.

Recognized citizenship exists when the state or nation publicly recognizes an individual or group as a legitimate, legal, and valued member of the polity and provides the individual or group full rights and opportunities to participate. Although recognized citizenship status gives individuals and groups the right and opportunity to fully participate in the civic community of the nation-state, it does not require their participation. Individuals who have state-recognized citizenship status participate in the polity at very different levels, including nonparticipation.

Participatory citizenship is exercised by individuals and groups who have been granted recognized citizenship by the nation-state. It takes place when individuals with citizenship rights take actions as minimal as voting to influence political decisions in their communities, nations, and the world to actualize existing laws and conventions. An example of participatory citizenship is the action taken by civil rights groups to enable African Americans to vote after the Voting Rights Act was signed into law by President Lyndon B. Johnson on August 6, 1965.

Transformative citizens take action to implement and promote policies, actions, and changes that are consistent with values such as human rights, social justice, and equality. The actions that transformative citizens take might—and sometimes do—violate existing local, state, and national laws. Examples are actions taken by transformative citizens such as Mahatma Gandhi, Martin Luther King Jr., and Rosa Parks that violated prevailing laws but helped to actualize values such as human rights and social justice and to eliminate institutionalized discrimination and racism.

MAINSTREAM AND TRANSFORMATIVE CITIZENSHIP EDUCATION

Citizenship education must be reimagined and transformed to effectively educate both citizen and noncitizen students. To reform citizenship education, the knowledge that underlies its construction needs to shift from *mainstream* academic knowledge to *transformative* academic knowledge. Mainstream knowledge reinforces traditional and established knowledge in the social and behavioral sciences as well as the knowledge that is institutionalized within the popular culture and within the nation's schools, colleges, and universities (J. Banks 1993). Transformative academic knowledge consists of paradigms and explanations that challenge some of the key epistemological assumptions of mainstream knowledge (Collins 2000; Harding 1991; Homans 1967). An important purpose of transformative knowledge is to improve the human condition. Feminist scholars and scholars of color have been among the leading constructors of transformative academic knowledge (Harding 1991; Collins 2000; Takaki 1993, 1998).

Mainstream citizenship education is grounded in mainstream knowledge and assumptions and reinforces the status quo and the dominant power relationships in society. It is practiced in most social studies classrooms in the United States as well as within most other nations (Arthur, Davies, and Hahn 2008; J. Banks 2017a; Parker 2003) and does not challenge or disrupt the class, racial, and gender discrimination within the schools and society. It does not help students to understand their multiple and complex identities, the ways in which their lives are influenced by globalization, or what their role should be in a global world. The emphasis is on memorizing facts about constitutions and other legal documents, learning about various branches of government, and developing patriotism to the nation-state (Westheimer 2007). Critical thinking skills, decision making, and civic action are not important components of mainstream citizenship education.

Transformative citizenship education needs to be implemented within the schools in order for both citizen and noncitizen students to attain clarified and reflective cultural, national, regional, and global identifications and to understand how these identities are interrelated and constructed. The transformative curriculum helps students to acquire the knowledge, skills, and values needed to become social critics who can make thoughtful decisions and implement their decisions in effective personal, social, and civic actions. In other words, reflective decision-making and civic action are the primary goals of a transformative and empowering curriculum.

A transformative civic education curriculum helps students to reconceptualize the human experience in both the United States and the world; to view the human experience from the perspectives of diverse cultural, racial, ethnic, and linguistic groups; and to construct their own versions of the past, present, and future. In the transformative curriculum, multiple voices are legitimized—the voices of textbooks, literary and historical writers, the voices of teachers, and the voices of students from diverse groups. Students construct their own versions of the past, present, and future after listening to and contemplating the multiple and diverse voices in the transformative classroom.

The transformative curriculum teaches students to think and reflect critically on the materials they read and the voices they hear. James Baldwin (1985), in a classic essay, "A Talk to Teachers," states that "the main purpose of education . . . is to create in a person the ability to look at the world for himself, to make his own decisions, to say to himself that this is black or this is white, to decide for himself whether there is a god in heaven or not. To ask questions of the universe, and then to live with those questions, is the way he achieves his identity" (326). Although Baldwin believed that thinking should be the main purpose of education, he also believed that no society was serious about teaching its citizens to think. He writes further, "But no society is really anxious to have that kind of person around. What society really, ideally, wants is a citizenry which will simply obey the rules of society. If a society succeeds in this, that society is about to perish" (326).

Transformative citizenship education also recognizes and validates the cultural identities of students. It is rooted in transformative academic knowledge and enables students to acquire the information, skills, and values needed to challenge inequality within their communities, their nations, and the world; to develop cosmopolitan values and perspectives; and to take actions to create just and democratic multicultural communities and societies. Transformative citizenship education helps students to develop decision-making and social action skills that are needed to identify problems within society, to acquire knowledge related to their home and community cultures and languages, to identify and clarify their values, and to take thoughtful individual or collective civic action (J. Banks and C. Banks 1999). It also fosters critical thinking skills and political literacy (Moodley and Adam 2004), skills and knowledge that are urgently needed because populist revolts in a number of Western nations are resulting in the election of conservative, xenophobic, and authoritarian politicians who seriously threaten democracy, which is fragile and requires renewal in each new generation.

NOTES

Acknowledgments: I am grateful to these colleagues who prepared discerning and helpful comments on an earlier draft of this chapter that enabled me to strengthen it: Angela M. Banks, Sandra Day O'Connor College of Law, Arizona State University; Cherry A. McGee Banks, University of Washington, Bothell; Carlos F. Diaz, Florida Atlantic University; and Yiting Chu, University of Louisiana at Monroe.

1. Kymlicka calls this approach "cosmopolitan human rights education." I call it "human rights cosmopolitan education" in this chapter.

REFERENCES

Abu El-Haj, Thea R. 2007. "'I Was Born Here, but My Home, It's Not Here': Educating for Democratic Citizenship in an Era of Transnational Migration and Global Conflict." *Harvard Educational Review* 77 (3): 285–316.

Arthur, James, Ian Davies, and Carole Hahn, eds. 2008. *Education for Citizenship and Democracy*. London: Sage.

Australian Government. 2008. "Apology to Australia's Indigenous Peoples." February 13, 2008. www.australia.gov.au/about-australia/our-country/our-people/apology-to-australias-indigenous-peoples.

Baldwin, James. 1985. "A Talk to Teachers." In *The Price of the Ticket: Collected Nonfiction 1948–85*, 325–32. New York: St. Martin's.

Banks, Angela M. 2017. "Citizenship, Culture, and Race in the United States." In *Citizenship Education and Global Migration: Implications for Theory, Research, and Teaching*, edited by James A. Banks, 61–85. Washington, DC: American Educational Research Association.

Banks, James A. 1993. "The Canon Debate, Knowledge Construction, and Multicultural Education." *Educational Researcher* 22 (5): 4–14.

———. 2006. *Race, Culture, and Education: The Selected Works of James A. Banks*. London: Routledge.

———. 2007. *Educating Citizens in a Multicultural Society*. 2nd ed. New York: Teachers College Press.

———. 2008. "Diversity, Group Identity, and Citizenship Education in a Global Age." *Educational Researcher* 37 (3): 129–39.

———, ed. 2009. *The Routledge International Companion to Multicultural Education.* London: Routledge.

———. 2015. "Failed Citizenship, Civic Engagement, and Education." *Kappa Delta Pi Record* 51: 151–54.

———. 2016. *Cultural Diversity and Education: Foundations, Curriculum, and Teaching.* 6th ed. London: Routledge.

———, ed. 2017a. *Citizenship Education and Global Migration: Implications for Theory, Research, and Teaching.* Washington, DC: American Educational Research Association.

———. 2017b. "Failed Citizenship and Transformative Civic Education." *Educational Researcher* 46 (7): 366–377.

Banks, James A., and Cherry A. Banks, with Ambrose A. Clegg Jr. 1999. *Teaching Strategies for the Social Studies: Decision-Making and Citizen Action.* 5th ed. New York: Longman.

Benhabib, Seyla. 2004. *The Rights of Others: Aliens, Residents, and Citizens.* Cambridge: Cambridge University Press.

Bhabha, Jacqueline. 2014. *Child Migration and Human Rights in a Global Age.* Princeton, NJ: Princeton University Press.

Bosniak, Linda. 2006. *The Citizen and the Alien: Dilemma of Contemporary Membership.* Princeton, NJ: Princeton University Press.

Brodkin, Karen. 1998. *How the Jews Became White Folks and What That Says About Race in America.* New Brunswick, NJ: Rutgers University Press.

———. 2016. "How Jews Become White Folks—and May Become Nonwhite under Trump." *Forward.* December 6, 2016. http://forward.com/opinion/356166/how-jews-became-white-folks-and-may-become-nonwhite-under-trump/.

Broome, Richard. 1982. *Aboriginal Australians: Black Response to White Dominance 1788–1980.* Sydney: George Allen and Unwin.

Carens, John H. 2013. *The Ethics of Immigration.* New York: Oxford University Press.

Chozick, Amy. 2017. "Raids of Illegal Immigrants Bring Harsh Memories and Strong Fears." *New York Times,* January 2, 2017. www.nytimes.com/2017/01/02/us/illegal-immigrants-raids-deportation.html.

Clapham, Andrew. 2007. *Human Rights: A Very Short Introduction.* New York: Oxford University Press.

Cohen, Cathy J. 2010. *Democracy Remixed: Black Youth and the Future of American Politics.* New York: Oxford University Press.

Collins, Patricia H. 2000. *Black Feminist Thought: Knowledge, Consciousness, and the Politics of Empowerment.* 2nd ed. New York: Routledge.

Cross, William E., Jr. 1991. *Shades of Black: Diversity in African-American Identity.* Philadelphia: Temple University Press.

Dewey, John. 1938. *Experience and Education.* New York: Macmillan.

Doosje, Bertjan, Annemarie Loseman, and Kees van den Bos. 2013. "Determinants of Radicalization of Islamic Youth in the Netherlands: Personal Uncertainty, Perceived Injustice, and Perceived Group Threat." *Journal of Social Issues* 69 (3): 586–604.

Gonzales, Roberto G. 2016. *Lives in Limbo: Undocumented and Coming of Age in America.* Oakland: University of California Press.

Greenbaum, William. 1974. "America in Search of a New Ideal: An Essay on the Rise of Pluralism." *Harvard Educational Review* 44 (3): 411–40.

Gutmann, Amy. 2004. "Unity and Diversity in Democratic Multicultural Education: Creative and Destructive Tensions." In *Diversity and Citizenship Education: Global Perspectives,* edited by James A. Banks, 71–96. San Francisco: Jossey-Bass.

Haberman, Maggie, and Niraj Chokshi. 2017. "Ivanka Trump Calls for Tolerance after Threats on Jewish Centers." *New York Times,* February 20, 2017. www.nytimes.com /2017/02/20/us/politics/ivanka-trump-jewish-community-centers.html?_r = 0.

Hahn, Carole L. 1998. *Becoming Political: Comparative Perspectives on Citizenship Education.* Albany: SUNY Press.

Harding, Sandra. 1991. *Whose Science? Whose Knowledge? Thinking from Women's Lives.* Ithaca, NY: Cornell University Press.

Helms, Janet E., ed. 1993. *Black and White Racial Identity: Theory, Research, and Practice.* Westport, CT: Praeger.

Hess, Diana E., and Paula McAvoy. 2015. *The Political Classroom: Evidence and Ethics in Democratic Education.* New York: Routledge.

Homans, George. C. 1967. *The Nature of Social Science.* New York: Harcourt.

Kymlicka, Will. 2017. "Foreword." In *Citizenship Education and Global Migration: Implications for Theory, Research, and Teaching,* edited by James A. Banks, xi–xvii. Washington, DC: American Educational Research Association.

Levinson, Meira. 2012. *No Citizen Left Behind.* Cambridge, MA: Harvard University Press.

Lomawaima, K. Tsianina, and Teresa L. McCarty. 2006. *"To Remain an Indian": Lessons in Democracy from a Century of Native American Education.* New York: Teachers College Press.

Lyons-Padilla, Sarah, Michele J. Gelfand, Hedieh Mirahmadi, Mehreen Farooq, and Marieke van Egmond. 2015. "Belonging Nowhere: Marginalization and Radicalization Risk among Muslim Immigrants." *Behavioral Science and Policy* 1 (2): 1–12.

Maira, Sunaina. 2004. "Imperial Feelings: Youth Culture, Citizenship, and Globalization." In *Globalization, Culture, and Education in the New Millennium,* edited by Marcelo M. Suárez-Orozco and Desirée B. Qin-Hilliard, 203–34. Berkeley: University of California Press.

Malin, Heather, Parissa J. Ballard, Maryam L. Attai, Anee Colby, and William Damon. 2014. *Youth Civic Development and Education: A Consensus Report.* Stanford, CA: Stanford University, Center on Adolescence; Seattle: University of Washington, Center for Multicultural Education.

Moodley, Koogila, and Heribert Adam. 2004. "Citizenship Education and Political Literacy in South Africa." In *Diversity and Citizenship Education: Global Perspectives,* edited by James A. Banks, 159–83. San Francisco: Jossey-Bass.

Motomura, Hiroshi. 2006. *Americans in Waiting: The Lost Story of Immigration and Citizenship in the United States.* New York: Oxford University Press.

Nguyen, Diem T. 2012. *Vietnamese Immigrant Youth and Citizenship: How Race, Ethnicity, and Culture Shape Sense of Belonging.* El Paso: LFB Scholarly Publishing.

Nussbaum, Martha. 2002a. "Education for Citizenship in an Era of Global Connection." *Studies in Philosophy of Education* 21: 289–303.

———. 2002b. "Patriotism and Cosmopolitanism." In *For Love of Country,* edited by Martha Nussbaum and Jay Cohen, 2–17. Boston: Beacon Press.

Osler, Audrey. 2016. *Human Rights and Schooling: An Ethical Framework for Teaching Social Justice*. New York: Teachers College Press.

Parker, Walter C. 2003. *Teaching Democracy: Unity and Diversity in Public Life*. New York: Teachers College Press.

———. 2017. "Towards a Powerful Human Rights Curriculum in Schools: Problems and Possibilities." In *Citizenship Education and Global Migration: Implications for Theory, Research, and Teaching*, edited by James A. Banks, 457–81. Washington, DC: American Educational Research Association.

Pontifical Academy of Sciences and Pontifical Academy of Social Sciences. 2017. "Final Statement of the Workshop on Humanitarianism and Mass Migration." January 17–19, 2017. www.pass.va/content/scienzesociali/en/events/2014–18/migration_ucla.html.

Spring, Joel. 2004. *Deculturalization and the Struggle for Equality: A Brief History of the Education of Dominated Cultures in the United States*. 4th ed. New York: McGraw-Hill.

Starkey, Hugh. 2017. "Globalization and Education for Cosmopolitan Citizenship." In *Citizenship Education and Global Migration: Implications for Theory, Research, and Teaching*, edited by James A. Banks, 39–60. Washington, DC: American Educational Research Association.

Suárez-Orozco, Carola, Mona M. Abo-Zena, and Amy K. Marks, eds. 2015. *Transitions: The Development of Children of Immigrants*. New York: NYU Press.

Suárez-Orozco, Carola, Hirokazu Yoshikawa, Robert Teranishi, and Marcelo M. Suárez-Orozco. 2011. "Growing Up in the Shadows: The Developmental Implications of Unauthorized Status." *Harvard Educational Review* 81 (3): 438–72.

Suárez-Orozco, Carola, Hirokazu Yoshikawa, and Vivian Tseng. 2015. *Intersecting Inequalities: Research to Reduce Inequality for Immigrant-Origin Children and Youth*. New York: William T. Grant Foundation. http://wtgrantfoundation.org/library/uploads/2015/09/Intersecting-Inequalities-Research-to-Reduce-Inequality-for-Immigrant-Origin-Children-and-Youth.pdf.

Takaki, Ronald. 1993. *A Different Mirror: A History of Multicultural America*. Boston: Little, Brown.

———. 1998. *Strangers from a Different Shore: A History of Asian Americans*. Boston: Little, Brown.

UNHCR (United Nations High Commissioner for Human Rights). 1966. *International Covenant on Economic, Social, and Cultural Rights*. www.refworld.org/docid/3ae6b36c0.html.

Valenzuela, Angela. 1999. *Subtractive Schooling: US–Mexican Youth and the Politics of Caring*. Albany: SUNY Press.

Vizguerra, Jeanette. 2017. "Why I Will Not Leave." *New York Times*, February 25, 2017. www.nytimes.com/2017/02/24/opinion/why-i-will-not-leave.html?_r = 0.

Westheimer, Joel, ed. 2007. *Pledging Allegiance: The Politics of Patriotism in America's Schools*. New York: Teachers College Press.

Westheimer, Joel, and Joseph Kahne. 2004. "What Kind of Citizen? The Politics of Educating for Democracy." *American Educational Research Journal* 41: 237–69.

Yoshikawa, Hirokazu. 2011. *Immigrants Raising Citizens: Undocumented Parents and Their Young Children*. New York: Russell Sage Foundation.

12

REFUGEES IN EDUCATION

What Can Science Education Contribute?

Pierre Léna

During the last two decades, in scores of countries, both developed and developing ones, scientists, often eminent ones, have stimulated a deep analysis of what science education should be today, aiming at *all* children, essentially those in primary schools and sometimes those in middle schools. Hence, a wealth of pilot projects has blossomed, impacting millions of children in the age group of six to eleven or so in diverse social surroundings and conditions (Léna 2012). More specifically, *science* here refers to the natural sciences, although some of the pilots have included mathematics. The main reason for this mobilization of scientists and educators is that the natural sciences were being poorly taught at the primary and middle-school levels in many educational systems, leaving many students uninterested or bored, or were not even taught at all, as a number of international studies have confirmed.

This movement, known as Inquiry-Based Science Education (IBSE), focuses on providing teachers with professional training and adequate resources for implementing an active pedagogy in the classroom. In parallel with its grassroots actions, the movement, which has been gaining momentum with the support of a number of science academies (IAP 2017) and industrial companies (e.g., Siemens Stiftung in Germany), has developed the rationales supporting this pedagogy, analyzed its impact on children and society, and proposed assessment tools. IBSE designates the implementation of a specific pedagogy to teach natural sciences (*inquiry*); it is not a set of subjects to be addressed in schools like the STEM aggregate subjects (science, technology, engineering, and mathematics) or the STEAM subjects (the STEM subjects plus art and design, and eventually a number of other school subjects); those programs, unlike the IBSE approach, do not specifically designate a particular way to teach the content they address. Progressively over the last two decades, IBSE pedagogy has gained wide acceptance.

IBSE has explored deep changes in science education during a time when international assessments such as the Programme for International Student Assessment (PISA) (since 2000) and Trends in International Mathematics and Science Study (TIMSS) (since 1995) have regularly provided a wealth of educational indicators for more than sixty countries (PISA 2015a; NCES n. d.). PISA primarily focuses on three domains: reading, mathematics, and natural sciences. Mastery of these subjects is considered essential for youngsters aged fifteen in their daily lives, no matter what their future professional choices will be. One notes that two out of the three domains deal with scientific content. This focus corresponds to an increasing interest among those in educational systems and political circles in the role of science in today's world and the need for specific cognitive qualities and skills, recognized as communicated through a proper science education, in order to understand the world as a citizen and to make one's way in it as a professional. Educational systems react slowly to change, and a systemic approach to transforming science education, although necessary, has not yet been undertaken in many countries. One reason for the delay is the magnitude of the effort required to transform teachers' pedagogy. This effort goes far beyond the simple and relatively easy publication of a new curriculum by a government.

In most cases, these pilots have been implemented in normal schools, where a multicultural context often exists, especially in countries hosting a large number of international migrants or refugees, such as France, Germany, and the United Kingdom. On the other hand, among the countries where large numbers of internally displaced persons (IDPs) exist—with a worldwide total reaching 24.5 million (IDMC 2017)—only a few, with six million IDPs, have developed such pilot projects in cooperation with France, including Colombia (*Pequeños Científicos* n. d.) and Pakistan (PSF 2017). In China, internal migrations from villages to large cities are displacing millions of people not accounted for in the previous statistics. Unfortunately, the likely mixing of students in China's urban schools that have implemented the important pilot science project "Learning by Doing (做中学)" (Wei Yu 2012) has not been documented. Despite some unsuccessful attempts,[1] to date, no similar pilot projects have been specifically developed for refugee children or in refugee camps.

Since 2014, in eleven of the fourteen largest refugee-hosting nation-states, a model leading to the hosting of refugee children in the schools within the national education system has been adopted, at least in principle. For children from international migrant families, either documented or not, the rule is generally to accept them in the national schooling system (Dryden-Peterson, chapter 10, this volume. In these cases, the presence of such children in regular schools leads to deep changes in the classroom composition. In France, for example, despite the fact that on average immigrant pupils represent less than 10 percent of the school population, one easily finds suburban primary or middle schools with more than twenty nationalities, mostly of developing countries, represented in a single class. Among these students, especially the youngest ones, one observes an extremely unequal mastery of the country's language, which is often not spoken at all at home. Similar mixing in the suburbs hosting immigrants and refugees can be found in London, Berlin, Stockholm, and many other large cities.

This chapter presents the rationale and evidence for considering science education, addressing children and teenagers, as an important tool for overcoming barriers of language, religion, and culture. Focusing on multicultural contexts in which migrants and international refugees are mixed, I outline some lessons learned from the previously mentioned pilot projects. Indeed, science education is also giving these children access to science itself, an essential and universal element in the development of humanity of which there is no reason to deprive them. Providing similar learning experiences for children living for long periods of time in refugee camps—whether they are internally displaced, as in Sudan, or internationally displaced, as in Turkey, Lebanon, or Jordan—would be a great challenge but would also probably provide a great opportunity for these children.

SCIENCE EDUCATION: A WAY
ACROSS CULTURAL BOUNDARIES

Parents know that most children are naturally curious. As soon as they are born, infants explore the world with their senses and progressively try to make sense out of their experiences. The development of language recognition and structuration begins long before words can be spoken when the pharynx becomes adequately developed. Neurosciences are exploring this emergence in great detail (Dehaene 2015) to the point where an infant can be described as a "scientist in the crib" (Gopnik, Meltzoff, and Kuhl 2000). Curiosity may have played an important role during human evolution by providing a definite selection advantage in the sense of innovating, escaping from predators, searching for food, and creating tools or weapons.

Parents also know that at the age of three and beyond, children ask many questions about the world and its phenomena, asking for causes and sometimes proposing surprising and highly logical answers. Although one can debate about the universal, or on the contrary, the not so common, nature of curiosity (Loewenstein 1994), there is no doubt that its existence is the very foundation of science—as it is the main driver of adult science researchers. Most scientists have told how their interests and scientific careers were rooted in their early youth. The testimony of Isaac Newton (1642–1727), a genius writing to a friend a few weeks before his death, deserves to be quoted: "I do not know what I may appear to the world, but to myself I seem to have been only like a boy playing on the seashore, and diverting myself in now and then finding a smoother pebble or a prettier shell than ordinary, whilst the great ocean of truth lay all undiscovered before me" (quoted in Westfall [1980] 1994, 866).[2] One finds similar emotional reactions related to an early discovery of chemistry's marvels in the reminiscences of neuroscientist Oliver Sacks (2001).

The common observations of children conducting hands-on experiments in a science museum or exploring in a classroom confirm this early interest. Exploring and playing are often presented in parallel as two "natural" and universal ways in which children develop in order to enter into a relation with the world and their peers. Playing, as well as exploring, can cross linguistic and cultural barriers; this crossing is commonly observed in multicultural contexts such as schools or streets. It is the basic reason to believe that science may represent a fertile entry point in relevant strategies for educating migrants and refugees as well as regular students in multicultural classrooms.

But curiosity and questioning ability, if not nourished, will soon fade away. So many youngsters, and later adults, use the marvels of today's technology without the slightest questioning about the way in which it works. Beyond the entry point provided by natural curiosity, education has to create and structure a process for attaining knowledge that accompanies the cognitive development of the child from early age to maturity. This need is even more relevant today since the advent of overwhelming and readily available "information." How best to educate children? This question has been debated since children and schools first existed. From the Confucian principles of absolute submission to the teacher to the *Fais ce que voudras* ("Do what you want") motto in the *Abbaye de Thélème* of François Rabelais or in *Summerhill* (Neel 1960), every principle and its opposite have been proposed and argued. Strangely enough, it does not seem that educating children in the natural sciences from an early age on has suffered from such opposing views. From Socrates to Ibn al-Haytham[3] and Jan Comenius, from John Dewey and Michael Faraday to Henri Bergson, from Maria Montessori to Jean Perrin,[4] from Frank Oppenheimer[5] to Bruce Alberts,[6] the principles of an inquiry pedagogy have been enunciated by scientists, philosophers, and educators; experimented with by thousands of teachers; and validated (if needed!) by researchers (Minner, Levy, and Century 2010; LASER 2016).

The great scientist Ibn al-Haytham (965–ca. 1040), in his *Kitab Al-Manadhir* ("Book of Optics"), gives a perfect definition of *inquiry*: "We begin by observing the reality. . . . We try to choose solid observations, with results not depending on the way we make the measurements. We continue by deepening our observations and measurements, submitting our hypothesis to critical analysis, being careful in our conclusions. . . . In everything we do, our goal must be the balance and not the arbitrary, the search of truth and not the choice of an opinion. . . . Nevertheless, we are only human beings, subject to human weakness, against which we must fight with all our strength. May Allah help us in all our enterprises" (Ibn al-Haytham [n. d.] 1989). The French philosopher Henri Bergson (1859–1941) makes the connection with education: "One [in science lessons] mainly presents results. Would it not be better to [begin with] methods? They [the students] would be immediately invited to practice, to observe, experiment, invent. How then would one be listened to!" (Bergson [1934] 1969, 60).

What is Inquiry-Based Science Education? Here, I give the definition adopted by the US National Research Council and adopted with a widespread international consensus: "IBSE means students progressively developing key scientific ideas through learning how to investigate and build their knowledge and understanding of the world around [them]. They use skills employed by scientists such as raising questions, collecting data, reasoning and reviewing evidence in light of what is already known, drawing conclusions and discussing results. This learning process is all supported by an inquiry-based pedagogy, where pedagogy is taken to mean not only the act of teaching but also its underpinning justifications" (Harlen 2013, 12).

This definition is entirely consonant with similar principles elaborated in 1995 by the *Académie des sciences* in France (for the project *La main à la pâte*), where students confronted with natural phenomena make observations and ask questions, do experiments and explore hypotheses, and present their own views to other students and the teacher, using their imagination and developing an appropriate language to express their findings (Charpak 1996; Charpak, Léna, and Quéré 2005). This whole process is guided by the teacher and is concluded by a summary to be learned and remembered by the student. Successive lessons are prepared in order to progressively build some solid knowledge, which can then be assessed. In a word, *learning* science is more efficient when accompanied by *discovering, reasoning,* and *understanding*. Needless to say, such a "horizontal" process, compared to a "vertical" one downward from teacher to student, is highly demanding for the teacher, and its success depends on the adequacy of the teacher's preparation.

Let me present here an important commentary on mathematics education. As mentioned earlier, IBSE specifically deals with natural sciences, with their broad spectrum extending from physics to life sciences, from astrophysics to earth sciences, a spectrum continuously increasing in diversity and scope in order to understand the natural world. Mathematics is indeed also a science, and one that is not without some references to experimental processes in the ways in which children or scientists experience the world around them—with numbers (leading to arithmetic and algebra) or shapes (leading to geometry). But the construction of abstract objects and of mathematical rules is further deployed with a predominant use of logic and with a limited (or even without any) connection with natural objects. Contrary to the teaching of natural sciences, the teaching of mathematics, which in school is often limited to the practice of useful, convenient algorithmic rules (calculus), is everywhere considered an essential part of basic science education—as is reflected in the universal motto "Reading, writing, counting." Hence, the mathematical sciences may also suffer from inadequate teaching, but this teaching possibly requires somewhat different principles of inquiry. This delicate point has been explored in depth in the recent project of science education *Fibonacci,* supported by the European Union (Artigue and Baptist 2012).

PREPARING YOUTH FOR THE CHALLENGES OF THEIR LIVES

The main goal of science education, taught at an early age, is to better prepare children to develop their personalities, understand the world they live in, and acquire the necessary skills—intellectual as well as manual—to make their future way as adults in the complex societies of our times. Being capable of sound judgment, developing a critical mind, cultivating self-confidence and creativity, balancing their emotional and rational responses in the face of natural phenomena, being able to express themselves accurately and to communicate peacefully with others appear to be essential skills for them, and there is no disputing the need to cultivate them.

We assert, and have observed, that science education is a remarkable tool for reaching these goals, indeed, not excluding the roles of other fields of knowledge. We also assert that this sharing of science, a legacy of the efforts and creations made since the dawn of humanity, should be made accessible to all, including those placed in the poorest educational conditions.

BIG IDEAS IN SCIENCE EDUCATION

What should these children learn? There is the question about what content or subjects should be taught, that is, the question of curricula. The amount and diversity of available scientific knowledge has led to the question of what should be the optimum content of a science curriculum, beginning at an early age (Grade 1 or even preschool), that would be reasonably common for all students until the age of fifteen or so (Grade 9). In addition to the study of the natural sciences themselves, the inclusion of technology, informatics, engineering, and health education provides new fields to be covered, thus making many connections to the natural sciences. Is it possible to enunciate a limited number of fundamental ideas *of* science as well as ideas *about* science that should be the backbone of IBSE progressions from Grades 1 through 9? This question has recently been explored under the term *big ideas* (Harlen 2015). These may provide an interdisciplinary and manageable focus on the main science concepts that will help children, teenagers, and other students to possess an efficient "reference system" in order to understand the world around them.

SUSTAINABLE DEVELOPMENT AND CLIMATE CHANGE

Humanity is entering an extremely difficult period in which the global issues of sustainability will be the challenges for the decades to come. Climate change is a threat that requires urgent action in politics, the economy, finance, energy production, and agriculture, as documented in the periodic reports of the Intergovernmental Panel on Climate Change (IPCC). In order to prepare societies for such considerable changes of behavior and mindset over long periods of time, education is a precious and necessary tool. This situation is recognized by the United Nations in its *Seventeen Sustainable Development Goals* (United Nations 2015), by UNESCO (2016) in its report *Education for People and the Planet*, and especially by article 12 of the Paris Agreement (2015; COP21 2015), which reads: "Parties shall cooperate in taking measures, as appropriate, to enhance climate change education, training, public awareness, public participation and public access to information, recognizing the importance of these steps with respect to enhancing actions under this Agreement." It is also the subject of a whole chapter entitled "Education and Spiritual Ecology" in Pope Francis's (2015) Encyclical Letter *Laudato Si'*. Only a small fraction of curricula in the world deal with these subjects, and this situation probably explains the ignorance of large parts of the population, even in developed countries, regarding their understanding and acceptance of the facts that science is providing about climate or the causes of climate change that scientists have identified.

Hence, focusing on these new and urgent issues becomes a necessity for the "traditional" IBSE. Recently, a number of authors have explored the issue of children and sustainable development as it relates to "an ecological education in a globalized world" (Battro, Léna, Sorondo, and von Braun 2016, book subtitle), paying special attention to the multicultural mixing of student populations. By promoting active learning in science, IBSE has already given millions of students much more initiative and has played a more active role than is provided in a classical, more vertical type of learning system. But more needs to be done to empower students. Climate and environmental issues offer such opportunities since they may call for the personal engagement of children to act and become agents of change, not only to understand and learn. This approach has been successfully explored in Peru, India, Bangladesh, and Ghana (von Braun 2016). *La main à la pâte* has developed modules on climate (Hirtzig, Wilgenbus, and Zimmermann 2015), but more ambitious action is needed to really make populations understand the issues of future climatic impacts and take necessary action (Wilgenbus 2016). Developing guidelines and resources for teachers that would be helpful for their classroom activities on the basis of the IPCC regular reports would require that a considerable effort be undertaken at the international level in order to fill the gap existing today (IAP 2017b). Needless to say, climate refugees and their children are primarily concerned about understanding the causes of and possible remedies for their fate and suffering.

IMPLEMENTING INQUIRY-BASED SCIENCE EDUCATION: CHALLENGES AND SUCCESSES

It is not appropriate to present details here on the implementation of the IBSE pedagogy in classrooms dealing with natural sciences. The topic has been explored in many instances, accompanying the development of the previously mentioned pilot projects during the last two decades (Harlen and Léna 2014). The main effort has been to train primary school teachers in basic science education in order to provide them with help and support and to give them self-confidence. Most of these teachers have little scientific knowledge; for them, science is something too often learned from a textbook as a collection of facts to know, of recipes to memorize. How could these teachers practice something different with their students? The process of building evidence from observation or experimentation is quite often absent from their mind and practice; this situation must be changed to empower them to focus on inquiry and practice a more creative pedagogy.

HELPING TEACHERS

We have found that it is most effective to put teachers in the very situations in which they will later place their students and to ask them to carry out the requested investigation in groups. This strategy is to let the teacher's curiosity become alive, opening his or her eyes before a natural phenomenon, questioning false evidence or a priori ideas, listening to another person's hypothesis or model, defining and then attempting an experiment or a measurement, finding the right words to express the conclusions—in short, exploring the very process of a scientific investigation. Indeed, the implementation of this method has to be guided, so guidance by scientists is invaluable here. We have applied these simple rules in many different cultural contexts and have verified their effectiveness.

When the teacher is again in front of the students, he or she will not be surprised to find among the students the same kind of hesitation, misconceptions, and inappropriate vocabulary that he or she had encountered during the training. It takes several training sessions, including getting feedback, for teachers to become trained in this pedagogy and to progressively become "inquiry experts" who are then able to train other teachers at their schools.

Since the mid-1990s, such initiatives for teachers' professional development in basic science education have been undertaken at various levels: local, national, regional, and global. Australia with Primary Connections, Chile with *Enseñanza Ciencias Basada en la Indigacion*, Colombia with *Pequeños Cientificos*, China with *Zuo Zhong Xue*, France with *La main à la pâte*, Germany with the *Haus der kleinen Forscher*, Italy with *Scientia Inquirendo Dicere*, Malaysia with *Learning by Doing*, and Mexico with *Innovec* are current examples of IBSE implementation at local or national levels. In the United States, where education is not centralized, the National Academy of Sciences, relayed by the Smithsonian Institution, has advanced the concept of inquiry through a large number of high-quality publications, intending to provide standards to guide education boards at state and local levels (National Research Council 2000). It is remarkable to observe that in all of these programs, with no exceptions, leading scientists, physicists, chemists, biologists, and engineers have been at the forefront of the movement to ensure that the strategies presented to teachers adequately reflect the IBSE principles—namely, to have students understand how science works rather than to merely memorize scientific content and facts (Alberts 2009; Nuffield 2017).

These efforts have also produced a great wealth of resources to help teachers in the classroom. The Internet is a remarkable tool for allowing their broad distribution and for facilitating interactions among teachers at a national level, as *La main à la pâte* does in France, or at a regional one, as is done in Europe (Harlen and Léna 2014) or has been attempted in many Latin American countries.

Given the great number of teachers requiring guidance in order to be transformed into good IBSE practitioners, ambitious national plans have been successfully conceived and developed, first in the United Kingdom since 2006 by the National Science Learning Centers (Holman 2016), then in France since 2012 (*Maisons pour la science* 2017). In the future, these very effective strategies might inspire similar actions to be undertaken for a whole region such as Africa. One such project, Centers for Science Education in Africa, the Mediterranean, and Europe (CESAME), is currently being discussed among European, Mediterranean, and African academies (CESAME 2017). These strategies may also inspire ways to train teachers dedicated to refugees or migrants in humanitarian camps if it becomes possible to develop science education there.

INTEREST IN SCIENCE IS UNIVERSAL

Circumstances have led *La main à la pâte* to implement IBSE in countries with teachers of very different qualities and training and with students of very diverse social statuses. It has been quite rewarding to observe that this pedagogy has been well received despite its implementation in such diverse situations. Here, I especially focus on implementations made within difficult schooling contexts and will provide some insights about the results. Some of the countries (Colombia, Cambodia, Venezuela, and South Africa) have been evaluated in a somewhat homogenous frame of

TABLE 12.1 Implementation of IBSE in various developing countries

Country	Beginning year	Teachers trained	Number of schools/students	Partnerships
Cambodia	2002	600	22,000 students	Ministry of Education, French cooperation, *Lamap*
Columbia	2000	3,000	300 to 400 students	Universidad Los Andes, *Lamap*
South Africa	2012	30	10 schools	SA Academy of Sciences, *Lamap*
Venezuela	2009	2,500	55,000 students	Academy of Sciences, *Lamap*
Haiti	2012	440	22,000 students	Education Ministry (Haiti), *Lamap*
Lebanon	2015	19	—	French cooperation, *Lamap*

NOTE: *Lamap* stands for the foundation *La main à la pâte* in France.
SOURCE: Table constructed from a series of papers in *Resolis* 2016.

analysis (*Resolis* 2016) and are presented in table 12.1, showing the possibility of acting on a large scale as long as the program extends for a sufficient period of time.

It is also interesting to examine extreme cases in which implementing science education in primary schools might appear to be a luxury given the extremely difficult social or political conditions, such as Haiti (TEH 2017) and Madagascar (Défi 2017). In both cases, several IBSE strategies are ensuring the success of this implementation, which has been well received by teachers as well as families—namely, developing the ability to observe and to reason from observation of the environment, familiar phenomena, or objects; promoting experimental or manual skills; connecting science and language acquisition; creating links between traditional knowledge and "modern" science, even if very elementary, as explored with the Mapuche Indians in Chile (Siemens Stiftung 2017); and familiarizing families with the learning process employed at school.

Most of these actions enable researchers to verify the pertinence of the previously enunciated ideas: curiosity is present among most children, boys as well as girls, with no gender difference; elementary scientific reasoning can be taught based on the immediate environment of the child (savanna, forest, city suburbs); cognitive skills are progressively developed, including the linguistic ability to designate or describe with accurate words—orally or in writing, or with elementary schemas—the experimental process. The families are interested in the ways in which their children explore the world and communicate their discoveries at home; the universal language of science allows schools to break down the barriers between students of different origins.

In order to demonstrate this last point, I refer to an example developed by local teachers and education actors in Nogent-sur-Oise, France. This area north of Paris is

FIGURE 12.1. In the Grand Amphithéâtre de la Sorbonne in Paris, celebrating the twentieth anniversary of *La main à la pâte*, children from the Nogent-sur-Oise pilot center enact a detective story on the physical states of water with Sciences on Stage (http://lamap-nogent.rep.ac-amiens.fr/?page_id=1045). Photo credit: Teresa Suarez.

characterized by a mixed population from various waves of immigration during the last decades, social tensions connected with Muslim fundamentalists, and high rates of unemployment. A pilot center of *La main à la pâte* has been operated there continuously since 1998 by a local and remarkable teacher, Nicolas Demarthe, to explore how science education may provide a focus of interest and learning for students in primary school and then as they move on to middle school. For example, the classical topic of *phase transition* (e.g., the boiling or freezing of water), a phenomenon that is part of the everyday experience of children and families, has been for a year long the focus of a play written and then enacted on stage by the students, accompanied by classroom experiments and written descriptions of their observations and creative writing in French (Nogent 2017). The play was presented to an audience of community leaders, parents, and the local public (see fig. 12.1). Despite the extreme diversity of cultural and family backgrounds—or rather, thanks to the richness of this diversity—the whole process has been a great success in learning and community building. Again, the universality of science has played its role.

The human impact of natural disasters is increasing in proportion to the number of humans exposed to them in unhealthy environments or poor habitats. In addition, climate change induces more extreme events (drought, floods, heat waves), having the same result of displacing people. In 2015 alone, such disasters displaced 19.2 million persons (Sánchez-Terán 2017). Education in such locations is a critical remedy for the worst aspects of these disasters. Let me remind you of the 2010 Haiti earthquake, in which many people died rushing into their homes instead of staying outside because they believed in the sacred nature of house protection. Let me also remind you of the story of a young English girl who in 2004, on the beach of Phuket in Thailand, saved many lives because she had learned at school what a tsunami was—specifically, the phenomenon of water retreating before the arrival of the deadly wave on the beach. She shouted to warn her mother and the people around her, with the deep conviction that science had to be believed. *La main à la pâte* has produced resources to help teachers in countries such as Indonesia and the Philippines facing such events (Wilgenbus, Faure, and Schick 2016).

In all of these cases, an organized, properly supported long-term process is an absolute requirement for achieving significant and long-lasting results. It is not so much a matter of cost but of persistent effort and support. When these are lacking, or when the circumstances are too adverse, failure occurs. I could cite our early failures in Egypt (the rigidity of the education system as opposed to giving children more initiative), in Israel/Palestine (the Gaza wars), and in some African countries where the local support of education authorities has failed, hampering the long-term sustainability of programs (Senegal). But even in these cases, useful lessons were learned.

PERSPECTIVES

Science education can only be a small fraction of any effort aimed at improving the conditions of learning in the world at a time of intense migrations and multiplication of refugees. Fighting the causes of such population displacement should be the main goal. Nevertheless, it is unacceptable to let millions of children grow up with little or even no access to education in general and to science education as part of it. In this context, the experiences and international efforts made during the last two decades to implement rejuvenated science education in various social contexts may be a starting point to amplify the effort on a more global scale and with motivated partners such as the United Nations, UNICEF, UNESCO, the science academies, InterAcademy Partnership, the International Council of Science (ICSU, since 2018 International Science Council), IPCC, private foundations, and nongovernmental organizations (NGOs), among others.

In countries where large refugee camps exist (Lebanon, Jordan, Sudan), scientists and local academies may be mobilized to implement some science activities in the camps. An adaptation of existing resources, the development of simple experimental material in kits, and the use of pictograms to facilitate the communication are easily conceivable. People acting as teachers could be trained along with regular teachers in practice sessions in order to implement the rudiments of IBSE. The experience gained from such pilot projects in multicultural surroundings would then be invaluable since it would amply demonstrate both the universality of science and the universality of children's curiosity. Connecting the educational content with the personal experience of a refugee child, which is often marked by terrible trauma (see Betancourt, chapter 6; Mollica, chapter 5; Stathopoulou, chapter 7, all in this volume), is an additional and difficult challenge. Yet experimenting with science education delivered to severely handicapped children has proven that, even in extreme situations, curiosity and the desire to know and understand natural phenomena do remain active (Ferrand-Heitz and Saltiel 2017). An interesting and recent development is the action of the *Haus der kleinen Forscher Stiftung* in Germany, which uses science education and inquiry pedagogy to contribute to the integration of refugee children into schools (Haus der kleinen Forscher 2017).

The 2015 PISA study addressing the natural science skills of youngsters aged fifteen in seventy-two countries and economies provides an interesting confirmation of the transcultural interest in science, correlated with good academic results obtained in countries of different cultures. On average across countries with relatively large immigrant student populations, attending a school with a high concentration of immigrant students is not associated with poorer student performance, after accounting for the school's socioeconomic intake. However, this positive finding must be balanced with another conclusion that reflects all of the social difficulties of these students: on average across OECD countries, and after taking their socioeconomic statuses into account, immigrant students are more than twice as likely as their nonimmigrant peers to perform below the baseline level of proficiency in science. Yet 24 percent of disadvantaged immigrant students are considered resilient (PISA 2015a). The next PISA study (2018) is planning to address more specifically the effects of a multicultural environment on students' proficiency in science; this study promises to be highly interesting and should help in the sharing of our scientific understanding of nature with these children.

NOTES

1. A science project was developed between *La main à la pâte* and the Israel-Palestine Science Organisation (IPSO) to implement IBSE in schools within Palestinian refugee camps with multilingual tools (Arabic, Hebrew, English, and French) and support from the European Union, but since the Gaza War (2008–09), any progress has been blocked.

2. Citation refers to the French edition; English translation of quotation from www .brainyquote.com/quotes/quotes/isaacnewton387031.html.

3. Ibn Al-Haytham (Alhazen) was an Arab Muslim scientist, mathematician, astronomer, and philosopher (965–1040). He was the first to correctly interpret vision as the receiving of light from an object (and not the eye "illuminating" the object). He is widely considered to have been an early proponent of the belief that a hypothesis must be proven by experiments based on confirmable procedures or mathematical evidence, as illustrated by the quotation from his famous *Book of Optics*.

4. Jean Perrin (1870–1942), a French physicist, was a Nobel laureate in Physics in 1926 for the experimental demonstration of the existence of atoms. He created the *Palais de la Découverte*, the first hands-on science museum, in Paris.

5. Frank Oppenheimer (1912–85), American physicist and brother of Robert Oppenheimer, was the creator of San Francisco's Exploratorium.

6. Bruce Alberts (1938–), an American molecular biologist who chaired the US National Academy of Sciences, has promoted science education worldwide and introduced this field into the journal *Science* when he was its editor-in-chief.

REFERENCES

Alberts, Bruce. 2009. "Redefining Science Education." Editorial. *Science* 323: 75.

Artigue, Michèle, and Peter Baptist, eds. 2012. *Inquiry in Mathematics Education*. Fibonacci Project. www.fondation-lamap.org/sites/default/files/upload/media/minisites/action_internationale/inquiry_in_mathematics_education.pdf.

Battro, Antonio M., Pierre Léna, Marcelo Sánchez Sorondo, and Joachim von Braun, eds. 2016. *Children and Sustainable Development: Ecological Education in a Globalized World*. Basel: Springer International Publishing.

Bergson, Henri (1934) 1969. *La Pensée et le Mouvant*. Paris: Presses Universitaires de France.

CESAME (Centers for Science Education in Africa, the Mediterranean, and Europe). 2017. *CESAME (Centers for Science Education in Africa, the Mediterranean, and Europe)*. www.academie-sciences.fr/en/Interacademic-action/aemase-2017.html.

Charpak, Georges, coord. 1996. *La main à la pâte. Les sciences à l'école primaire*. Paris: Flammarion.

Charpak, Georges, Pierre Léna, and Yves Quéré. 2005. *L'Enfant et la science. L'aventure de La main à la pâte*. Paris: Le Pommier.

COP21 (Conference of Parties, No. 21). 2015. *United Nations Framework Agreement for Climate Change*. http://unfccc.int/paris_agreement/items/9485.php.

Défi. 2017. *Le défi de la formation et de l'éducation*. www.ongdefi.org/. (*Défi*, which means "challenge" in French, is an NGO inspired by IBSE [Inquiry-Based Science Education] and acting in Madagascar, Haiti, and Benin.)

Dehaene, Stanislas. 2015. "*L'engagement actif, la curiosité et la correction des erreurs*" [Active engagement, curiosity and correcting mistakes]. Lesson given at the Collège de France, February 3, 2015. www.college-de-france.fr/site/stanislas-dehaene/course-2015–02–03–09h30.htm.

Ferrand-Heitz, Marie Hélène and Edith Saltiel. 2018. "Science and Investigation: Teaching for Sustainable Learning to Students with Disabilities." *Review of Science, Mathematics and ICT Education* 12 (1).

Gopnik, Alisa, Andrew N. Meltzoff, and Patricia K. Kuhl. 2000. *The Scientist in the Crib: What Early Learning Tells Us about the Mind*. New York: William Morrow.

Harlen, Wynne. 2013. *Assessment and Inquiry-Based Science Education: Issues in Policy and Practice*. Global Network of Science Academies (IAP), Science Education Program. www.interacademies.net/activities/projects/12250.aspx.

Harlen, Wynne, ed. (2010) 2015. *Principles and Big Ideas of Science Education*. Revised edition of *Working with Big Ideas in Science Education*. United Kingdom: Association for Science Education.

Harlen, Wynne, and Pierre Léna, eds. 2014. *The Legacy of the Fibonacci Project to Science and Mathematics Education: A Systemic Approach for Sustainable Implementation and Dissemination of Inquiry Pedagogy, Tested in Primary and Secondary Schools throughout Europe (2010–13)*. www.fondation-lamap.org/sites/default/files/upload/media/minisites /international/Fibonacci_Book.pdf.

Haus der kleinen Forscher [House of the young researchers]. 2017. https://integration .haus-der-kleinen-forscher.de.

Hirtzig, Mathieu, David Wilgenbus, and Gabrielle Zimmermann. 2015. *The Ocean, My Planet . . . and Me*. Paris: Le Pommier.

Holman, John. 2016. "Professional Development of Teachers at the Science Learning Centers in the UK." In *Children and Sustainable Development: Ecological Education in a Globalized World*, edited by Antonio M. Battro, Pierre Léna, Marcelo Sánchez Sorondo, and Joachim von Braun, 283–90. Basel: Springer International Publishing.

Ibn al-Haytham. (n. d.) 1989. *The Optics of Ibn al-Haytham [Kitab Al-Manadhi]*. Translated from Arabic by A. I. Sabra. Books I–III: *On Direct Vision: English Translation and Commentary*. Vol. 40 of *Studies of the Warburg Institute*. London: Warburg Institute, University of London.

IAP (InterAcademy Partnership). 2017a. "InterAcademy Partnership Science Education Program." http://interacademies.net/ProjectsAndActivities/Projects/12250/18276.aspx.

———. 2017b. "Statement on Climate Change and Education." www.interacademies .org/38806/IAP-Statement-on-Climate-Change-and-Education.

IDMC (Internal Displacement Monitoring Centre). 2017. *Global Internal Displacement Database*. Norwegian Refugees Council. www.internal-displacement.org/database/.

LASER (Leadership and Assistance for Science Education Reform). 2016. Washington, DC: Smithsonian Institution. http://ssec.si.edu/laser-i3/.

Léna, Pierre. 2012. "Education in Science: Its Values and the Role of the Scientific Community." Supplement 1, *Rendicoti Lincei. Scienze Fisiche e Naturali* 23: S13–S16. doi:10.1007 /s12210-012-0195-z.

Loewenstein, George. 1994. "The Psychology of Curiosity: A Review and Reinterpretation." *Psychological Bulletin* 116: 75–98.

Maisons pour la science [Houses for science]. 2017. Accessed June 20, 2018. www.maisons-pour-la-science.org/.

Minner, Daphne D., Abigail J. Levy, and Jeanne Century. 2010. "Inquiry-Based Science Instruction: What Is It and Does It Matter? Results from a Research Synthesis, Years 1984 to 2002." *Journal of Research in Science Teaching* 47: 474–96.

National Research Council. 2000. *How People Learn*. Washington, DC: National Academy Press.

NCES (National Center for Education Statistics. n. d. *Trends in International Mathematics and Science Study*). https://nces.ed.gov/timss/.

Neel, Alexander S. 1960. *Summerhill: A Radical Approach to Child Rearing*. New York: Hart.

Nogent. 2017. "The *Nogent-sur-Oise* Pilot Center and the '*Sciences en Scène*' [Sciences on stage] Achievements." http://lamap-nogent.rep.ac-amiens.fr/?page_id = 1045/.

Nuffield Foundation. 2017. "How Science Works." www.nuffieldfoundation.org/science-society/how-science-works/.

Paris Agreement. 2015. *UN Sustainable Development Knowledge Platform.* https://sustainabledevelopment.un.org/frameworks/parisagreement/.

Pequeños Científicos. n. d. Accessed June 12, 2018. http://pequenoscientificos.org/index.html/.

PISA (Programme for International Student Assessment). 2015a. "PISA 2015 Results in Focus." https://www.oecd.org/pisa/pisa-2015-results-in-focus.pdf.

———. 2015b. *Programme of International Student Assessment (PISA).* http://www.oecd.org/pisa/.

Pope Francis. 2015. *Laudato Si': For the Care of Our Common Home.* http://laudatosi.com/watch/.

PSF (Pakistan Science Foundation). 2017. *Pakistan Science Foundation.* http://www.psf.gov.pk/lamap.aspx/.

Resolis. 2016. "Science Education: *La main à la pâte* abroad." Special issue, *Resolis* 9 (April). www.resolis.org/.

Sacks, Oliver. 2001. *Uncle Tungsten: Memory of a Chemical Boyhood.* New York: Vintage.

Sánchez-Terán, Gonzalo. 2017. "The Global Forced Migrations and the Education of Children." Paper presented at the Workshop on Humanitarianism and Mass Migration, UCLA, Los Angeles, January 18–19, 2017.

Siemens Stiftung. 2017. *The "Experimento" Program, Siemens Foundation.* https://www.siemens-stiftung.org/en/projects/experimento/.

TEH *(Transformer l'Enseignement en Haïti).* 2017. *Transformer l'Enseignement en Haïti (TEH).* http://teh.fondation-lamap.org/teh/.

UNESCO (United Nations Educational, Scientific, and Cultural Organization). 2016. *Education for People and Planet: Creating Sustainable Futures for All.* http://unesdoc.unesco.org/images/0024/002457/245752e.pdf.

United Nations. 2015. *Sustainable Development Goals.* https://sustainabledevelopment.un.org/sdgs/.

von Braun, Joachim. 2016. "Children as Agents of Change for Sustainable Development." In *Children and Sustainable Development: Ecological Education in a Globalized World,* edited by Antonio M. Battro, Pierre Léna, Marcelo Sánchez Sorondo, and Joachim von Braun, 17–30. Basel: Springer International Publishing.

Wei, Yu. 2012. 十年 "做中学" 为了说明什么 [Ten years to explore "Learning by Doing" in schools]. Beijing: China Science and Technology Press.

Westfall, Robert. (1980) 1994. *Newton 1642–1727.* French edition. Paris: Flammarion. Originally published as *Never at Rest: A Biography of Isaac Newton.* Cambridge: Cambridge University Press.

Wilgenbus, David. 2016. "Educating Students in Sustainability: The Experience of *La main à la pâte.*" In *Children and Sustainable Development: Ecological Education in a Globalized World,* edited by Antonio M. Battro, Pierre Léna, Marcelo Sánchez Sorondo, and Joachim von Braun, 17–30. Basel: Springer International Publishing.

Wilgenbus, David, Cédric Faure, and Olivier Schick. 2016. *When the Earth Rumbles.* Paris: Le Pommier. www.fondation-lamap.org/en/11/when-the-earth-rumbles.

13
_____

LOST IN TRANSIT

Education for Refugee Children in Sweden,
Germany, and Turkey

Maurice Crul, Frans Lelie, Elif Keskiner,
Jens Schneider, and Özge Biner

The ongoing refugee crisis revealed two faces of both the European Union (EU) and the Europeans themselves: the beautiful face of empathy and heartwarming solidarity, and the ugly face of political bargaining and blunt indifference to refugees and their children. European policy makers and citizens acted upon Europe's core values, opening the borders for people fleeing war-torn Syria, Afghanistan, and Eritrea. Because of the conflicts in the Middle East and Africa, no fewer than 613,395 youngsters under the age of eighteen had applied for asylum in Europe between 2013 and 2015 (European Commission Education and Training Monitor 2016). In 2016, Europe admitted another one million refugees, an unprecedented number in the history of the European Union. At the height of the crisis in 2016, the city of Hamburg alone had to find four hundred new school places for refugee children each month. All over Europe empty buildings were turned into classrooms, and new teachers were hired on a daily basis. Volunteers helped people to acquire basic national language skills and navigate their new lives in a strange country. Chancellor Angela Merkel's *"Wir schaffen das!"* ("We make this happen!") was made a reality by huge numbers of city officials, social workers, school leaders, teachers, and—last but not least—an infinite army of European volunteers from all sectors of society. The response to this humanitarian drama showed both European administrators and citizens at their best.

But there is, unfortunately, another face of Europe, and it is this face that appears to have become dominant since the second half of 2016. It is one of harsh indifference toward refugees and their children, the face of European politics bargaining with the lives of desperate people. It is the face that turned away from refugee families stuck and forgotten in tents in the snow in Greece or Croatia in the winter of 2016–17 in Europe (Stathopoulou, chapter 7, this volume) and the exploitation of refugee children on the Turkish labor market, their families held hostage and in poverty by the deal struck between the EU and Turkey (Crul et al. 2017). UNICEF released a press statement in January 2017 stating that more than 380,000 Syrian children in Turkey were not attending school. This number amounts to about half of the refugee children in Turkey (ÇOÇA 2015). The majority of the children who do go to school are being taught in schools that are mostly in refugee camps by Syrian teachers teaching the Syrian curriculum. Turkish second-language teaching is not provided in public schools. This generation of young children—we call them "the locked-out refugee generation"—who cannot return to Syria anytime soon will be left empty-handed. The destiny of these children, who should all be in school, has been outsourced by the European Union to the camps in Turkey and the margins of Turkish cities.

This chapter will consider the situation of refugee children in Sweden and Germany and contrast it with the situation of refugee children in Turkey. What does it mean for refugee children to be "lost in transit" in Turkey? But also, what does it mean for refugee children to be incorporated into school in Sweden as compared with their incorporation in Germany? There are also major differences regarding the incorporation of refugee children into schools within Europe.

GOING BEYOND THE STATE OF THE ART

The research debate on the so-called "refugee crisis in Europe" has largely been addressing issues like border control, EU policies (or the lack thereof), and the political backlash in the form of anti-immigrant sentiment. But follow-up questions about the integration of refugees and their children into society, education, and work are slowly beginning to appear on the agenda. Policy makers and practitioners across Europe and in Turkey are struggling to offer education to these new refugee children (EUROCITIES 2017). Researchers in Europe and Turkey have started to monitor these efforts. It will probably take a few years before the first results of most of these studies are published. However, in Europe there is already a body of research based on previous waves of refugees in the 1990s, when people fled from war-torn Yugoslavia, Iran, Iraq, Afghanistan, and Somalia—some of the same countries from which people are coming today.

Compared with the overwhelming research done on children of immigrants in Europe, much less attention has been paid to refugee children in educational systems (Crul et al. 2017). Furthermore, refugee children are often not specially targeted in either national or international surveys like the Programme for International Student Assessment (PISA) of the Organization for Economic Cooperation and Development (OECD) (Bloch et al. 2015). While, for instance, data on the school results of children of labor migrants or former colonial immigrant groups in Europe are readily available at a national or even a city level, similar data are often lacking for refugee children in Europe. However, the limited data show that refugee children usually face many more obstacles than other children of immigrants do (McBrien 2005; Bloch et al. 2015; Suárez-Orozco, Bang, and Kim 2011; PPMI 2013; Sirin and Rogers-Sirin 2015).

A further observation is that the usual differentiation between children of immigrants who were born in the country and children who arrived with their families during the compulsory school period (the in-between generation) is mostly not made for refugee children. However, education research has demonstrated time and again that this distinction is an important one to make when seeking to explain the variation in outcomes both within and between groups (Bloch at al. 2015, 15; Crul, Schneider, and Lelie 2012; Crul, Herzog-Punzenberger, et al. 2012; Heath and Brinbaum 2007; Holdaway, Crul, and Roberts 2009; OECD 2010). There also appears to be little literature on the development of refugee children's school careers over time. Until now, most research has focused on the limited period of *welcome, introduction,* or *submersion classes.* Of course, these classes are a crucial element in helping children get off to a successful start in education, but they only tell part of the story. What happens after these classes is equally important. To what sort of educational track are children admitted? Do they still receive second-language support or other additional support? Are they allowed to continue their studies after compulsory education?

Finally, much research within refugee studies focuses on what Jenny Nilsson and Nihad Bunar (2016, 401) call singular factors, such as trauma or individual background factors. Little attention has been paid to the importance of institutional factors in education that influence the school careers of refugee children. We will argue in this chapter that institutional arrangements such as the way in which welcome classes and second-language education are organized or whether or not there is access to education beyond compulsory school age have a huge impact on the incorporation of refugee children into a country's educational system.

EXPLANATION OF OUR COMPARATIVE RESEARCH APPROACH

The comparison we will make among Sweden, Germany, and Turkey is based on relevant existing literature in the three countries on refugee children in education. An important gap in the present body of research is caused by the compartmentalization of the literature. Some research papers concentrate on primary school children, others on secondary school children, and others still on refugee students past compulsory school age. Focus also diverges among welcome classes, second-language education, and possibilities for vocational education and apprenticeships.

In this chapter we will try to connect the dots among the different studies that report on different age groups and discuss refugee children in different forms of education. For this approach, we will make use of studies specifically aimed at refugee children as well as more general studies on children of immigrants published in English and in the national languages. We will also incorporate our knowledge of the impact of different institutional arrangements on the school careers of children of immigrants. The importance of the impact of differences in national school systems on children of immigrants is well documented (see, for instance, Crul, Herzog-Punzenberger, et al. 2012; Keskiner 2013; Schnell 2012). Theoretically, the impact of national educational institutions on children of immigrants is formulated in the Comparative Integration Context Theory (Crul and Schneider 2010; Crul and Mollenkopf 2012; Crul et al. 2012a). We will use this theoretical and analytical framework to compare the three countries.

There were a number of reasons for selecting these three countries in particular. First, they are among the countries that have received the highest numbers of refugees from the conflicts in Syria, Eritrea, Afghanistan, and Iraq and therefore have the highest numbers of refugee children entering their educational systems. Secondly, they have very different institutional arrangements for integrating refugee children into education. This factor makes it important and useful to compare them. Thirdly, we specifically included Turkey because of the EU–Turkey arrangement, which includes exchanges between the EU and Turkey in terms of policy making with regard to Syrian refugee children. It is important to note that *most* refugee children who fled Syria, Afghanistan, Eritrea, or Iraq reside outside of Europe and are entering (provided they have access to education) the educational systems in neighboring countries such as Jordan, Lebanon, Ethiopia, Pakistan, or Turkey. It is urgent to include the case of Turkey here because refugees are more often than not "lost in transit" in neighboring countries for many years without any opportunity to settle in a country of their own choosing. These situations have become the norm in many African countries, and we argue that this specific type of incorporation should be studied alongside incorporation into countries where people were able to flee to a destination of their own choosing.

The different ways in which the three countries incorporate refugee children are very illuminating, both in terms of the consequences for educational success and for studying good practices. We have organized this chapter with a separate section on each country being studied, in which we describe the incorporation around seven key institutional arrangements that we have identified as being influential for the school careers of refugee children: (1) preschool arrangements; (2) entrance into compulsory education; (3) welcome, submersion, or introduction classes; (4) second-language instruction; (5) additional teacher support; (6) tracking; (7) education after compulsory schooling.

We begin each country section with a short statement about the overall vision of incorporating refugee children into the national school system. We roughly categorize the Turkish approach as a form of limited integration, with many children not attending school and a large group being taught in a parallel school system instead of being integrated into the Turkish national school system. The German approach aims for full integration of these students into the German school system, but their integration is largely limited to access to the lowest forms of vocational education. The Swedish approach offers unlimited access to education even beyond compulsory education, with the explicit purpose of providing equal access to all types of education, including academic forms. The country paragraphs will offer extensive proof of how these different views are shaped in practice within national education systems. In the concluding paragraph, we will discuss the theoretical implications of our findings and our contribution to the fast-growing field of refugee studies.

Our comparison of the three countries comes with some limitations. The challenges faced by Turkey are obviously very different from those faced by Germany or Sweden. The number of refugees entering Turkey is much higher than the number of those entering Sweden, as demonstrated by the following statistics on Syrian refugees in Turkey. According to the most recent report by UNICEF in December 2016, there are 2.8 million Syrian refugees being hosted in Turkey. Fewer than 10 percent reside in refugee camps, and children between the ages of five and seventeen make up around 870,000 of this population. This high influx has placed much greater demands on the existing school facilities and resulted in many temporary solutions to deal with the reality on the ground. Furthermore, it is crucial to underscore that from 2005 to 2013, Turkey had been undergoing a shift from being a transition country to being a host country with regard to its refugee regime (Biner 2014, 2016).[1] Unlike countries such as Germany and Sweden, where there is an established institutional regime of refugee incorporation, Turkey has had to deal with a huge influx of refugees while in the process of setting up its refugee incorporation legislation. With no infrastructure to host refugees or their children, the Turkish state seems to address and resolve the matters ad hoc.

Different refugee populations came to the three countries, resulting in different challenges with regard to education. In Sweden, for instance, an additional challenge is that about half of the refugee children are unaccompanied minors (Rydin et al. 2012, 185; Çelikaksoy and Wadensjö 2015). A proper comparison would therefore require a comparison of similar groups that arrived during the same period under similar conditions and with similar educational histories in their countries of origin. Such detailed studies are not yet available. We are aware of these limitations, but, at the same time, we think this factor should not prevent us from looking into differences in both the opportunities and the obstacles that school systems and legal regulations present in these different countries.

REFUGEE CHILDREN IN AND OUT OF EDUCATION IN TURKEY: THE LOCKED-OUT REFUGEE GENERATION

Vision

Turkey is an example of a country where access to school even for children of compulsory school age is still not assured and where policies in the last five years have led to creating a parallel school system (see Crul et al. 2017). Turkey is a party to the United Nations Convention on the Rights of the Child, Article 22 of which obliges the signatory countries to provide protection and schooling to all asylum-seeking and refugee children. Furthermore, Turkish law (5395) obliges the Turkish state to provide education and protection to minors irrespective of their nationality. Despite this legal requirement, about half of the refugee children are *not* participating in education. Most of the children who can access education are attending temporary education centers, where they follow a Syrian curriculum. In 2017, the Turkish government made a start, closing temporary education centers and transferring the Syrian children to regular public schools.

Preschool

In Turkey, preschool is generally private, so public preschool facilities are therefore very limited. There are a few private preschools for Syrian refugee children in Istanbul and Gaziantep. Official reports do not provide any information about whether such facilities exist in the refugee camps. A recent report by Bülent Aras and Salih Yasun (2016) states that preschool education and first-grade participation in public schools are in the government mandate; hence, Syrian children who would like to attend these classes can do so in public institutions, but to date no data have been provided with regard to what is actually happening.

Access to Compulsory Education

Although 90 percent of the children in the refugee camps attend school, these children only comprise 13 percent of Syrian children of school age living in Turkey. Turkey is legally bound to provide schooling to refugee children irrespective of their status. In October 2014, a new regulation, the Temporary Protection Regulation (TPR), became the main domestic legislation to govern Turkey's de facto temporary protection of Syrian refugees in the areas of education, health, and social protection. The TPR was expected to ease the process of enrollment in schools (ÇOÇA 2015).[2] Syrian children have three main options for accessing compulsory education: the first is to enroll in a Turkish public school; the second is to enroll in a Temporary Education Center (TEC); and the third is to attend a private school set up by Syrian organizations or donors, but these are limited in number and mostly located in the cities of Gaziantep and Istanbul. Most Syrian refugee children until the summer of 2017 were being educated in Temporary Education Centers, which operate at the primary and secondary education levels both within and out-side the refugee camps. TECs provide instruction in Arabic and follow a curricu-lum set up by the Syrian Interim Government's Ministry of Education that has been adjusted and approved by the Turkish Ministry of Education (HRW 2015). Lessons are taught by Syrian teachers who are selected and contracted by the Turk-ish state as "volunteers" as they do not have work permits. Payment is arranged through UNICEF. Although these centers began as private initiatives, they were brought under the domain of the Turkish Ministry of Education in 2014, becom-ing public institutions through a fast-track intervention. Since then, the Turkish Ministry of Education has decided in each instance whether or not an educational initiative may be called a Temporary Education Center and who can teach there. The curriculum is determined in cooperation between the Syrian Interim Govern-ment's Ministry of Education and the Turkish Ministry of Education. Educational supplies are provided by UNICEF (see report). According to the December 2016 UNICEF report, 78 percent of Syrian refugee students enrolled in education attend Temporary Education Centers, and the rest go to other educational institutions (mainly Turkish public schools) (UNICEF 2016).[3]

The third option components—private schools—are not known as TECs. These institutions are mostly found in Istanbul and Gaziantep, but participation by the Syrian population in these private, fee-based institutions is limited. Up until the summer of 2017, most of the Syrian children in education were being taught in TECs, followed by those in Turkish public schools. According to the 2016 UNICEF report, a total of 490,000 were enrolled in school, but as this figure only accounts for 56 percent of the total number of Syrian children in Turkey between the ages of five and seventeen, around 380,000 Syrian children were at that moment out of school (UNICEF 2016).

There are various reasons for this lack of participation in compulsory educa-tion. Being in limbo with regard to their legal status, Syrian refugee families are experiencing severe economic hardship, and this condition forms a major imped-iment to accessing education (HRW 2015). The fact that Syrian refugees have no permission to work has created a huge labor black market in Turkey, and this development, in combination with the poverty endured by these families due to the war, has created a situation in which child labor has become common among Syrian children (Mutlu, Kirimsoy, and Antakyalioglu 2016; Aras and Yasun 2016). Additionally, many Syrian families are not well informed about their children's right to education. The Ministry of Education recently cooperated with UNICEF in a project to inform Syrian parents of this right (Aras and Yasun 2016, 5). Other common reasons include unsystematic implementation and arbitrary practices on the part of local state agencies when providing Syrian children access to public schools or resolving difficulties regarding transport.

Welcome Classes

In Turkey, it is difficult to talk systematically about welcome classes on the national scale. Students enrolling in public schools are not required to attend a welcome class. However, since their incorporation into the public domain, the Turkish state seems to be treating the Temporary Education Centers as transition institutions, which could be seen as a form of welcome classes to facilitate the full transition of students into the national education system. According to our colleague Özge Biner's fieldwork with TEC organizations, Syrian teachers working in İzmir have said that in the coming years, TEC will provide these courses for a limited period of time and that Syrian students will be directly transferred to Turkish public schools after completing these welcome classes. Therefore, the current expectation is that TECs will function as institutions to prepare Syrian refugee students for entrance into the Turkish public education system.

Second-Language Education

For Turkey, our literature overview shows that, next to the economic hardships that force many children into the labor black market, lack of national language proficiency is the main obstacle Syrian children face in accessing education. With the exception of the Turkmen ethnic minority, who speak Turkish, Syrian refugee children do not speak Turkish; their most common languages are Arabic and Kurdish. As of publication of this book, there is no systematic Turkish-language training in the public schools. Upon enrolling in a Turkish public school, pupils take a test to determine their level and are then assigned to a class where they immediately study along with the other pupils, with no additional Turkish-language training. Turkish-language courses seem to be handled at the local level with initiatives from the municipalities or nongovernmental organizations (NGOs), but these efforts remain very limited. A recent study in Istanbul by Auveen Woods and Nihal Kayali (2017) underscores that education is the most complex problem that municipalities have to deal with regarding the refugees. They mention that although there are initiatives to supply Turkish courses, they are few and only available in a small number of places.

At the beginning of 2017, the Turkish government started to urge Temporary Education Centers that teach in Arabic to provide Turkish-language courses. These classes are taught by regular Turkish schoolteachers at schools where the TECs are located. Although it is hard to assess this implementation systematically on a national scale, Biner's fieldwork and interviews with official actors confirm that the hours of Turkish-language teaching have increased. This condition also relates to the fact that the Turkish authorities want eventually to transfer Syrian students to mainstream education and therefore regard the TECs as a transition phase. This view reflects a change in the Turkish state's attitude regarding the integration of Syrian refugee children. Biner's fieldwork in Izmir illustrates how the state has increased children's participation during a short period. According to an interview with a schoolteacher in Izmir, the Ministry of Education had launched an initiative to increase the number of Syrian children attending school in Izmir. Hence, they pressured school officials to visit neighborhoods where refugees reside with lists of registers for enrolling their children in school. In 2016, a total of 3,500 Syrian children were attending school. By 2017, this number had increased to 11,000 (3,000 going to regular public schools and 8,000 attending TECs). In Izmir, Turkish-language teaching in TECs increased from five hours per week to fifteen hours per week during this period.

Lack of sufficient Turkish-language training is leading to different results for younger and older children. While younger Syrian children learn Turkish faster (and are therefore doing better in school and are integrating more quickly), a lack of language proficiency among older children is leading to their becoming isolated in classrooms, causing them to drop out—provided that they are even accepted for enrollment in the first place. Many of these older children end up working in sweatshops under extremely low-paid and difficult conditions (HRW 2015; Aras and Yasun 2016; Woods and Kayali 2017).

Additional Support Teachers

Turkey does not require schools to assign support personnel to refugee children. Although counseling facilities are available in public schools in Turkey, they do not seem to be equipped to support Syrian children who have suffered serious traumas.

Tracking

In Turkey, the newly adopted 4+4+4 system requires children to begin compulsory education at the age of six and to attend school until the age of eighteen. Although the system has no specific tracking moment, there are significant distinctions between selective and nonselective educational institutions and the quality of education in both the private and public domains. These distinctions become crucial when one is trying to gain access to higher education. The studies reviewed for this chapter only mention the participation of Syrian children in nonselective public education and temporary education centers (ÇOÇA 2015; HRW 2015; Mutlu, Kirimsoy, and Antakyalioglu 2016).

Education after Compulsory Education

With regard to higher education in Turkey, there are provisions to allow Syrian university students to enroll in seven higher education institutions near the Syrian border that have a "special student" status. According to the Turkish Higher Education Institutions (YÖK), 3,397 male and 2,163 female Syrian students were enrolled at a higher education institution in the academic year 2014–15 (Mutlu, Kirimsoy, and Antakyalioglu 2016, 42).

Legal arrangements have been made to enable Syrian refugees to attend higher education institutions irrespective of whether they attended a Turkish public school or Temporary Education Center. To begin with, students with a high school diploma must pass an accreditation exam that was designed for Syrian students and first administered in 2016. Next, Syrian students must take the university entrance examination designed for foreign students (YOS). If they pass both examinations, they can enroll in a Turkish university on the basis of the 10 percent quota that each university has for foreign students (Aras and Yasun 2016). Furthermore, students are expected to display a certain degree of Turkish-language proficiency, which is determined as C1 level by the Türkçe Öğretim Merkezi (TOMER).[4] If they have not yet attained this level, they can take a preparatory year to learn Turkish. These prep years, however, are not offered by all Turkish universities. Upon admission, Syrian students are charged a fee, which varies across universities and departments. There are scholarship opportunities for Syrian students, such as funding from the Presidency for Turks Abroad and Related Communities, and the United Nations High Commissioner for Refugees (UNHCR) is setting up a scholarship for higher education students. Aras and Yasun (2016) also mention that there are plans in progress to offer a one-year course for learning academic Turkish. We were not able to find any information on adult education for Syrian refugees. All the restrictions mentioned, both formal and financial, result in very low numbers of Syrian students in Turkey's universities.

GERMANY

Vision

In contrast to the situation in Turkey, refugee children may enter the German national school system, but the way in which they are incorporated does not give them opportunities for educational success that are equal to those available to pupils of native descent (see Crul et al. 2017; EUROCITIES 2017). In Germany most policy measures are aimed at (and limited to) the transitional phase of welcome or international classes. Refugee children often spend one or two years in parallel welcome classes. This situation, combined with early tracking at age ten, means that refugee children often end up in the (lowest) vocational track called *Hauptschule.* A brochure (UMF 2010) for unaccompanied minors in Germany is quite telling: "In Germany, all children and teenagers under the age of sixteen have the right and duty to go to school. This is called compulsory attendance. Usually you would start off with the '*Hauptschule,*' where you have the possibility of getting a '*Hauptschuleabschluss*'" (secondary school qualification).

Only a small percentage of pupils of German descent go to *Hauptschule,* and many German parents avoid this school track at all costs because it offers few prospects for obtaining a good apprenticeship placement and often leads to problems in entering the labor market. For many teachers and policy makers, however, *Hauptschule* seems to be the highest possible option for refugee children (see also Niemeyer 2014, 46).

Preschool

In Germany compulsory school starts at age five or six, depending on which *Bundesländ* (state) one lives in. This relatively late start makes access to preschool very important. It also means that a relatively large age group is affected by the institutional arrangements for preschool that have been made available—or not.

The development of preschool facilities for disadvantaged children and children of immigrants in Germany has been strongly stimulated during the last decade. Previously, preschool was mostly available for working mothers and came with considerable costs. As far as we know, there are no figures specifically on the inclusion of refugee children in preschool facilities. As soon as parents receive official asylum status, they will, in principle, be treated as equally as parents of native descent are. Costs for child care differ between *Bundesländers* and even between cities. Some cities, like Hamburg and Berlin, make an extra effort to include young refugee children in preschool. However, in some cities or *Bundesländer*, such inclusion is not considered something that requires an active approach because preschool does not fall under compulsory education. Consequently, it appears that not many young refugee children attend preschool. This situation means that by the time they enter elementary school at the age of six, they already have a huge deficit in German as a second language.

Access to Compulsory Education

Compulsory education in Germany covers the age range between six and sixteen. The right to attend compulsory education is guaranteed by law. European regulations stipulate that children should be included in education within three months (Article 14, paragraph 1, European Regulations 2003/9/EG). There are no additional legally binding limits in Germany. In practice, the time lapse between entering the country and entering school amounts to three months or even up to six months. Education for school-aged children has often been arranged in an improvised manner, especially during the past two years, when many refugee families were being housed in temporary shelters and camps, and people had to move several times before being accommodated in more permanent centers for asylum seekers.

German-language courses in the reception centers are mandatory in theory, but school attendance is not compulsory for children who are still in the process of status definition and who therefore do not yet have residence permits (Bourgonje 2010, 47). As a result, small groups of children of compulsory school age are not attending school, and the quality and amount of schooling these children receive is also being affected (47). For instance, in some cases children were receiving language education in asylum seekers' centers for only a few hours a day instead of going to a regular school.

International Classes and Welcome Classes

In Germany children attend welcome classes or international classes for one or two years before being transferred to regular classes. Depending on the state, city, or even the school, this teaching can be followed by more assistance with German as a second language if their German-language skills are still insufficient. There are some preparation classes attached to *Gymnasia,* the highest level of secondary education and the preacademic track, but in general pupils attending preparation classes in secondary school are in *Hauptschule* or *Realschule,* lower- and middle-level vocational education. The sheer number of refugee children in Germany in the past two years has been overwhelming, and the task at the level of *Bundesländer* and cities has therefore been gigantic.

Second-Language Education

There is second-language support in elementary school in Germany (up to age ten or twelve, depending on the *Bundesland*). Niemeyer (2014, 57) emphasizes in her study that it is important to note that "nowhere is it stated that German as a second language has to be taught in school." The Mercator Institute recently released a report (Massumi et al. 2015) stating that teacher training in second-language education is still insufficient (see also Niemeyer 2014, 47). Study methods and techniques for second-language education were often lacking in the past (Niemeyer 2014, 48). Some German schools have a separate second-language teacher, while in others, schoolteachers receive additional training in second-language teaching, but this training usually consists of just one day (Niemeyer 2014). In daily practice, it is these regular teachers with scarce training who provide additional second-language instruction in the classroom (Niemeyer 2014, 57). However, new programs in second-language education are expanding quickly. In 2014, second-language teacher training was only compulsory for schoolteachers in one *Bundesland.* Today it is required in five *Bundesländer.* In Germany, second-language instruction is regarded as additional to regular language instruction. As a result, the extent to which extra materials are used and the quality and number of hours of second-language instruction provided will differ from school to school and from teacher to teacher.

Additional Support Teacher

Schools in Germany are not obliged to assign an additional support teacher for refugee children. Support therefore varies and depends on the regular existing support structure in schools. It appears that teachers often take up this role (Niemeyer 2014, 47).

Tracking

The starting situation of refugee children is crucial because of the effect of tracking and early selection in Germany. In general, we can say that the age of arrival determines the extent to which children are hindered by the general institutional arrangements of early selection and tracking.

At the age of sixteen (or even fifteen at some schools), *Hauptschule* or *Realschule* pupils are supposed to enter an apprenticeship track. Second-language difficulties, however, often make it impossible for refugee children to find an apprenticeship. It has already been clearly established that German-born children of immigrants (the second generation) face discrimination when trying to find an apprenticeship (Crul et al. 2012a). For refugee children, who mostly have not been born in Germany, the chances of finding an apprenticeship slot are often even bleaker because of their German-language deficits, lack of experience with the system, and poor grades they have received as a result (Niemeyer 2014, 16). Furthermore, there is competition for apprenticeship positions among pupils who have diplomas from different educational tracks. It comes as no surprise that those with a *Gymnasium* diploma are the most favored by employers, followed by those with a *Realschule* diploma. Children with a *Hauptschule* diploma have the least opportunity to obtain an apprenticeship (Crul et al. 2012a). This situation has serious adverse consequences for these young people since leaving school without having completed an apprenticeship in a system that relies so heavily on them makes it extremely difficult for these students to enter the labor market and find a steady job. More often than not, it is an apprenticeship that opens the door to one's first paid job.

Access to Education after Compulsory School Age

In Germany, compulsory school ends at age sixteen. There are no formal obligations for *Bundesländer* or cities to provide education beyond compulsory school. This condition severely limits the options for young people arriving in Germany between the ages of sixteen and eighteen without a high school diploma. This situation is true even for pupils who were on their way to higher education (for instance, attending the last years of lyceum) in their country of origin. Most of the programs in the various *Bundesländer* only offer these youngsters short vocational education programs. Another problematic aspect of these programs is finding enough internship and apprenticeship places in the private sector since this practical component is an important element in the German "dual system" of vocational training.

A positive aspect of Germany's educational system is that there are plenty of possibilities and programs for adult education, including programs for obtaining school qualifications and language certificates. However, the problem in the German system is the lack of information and the costs of these programs. In the face of the refugee crisis, many institutions for adult education started to offer free courses at least at the basic level, but sometimes the costs are also shouldered by the government. The state-owned *Volkshochschulen* in particular have played an important role in this development—something they had done in the past for previous waves of immigrants and refugees. Quite new has been the initiative taken by universities to offer free language courses to refugees (often organized by student organizations), to recognize voluntary help to refugees as internships, and to establish mechanisms for the recognition of foreign diplomas and school certificates.

SWEDEN

Swedish Vision of Equal Chances

There are substantial differences between the Swedish vision of incorporating refugee children in education and those of Turkey or Germany. However, these differences do not mean that conditions in Sweden are optimal for refugee children. There is also much to be criticized, and many Swedish researchers have expressed criticism, perhaps to an even greater extent than critics have about other countries' educational systems for refugees. The Swedish approach differs from the other countries' systems at almost every level, from providing access to education beyond compulsory education to limiting the duration of welcome classes and integrating children into regular classes with sustained second-language education at an early stage. The important thing to note here is that these interventions are interrelated. For example, it is only possible to have short welcome classes if there is sustained second-language support in regular classes.

Institutional arrangements have been put in place for refugee children to give them the same opportunities that children of native descent have. Although this goal is not being fulfilled, refugee children in Sweden are gaining access to higher education in far greater numbers than those in Germany or Turkey are.

Preschool

In Sweden refugee children of preschool age receive treatment equal to that given children with Swedish citizenship regardless of their status, even in noncompulsory education (Niemeyer 2014, 17). If a preschool-aged child arrives in Sweden, she may attend what is called *open preschool*, which is free of charge. In the larger cities, where a high proportion of children have a mother tongue other than Swedish, there are special preschools focusing specifically on Swedish-language acquisition (Rydin et al. 2012, 197). However, not all refugee parents are aware that they can send their children to preschool free of charge. Consequently, a lower proportion of young refugee children than of children of Swedish descent attend preschool . However, many more refugee children attend preschool in Sweden than in

Germany, let alone Turkey, and are therefore able to enter elementary school with at least some knowledge of the Swedish language.

Access to Compulsory School

Like all EU countries, Sweden is legally obliged to allow children of refugees to enter compulsory school within three months of their arrival. Sweden, however, has gone further and introduced a regulation to limit this period to one month after arrival (Rydin et al. 2012, 193). Nilsson and Bunar (2016, 403) report that some children who are still in asylum seekers' centers have access to 10 to 50 percent less schooling than regular school children do and are often only taught a limited number of school subjects (Rydin et al. 2012, 199). School attendance is not compulsory for children without an official asylum permit. As a result, some parents who are still in the application process do not send their children to school (Nilsson and Bunar 2016).

Welcome Classes

The situation in Sweden varies widely among schools. However, the general policy in Sweden is to only keep children in welcome classes for a very short period. Examples of schools keeping children in such classes for only two or three weeks are described as ideal cases (Rydin et al. 2012, 204). Pupils are then transferred as quickly as possible to regular classes, which often provide additional courses focusing on second-language education. This approach is partly enabled by the fact that Swedish schools offer second-language education as a regular subject from elementary school until the end of upper-secondary school, making it easier to incorporate students with migration backgrounds—both refugees and others—into regular classes after a short period of time. Part of the philosophy behind limiting the time spent in welcome classes is that refugee children should not be segregated from the other pupils. The belief is also that it will be easier for refugee children to pick up Swedish if they are together with pupils who can speak Swedish with them.

Second-Language Education

The subject Swedish as a Second Language (SSL) is available in Sweden at both elementary and upper-secondary school (up to age eighteen). The head teacher decides which students need to follow SSL (Rydin et al. 2012, 196). The fact that second-language education is also offered in upper-secondary schools is particularly important for refugee children who arrive in Sweden after the age of eleven. This group attends regular classes with extra support in Swedish as a second language very soon after they enter the educational system. It is important to note that in Sweden, SSL courses use separate teaching materials (syllabus) and instruction that are equivalent to those used for teaching Swedish as a first language (Bourgonje 2010, 48, 50). Specially trained teachers teach SSL (Nilsson and Bunar 2016, 409).

Some reports, however, stipulate that the status of these teachers is considered lower than that of regular teachers who teach Swedish as a first language (Bourgonje 2010, 50; Nilsson and Bunar 2016, 409). One can choose to take Swedish as a Second Language as an exam subject in *Gymnasium,* and the grade for the subject counts as a normal entrance grade for university (Rydin et al. 2012, 196).

Additional Support Teacher

In Sweden a person is assigned to support pupils who have attended an international or welcome class. Schools are obliged to allocate this additional support through a support teacher. This teacher starts giving support once pupils are transferred to a regular class (Bourgonje 2010, 48–50; Niemeyer 2014, 23, 55). This could be individual support or support in a small group or even in a regular class (Niemeyer 2014, 23). This arrangement appears to be an ideal situation. Reports, however, note that in practice, support teachers often lack the time to give proper guidance to their pupils.

Tracking

The first selection point in Sweden is at the age of fifteen, when students choose or receive recommendations for different programs within *Gymnasium.* Although the choice made at this point limits options for further education, all programs provide access to higher education. However, students who go on to more vocationally oriented programs at the age of fifteen often enter a form of postsecondary vocationally oriented education at the age of eighteen that is not part of the higher education system. Aycan Çelikaksoy and Eskil Wadensjö's (2015) report, which focuses on unaccompanied minors, presents some educational outcomes of refugee children. The group of unaccompanied minors is more at risk than children who came with their parents are. But even this group achieves educational results that far exceed those of refugee children in Germany or Turkey. Of the nineteen-year-olds, 77 percent of the females and 88 percent of the males were still enrolled in school in Sweden (Çelikaksoy and Wadensjö 2015, 15). Even about half of the group of twenty-one-year-olds were still in education. Forty percent of men between the ages of twenty-four and twenty-seven still in education were in undergraduate training, while another third were in adult education. Approximately a quarter of the women still in education were in undergraduate education, and about half were in adult education (Çelikaksoy and Wadensjö 2015, 16). The figures show that a considerable number of these refugee children, who are considered at high risk, reach higher education in Sweden.

Access to Education after Compulsory School

In Sweden compulsory education ends at age sixteen, but pupils who are still in upper-secondary school when they turn seventeen or eighteen have the right to continue their education as regular students do, even if they do not have official asylum-seeker status. This point is important because unaccompanied minors in particular often arrive between the ages of fifteen and seventeen (Çelikaksoy and Wadensjö 2015, 14). Young adults arriving after the age of eighteen can attend general adult education or Swedish for Immigrants (SFI) classes for adults to learn basic Swedish.

Adult education in Sweden is much more of a mainstream institution than it is in Germany. There is therefore much greater awareness of this option among refugees. Adult education was also an important entrance route into the educational system for migrants in the past. Many first-generation Turkish and Yugoslavian migrants went to adult education to learn Swedish as a second language. Therefore, adult education in Sweden is now very much attuned to the needs of the new arrivals. An adult education diploma can be used to enter higher education or a form of postsecondary education.

In this chapter we have compared the incorporation of refugee children into the educational systems of Turkey, Germany, and Sweden based on a review of the literature. We identified seven institutional arrangements as being influential for the school careers of refugee children: (1) preschool arrangements; (2) entrance into compulsory education; (3) so-called welcome, submersion, or introduction classes; (4) second-language instruction; (5) additional teacher support; (6) tracking; (7) education after compulsory school. We used the comparative integration context theory developed for studying the school careers of children of immigrants as a theoretical framework to examine how these institutional arrangements influence both access to education and the way in which the school careers of refugee children develop. On the surface, it would appear that these three countries have put very similar policies in place. In the initial period following arrival, the emphasis is on providing temporary housing, and NGOs often provide a range of educational and other activities for children. When families and children are in a more permanent setting, children are initially taught in classes parallel to regular school classes together with other refugee children. There are also similarities in the academic discussions in the three countries. In all three there is debate about how long pupils should be kept in separate classes, the appropriate intensity of second-language teaching, and how the mother tongue should be used to incorporate children into school. When, however, we look more precisely at how institutional arrangements are organized, we see huge differences in both access to education and the educational opportunities provided to refugee children in the three countries.

The first major difference among the three countries concerns access. Turkey has no consistent institutional arrangements in place to incorporate refugee children into the Turkish school system. Most young children are placed in a parallel Arabic-speaking school system. Only half of the pupils of compulsory school age attend school. Either their parents cannot afford to send them to school, or they are not able to enter Turkish-language schools. In Germany all pupils of compulsory school age are placed in schools. But children younger (under the age of five or six) or slightly older than compulsory school age (eighteen and older) have only very limited access to education. Sweden has established institutional arrangements to provide access to the Swedish school system, even before and beyond compulsory school age. Consequently, access to education for refugee children looks very different across the three countries.

A second major difference is how educational placement influences the school careers of refugee children. The way in which institutional arrangements (short welcome classes, sustained second-language support, and late tracking) are organized in Sweden provides a full range of educational options, including access to academic tracks and higher education. In Germany the long duration of welcome classes and the limited support for second-language instruction only provide limited access to lower vocational education in practice. In Turkey the parallel school system based on a Syrian curriculum makes it very difficult for refugee children to progress to a Turkish high school, basically limiting their educational possibilities to elementary school.

Syrian refugee children have ended up both in European countries like Germany and Sweden and in neighboring countries. About a third of Syrian refugee children are now residing in Europe and are being incorporated into European schools. Two-thirds of Syrian refugee children are in neighboring countries such as Turkey, Lebanon, and Jordan. The educational provisions for Syrian children in Turkey are part of the EU–Turkey deal. The research findings in Turkey demonstrate the detrimental effects of the EU–Turkey deal for refugee children in terms of both access and educational opportunities. The EU–Turkey deal has created a unique situation in which, for the first time ever, the European practice of dealing with refugees and their children has been linked with the Turkish practice. A core political argument for the EU–Turkey deal states that if the right conditions are created for refugees and their children in Turkey, they will no longer need to come to Europe. In many African countries, refugees have been living in camps for more than twenty years. Their fate is often out of the public eye because there is no direct European involvement. This time, the EU is directly collaborating with Turkey to deal with refugees and their children. Our findings show that the circumstances in Turkey do not remotely meet the minimum criteria set for refugee children in Europe. In order to bring the incorporation of refugee children into the educational system in line with European practice, the Turkish government has to provide refugee students access to the Turkish school system and introduce Turkish as a second language in these schools. The first steps toward achieving these outcomes are now being made. However, this effort will come too late for some of the children. This generation, effectively "locked out" of educational opportunities, got lost in transit.

The case of Sweden could serve as an example for both Germany and Turkey. Many of the influential institutional differences we discovered among the three countries were revealed when studying how things actually worked in practice. This kind of examination requires that researchers go beyond official statements on education for refugee children. For example, no policy document states that refugee children are not allowed to attend *Gymnasium* in Germany, but in practice this option is effectively out of reach for them. Even if Syrian refugee children have attended a *lyceum* in Aleppo or Damascus with subjects similar to those offered in a *Gymnasium* in Germany, they will still be transferred to the lowest forms of vocational education in Germany. And, of course, the official policy in Turkey is that Syrian refugee children can attend high school, but in reality it is difficult for them to gain access to a Turkish high school or to successfully participate in a high school that does not provide Turkish second-language teaching.

It is therefore essential to examine how things are actually organized and implemented in practice. This factor is perhaps most visible in the area of second-language instruction, which is provided in all three countries. It is very difficult to find reliable information on second-language instruction in Turkey, but experts say that it has been virtually absent in most schools so far. In Germany, it is only offered in parallel classes and is not continued when students are transferred to regular classes. By contrast, Sweden provides sustained second-language support at all school levels, administered by properly trained teachers using specifically developed teaching materials, so this arrangement is not an obstacle for students entering academically oriented programs.

Some of the institutional policies in place are general arrangements that also hinder the larger group of pupils of immigrant descent. The system of early tracking in Germany is, for instance, highly problematic for children from minimally educated immigrant families. But the negative effect seems to be multiplied for refugee children because they are separated into parallel welcome classes. Because of the huge emphasis on second-language skills in these welcome classes, students fall behind in regular subjects and end up only being able to access the lowest forms of vocational education. Due to the lack of sustained second-language support after their transferral to regular classes, pupils are unable to keep up in more academically demanding classes.

When evaluating the differences among institutional arrangements, it is important to consider the different arrangements in relation to each other. Often, several negative institutional arrangements can create an accumulation of disadvantage. Refugee children who are placed in the lowest vocational tracks in Germany, for instance, go to school with children with severe learning and behavioral problems because they are overrepresented in these tracks. The school climate in these classes is problematic and not very conducive to learning.

Certain institutional arrangements have negative effects that only become visible in the long term. In Turkey, using Syrian teachers to give lessons to elementary-school children in Arabic is a short-term solution that enables these children to attend school, but in the long term it blocks their transfer to regular Turkish high schools, and in the worst case, it limits their educational access to only elementary school.

The comparative integration context theory has proven to be a useful framework for studying institutional arrangements that either hinder or help refugee children in an educational system. Applying the same theoretical framework to refugee children that we had previously used for children of immigrants makes it possible to see the differences between the two groups. For children of immigrants, the macro level in the form of school system characteristics is most important. These macro system differences are also important for refugee children, but meso-level factors are also crucial. Differences in the way in which second-language education or welcome classes are organized within the same school system also have a huge impact. This is an important complementary finding that demonstrates that the comparative integration context theory provides different outcomes, giving students different migration trajectories. This finding once more underscores the importance of gathering data for each group separately. The outcomes also show that fine-tuning institutional arrangements can make a huge difference. We can counter many of the negative effects of the so-called refugee crisis by putting better institutional arrangements in place.

NOTES

1. Turkey is one of the few countries that maintain the rule of geographic reservation as set out in the 1951 Geneva Convention. Accordingly, the asylum system does not offer refugee status to non-European asylum seekers but merely provides them with temporary status. Until recently, the official asylum and refugee policy had only been based on a few regulations, and the lack of national legislation for non-European refugees had been a crucial factor in the way in which refugees were governed. However, in April 2013, Turkey adopted, for the first time, a Law on Foreigners and International Protection that attempts to establish a codified legal framework for asylum.

2. Local authorities are now held responsible for monitoring the registration of Syrian refugees in public schools to ensure their access to education (ÇOÇA 2015). In order to enroll, children must be registered with the local police office or the Disaster and Emergency Management Presidency, the state institution running the majority of refugee camps for Syrians.

3. The most reliable Turkish resource we could find states that among the Syrian students who attended school, 65 percent attended TEC, 3 percent attended private schools,

and 32 percent attended Turkish public schools. http://www.egitimreformugirisimi.org/tr/node/1823.

4. Türkçe Öğretim Merkezi (TOMER) is an educational institution of Ankara University; it is the most renowned organization providing Turkish-language training.

REFERENCES

Aras, Bülent, and Salih Yasun. 2016. *The Educational Opportunities and Challenges of Syrian Refugee Students in Turkey: Temporary Education Centers and Beyond.* IPC Policy Brief. http://ipc.sabanciuniv.edu/publication/the-educational-opportunities-and-challenges-of-syrian-refugee-students-in-turkey-temporary-education-centers-and-beyond/?lang = en.

Biner, Özge. 2014. "From Transit Country to Host Country: A Study of 'Transit' Refugee Experience in a Border Satellite City, Van, Eastern Turkey." In *Migrants and Politics of Migrations: Policies, Practices, and Trends in Turkey,* edited by Tokat Karaçay, Ayşem Biriz, and Üstünbici Ayşen, 120–32. Istanbul: ISIS Press.

———. 2016. *Türkiye'de Mültecilik: İltica, Yasallık ve Geçicilik* [Refugeehood in Turkey: Asylum, legality, and temporality]. Istanbul: İstanbul Bilgi University Press.

Bloch, Alice, Milena Chimienti, Anne-Laure Counilh, Shirin Hirsch, Giovanna Tattolo, Laurence Ossipow, and Catherine Wihtol de Wenden. 2015. *The Children of Refugees in Europe: Aspirations, Social and Economic Lives, Identity and Transnational Linkages. Final Report.* Working paper. Geneva: Swiss Network for International Studies.

Bourgonje, Paloma. 2010. *Education for Refugee and Asylum-Seeking Children in OECD Countries: Case Studies from Australia, Spain, Sweden, and the United Kingdom.* Brussels: Education International.

Çelikaksoy, Aycan, and Eskil Wadensjö. 2015. *Unaccompanied Minors and Separated Refugee Children in Sweden: An Outlook on Demography, Education, and Employment.* Mannheim: IZA paper, no. 8963.

ÇOÇA (Çocuk Çalışmaları Birimi). 2015. *Suriyeli Mülteci Çocukların Türkiye Devlet Okullarındaki Durumu Politika ve Uygulama Önerileri* [The conditions of Syrian refugee children in Turkish public school and policy advice for implementation]. Istanbul: İstanbul Bilgi Üniversitesi.

Crul, Maurice, Barbara Herzog-Punzenberger, Philipp Schnell, Rosa Aparicio-Gomez, and Marieke Slootman. 2012. "Which National School Systems Provide the Best Opportunities for Success? School Careers of Second-Generation Turks in Seven European Countries." In *The European Second Generation Compared: Does the Integration Context Matter?,* edited by Maurice Crul, Jens Schneider, and Frans Lelie, 101–64. Amsterdam: Amsterdam University Press.

Crul, Maurice, Elif Keskiner, Jens Schneider, Frans Lelie, and Safoura Ghaeminia. 2017. "No Lost Generation: Education for Refugee Children: A Comparison between Sweden, Germany, the Netherlands, and Turkey." In *The Integration of Migrants and Refugees,* edited by Rainer Baubock and Milena Tripkovic, 62–80. Florence: European University Institute (EUI).

Crul, Maurice, and John Mollenkopf. 2012. *The Changing Face of World Cities: Young Adult Children of Immigrants in Europe and the United States.* New York: Russell Sage Foundation.

Crul, Maurice, and Jens Schneider. 2010. "Comparative Integration Context Theory: Participation and Belonging in New Diverse European Cities." *Ethnic and Racial Studies* 33 (7): 1249–68.

Crul, Maurice, Jens Schneider, and Frans Lelie. 2012a. *The European Second Generation Compared: Does the Integration Context Matter?* Amsterdam: Amsterdam University Press.

EUROCITIES. 2017. *Cities' Actions for the Education of Refugees and Asylum Seekers.* Brussels: EUROCITIES.

Heath, Anthony, and Yaël Brinbaum. 2007. "Explaining Ethnic Inequalities in Educational Attainment." *Ethnicities* 7: 291–305.

Holdaway, Jennifer, Maurice Crul, and Catrin Roberts. 2009. "Cross-National Comparison of Provision and Outcomes for the Education of the Second Generation." *Teachers College Record* 111 (6): 1381–1403.

HRW (Human Rights Watch). 2015. "'When I Picture My Future, I See Nothing': Barriers to Education for Syrian Refugee Children in Turkey." New York: HRW. www.hrw.org/sites/default/files/report_pdf/turkey1115_reportcover_web.pdf.

Ingleby, David, and Sander Kramer. 2012. "Country Report: Netherlands." In *Integrating Refugee and Asylum-Seeking Children in the Educational Systems of EU Member States,* edited by Andrey Nonchev and Nikolai Tagarov, 279–304. Sofia, Bulgaria: Center for the Study of Democracy.

Keskiner, Elif. 2013. "Generation in Transition: Youth Transitions among Native-Born Descendants of Immigrants from Turkey." PhD diss., University of Amsterdam, Amsterdam.

Massumi, Mona, Nora von Dewitz, Johanna Grießbach, Henrike Terhart, Katarina Wagner, Kathrin Hippmann, and Lale Altinay. 2015. *Neu zugewanderte Kinder und Jugendliche im deutschen Schulsystem* [Newly migrated children and youths in the German school system]. Cologne, Germany: Mercator Institute.

McBrien, Lynn. 2005. "Educational Needs and Barriers for Refugee Students in the United States: A Review of the Literature." *Review of Educational Research* 75 (3): 329–64.

Mutlu, Yesim, Emrah Kirimsoy, and Sahin Antakyalioglu. 2016. *Bulanık Mekanlarda Gölgede Kalanlar Suriyeli Mülteci Çocuklar ve Vatansızlık Riski Araştırma Raporu* [Shadowed in misty waters: Syrian refugee children and their risk of statelessness]. Research report by Gündem Çocuk Derneği. Ankara: Sen Matbaa.

Nilsson, Jenny, and Nihad Bunar. 2016. "Educational Responses to Newly Arrived Students in Sweden: Understanding the Structure and Influence of Post-Migration Ecology." *Scandinavian Journal of Educational Research* 60 (4): 399–416.

Niemeyer, Maya. 2014. "The Cultural and Social Capital of Unaccompanied Refugee Minors." Masters thesis, Stockholm University, Stockholm.

OECD (Organization for Economic Cooperation and Development). 2010. *PISA 2009 Results: What Makes a School Successful? Resources, Policies and Practices.* Vol. 4. PISA, OECD.

PPMI (European Commission of Education and Training). 2013. *Study for Educational Support for Newly Arrived Migrants.* Brussels: PPMI.

Rydin, Ingegerd, Monica Eklund, Sara Högdin, and Ulrika Sjöberg. 2012. "Country Report: Sweden." In *Integrating Refugee and Asylum-Seeking Children in the Educational Systems of EU Member States,* edited by Abdrey Nonchev and Nikolai Tagarov, 182–215. Sofia, Bulgaria: Center for the Study of Democracy.

Sirin, Selcuk, and Lauren Rogers-Sirin. 2015. *The Educational and Mental Health Needs of Syrian Refugee Children.* Brussels: Migration Policy Institute.

Schnell, Philipp. 2012. "Educational Mobility of Second-Generation Turks in Cross-National Perspective." Dissertation manuscript, University of Amsterdam, Amsterdam.

Suárez-Orozco, Carola, Hee Jin Bang, and Ha Yeon Kim. 2011. "'I Felt Like My Heart Was Staying Behind': Psychological Implications of Family Separations and Reunifications for Immigrant Youth." *Journal of Adolescent Research* 26 (2): 222–57.

UMF (*Bundesfachverband Unbegleitete Minderjährige Flüchtlinge e. V.*) (Federal Association for Unaccompanied Minor Refugees). 2010. *Welcome to Germany! A Guide for Unaccompanied Minor Refugees.* Munchen, Germany: UMF.

UNICEF. 2016. *UNICEF Turkey Humanitarian Situation Report 2016.* http://reliefweb.int /report/turkey/unicef-turkey-crisis-humanitarian-situation-report-december-2016.

Woods, Auveen, and Nihal Kayali. 2017. *Engaging Syrian Communities: The Role of Local Government in Istanbul.* IPC Research Report. Istanbul: Istanbul Policy Center. http:// ipc.sabanciuniv.edu/publication/english-engaging-syrian-communities-the-role-of-local-government-in-istanbul/?lang=en.

14

FROM THE CRISIS OF CONNECTION TO THE PURSUIT OF OUR COMMON HUMANITY

The Role of Schools in Responding to the Needs of Immigrant and Refugee Children

Pedro A. Noguera

INTRODUCTION: THE CRISIS OF CONNECTION

Throughout the ages we have [had] to rediscover that our community is not only made [up] of . . . highly motivated competing individuals . . . but that it [also] includes fragile, vulnerable, suffering individuals who reveal to [us] our own fragility, our own vulnerability. . . . This fundamental discovery is at the heart of our humanity.

—XAVIER LE PICHON (2009, 3)

We are in the midst of a crisis of connection on a global scale, and the signs of its presence are ubiquitous. The crisis of connection is at the core of our inability to overcome and transcend differences in nationality, race, religion, social class, and political ideology so that we can act affirmatively on common *human interests*. The crisis is frequently manifested as an "empathy gap," an inability to act with compassion in response to human suffering. This is particularly the case when it involves those we treat and regard as the Other. The empathy gap in turn obstructs our ability to pursue our common interests as human beings and to ensure our collective need for peace, security, food, water, shelter, and environmental stability. The crisis of connection exacerbates other problems such as our ability to prevent war, to combat terrorism and violence, and to counter poverty, hunger, and disease, because it produces a tolerance for knowing that others are suffering and normalizes increasingly common forms of brutality.

Signs of the crisis of connection are particularly evident in the international response to the global refugee crisis. As millions of people are displaced from their homes and forced in many cases to risk their lives as they attempt to flee war, hunger, and violence, a yawning empathy gap acts as a formidable obstruction to the development of humane and creative responses to suffering. According to the United Nations Refugee Council, as many as sixty-five million people throughout the world have been forcibly displaced from their homes (UNHCR 2015). If they manage to find refuge in another nation, many of these refugees and undocumented immigrants often end up trapped in modern forms of slavery, subjected to a trade and form of bondage now referred to as "human trafficking," while many others languish indefinitely in refugee camps. The tepid, ineffectual response to the global refugee crisis has been reinforced and exacerbated by our acceptance of grotesque inequalities in wealth and access to resources, an imbalance that drives at least some of the refugee crisis and often threatens the quality of life in places where the displaced wait to be settled.

The crisis of connection may not be the cause of the current refugee crisis, but it is certainly a factor that has paralyzed politicians from reacting creatively and effectively to the enormous challenges we face. To the degree that war and violence are accepted as "normal" or "inevitable" in certain communities or parts of the world, to the degree that the signs of global warming are ignored because they are felt most directly in remote corners of the Pacific or South America, or to the degree that we learn to tolerate large numbers of people drowning after the woefully inadequate vessels they attempt to travel in capsize, it becomes clear that the crisis of connection is exacting deadly consequences. In the United States we learned long ago to tolerate millions of mentally ill people living on our streets or filling our nation's prisons. Under the new Trump administration, there is now a question of whether Americans will turn their backs entirely on the refugees who seek asylum in US territory. Fear and indifference are often at the core of the crisis of connection, and it is becoming increasingly clear that they may serve as the fuel and provide the rationale for a new immigration policy.

The crisis of connection deludes us into believing that the problem of unaccompanied minors who have arrived from Central America in recent years is not "ours." It lulls us into believing that if we did not cause these young people to leave their homes and to risk their lives to enter the United States, then we, the safe and unaffected, are not responsible for addressing the problem. We treat the gang violence of El Salvador, Honduras, and Guatemala as "their" problem, even though the gangs that terrorize impoverished barrios and towns there originated on the streets of Los Angeles. Why worry about refugees unless they move into our neighborhoods? Why worry about war in Africa or the Middle East unless one of the "terrorists" comes to our community, and one of our loved ones is shot? Why not build a wall and demand that Mexico pay for it if we see the world not as a unitary whole but as one with borders that divide and separate?

There is a logic that drives the crisis of connection, and it is evident in the US response to the international refugee crisis. It was one of the factors that prompted nearly half of the nation's voters to elect Donald Trump (Agiesta 2016). Obviously, his calls to ban Muslims from entering the country and to keep outsiders—the terrorists, the rapists, the foreigners taking "our jobs"—out resonated with many of them. Wise actions and policies to manage immigration and respond humanely to the needs of the millions of undocumented people are difficult if not impossible to enact when large portions of the population resent, fear, feel disconnected from, and are unable to empathize with the suffering of others. Indifference is invariably a source of fuel and sustenance for resentment that politicians can use to bolster their campaigns, a narcotic that makes it possible for hardships experienced by others to fester, spread, and become more severe. The crisis of human connection obstructs empathy and blocks the emergence of creative solutions or even consideration of serious responses to problems large and small.

PUBLIC SCHOOLS AND AMERICA'S
RESPONSE TO UNDOCUMENTED CHILDREN

Challenges related to the empathy gap and the crisis of connection are playing out in many schools throughout the United States today. Unlike other institutions, public schools have historically been required by law to serve *all children* (Fass 1991). Historically, this requirement has included undocumented children and the children of refugees.[1] While some of the receiving schools have reacted to the inclusion of these children with hostility and resentment, others have responded with humanity and care. More often than not, schools respond without guidance or adequate resources to address the needs of the newly arrived, and for those reasons it is not surprising that these children often struggle.

In this chapter, I analyze some of the struggles that are playing out in schools throughout the US today as they attempt to address the needs of some of our most vulnerable children—unaccompanied minors and undocumented youth generally. I do so in an attempt to ascertain what they tell us about the potential for modern society to move beyond the empathy gap and reduce the crisis of connection. James A. Banks (chapter 11, this volume) has described the inadequacy of the state's response to the arrival of refugees as a form of "failed citizenship." The failure he points out lies not with the immigrants but with the inability of the modern state to enact policies and procedures to integrate them into the new societies within which they reside. If American society is to adopt a more humane approach to immigrants and refugees, schools will be at the forefront of figuring out how to do so. My examples illustrate what we might expect and hope for if the crisis of connection is addressed, and the empathy gap is closed.

FROM ALIENATION AND FEAR TO
TRUST AND EMPATHY

French sociologist Emile Durkheim ([1897] 1951) documented the crisis of connection and its presence in Western society more than two hundred years ago in his seminal work *Suicide: A Study in Sociology*. Through an empirical study of suicide in mid-nineteenth-century France and Germany, Durkheim discovered interesting and unmistakable patterns: those who were most socially isolated were more likely than others to commit suicide. What is most remarkable about Durkheim's finding is that wealth and status did not reduce the likelihood of suicide; rather, they increased the possibility of its occurrence. Durkheim found that wealthy single Protestant men were more likely to commit suicide than married working-class Catholic or Jewish women were. He discovered that vulnerability to committing suicide increased with alienation and isolation and that the correlates of success—income, education, and status—were actually factors that contributed to risk. Although his work did not produce clarity related to the causes of suicide, he posited that the pervasive alienation and anomie that accompanied the industrialization, urbanization, and secularization of Western society were responsible for the increase in self-inflicted deaths.

More than 150 years later, sociologist Eric Klinenberg (2002) identified patterns in the ways that humans respond to crises that correspond strikingly to those of Durkheim. Studying mortality patterns in the aftermath of a devastating heat wave in Chicago in July 1995, Klinenberg discovered a pattern that was quite revealing: while the elderly were generally more likely to die from the effects of extreme heat than others were, their likelihood of dying was substantially greater if they lived alone or resided in a building where they were isolated from other residents. Klinenberg learned that it was actually not the heat that killed people but instead the lack of support from others and various forms of social disintegration (anomie)—including the institutional abandonment of poor neighborhoods and the retrenchment of public assistance programs—that contributed to the high fatality rates (see Klinenberg 2002).

Klinenberg's research reinforced a finding that social scientists have been aware of for some time: people need people. Put differently, individuals who are rich in social capital—the resources and benefits one derives from participation in social networks (Coleman 1988; Woolcock 1998)—receive tangible benefits that are often not available to those who lack social capital. These benefits can include access to information, jobs, housing, safety, social support, and other forms of material assistance. When individuals are embedded within social networks, they generate and benefit from bonds of reciprocity with others who also participate in the network. For example, a neighborhood watch group may provide enhanced security to its members when they simply watch each others' homes; parent groups furnish members with valuable

information about babysitters and schools; and religious and civic organizations provide members with access to jobs and information about housing, health care, and a
wide variety of other resources and services. Political scientist Robert D. Putnam
(2000) has argued that when these ties whither and people become more isolated, the
social fabric that holds society together begins to fall apart.

In his most recent book *Our Kids,* Putnam (2015) argues that growing inequality, the shrinking of the American middle class, and the loss of secure union jobs
have imperiled what is commonly thought of as the American Dream: the possibility that America can be a land where hard work and talent are rewarded with
opportunity and social mobility. Putnam reflects on the state of his hometown,
Clinton, Ohio, a small blue-collar city that managed to send 80 percent of its children to college in 1964, the year that he graduated from high school. Today, the
same town bears all the marks of racial and class segregation, deindustrialization,
and capital flight. Most of its residents are trapped in a perpetual cycle of poverty
and downward mobility, ravaged by the effects of growing inequality. Only those
with means, particularly those with high incomes who live in large homes along
the shores of Lake Erie, consistently send their children to college today.

What went wrong? Can things be reversed? As hostility toward immigrants has
increased in the United States, a growing number of activists and advocates are
asking, must we accept a society in which suffering and despair are dismissed as
foreign problems, in which widespread hopelessness festers, and in which large
numbers of immigrants live in fear of deportation? For educators who are on the
front lines of the refugee crisis in many communities, the critical question is, Can
public schools become centers of support and beacons of hope for refugees and the
undocumented despite growing fear and hostility?

RESPONDING TO THE NEEDS OF IMMIGRANT CHILDREN
BY OVERCOMING THE CRISIS OF CONNECTION

As we contemplate how to address the global refugee crisis and consider what it might
take to move beyond the fear and xenophobia that have been generated in response,
it is important to consider how and why the empathy gap has become an impediment
to the development of innovative responses to the needs of immigrant children and
what might be done to overcome it. Focusing on the crisis of connection does not
mean that we ignore the substantive challenges faced by undocumented people or
refugees—poverty, trauma, lack of adequate housing, and enormous legal challenges,
to name just a few. To do so would be naïve and unrealistic. However, it might be possible to devise creative responses if we were to focus on actions that can be taken
locally, particularly in schools, involving those most directly affected.

Since 1990, the United States has experienced the greatest influx of immigrants in
its history, surpassing even the unparalleled increase in immigration that occurred

between 1900 and 1910 (Grieco et al. 2012). With a steady increase in the number of immigrants during the last decade (C. Suárez-Orozco, M. Suárez-Orozco, and Todorova 2008) and a recent crisis triggered by a sudden rise in the number of unaccompanied minors arriving at the border from Central America (Park 2014), the United States has been in the throes of a tumultuous conflict over how to respond to the current influx. The nation's total immigrant population reached a record forty million, or 12.9 percent of the US population, in 2010 (Grieco et al. 2012), and it is estimated that as much as 30 percent of the total immigrant population is composed of undocumented immigrants (Pew Hispanic Research Center 2013).

Public schools in communities experiencing dramatic increases in immigrant populations are confronted with the enormous challenge of figuring out how to respond to their needs. For the most part, schools have received relatively little guidance from the federal or state government in how to handle the tasks of integrating and educating immigrant children. Reports from schools and data collected on the performance of immigrant children indicate that many schools lack the expertise and resources needed to address these children's learning needs. In many school districts recent immigrant students have the highest dropout rates and lowest rates of high school graduation and college attendance (Rodriguez 2014). They are also frequently overrepresented in special education, often due to a tendency in many districts to misdiagnose challenges in language acquisition as a form of disability (Figueroa 2005).

In some communities the political backlash against the growing presence of immigrants has negatively influenced how local schools have responded to the needs of immigrant children (Olson 1997). Despite the large number of Americans with immigrant origins, overt hostility toward newcomers has been a regular occurrence throughout US history (Roediger 1991). In recent years, the political backlash against the influx of new immigrants has led to the enactment of local and state ordinances in states such as Georgia, Arizona, and Pennsylvania intended to make it more difficult for undocumented immigrants to work, drive a car, obtain health services, or even rent a home (Yoshikawa 2011).

Immigrant youth often face a number of challenges directly related to their adjustment to life in the United States that place them at greater risk of experiencing negative life outcomes. The challenges are particularly acute for Mexican and Central American youth, whose families are typically poor, have low levels of education, work at low-wage (and often dangerous) jobs, and are more likely to be undocumented (C. Suárez-Orozco and M. Suárez-Orozco 2002; Smith 2006). Some of these challenges include stress related to acculturation and social adjustment (C. Suárez-Orozco, M. Suárez-Orozco, and Todorova 2008) and instability caused by difficulty in maintaining ties with family members abroad (Bartlett and García 2011). Existing research suggests that when these risks are not addressed, immigrant students often experience a heightened degree of vulnerability to negative social, psychological, and educational outcomes (Thom 1998; C. Suárez-Orozco, M. Suárez-Orozco, and Todorova 2008; Perreira and Ornelas 2011; Conchas and Vigil 2010; Rodriguez 2014).

In many schools that serve recent immigrants, a student's inability to speak English fluently, or more precisely, to display a command of academic literacy is used as a justification for segregating the student from her or his English-dominant peers and placing the student in courses designated for English language learners (ELLs).[2] While such placements are frequently rationalized as a way to ensure that recent immigrant students learn English in a "sheltered" environment, classes designated for students who speak English as a second language (ESL) are often not staffed by qualified teachers, and courses designated to help ELLs often serve as a means through which immigrant students are tracked and marginalized (Noguera and Wing 2006; Kao, Vaquera, and Goyette 2013). In many school districts, large numbers of immigrant children fail to acquire proficiency in English and in many cases lose proficiency in their native language as well (Gandara and Rumberger 2009). Once students have been enrolled in ESL courses, they frequently are unable to access the courses needed to fulfill the requirements for college (Gandara and Contreras 2009; Stanton-Salazar 2001; Noguera and Wing 2006). Tracking on the basis of language difference is one of the factors that have been cited by researchers as contributing to the high dropout rates that are common among recent immigrant students (Gandara and Rumberger 2009).

In many cases, immigrant parents, especially the undocumented, do not know how to advocate for their children. Accustomed to trusting the educators and schools that their children attended in their native country and lacking the language skills and social capital to navigate US schools and the legal barriers that often obstruct access to services, many are unable to advocate effectively for the needs of their children (García-Coll et al. 2002, Kasinitz et al. 2008). Additionally, immigrant children often acculturate more quickly than their parents do, so they frequently acquire skills in English and become familiar with the rules and customs of the new society more rapidly than their parents do. When this occurs, an imbalance in the relationship between parent and child often results as the child assumes the responsibility of translator and negotiator with landlords, service providers, and the school system (Orellana 2009; Olsen 1997; Giguère, Lalonde, and Lou 2010).

In the sections that follow, I present three case studies that demonstrate how some schools have responded creatively to the educational needs of immigrant youth and overcome the political hostility and indifference that often characterize the way these youth have been treated elsewhere. In such schools, confronting the crisis of connection by developing trust and a sense of community has been central to the effort to improve academic outcomes. I use these cases in the hope that by my drawing attention to the approaches they have taken, other schools and communities might feel inspired and compelled to take similar actions.

CASE 1: OVERCOMING VIOLENCE BY
ADVANCING COMMON INTERESTS

In fall 1998, several schools in the San Francisco Bay Area experienced a series of incidents involving interracial violence. The violence involved different groups at different schools, but in each case, immigrant youth were targeted and victimized. At Castlemont (Oakland) and Richmond High Schools, the conflicts were between blacks and Latinos (mostly Central Americans). At Skyline High School (Oakland) the primary conflicts occurred between blacks and Asians (largely recent immigrants from Southeast Asia). And at El Cerrito and Berkeley High Schools, various groups (white, black, Latino, and Asian) were fighting each other. There seemed to be no consistent or single cause linking the violence across the five schools, but it was occurring frequently and seemed to be spiraling out of control. On numerous occasions, dozens of police officers were deployed to the schools to quell what the police described as "riots" involving large numbers of students. To make matters worse for the local police, these incidents were occurring during roughly the same time period.

The police complained to district officials in all four cities that it was not their job to stop the violence, and they made it clear that they could not station police officers indefinitely at the schools. District officials were at a loss about what to do. They did not understand what was causing the outbreak of violence and had no idea of what they should do to prevent further episodes. After a third week of fighting, two of the school districts approached a research firm, Arts, Resources, and Curriculum (ARC), for help in devising a strategy to respond to the violence. The firm came up with a novel idea: they would create multiracial student-run groups called Youth Together (YT) on each of the five campuses so that students could take the lead in addressing the issue. I was asked to serve as the evaluator of their efforts.

In approaching their work, Youth Together devised a novel strategy. Rather than bringing young people together to talk about the conflicts that had occurred, they started by bringing a multiracial group of students together to talk about their experiences at schools. The conversation quickly raised a number of serious complaints about the condition of their schools, and within a short period of time, students on each of the five campuses began to see that they had a great deal in common in their complaints. YT decided that rather than simply air their concerns, the students should develop school-change campaigns and organize with others to carry them out. The campaigns varied in focus and were devised by the students based on their perception of which issues were of greatest concern. At Richmond and El Cerrito High Schools, students signed petitions and marched to the school board to demand access to bathrooms (these were locked while classes were in session due to safety concerns). At Berkeley and Skyline High Schools, students called for the creation of ethnic studies classes. At Castlemont High

School, black and Latino students marched together to demand that a new cafeteria be built (for more than two years the students had been eating outdoors, even in the rain).

Our research team documented the YT efforts and evaluated their impact at each school. We did this by surveying administrators, teachers, and students to assess how the school's climate had been affected by the change campaign. Remarkably, not only had the violence subsided within a short period of time (in six to eight weeks), but the perception of safety and morale of students and staff at all of the schools had improved. The following comment from a Richmond High School student helps to explain the dramatic turnaround, "Most of the fights were caused by stuff that happened outside of school and crept in. Because we didn't even know each other, we didn't trust each other. When Youth Together brought us together, we started to see that we had a lot in common. As we began working together to get access to the bathrooms, we began to see that we were fighting over nothing. We had more in common than we realized" (November 15, 1998).

Similar responses were expressed at the other schools. One teacher at Berkeley High acknowledged that adults had unintentionally helped to create a climate in which violence was likely because they had done so little to bring students together, "We like to celebrate the diversity of this school, but actually it's very segregated from within. Our classes are tracked, and even the clubs and sports teams are mostly segregated. Our ESL students don't even attend classes with other kids. How can we expect kids to learn how to respect each other when they aren't learning together?"

Our study found that by getting students to work together to improve their schools and promote their common interests, the schools not only experienced a reduction in hostility, conflict, and fear, but students from different racial backgrounds also began to forge bonds based on solidarity and trust (for the evaluation report, see Noguera and Bliss 2001). Such relationships are especially important for recent immigrant students, who have a limited understanding of race and racism in America and are often marginalized and segregated within schools. By working with classmates they once feared or regarded as threatening and by engaging in efforts to improve the quality of their schools, the immigrant students not only experienced a reduction in violence but also became more integrated into their schools.

It is important to note that in order to even consider these types of solutions to racial conflict, the schools had to stop relying exclusively on security measures to address the conflict. They had to take what some might regard as a tremendous risk: listening to the perspectives of students. Recognizing that listening to students can be helpful to schools compels those in leadership to see students as legitimate partners in the educational process. As the next case illustrates, such recognition can be of enormous benefit to schools.

CASE 2: LISTENING TO STUDENTS TO IMPLEMENT
SCHOOL IMPROVEMENT

In 2001, I was approached by the former Boston school superintendent, Dr. Tom Paizant, to help him figure out how to improve several of the high schools in the school district. Like most urban school districts across the country, Boston had experimented with a number of reforms in an attempt to raise achievement at its schools. Many of the most troubled schools served recent immigrants who struggled with academic English. In light of the implementation of the newly devised Massachusetts Comprehensive Assessment for Students (MCAS), a high-stakes examination that all tenth graders were required to take, Paizant was looking for ways to help his schools improve. Under his leadership a number of different reforms had been implemented at each of the high schools, but after several years of effort, it was clear that while some schools were improving, several others were not.

Paizant wanted to know why progress was uneven at the district's schools and what could be done to improve the situation. After visiting several of the schools with him, I proposed what he and I considered a novel idea: we would study the impact of the reforms through the experiences of the students. We opted for this focus because we wanted to know whether students were experiencing the benefits that were intended by particular reforms. I proposed that we could undertake our study by shadowing fifteen students at ten different high schools. The groups would be representative of the schools with respect to race, ethnicity, immigration status, and gender, and they would include students with differing levels of academic achievement—five low, five medium, and five high.

Although the project had not been designed with an explicit focus on immigrant students, all ten of the schools served large immigrant populations from Latin America, Asia, and Africa. Over the course of the next two years, we followed our focal students to their classes; interviewed them, their teachers, and their parents periodically; and tracked their academic performance. We also collected school climate surveys that allowed us to compare the responses of our focal students with those of the larger population of students at each school. Specifically, we wanted answers to these questions: Did students report that they had developed closer, more supportive relationships with teachers as their schools were restructured and made smaller? Had they received better and more rigorous instruction as their schools prepared them for high-stakes exams? Had students who struggled academically received sufficient support? Did charter schools or pilot schools have greater success in meeting the needs of students than traditional public high schools did, and if so, why? For the immigrant students, who represented more than half of the sample, we were particularly interested in knowing how effectively the schools were meeting their academic needs since most were at the highest risk of failing the state exam.

The questions we posed were central to the larger policy debates that were occurring throughout the country regarding education reform. However, largely missing from these debates were the voices of students. There seemed to be an unstated assumption that if the adults got the reforms right, students would eventually achieve at higher levels. Our research at the schools allowed us to test the theories underlying the reform strategies. It also allowed us to elevate the voices of students so that their perspectives and experiences were considered, in many cases for the first time.

Over the course of two years, we began to notice significant discrepancies at several of the schools between what the adults claimed they were doing and what the students were actually experiencing. We went into classrooms serving students who had failed the state exam and were at risk of being denied diplomas if they did not eventually pass. Expecting to see rigorous, highly focused instruction, we more often than not saw disorganized teachers who frequently were unprepared to meet the needs of the students they served. For example, during one visit to a math class, a Honduran student we had been following informed us that he and his classmates usually played poker during class, but he suspected that because we were present, the teacher might make them do some work. Despite our presence, the students played poker anyway. Embarrassed by the obvious lack of educational focus, the teacher turned to us and said: "These kids refuse to do any work, so I let them play. They're probably learning more math playing poker than they would from my lesson anyway."

Observations of this kind were common at several of the schools. We observed students who were supposed to be preparing for high-stakes exams chatting, brushing their hair, and putting on makeup in class. At one school I saw the principal lock the front door to the school at 7:35 am, denying entry to students who arrived more than five minutes late (7:30 am was the official time school was supposed to start) until they could return with a note from a parent or an adult explaining their tardiness. I pointed out sarcastically that his tough tardy policy was creating a truancy problem, but he failed to note the irony of my observation.

At other schools we pointed out that many of the students lacked basic skills in literacy and math and were unlikely to pass the state's new high-stakes exam if the classes they took only focused on providing test-taking skills. This situation was particularly the case for recent immigrants who were still acquiring academic English fluency. However, even after sharing our findings with the schools, the disconnect between what the adults asserted they were doing in the name of reform and what the students were actually experiencing (and needing) remained; despite our efforts to reveal these contradictions, the issues remained unaddressed.

However, we also visited schools where relationships between students and teachers were strong, where immigrant students and English language learners received high-quality academic support and were able to clearly explain what they were learning in their classes and why it was important. What set these schools apart from the others appeared to be coherence in the organizational plan and the school's culture. Several researchers have found that when schools are organized around a clear mission, when they adopt strategies to ensure that the skills of professional staff match the learning capabilities of students, and when the beliefs, expectations, values, and norms are aligned with the school's mission and purpose, schools are more likely to be successful (Sarason 1971; Boykin and Noguera 2011; Bryk et al. 2010); Fullan and Quinn 2016). We learned that at such schools, students took their education seriously, both in word and in deed, not because they were afraid of failure but because they were fully integrated into the life of the school, and they accepted the premise upon which the school operated.

In contrast with students at the dysfunctional schools, students in the higher functioning schools also accepted responsibility for their education and did their part to maintain a safe, orderly environment. In a more detailed discussion of the findings (Noguera 2004), I describe how the strong, positive relationships we observed contributed to higher levels of school safety and student achievement. What is most important about these findings is that they run counter to official policies designed to promote school safety and higher achievement. Current education policies designed to promote safety generally emphasize the adoption of strict security measures including metal detectors, law enforcement, surveillance cameras, and zero-tolerance policies (Gottfredson 2001). Similarly, the policy lever used to promote increased student achievement has in recent years consisted almost exclusively of high-stakes testing and the elevation of academic standards (Elmore 1996; Darling-Hammond 2004). Our research at ten Boston high schools showed that the development of strong, positive relationships between teachers and students was more effective than heavy security measures in creating a safe and orderly environment. We also found that *hope* was more effective than *fear* in motivating students to achieve.

It is important to note that while positive relationships and a student-centered culture cannot be imposed upon a school, a coherent strategy for meeting student needs can be implemented when all stakeholders—teachers, students, and parents—are organized around a common vision. Research on school improvement (Bryk et al. 2015) has shown that when schools clearly define their problems and adopt research-based strategies to address them, they can experience steady, incremental improvement. This outcome is what occurred at Brockton (MA) High School, an urban school with a large immigrant population that is now widely regarded as a success story (Blankstein and Noguera 2015), and at several of the schools in our study.

While it may be easier to install a metal detector or surveillance cameras to address safety concerns than to work on improving the quality of relationships between children and the adults who serve them, the long-term benefits of the latter approach far outweigh the short-term relief provided by the former. However, if we fail to recognize that such "nontechnical" approaches might actually work to create trust, bridge the empathy gaps, and be more effective in realizing the goals of education, chances are they will never even be considered.

NOT GIVING IN TO FEAR: ACTING ON
OUR COMMON INTERESTS

I want to end with a story conveyed to me by a teacher from a school that illustrates the power of trust and community and the need for the courage to act on our common interests. I share this story because it serves as an excellent example of how we can overcome our fears through positive action that affirms the basic human values that are essential for living in a just, civil society.

The school in question was a small continuation high school[3] designed to serve students with a record of poor attendance, poor behavior, or both. Many of the students at the school had criminal records, and most had a long record of poor academic performance. One of the students, a well-known gang leader from El Salvador with a reputation for violence in the community, informed his counselor one morning that starting the next day, he was going to show up at school with a new identity—he was going to be a young woman. The student explained that he intended to change his name from Carlos to Carla, that he would dress as a woman, and that he wanted his choice to be respected. He informed the counselor that his parents had kicked him out of their house because they were unhappy with his new transgender identity. He also warned the counselor that he expected a violent reaction to news of her transformation from members of her own gang, who might feel betrayed by her decision.

The counselor reacted with alarm due to the likelihood of violence and immediately notified the school principal. The principal was equally alarmed by the possibility that there might be an outbreak of gang violence at his school, so at the end of the day, he called a meeting with the faculty and staff to warn them and figure out what should be done. Fearful of the violence they thought might occur, the staff immediately decided that the police should be notified and that the student should be banned from entering the school. However, while the adults were in the middle of their meeting, a small delegation of students arrived and asked for an opportunity to speak. They wanted the staff to know that they were aware of their classmate's decision to change her gender identity, and on their own, they had devised a plan to support her. Since Carla had been kicked out of her parents' home, she would start living with another student who was willing to take her in. The students also reported that they had organized themselves to take turns riding the bus with Carla to school each day to provide her with protection. Finally, they agreed that while she was in school, everyone would accept and respect her decision, and begin calling *her* by *her* preferred name and pronoun.

The school staff was shocked by the news shared by the students. Several spoke up and said how proud they were that the students had come together to support their classmate. One admitted how embarrassed she was because of the actions she and her colleagues had proposed—calling the police and banning the student— before hearing from the students. After further deliberation, the staff decided that they would support the students' approach and that together they would support the transgendered student. The following day the plan was implemented as proposed. No violence occurred, and ultimately Carla was able to complete the school year and graduate without any violent incidents happening at the school.

I share this final story because it serves as a poignant way of reinforcing the larger point of this chapter. Although the crisis of connection is real, rooted in history, and reinforced by divisions that have led to deep distrust and disconnection based on race, language, sexuality, gender, and nationality, the examples demonstrate that it might be possible for the crisis of connection to be overcome, at least in schools. Even for refugees and undocumented immigrants who are increasingly vilified, scorned, and denied access to basic human rights, schools can become centers of support and refuge where they can escape persecution and threats. The examples show that listening to students, developing caring relationships, and even countering racial violence by focusing on the common interest of students can all help to create schools where compassion is the norm and even the most vulnerable feel safe. Such examples remind us that it is possible to counter fear with empathy and that possibilities for addressing complex problems may be more likely if we focus directly on addressing the crisis of connection. Although these examples do not serve as proof that it will be easy to solve the global refugee crisis, they do suggest that creative strategies that focus on overcoming the empathy gap must be considered if we are to address the large, complex problems we face.

During the last few months, we have been inundated with news of mass drownings as boats carrying refugees capsize in the Mediterranean, of borders closing due to fears pertaining to terrorists attacks, and of mass arrests by immigration agents targeting the undocumented. Such incidents are occurring in communities throughout the United States (including in so-called sanctuary cities) and in a diverse array of countries throughout the world. The news is frightening, and the problem may seem overwhelming. Because the atrocities occur with such frequency, they can easily become accepted as the new normal. But why should we accept this condition? Normalization and complacency toward human suffering must be seen for what they are: threats to our collective future that can and must be resisted through creative forms of action. What we need are actions and strategies that assert our common interests as human beings and that further and promote empathy, trust, and goodwill.

The renowned French geophysicist Xavier Le Pichon (2009, 3) reminds us that "our humanity is not an attribute that we have received once and forever with our conception. It is a potentiality that we have to discover within us and progressively develop or destroy through our confrontation with the different experiences of suffering that will meet us throughout our life."

Like Le Pichon, I am under no illusion that the problems we face can be solved by simple solutions or small acts of kindness. However, I do believe that the best way to counter indifference and resentment, and the most effective way to revive a pragmatic form of optimism about the future of the planet and human society, is through deliberate actions that address our crisis of connection and that remind us that our common interests as human beings are worth acting upon.

NOTES

1. In 1982, the US Supreme Court ruled in *Plyler v. Doe* that states cannot constitutionally deny immigrant students, including the undocumented, free public education. See "Public Education for Immigrant Students: Understanding *Plyler v. Doe*," *American Immigration Council Report* (Oct. 24, 2012).

2. It is important to note that not all recent immigrants are English language learners, and not all ELLs are recent immigrants.

3. Continuation high schools are alternative schools that are designed to serve students with a track record of poor attendance and poor academic performance.

REFERENCES

Agiesta, Jennifer. 2016. "Partisan Gap Widens as Demographics Shift." *CNN Politics,* September 16, 2016, 1. www.cnn.com/2016/09/13/politics/pew-research-center-presidential-poll-election-2016/index.html.

Baig, Jalal. 2016. "Istanbul and the Empathy Gap: Why Was the West's Response Muted Compared to Paris or Brussels?" *Salon,* July 3, 2016. www.salon.com/2016/07/03/istanbul_and_the_empathy_gap_why_was_the_wests_response_muted_compared_to_paris_or_brussels/.

Bartlett, Linda, and Ophelia García. 2011. *Additive Schooling in Subtractive Times: Bilingual Education and Dominican Immigrant Youth in the Heights.* Nashville, TN: Vanderbilt University Press.

Blake, James. 2016. "Slavery as Free Trade." *AEON,* June 29, 2016.

Blankstein, Alan, and Pedro Noguera. 2015. *Excellence through Equity.* Alexandria, VA: ASCD.

Boykin, Alfred W., and Pedro Noguera. 2011. *Creating the Opportunity to Learn: Moving from Research to Practice to Close the Achievement Gap.* Alexandria, VA: ASCD.

Bryk, Anthony S., Penny Bender Sebring, Elaine Allensworth, Stuart Luppescu, and John Q. Easton. 2010. *Organizing Schools for Improvement: Lessons from Chicago.* Chicago: University of Chicago Press.

Bryk, Anthony S., Louis M. Gomez, Alicia Grunow, and Paul G. LeMahieu. 2015. *Learning to Improve: How America's Schools Can Get Better at Getting Better.* Cambridge, MA: Harvard Education Press.

Coleman, James 1988. "Social Capital in the Creation of Human Capital." Supplement, *American Journal of Sociology* 94: S95–S120.

Conchas, Gilbert Q., and James Diego Vigil. 2010. "Multiple Marginality and Urban Education: Community and School Socialization among Low-Income Mexican-Descent Youth." *Journal of Education for Students Placed at Risk* 15 (1–2): 51–65.

Darling-Hammond, L. 2004. "Standards, Accountability, and School Reform." *Teachers College Record* 106: 1047–85.

Durkheim, Emile. (1897) 1951. *Suicide: A Study in Sociology.* New York: Free Press.

Elmore, Richard. 1996. "The New Accountability in State Educational Policy." In *Performance-Based Strategies for Improving Schools,* edited by Helen Ladd, 16–22. Washington, DC: Brookings Institution Press.

Fass, Paula. 1991. *Outside In: Minorities and the Transformation of American Education.* New York: Oxford University Press.

Figueroa, Richard A. 2005. *"Dificultades o desabilidades de aprendizaje?"* Learning Disability *Quarterly* 28 (2): 163–67.

Fullan, Michael, and Joanna Quinn. 2016. *Coherence: The Right Drivers in Action for Schools, Districts, and Systems.* New York: Corwin Press.

Gandara, Patricia C., and Frances Contreras. 2009. *The Latino Education Crisis: The Consequences of Failed Social Policies.* Cambridge, MA: Harvard University Press.

Gandara, Patricia C., and Russell Rumberger. 2009. "Immigration, Language, and Education: How Does Language Policy Structure Opportunity?" *Teachers College Record* 111 (3): 750–82.

García-Coll, Cynthia, Daisuke Akiba, Natalia Palacios, Benjamin Bailey, Rebecca Silver, Lisa DiMartino, and Cindy Chin. 2002. "Parental Involvement in Children's Education: Lessons from Three Immigrant Groups." *Parenting: Science and Practice* 2 (3): 303–24.

Giguère, Benjamin, Richard Lalonde, and Evelina Lou. 2010. "Living at the Crossroads of Cultural Worlds: The Experience of Normative Conflicts by Second-Generation Immigrant Youth." *Social and Personality Psychology Compass* 4 (1): 14–29.

Gottfredson, Denise C. 2001. *Schools and Delinquency.* Cambridge, UK: Cambridge University Press.

Grieco, Elizabeth, Edward Trevelyan, Luke Larsen, Yesenia D. Acosta, Christine Gambino, Patricia de la Cruz, Tom Gryn, and Nathan Walters. 2012. *The Size, Place of Birth, and Geographic Distribution of the Foreign-Born Population in the United States: 1960 to 2010.* Population Division Working Paper No. 96. Washington, DC: US Census Bureau.

Kao, Grace, Elizabeth Vaquera, and Kimberly Goyette. 2013. *Education and Immigration.* Cambridge, MA: Polity Press.

Kasinitz, Philip, John H. Mollenkopf, Mary C. Waters, and Jennifer Holdaway. 2008. *Inheriting the City: The Children of Immigrants Come of Age.* New York: Russell Sage Foundation.

Klinenberg, Eric. 2002. *Heat Wave: A Social Autopsy of Disaster in Chicago.* Chicago: University of Chicago Press.

Le Pichon, Xavier. 2009. *ECCE Homo—Behold Humanity.* Paris: Templeton Foundation.

Noguera, Pedro A. 2004. "Transforming High Schools." *Educational Leadership* 61 (8): 43–65.

Noguera, Pedro, and Jean Yonemura Wing. 2006. *Unfinished Business: Closing the Achievement Gap in Our Nation's Schools.* San Francisco: Jossey Bass.

Olsen, Laurie. 1997. *Made in America: Immigrant Students in Our Public Schools.* New York: New Press.

Orellana, Marjorie Faulstich. 2009. *Translating Childhoods: Immigrant Youth, Language, and Culture.* New Brunswick, NJ: Rutgers University Press.

Park, Haeyoun. 2014. "Children at the Border." *New York Times,* Aug. 7. www.nytimes.com /interactive/2014/07/15/us/questions-about-the-border-kids.html.

Perreira, Krista M., and India J. Ornelas. 2011. "The Physical and Psychological Well-Being of Immigrant Children." *The Future of Children* 21 (1): 195–218.

Pew Hispanic Research Center. 2013. *US Population Projections: 2005–2050.* Washington, DC: Pew Hispanic Center.

Putnam, Robert D. 2000. *Bowling Alone: The Collapse and Revival of American Community.* New York: Simon and Schuster.

———. 2015. *Our Kids: The American Dream in Crisis.* New York: Simon and Schuster.

Rodriguez, Louie F. 2014. *The Time Is Now.* New York: Peter Lang.

Roediger, David R. 1991. *The Wages of Whiteness.* New York: Verso Press.

Sarason, Seymour Bernard. 1971. *The Culture of Schools and the Problem of Change.* Boston: Allyn and Bacon.

Smith, Robert. 2006. *Mexican New York: Transnational Lives of New Immigrants.* Berkeley: University of California Press.

Stanton-Salazar, Ricardo D. 2001. *Manufacturing Hope and Despair: The School and Kin Support Networks of US–Mexican Youth.* New York: Teachers College Press.

Suárez-Orozco, Carola, and Marcelo Suárez-Orozco. 2002. *Children of Immigration.* Cambridge, MA: Harvard University Press.

Suárez-Orozco, Carola, Marcelo Suárez-Orozco, and Irina Todorova. 2008. *Learning a New Land: Immigrant Students in American Society.* Cambridge, MA: Harvard University Press.

Thom, Linda H. 1998. "Immigration's Impact on Teen Pregnancy and Juvenile Crime." *Population and Environment* 18 (5): 57–72.

UNHCR (United Nations High Commissioner for Refugees). 2015. *Figures at a Glance: Global Trends, Statistical Yearbooks.* www.unhcr.org/en-us/figures-at-a-glance.html.

Woolcock, Michael. 1998. "Social Capital and Economic Development: Toward a Theoretical Synthesis and Policy Framework." *Theory and Society* 27: 151–208.

Yoshikawa, Hirakazu. 2011. *Immigrants Raising Citizens: Undocumented Parents and Their Young Children.* New York: Russell Sage Foundation.

15

CHILDREN OF IMMIGRANTS IN
THE UNITED STATES

Barriers and Paths to Integration and Well-Being

Mary C. Waters

Today the 43 million immigrants in the United States represent 13.4 percent of the US population, a percentage slightly lower than it was one hundred years ago. The US-born children of immigrants, the second generation, represent another 37.1 million people, or 12 percent of the population. Thus, the first and second generations together account for one out of four members of the US population. An estimated 11.3 million of these immigrants are undocumented. The successful integration of these immigrants and their children is necessary for the overall success of our society. The well-being of a quarter of our population ought to be one of our highest public policy priorities. As a society that has successfully integrated generations of immigrants and their children throughout its history, the United States should be a model for societies around the world that face similar challenges in the age of unprecedented human migration. In this chapter I review recent empirical trends in the United States, with the aim of addressing these questions: How well are we doing in integrating the children of immigrants? What policies facilitate or impede that integration? How does integration affect the well-being of the second generation? And how might the United States do much better?

I begin by reviewing the findings of a National Academy of Sciences (NAS) panel examining the integration of immigrants and their children across a wide array of social, political, and economic indicators (Waters and Pineau 2016). I led a team of eighteen social scientists who worked for two years to review the pace and direction of integration of the first and second generations into the American economy and society. While overall, the children of immigrants are integrating very well into American society, the report identified three major impediments to the successful integration and greater well-being of immigrants and their children—income inequality, racial and ethnic discrimination, and legal status. The first two are key aspects of American society that affect all Americans, whether they are immigrants or second generation. They are best ameliorated through *universal social policies* designed to help all Americans—policies to redistribute income and to establish a robust safety net, and policies to prevent racial discrimination and promote equality of opportunity.

Legal status, however, is a new impediment to immigrant integration, one that is much more widespread and consequential now than at any prior time in our nation's history. It is also a policy arena that only affects immigrants, their citizen children, and other family members and is not shared by other natives. In this sense, then, the specific problems of the undocumented and their families are separated from those of other Americans and require a specific *targeted policy intervention*. Legal status also connects the children of undocumented immigrants in the United States with refugee children around the world, a topic discussed elsewhere in this volume. Physically present in the host country yet not fully integrated and often defined out of civil society, these children face formidable barriers and many roadblocks to successful development.

Achieving successful immigration policy reform has proved impossible for legislators in the United States since 1986, and it has become much more difficult to imagine after the 2016 presidential election and the Republican control of the federal government. The demonization of the undocumented and the new policy of the United States to try to deport settled families are an affront to the basic human rights of more than 11 million people, also reverberating onto their 4.5 million citizen children. Social movements and political pressure will be necessary to improve and defend the situation of immigrants and their children, particularly the undocumented.

In this chapter's conclusion, I argue that the civil rights paradigm that is highly developed (although deeply contested) in the United States is inadequate for addressing the problems caused by documentation status. The exclusion faced by the undocumented and their children is better addressed by a human rights paradigm, one that is not as developed in American, as opposed to European, political culture but that holds strong moral authority and potential for claims making. I also suggest that the Catholic Church and other religious organizations have the potential to contribute greatly to the moral underpinnings of the movement that is needed to keep immigrant families together and to strengthen the next generation. The Catholic Church, along with other faith-based organizations, has long been a leader in nongovernmental action in immigrant integration. Faith-based institutions have great potential to also be moral leaders in the kinds of policy changes that are urgently needed in the United States going forward.

We are at a crossroads in immigration policy in the United States. The numbers of immigrants coming to the United States, the racial and ethnic diversity of new immigrants, the increasing complexity of the immigration system, and the politically fraught issue of undocumented migration have raised questions about whether the nation is being as successful in absorbing current immigrants and their descendants as it has been in the past. This issue was a central question reviewed in the NAS panel on immigrant integration (Waters and Pineau 2016).

The NAS panel defined *integration* as the opportunities for immigrants and their descendants to achieve their goals in a society through participation in major social institutions as well as to gain social acceptance. Greater integration implies parity of critical life chances with the native-born American majority. Integration is a twofold process: it happens both because immigrants experience change once they get here and because native-born Americans change in response to immigration. Yet integration may not always improve the well-being of immigrants and their children. Convergence with native-born Americans may make immigrants and their children better off, a result that is no doubt a major objective of the immigrants themselves. But it may also make them worse off. Many uneducated immigrants see their children achieve a higher level of education than their own. Yet many immigrants who arrive in very good health see their children's health deteriorate as they adopt American health behaviors and diets. The process of integration takes time, and it can be measured in two ways: for the first generation, by examining what has happened in the time since their arrival; for the second and third generations—the children and grandchildren of immigrants—by comparisons between earlier and later generations.

After reviewing a wide variety of indicators in the domains of education, occupations, family form, crime, and health, the NAS panel found that current immigrants and their descendants are successfully integrating into US society. When taken as a whole, the facts that today's immigrants come from different regions of the world and have racial and ethnic backgrounds that differ from those of earlier immigrants have not been insurmountable barriers to integration. However, this general picture masks important variation between and within groups and across domains. In all five realms, the children of immigrants are integrating in that they are converging with native-born Americans in outcomes over time. In terms of their education and occupations, there is an improvement overall in the well-being of the second generation. In terms of family form, crime, and health, persons of the second generation have experienced a decline in their well-being compared with that of their parents, as they become more like later-generation native-born Americans. After reviewing these empirical patterns, I discuss the policy environment and its effect on the second generation, arguing that we need different kinds of policies to facilitate the integration and well-being of the second generation.

EDUCATION

The educational progress of the children of immigrants depends greatly on the starting point of their parents and on conditions they face in the United States.

Immigrants are overrepresented at both the bottom and the top of the educational distribution: a sizable proportion come with advanced educational credentials. These differences in educational attainment also map onto source countries, with Asia and Africa sending immigrants with high educational attainment, and Latin America and the Caribbean sending immigrants with low attainment.

The patterns among selected large immigrant groups illustrate these trends (Waters and Pineau 2016, 247–56). Among men measured in 2013, Mexicans have the lowest average educational attainment (9.4 years), and 55 percent of the first generation have less than a high school degree, with only 5 percent having a college degree. The average educational attainment of Central Americans is also very low in the first generation (9.8 years); 48 percent of men have less than a high school degree while only 9 percent have a college education. Dominicans are less disadvantaged but still have overall low levels, averaging 11.8 years of education, 27 percent with less than a high school degree and 16 percent with a college degree.

The highest educational attainments among first-generation men are found in immigrants from Asia, followed closely by those from Africa, Canada, and Europe. Indians are the most educated, with an average of 16.3 years of education, and 83 percent have a college degree. They are followed by immigrants from Japan, Korea, and the Philippines, with very high average levels of education, extremely low numbers of people with less than a high school education (fewer than 1 percent of Koreans and Japanese), and very high numbers of people with college and beyond. Chinese and Vietnamese immigrants contain high numbers at the top of the educational distribution (58 and 30 percent, respectively, with college degrees) but also have relatively large numbers of immigrants at the bottom of the distribution (11 and 15 percent with less than a high school education). The patterns for women are fairly similar to those of men in all groups, with the average levels of education somewhat lower for women among the Asian and African groups and modestly higher among the Latino groups.

Overall, the educational profiles of these groups vary a lot by source country, and these national origin differences are also associated with undocumented status, which is not measured in census data. Mexicans and Central Americans have both the lowest educational attainments in the first generation and the highest proportion of undocumented people. Among Asian immigrants there is a relatively low proportion of undocumented, and the profile of high education among immigrants bodes well for the second generation, as the best predictor of a child's educational outcomes is her or his parents' educational attainment.

The very good news is that even with these different starting points, across all groups, the second (children of immigrants) and later (third-plus) generations show remarkable educational progress compared with that of the first generation. The second generation as a whole and second generation members of most contemporary immigrant groups meet or exceed the schooling level of the typical third- and higher-generation Americans. This finding is true for both men and women.

Overall, the average educational attainment for men goes from 12.1 years in the first generation to 13.9 in the second, surpassing the average educational attainment of third-plus- generation whites of 13.8 years. For women, the second generation has an average attainment of 14.0 years, also surpassing third-plus-generation whites, who average 13.9 years.

For the groups with overall low levels of education in the first generation, both men and women gain education from the first to the second generation. Among Mexican American men, for instance, average education rises from 9.4 years to 12.6 years in the second generation. Among women, the average education rises from 9.5 to 12.8 years. The percentage with less than high school education falls from 55 percent in the first generation to 15 percent in the second for men, and from 54 to 15 percent for women. The same strides are made by Central American men, who improve their average attainment from 9.8 to 13.4 years, and by women, who improve from 10.2 to 14.0 years. The percentage without high school education among Central American men falls from 48 percent to 8 percent, and for women from 43 percent to 5 percent. This is an impressive amount of educational mobility in one generation.

Among the Asian groups with exceptionally high educational attainment in the first generation, the Indians, Koreans, and Japanese show a decline in those with above a college degree between the first and second generations. This outcome likely reflects the selectivity among the first generation as well as differing patterns of immigration over time. Most of the other groups show modest increases in education by generation to equal or exceed those of native-born third-plus-generation whites.

Overall, the NAS panel concluded that the second generation of all groups was doing well and that the remaining deficits among three Latino second-generation groups (Mexicans, Central Americans, and Dominicans) were primarily due to the very low starting point of their immigrant parents. All of these data are very positive evidence of rapid educational integration. These findings are supported by other research pointing to educational progress for the children of immigrants, including rising high school completion rates of US-educated Hispanics from 1990 to 2010 (Murnane 2013) and a declining dropout rate that fell to a record low of 15 percent in 2012 (Lopez and Fry 2013). There has been steady and substantial improvement from 2003 to 2013 in how Hispanic fourth and eighth graders scored on standardized math tests (Pane 2014); and among recent high school graduates, for the first time a greater share of Hispanic graduates (49 percent) than white graduates (47 percent) are enrolled in college (Lopez and Fry 2013).

OCCUPATION

The occupational distributions of the first and second generations reveal a picture of intergenerational change and stability similar to the one for education. The groups that are concentrated in low-status occupations in the immigrant generation improve their occupational positions substantially in the second generation, although they do not reach parity with third- and later generation Americans. The second generation of immigrants from Mexico and Central America makes a large leap in occupational terms: 22 percent of second-generation Mexican men and 31 percent of second-generation men from Central America are in professional or managerial positions. The latter figure is not much lower than that for all later generation men. Second-generation men are, like their immigrant fathers, overrepresented in service jobs, though they have largely left agricultural ones.

Also, the job situations of the second generation improve in other ways. Second-generation Mexican men are less likely than their immigrant parents to take jobs in the informal sector, and they are more likely to receive health and retirement benefits through their employment, although not as often as later-generation men do. The robust representation of the first and second generations throughout the occupational spectrum implies that the US workforce increasingly welcomes immigrants and their children into higher-level jobs. This pattern of workforce integration is likely to continue to increase as the baby-boom cohorts complete their retirement over the next two decades.

HEALTH

In health, immigrants show better infant, child, and adult outcomes than the US-born population in general and better than US-born members of their ethnic group (Waters and Pineau 2016, 377–89). Compared with native-born Americans, immigrants are less likely to die from cardiovascular disease and all cancers combined; they also have a lower incidence of all cancers combined, fewer chronic health conditions, lower infant mortality rates, lower rates of obesity, a lower percentage who are overweight, fewer functional limitations, and fewer learning disabilities. Immigrants also have a lower prevalence of depression, the most common mental disorder in the world, and of alcohol abuse. US immigrants live longer, too. They have a life expectancy of 80.0 years, 3.4 years higher than that of the native-born population. Across the major ethnic categories (non-Hispanic whites, blacks, Asian/Pacific Islanders, and Hispanics), immigrants have a life expectancy advantage over their native-born counterparts.

Unfortunately, persons of the second generation adopt health behaviors similar to those of other Americans and lose the health advantages their parents had. For example, second-generation Hispanic and Asian adolescents have shown much higher rates of obesity than the first generation has (Singh, Rodriguez-Lainz, and Kogan 2013). Children of recent immigrants have encountered weight problems across socioeconomic (SES) status, and this finding was especially so for sons of non-English-speaking parents (Van Hook and Baker 2010). Rates of smoking and drinking also rise with generations as the rates of children and grandchildren of immigrants converge with those of other native-born Americans.

CRIME

Immigration is linked to lower crime rates, the opposite of what many Americans fear. Among men between the ages of 18 and 39, the foreign-born are incarcerated at a rate of one-fourth of that of the native-born. Areas, especially neighborhoods, with greater concentrations of immigrants have much lower rates of crime and violence than comparable nonimmigrant neighborhoods do. This phenomenon of lower rates of crime and violence for neighborhoods with high concentrations of immigrants is reflected not only across comparable areas but also over time. Immigrants also become integrated into US society in ways that are less welcome. Although they have much lower levels of crime in the first generation, the second and third generations have crime rates more similar to those of the native-born.

FAMILY FORM

Another arena in which well-being declines from the first to the second generation is in family formation patterns that change over time: their divorce rate and out-of-wedlock birth rates increase while the likelihood of their living in extended families with multiple generations under one roof declines (Waters and Pineau 2016, 358–68). Among all families headed by first-generation immigrants, children are concentrated in two-parent families in the major racial and ethnic groups, an arrangement that provides them with a number of important contextual advantages. These families are associated with lower risks of poverty, more effective parenting practices, and lower levels of stress. The prevalence of two-parent families continues to be high in the second generation, but the percentage of children in two-parent families declines substantially between the second and third generations, a situation similar to that of other native-born families. Since single-parent families are more likely to be impoverished, this development is a cause for concern.

PATHWAYS AND IMPEDIMENTS TO INTEGRATION AND WELL-BEING

The empirical patterns in integration identified by the NAS panel all point to rapid integration into American society—with immigrants coming to share both the positive and negative aspects of that society. The second generation shows educational and occupational progress, but within a society that is becoming more socioeconomically unequal over time. The second generation displays differential progress in outcomes that are highly stratified by race. As immigrants and their children become Americans, they are increasingly stratified by race as well—and share in both the ongoing discrimination and the legal apparatus that attempts to combat that discrimination. But there is one area that the second generation faces that is specifically tied to immigration—the lasting legacies of the undocumented status of their parents. I review each of these impediments to integration and well-being in turn.

Income Inequality

Immigrants and their children are overrepresented among American households with low education and low incomes. Although many Americans think nostalgically about the experiences of their immigrant and second-generation parents raising families in the mid-twentieth century, when income inequality was declining and an expanding economy provided many routes for upward mobility, current immigrants face very different circumstances. Immigrants from Italy and Poland who arrived in the United States in the early twentieth century saw their children and grandchildren come of age in an era of declining income inequality when a rising economic tide lifted all boats, especially workers at the bottom of the income distribution. This social mobility was a major factor in the integration of America's white ethnic immigrants (Alba 1990; Waters 1990). Today, immigrants who start at the bottom of the socioeconomic distribution share with all poor Americans the challenges of declining real wages and limited opportunities for social mobility in an increasingly unequal society (Noah 2012). Real hourly earnings for men without a high school education dropped 22 percent between 1980 and 2012; for high school graduates, they dropped by 11 percent. Only those with a college degree or higher have seen increases (Autor 2014). And while real wages for women with less than a college degree did not decline over this period, they experienced very modest growth.

Programs designed to help all families in these circumstances can provide support for the successful integration of immigrant families. In other words, immigrants with low skills and low education face declining wages over time, but it is not because they are immigrants but rather because of the dynamics of the labor market. Universal social policies to redistribute income and to pay a living wage to workers would help all Americans in this labor market position, not just immigrants. Benefits such as the Earned Income Tax Credit (EITC), increases in the minimum wage, support for unions and collective bargaining, and legislation such as the Affordable Care Act that provides universal access to health insurance are all programs that disproportionately aid immigrants because they are concentrated in the low end of the labor market, but the programs are universal in that they help all Americans in those economic circumstances (Danziger et al. 2016; Cancian and Danziger 2009).

Race

A second concern is race. The United States has a long history of shameful racial discrimination and prejudice, as well as a more noble history of mass resistance to that discrimination in the form of the civil rights movement and legal vigilance in prosecuting and preventing that discrimination since the mid-1960s. These two trends continue and are now complicated by the growing racial and ethnic diversity that immigration has fueled. Immigration has transformed American society through the growth in racial, ethnic, and religious diversity in the US population that has resulted in increased intergroup contact and the transformation of American communities and institutions. In 1970, 83 percent of the US population was non-Hispanic white; today, that proportion is about 62 percent, and immigration is responsible for much of that change. Hispanics have grown from just over 4.5 percent of the total US population in 1970 to about 17 percent today. Asians are currently the fastest-growing immigrant group in the country: they represented less than 1 percent of the population in 1970 but are 6 percent of it today. Black immigration has also grown: in 1970, blacks represented just 2.5 percent of immigrants; today, that number is 9 percent.

Ethnic and racial diversity resulting from immigration is no longer limited to a few states like California and New York that have histories of absorbing immigrants; today new immigrants are moving throughout the country, including such areas as the South that had not previously witnessed a large influx of immigrants. This movement has changed the landscape of immigration. The states with the fastest growth rates of immigrant population today are in the South and Midwest. The growth of immigrant populations, largely Hispanics, in new localities and in nonmetropolitan areas raises new challenges of integration and incorporation for many communities and small towns that are unaccustomed to minority and immigrant populations. At the same time, there are many localities in new destination areas that have adopted welcoming strategies to encourage immigrant workers and better integrate them into communities.

Immigrants have also contributed enormously to America's shifting patterns of racial and ethnic mixing in intimate and marital relationships. Today, about one of every six new marriages each year is an interracial or interethnic marriage (defined as a marriage that crosses the five major racial/ethnic groups in the US, white, black, Asian, Hispanic, and American Indian) which is more than twice the rate a generation ago (Bialik 2017). The overall picture suggests that the number of marriages between US natives and immigrants has increased significantly over time. Perhaps as a result, the social and cultural boundaries between native and foreign-born populations in the United States are much less clearly defined than they were in the past. Moreover, second- and third-generation immigrant minority populations are far more likely to marry native-born whites than their first-generation counterparts are. These intermarriages also contribute to the increase in mixed-race Americans. In the future the lines between what we today think of as separate ethno-racial groups may become much more blurred.

However, other racial and ethnic trends are much more troubling. The NAS panel found that patterns of immigrant integration are shaped by race. While there is evidence of integration and improvement in socioeconomic outcomes for blacks, Latinos, and Asians, their perceived race still matters, even after controlling for all their other characteristics. Black immigrants and their descendants are integrating with native-born non-Hispanic whites at the slowest rate. Asian immigrants and their descendants are integrating with native-born non-Hispanic whites most quickly, and Latinos are in between. The panel found some evidence of racial discrimination against Latinos and some evidence that their overall trajectories of integration are shaped more by the large numbers of undocumented in their group than by a process of racialization. It was not possible with the data available to the NAS panel to definitively state whether Latinos are experiencing a pattern of racial exclusion or a pattern of steady progress that could lead to a declining significance of group boundaries. What can be reasonably concluded is that progress in reducing racial discrimination and disparities in socioeconomic outcomes in the United States will improve the outcomes for the native-born and immigrants alike. Again, this projection points to universalist policy solutions that improve conditions for all non-white Americans, not specifically targeting immigrants per se.

Undocumented Status

An immigrant's legal status is a key factor in the individual's integration trajectory. Immigration statuses fall into four rough categories—permanent, temporary, discretionary, and unauthorized. These statuses lie on a continuum of precariousness and security, providing different rights to remain in the United States, rights to benefits and services from the government, ability to work, susceptibility to deportation, and ability to participate fully in the economic, political, social, and civic life of the nation. In recent decades, because of changes to immigration policy, these statuses have multiplied, creating different paths and roadblocks toward integration into American society.

Unlike many countries with large immigrant populations, the United States has neither an explicit federal policy for immigrant integration nor one specific government agency tasked with coordinating integration efforts. Instead, since the mid-1990s, the main focus of federal immigration policy has been on trying to hinder the integration of undocumented immigrants—through increased border enforcement, rising deportation rates, and policies designed to prevent the undocumented from being hired. Yet this approach fails in two major ways. First, it does not meet its first objective of preventing long-term integration since an estimated 11.3 million undocumented immigrants live and work in the country, and many of them are raising children. Indeed, the average length of stay among the undocumented has grown over this time, making them a more settled and partially integrated population. Second, these policies create obstacles to successful integration, not only for the undocumented people themselves but also for their children who are citizens, for other members of mixed-status households, and for the wider communities they inhabit.

Undocumented status itself carries a substantial wage penalty, perhaps as much as 17 percent for men and 9 percent for women (Waters and Pineau 2016). There are also large differences in returns to human capital by legal status. The shift in recent years to a more intense regime of border and internal enforcement of immigration laws coincided with a drop in the economic returns to a variety of forms of human and social capital, constraining both occupational attainment and earnings. This development means that undocumented parents are working longer hours for less pay to provide for their children, inflicting more of the problems of poverty on their children. In addition, undocumented students themselves are less likely than other immigrants to graduate from high school and enroll in college, an outcome that then undermines their future earnings capacity.

In the United States, state and local institutions and the private sector perform the bulk of what would be considered traditional integration functions such as providing language and civics education, job training, and assistance in accessing public benefits and institutions. Across the federal, state, and local levels there are a variety of policies and laws designed both to facilitate the integration of immigrants and to restrict the integration of certain segments of the immigrant population, primarily the undocumented. Sometimes federal and state policies work together, but they also sometimes function at cross-purposes. Some states and localities are providing in-state college tuition for undocumented immigrants, some provide driver's licenses to such immigrants, and some are even declaring themselves sanctuary cities; these approaches are at odds with federal enforcement policies and priorities. In other localities, there are restrictive laws, such as those prohibiting rentals to undocumented immigrants and authorizing local enforcement of federal immigration laws in ways that overreach federal legislation and are also at odds with federal government policies and priorities.

The confusing situation of legal status is further complicated by the fact that families can contain members with different legal statuses. Today, 5.2 million US children reside with at least one undocumented immigrant parent. The vast majority of these children—4.5 million—are US-born citizens. Included in this total are almost 7 percent of K–12 students, a situation that presents important challenges for schools. Because of mixed-status families, policies designed to halt the integration of undocumented immigrants or individuals with a temporary status can have the unintended effect of halting or hindering the integration of citizens and lawful permanent residents. Laws are often designed to apply to individuals, yet they frequently take effect through households and families, with measurable long-term negative impacts on children who are citizens. Thus, laws and practices intended to halt the integration of undocumented parents can have the unintended effect of depressing the integration of their children into US society.

The experiences of these families with undocumented members include many violations of the human rights laid out in the UN's (1948) Universal Declaration of Human Rights: the right of families to stay together (Article 16), the right to be treated equally before the law (Article 7), the right to work and to be paid fairly (Article 23), the right to political participation (Article 21), and the right to social services to provide a decent standard of living (Article 25). The citizen children of undocumented parents live with the knowledge that their parents can be deported at any time. Meanwhile, the children who are themselves undocumented face an additional looming U-turn in their integration experiences. Fully incorporated into elementary and high school, they "awaken to a nightmare" in young adulthood when they do not have the right to work, face possible deportation, and, in many parts of the country, are not eligible for financial aid to attend college (Gonzales and Chavez 2012). The "cruel experiment" that we are conducting involves denying full equality to these young people while at the same time teaching them that they are Americans in a land founded on the principle that all people are created equal (Smith 2013, 250).

Since 1996, the circumstances of the undocumented have become harsher. Both the 1996 Illegal Immigration Reform and Immigrant Responsibility Act and the 1996 Antiterrorism and Effective Death Penalty Act laid the legal groundwork for mass deportations of undocumented immigrants and greatly increased the deportations of legal immigrants who have been convicted of a felony. Furthermore, the Personal Responsibility and Work Opportunity Reconciliation Act, popularly known as Welfare Reform, broadened the restrictions on public benefits for undocumented immigrants. These laws have combined with administrative changes that also increased the integration of everyday policing and immigration data systems, leading to a sharp rise of what is called "internal enforcement." The administrative integration of immigration status into federal and state databases means that the everyday activities of the undocumented now expose them to the very real danger of deportation. A routine traffic stop for a broken headlight or an expired inspection sticker will trigger an alert about immigration status in the onboard computer in a patrol car. As a result, Immigration and Customs Enforcement (ICE) increasingly deports people who are settled immigrants, not just those apprehended at the border. Deportations of undocumented immigrants have soared from an average of 20,000 per year before the mid-1990s to 400,000 per year since 2008. Between July 2010 and October 2012, more than 200,000 undocumented parents with US-born children were deported (Vicens 2014). Since the Trump administration took office in January 2017, ICE has targeted all undocumented people in the United States. This is a change in policy from that of the Obama administration, which had prioritized the apprehension of undocumented people who had been convicted of a serious crime. The Trump administration is apprehending people without criminal records and who are long-term residents, greatly increasing fear among settled families.

The insecurity and stress that undocumented families experience are harming children (Yoshikawa, C. Suárez-Orozco, and Gonzalez 2016). Research has shown that children of undocumented parents are less likely than their peers to receive benefits for which they are legally eligible (Yoshikawa 2011). They are also more likely to experience anxiety and depression in adolescence and to have lower levels of educational attainment in middle childhood (Brabeck and Xu 2010). Undocumented immigrants and their relatives live in constant fear of being apprehended, and families often separated by the deportation process (Dreby 2012; Hagan, Rodriguez, and Castro 2011). Recent research suggests that for children living in high-poverty and violent neighborhoods, elevated levels of toxic stress can create long-lasting adverse health effects that can even affect future generations through epigenetic changes (Fox and Shonkoff 2011; Thompson 2014). While no systematic research yet exists, it would not be surprising if future studies find the same adverse health outcomes for children living with the anxiety that their undocumented parents could be deported. Undocumented status of parents, like poverty, is a risk factor for children's emotional well-being, cognitive development, and educational attainment.

Congress has repeatedly failed to pass comprehensive immigration reform to address the status of these undocumented families. The one brief bright spot in this area was the executive order of President Barack Obama in June 2012 that allowed young people who had entered the country as minors and who met certain conditions to qualify for Deferred Action for Childhood Arrivals (DACA). The DACA program allowed people who were currently in school or who had graduated from high school and who had not been convicted of a serious crime to apply for two-year work permits that allowed them to work legally and that freed them from fear of deportation. Research has found that this temporary legal status had beneficial effects on recipients (Hainmueller et al. 2017; Abrego 2017). This program was a precarious fix for these young people, however, and the Trump administration ended the program on September 15, 2017. Since then legal challenges both to the program and to its termination have been moving through the courts. Approximately 690,000 young adults had DACA and are at risk of losing it. Many other "DREAMers," or young people brought to the US as children who are undocumented, are at risk of deportation and are prevented from working.

CIVIL AND HUMAN RIGHTS

Many scholars have compared the experience of undocumented immigrants to the denial of rights to blacks in the period between the Civil War and the civil rights movement in the 1960s (e.g., Rodriguez 2013). Indeed, there are now more undocumented people living in the country with very few rights than there were black people living in the South under the Jim Crow system before the civil rights movement. In addition, the DREAMers movement of undocumented young people is modeled after the civil and gay rights movements (Nicholls 2013). These young people have held demonstrations and sit-ins modeled on the strategies of the civil rights movement (Altschuler 2011) and have "come out" as undocumented, using tactics from the gay rights movement.

Yet the civil rights movement demanded *civil* rights for African Americans who, as *citizens,* were entitled to protection from discrimination and to civic participation—most crucially, the right to vote. As Gunnar Myrdal (1944) pointed out, this was an "American Dilemma" because blacks were included as Americans yet denied these American rights. In contrast, although many undocumented immigrants have assimilated into American society, they are legally defined as "not Americans" and cannot, by definition, lay claim to civil rights. When opponents of unauthorized immigration carry signs with slogans such as "What part of illegal do you not understand?" and define people as "illegal aliens," they are stressing the stark legal barrier between "us" and "them." In sum, discrimination against unauthorized immigrants is not only legal; it is in many ways also required by the law.

As such, we need a new model for a movement to champion the rights of undocumented immigrants in American society—one that stresses their *human* rights, not their civil rights (Waters and Kasinitz 2016). The United States has little experience with movements based in the human rights tradition, yet a legal human rights framework can provide a strong basis for challenging laws that discriminate against people because of their citizenship status and deny them access to health care, public housing, higher education, and the labor market. It is time to move beyond the civil rights framework that has not been able to protect these undocumented families and to recognize their basic human right to inclusion in the society we all share.

One basis of support for changing the immigration laws in the United States is appealing to moral and religious values. Two-thirds of Catholics, along with 58 percent of mainline Protestants, support a path to citizenship for the undocumented (Jones et al. 2014). A recent poll by the Public Religion Research Institute (prri.org) showed that there is strong agreement among Americans about the moral values that should guide immigration reform. These include keeping families together (84 percent), protecting the dignity of every person (82 percent), and following the Golden Rule, defined as "providing immigrants the same opportunities I would want if my family [were] immigrating to the United States" (69 percent) (Cox, Navarro-Rivera, and Jones 2013). These values cross party lines and allow for a rare consensus in our partisan environment. There is great potential for finding common ground and moving forward based on a position of welcoming the stranger if these values are foregrounded in the immigration debate. Yet rarely do politicians begin with a moral position on immigration. They are far more likely to discuss jobs or legal status or crime when approaching the issue.

It is with that hope that I welcome Pope Francis's support for migrants and the social teaching of concern for basic human rights. The United States is a very religious society, so if we can actively involve religious traditions in America to organize on behalf of the human rights of the undocumented, we may have a chance to transform the immigration debate. Social science research tells us that the children of immigrants are making great strides in integrating into American society. Legal status remains a pressing and formidable barrier that is tearing families apart and denying human rights to millions of people. Past models of social change in the United States, most notably the civil rights paradigm, are difficult to use when advocating for noncitizens. A morally based appeal to human rights, led by religious organizations and appealing to the better parts of our nature, can be a potent force for change. It is time to begin this important work.

REFERENCES

Abrego, Leisy J. 2018. "Renewed Optimism and Spatial Mobility: Legal Consciousness of Latino Deferred Action for Childhood Arrivals Recipients and Their Families in Los Angeles." *Ethnicities* 18 (2): 192–207.

Alba, Richard. 1990. *Ethnic Identity: The Transformation of White Identity*. New Haven: Yale University Press.

Altschuler, Daniel. 2011. "The Dreamers Movement Comes of Age." *Dissent Magazine,* May 16, 2011. www.dissentmagazine.org/online_articles/the-dreamers-movement-comes-of-age.

Autor, David. 2014. "Skills, Education, and the Rise of Earnings Inequality among the Other 99 Percent." *Science* 334 (6186): 843–51.

Bialik, Kristen. 2017. "Key Facts about Race and Marriage, 50 Years after Loving v. Virginia." Pew Research Center June 12, 2017. http://www.pewresearch.org/fact-tank/2017/06/12/key-facts-about-race-and-marriage-50-years-after-loving-v-virginia/

Brabeck, Kalina, and Qingwen Xu. 2010. "The Impact of Detention and Deportation on Latino Immigrant Children and Families: A Quantitative Exploration." *Hispanic Journal of Behavioral Sciences* 32 (3): 341–61.

Cancian, Maria, and Sheldon Danziger. 2009. *Changing Poverty, Changing Policies*. New York: Russell Sage Foundation.

Cox, Daniel, Juhem Navarro-Rivera, and Robert P. Jones. 2013. *Citizenship, Values, and Cultural Concerns: What Americans Want from Immigration Reform*. Washington, DC: Public Religion Research Institute. www.prri.org/research/2013-religion-values-immigration-survey/.

Danziger, Sandra K., Sheldon Danziger, Kristin Seefeldt, and H. Luke Shaefer. 2016. "From Welfare to Work-Based Safety Net: An Incomplete Transition." *Journal of Policy Analysis and Management* 35 (1): 231–38.

Dreby, Joanna. 2012. "The Burden of Deportation on Children in Mexican Immigrant Families." *Journal of Marriage and the Family* 74 (4): 829–45.

Fox, Nathan A., and Jack P. Shonkoff. 2011. "How Persistent Fear and Anxiety Can Affect Young Children's Learning, Behavior, and Health." *Early Childhood Matters* 116 (June): 8–14.

Gonzales, Roberto G., and Leo R. Chavez. 2012. "Awakening to a Nightmare: Abjectivity and Illegality in the Lives of Undocumented 1.5-Generation Latino Immigrants in the United States." *Current Anthropology* 53 (3): 255–81.

Hagan, Jacqueline, Nestor Rodriguez, and Brianna Castro. 2011. "Social Effects of Mass Deportations by the United States Government, 2000–2010." *Ethnic and Racial Studies* 34 (8): 1374–91.

Hainmueller, Jens, Duncan Lawrence, Linna Marten, Bernard Black, Lucila Figueora, Michael Hotard, Tomas R. Jimenez, Fernando Mendoza, Maria I. Rodriguez, Jonas J. Swartz, and David D. Laitin. 2017. "Protecting Unauthorized Immigrant Mothers Improves Their Children's Mental Health" *Science* 357 (6355): 1041–1044.

Jones, Robert P., Daniel Cox, Juhem Navarro-Rivera, E. J. Dionne, and William A. Galston. 2014. *Citizenship, Values, and Cultural Concerns: What Americans Want from Immigration Reform.* Washington, DC: Public Religion Research Institute.

Lopez, Mark, and Richard Fry. 2013. "Among Recent High School Grads, Hispanic College Enrollment Rate Surpasses That of Whites." Washington, DC: Pew Research Center. September 4, 2013. www.pewresearch.org/fact-tank/2013/09/04/Hispanic-college-enrollment-rate-surpasses-whites-for-the-first-time/.

Murnane, Richard J. 2013. "US High School Graduation Rates: Patterns and Explanations." *Journal of Economic Literature* 51 (2): 370–422.

Myrdal, Gunnar. 1944. *An American Dilemma: The Negro Problem and Modern Democracy.* New York: Transaction.

Nicholls, Walter J. 2013. *The DREAMers: How the Undocumented Youth Movement Transformed the Immigrant Rights Debate.* Stanford, CA: Stanford University Press.

Noah, Timothy. 2012. *The Great Divergence: America's Growing Inequality Crisis and What We Can Do About It.* New York: Bloomsbury Press.

Pane, Natalie E. 2014. *Math Scores Add Up for Hispanic Students: States and School Districts Notable for Recent Gains by Hispanic Students in Mathematics.* Publication #2014–59. Bethesda, MD: Child Trends Hispanic Institute.

Rodriguez, Cristina M. 2013. "Immigration, Civil Rights, and the Evolution of the People." *Daedalus* 142 (3): 228–41.

Singh, Gopal K., Alfonso Rodriguez-Lainz, and Michael D. Kogan. 2013. "Immigrant Health Inequalities in the United States: Use of Eight Major National Data Systems." *Scientific World Journal* 2013. Article ID 512313, 21 pages.

Smith, Robert C. 2013. "Mexicans: Civic Engagement, Education, and Progress Achieved and Inhibited." In *One out of Three: Immigrants in New York in the Twenty-First Century,* edited by Nancy Foner, 246–66. New York: Columbia University Press.

Thompson, Ross A. 2014. "Stress and Child Development." *The Future of Children* 24 (1): 41–59.

UN (United Nations). 1948. *The Universal Declaration of Human Rights*. www.un.org/en /documents/udhr/.

Van Hook, Jennifer, and Elizabeth Baker. 2010. "Big Boys and Little Girls: Gender, Acculturation, and Weight among Young Children of Immigrants." *Journal of Health and Social Behavior* 51: 200–14.

Vicens, A. J. 2014. "The Obama Administration's Two Million Deportations, Explained." *Mother Jones,* April 4, 2014. www.motherjones.com/politics/2014/04/obama-administration-record-deportations.

Waters, Mary C. 1990. *Ethnic Options: Choosing Identities in America*. Berkeley: University of California Press.

Waters, Mary C., and Phillip Kasinitz. 2016. "The War on Crime and the War on Immigrants: Racial and Legal Exclusion in Twenty-First-Century United States." In *Fear, Anxiety, and National Identity: Immigration and Belonging in North America and Europe,* edited by Nancy Foner and Patrick Simon, 115–43. New York: Russell Sage Foundation.

Waters, Mary C., and Marisa Gerstein Pineau, eds. 2016. *The Integration of Immigrants into American Society*. Washington, DC: National Academies Press.

Yoshikawa, Hiro. 2011. *Immigrants Raising Citizens: Undocumented Parents of Young Children*. New York: Russell Sage Foundation.

Yoshikawa, Hiro, Carola Suárez-Orozco, and Roberto Gonzalez. 2016. "Unauthorized Status and Youth Development in the United States: Consensus Statement for the Society on Research on Adolescence." *Journal of Research on Adolescence* 27 (1): 4–19.

16
___

IMPROVING THE EDUCATION AND SOCIAL INTEGRATION OF IMMIGRANT STUDENTS

Francesca Borgonovi, Mario Piacentini,
and Andreas Schleicher

Many countries that are members of the Organization for Economic Cooperation and Development (OECD), especially in Europe, have seen a sharp increase in the number of immigrants entering their territories—including unprecedented numbers of asylum seekers and children. An estimated 4.8 million migrants arrived in OECD countries in 2015, an increase of about 10 percent relative to those arriving in 2014, with family reunification and free movement each accounting for about a third of these entries (OECD 2016a; OECD 2015a). The recent wave of migration has reinforced a long and steady upward trend in the share of the immigrant population in OECD countries, which has grown by more than 30 percent and has become increasingly diverse since 2000 (OECD/EU 2015). Over this period, many former OECD emigration countries such as Ireland, Italy, and Spain became destination countries; before the global economic crisis, immigration rates in these countries were sometimes as large as those of traditional OECD immigration countries (OECD 2015b).

Accommodating the unprecedented inflows of migrant children into education systems is one of the key challenges that host countries will face in the upcoming years. Children represent a significant portion of global migration flows, especially within refugee populations. According to a 2015 UNICEF report, one in eight migrants worldwide is a child, while the share of children among refugees is more than one half, and it has doubled between 2005 and 2015 (UNICEF 2015). Migration flows are profoundly changing the composition of classrooms in OECD countries. Between 2006 and 2015, the share of immigrant students rose by 3 percent on average across OECD countries and by more than 5 percent in Austria, Canada, Ireland, Luxembourg, New Zealand, Norway, Qatar, Sweden, Switzerland, the

United Kingdom, and the United States.[1] More than one in two students participating in the 2015 wave of the Programme for International Student Assessment (PISA) in Luxembourg, Macao (China), Qatar, and the United Arab Emirates had an immigrant background, as did close to one in three students in Canada, Hong Kong (China), and Switzerland.

The response of education systems to migration shocks has immediate consequences on the public perception of countries' abilities to cope with migration flows, but it also impacts the long-term economic and social consequences of migration. While migration flows can create some difficulties for host communities, they also represent an opportunity for countries that face aging native-born populations and the threat of labor and skill shortages (Boeri et al. 2012; Cerna 2016; EMN 2011; OECD/EU 2014). Education systems determine immigrants' ability to eventually participate in the labor markets of host countries, to contribute to welfare arrangements, and to feel part of their communities. Effective education and, more generally, social policies are necessary for host countries to successfully integrate migrant children into society and unlock the potential benefits of migrant inflows.

When families move to a new country, it is often because parents hope to offer their children a better living standard and a brighter future. However, children of immigrants have to overcome many barriers in order to succeed in school. For some, the lack of familiarity with the language of instruction and precarious living conditions can turn the first years spent in their new country into a particularly stressful experience. Research shows that the academic outcomes of immigrant students are shaped by various family and community characteristics, the social and educational policies of host countries, and the attitudes of natives toward immigrants (Berry et al. 2006; Levels, Dronkers, and Kraaykamp 2008). Assessing and explaining the efficacy of different education and social policies require an exhaustive understanding of the relative importance of these factors and the ways in which they interact. To this end, empirical research should focus on the confluence of the individual, local, and international aspects of migration and its associated hardships.

Immigration is not affecting all countries in the same way, and not all countries face the same challenges, given differences in their locations, migration histories, and selectivity of migration policies. However, countries that are currently facing changes in the volume or composition of immigration flows can learn from what others have done in the past to address the challenges of diversity. Since 2000, PISA has been collecting detailed information at the individual level on the academic performance of fifteen-year-old students enrolled in school in more than seventy education systems worldwide. PISA data can shed light on patterns of successful migrant integration in school and society, which can inspire and redirect future efforts of researchers and policy makers.

Student-level data from PISA highlights the great diversity of backgrounds that immigrant students possess and the circumstances that they encounter in different destination countries. Recognizing that individual circumstances matter and are related to outcomes can ensure that each student is acknowledged for his or her unique value and potential. Oftentimes, a generic label of "educational liability" is attached to immigrant students, and not enough efforts are put in place to identify who these students are and what they can do. PISA has consistently shown that children of immigrants differ widely in their cultural and language customs, socio-economic status, and readiness to integrate into their host communities, as measured by language fluency and the migration history of their families. They also bring a wide range of skills, knowledge, and motivation to their schools—useful assets that can enrich an educational system and society at large.

The rich information on background characteristics of immigrant students in PISA can be used to shed light on the factors behind inequalities in outcomes for immigrants and nonimmigrants. Immigrant students often face the double disadvantage of coming from nonnative speaking and socioeconomically disadvantaged backgrounds (Crul, Schneider, and Lelie 2012). Immigrant students from poor households have to overcome barriers that compound the effects of material deprivation, including attending schools with fewer resources and higher concentrations of other disadvantaged students (Cebolla-Bollado and Garrido Medina 2011). In this light, any (dis)advantage that results from language proficiency or country of origin is best understood and documented when compared with the outcomes of nonimmigrant youth of similar socioeconomic status. Looking at how multiple forms of disadvantage influence student performance is also a way of analyzing the resilience of immigrant students. Despite poverty and unfamiliarity with the prevailing language and culture, many immigrant fifteen-year-olds still manage to perform relatively well. Greater knowledge about the determinants of resilience can be used to boost the potential of migrants to make exceptional contributions to their host countries.

Most importantly, analysis and further development of PISA data on immigrant students can support policy changes to give all children opportunities that are proportionate to their needs. Indeed, immigrant students' education and integration outcomes are affected by institutional features of host-country education systems such as early stratification practices (Buchmann and Parrado 2006; Heath and Brinbaum 2014; Crul et al. 2017; Crul, Schneider, and Lelie 2012). For example, given a similar level of academic potential, immigrant students are more likely than their nonimmigrant peers to be delayed in their progression through school grades.

In order to evaluate differences across countries in social and emotional aspects related to immigrant students' integration, this chapter analyzes student performance on PISA standardized tests in conjunction with levels of self-reported life satisfaction and sense of belonging. Students' subjective evaluations of their degree of connection with the school environment and whether their need to feel a part of the school community is being met can be seen as important indicators of a school's ability to foster a sense of well-being that is not related to academic achievement (Maslow 1954; Deci and Ryan 1991; Vallerand 1997; Baumeister and Leary 1995).

This chapter summarizes the results of recent analyses of PISA data on immigrant students and discusses ways to enhance the relevance of PISA for analysis of integration issues. The chapter is organized as follows: we first present the data and methods used; next, we illustrate findings on immigrant students' outcomes; finally, we conclude by discussing policy implications and directions for future research, policy analysis, and data collection.

DATA AND METHODS

This study uses data from the OECD Programme for International Student Assessment (PISA), a triennial large-scale international survey that measures the knowledge and skills of representative samples of fifteen-year-old students in more than sixty education systems worldwide.[2] The primary goal of PISA is to assess performance in reading, mathematics, and science literacy. In each PISA survey wave, three subject domains are tested, and one of the three is assessed as the major domain. PISA 2000 and 2009 focused on reading, PISA 2003 and 2012 focused on mathematics, and PISA 2006 and 2015 focused on science. The primary PISA instruments are a two-hour test and a background questionnaire designed to take between thirty and thirty-five minutes for students to complete. The main domain receives a substantially larger portion of testing time and greater focus in the background questionnaires, in which students are asked about their engagement, attitudes, and dispositions toward such subjects. For example, in 2009, when reading was the main domain, students reported on their reading practices and attitudes; in 2012, students reported on their self-beliefs toward mathematics; in 2015, the student background questionnaire explored students' self-beliefs toward science.

The PISA questionnaires provide additional data that are extremely valuable for the study of immigrant students. Participants are asked about their social and emotional well-being, whether they were born in the country where they are being tested, whether they speak the test language at home, their age of arrival in the testing country, and whether their parents were born abroad. A selected number of participating countries also asked students to report their country of birth or their parents' country of birth.

The research reported in this study primarily uses the PISA 2015 and PISA 2012 datasets, the most recent editions of PISA. Some analyses are based on a pooled data set across cycles to overcome small sample size issues when examining specific groups of students with an immigrant background and their outcomes. PISA is conducted on two-stage stratified representative samples of students enrolled in lower secondary or upper secondary institutions and aged between fifteen years and three months and sixteen years and two months. The two-stage sampling strategy means that schools are sampled first, and then students are sampled within sampled schools.[3] Comprehensive documentation regarding the sampling design, response rates, questionnaire items, quality assurance, scale construction, and appropriate weighting procedures, which we follow in all analyses presented, is provided in the PISA Technical Reports.

When discussing the outcomes of students in this chapter, we refer to students as having an immigrant background if they either reported that they were foreign-born or reported that both of their parents were foreign-born (therefore students with one parent who was foreign-born and one who was not were considered not to have an immigrant background). Some analyses further distinguish between first- and second-generation immigrants. First-generation immigrant students are students who were not born in the same country as the one where the assessment is being administered; second-generation students are those who have foreign-born parents but who were born in the country where the assessment is being administered.

Countries differ in the degree to which their population of fifteen-year-olds is included in the PISA target population and is represented in PISA data, leading to potential biases in the analysis. PISA only considers students who are enrolled in lower or upper secondary schools and who have at least basic language proficiency in the language in which instruction takes place. This qualification implies that students who have just migrated to a new country and are not in school and/or have very poor language skills are not part of the PISA target population. Therefore, immigrant students, especially those who have recently migrated, are likely to be underrepresented in PISA data. This issue must always be considered when interpreting results in our study.

We consider three related dimensions of students' outcomes: academic performance, sense of belonging at school, and life satisfaction. Achievement scores in PISA are based on Item Response Theory (IRT) models, and students' response patterns to specific questions in their assessments are used to impute plausible value scores of students' achievement. PISA estimates for each student and for each assessment domain a set of plausible values (five until 2012, ten starting in 2015) that can be used to assign to each student a probability estimate of his or her achievement on problems at different levels of difficulty (OECD 2014). The key performance indicators are students' performance in reading, mathematics, and science. The unique feature of PISA is that its assessment frameworks are designed to identify students' ability to apply what they have learned in class to problem situations that they have not previously encountered. Information processing skills are examined not by drawing on curricular knowledge but by embedding test questions in real-life situations and scenarios that fifteen-year-olds may have encountered or experienced. This feature means that all the PISA tests have a high reading load and, as a result, may be particularly challenging for students who mainly speak a language at home that is different from the assessment one. Students' sense of belonging at school was examined by asking students to report on a four-point Likert scale ranging from "strongly agree," to "agree," "disagree," and "strongly disagree" to indicate whether they felt that they belonged at school. PISA 2015 asked students to report how satisfied they were with their lives overall. Measures of overall life satisfaction are based on self-reports and include both single-item and multiple-item measurement instruments (Huebner and Gilman 2014; Myers and Diener 1995). PISA 2015 employed the widely used question asking students to rate their current life satisfaction level on a scale from "0—not at all satisfied" to "10—completely satisfied."

Several of the analyses developed in this chapter introduce controls for students' socioeconomic status as measured by the PISA index of economic, social, and cultural status (ESCS). The ESCS index is a continuous variable standardized to have a mean of 0 and a standard deviation of 1 across OECD countries based on students' self-reports on their parents' educational attainment and occupational status as well as on the educational, cultural, and consumer durable resources available in their homes.

RESULTS

Performance

Performance Differences between Immigrants and Nonimmigrants.   Science was the main domain of assessment of PISA 2015, and reading is particularly relevant for immigrants because it is the domain in which language proficiency plays the largest role. Results from PISA 2015 indicate that in most countries first-generation immigrant students perform worse than students without an immigrant background, and second-generation immigrant students perform somewhere between the two (OECD 2016b). Although migrants generally have lower relative performance when compared with students without an immigrant background in their country, many can perform at very high levels by international standards. Results indicate that the performance gap between first-generation students and students without an immigrant background tends to be wider in reading than in science. This finding suggests that language barriers to text comprehension may be key in explaining the gap in academic performance between these two groups of students.

Beyond differences in mean performance, a major concern for countries and economies around the world is that immigrant students are more likely than their nonimmigrant peers to leave the school system without having attained a baseline level of skills—an indicator of the inclusiveness of these systems. Analyses of PISA data reveal that, on average across OECD countries, as many as 39.1 percent of first-generation immigrant students and 29.5 percent of second-generation immigrant students performed below proficiency level 2 in the PISA 2015 science assessment. By comparison, only 18.9 percent of students without an immigrant background were low performers in science.

Among countries with relatively large immigrant student populations, such as Canada, Estonia, Hong Kong (China), Ireland, Macao (China) and Singapore, fewer than 20 percent of both first- and second-generation immigrant students performed below level 2 in science. These are all countries and economies with a mean performance above the OECD average and in which high performance standards are achieved across the board regardless of immigrant background. By contrast, in Ciudad Autonoma de Buenos Aires (Argentina) (hereafter "CABA"), Costa Rica, Greece, Jordan, and Qatar more than four in ten immigrant students, both first- and second-generation, performed below proficiency level 2. These are countries and economies with mean performance in science below the OECD average. Results for mathematics closely mirror those of science: on average across OECD countries, 39.7 percent of first-generation immigrant students and 30.5 percent of second-generation immigrant students scored below proficiency level 2, whereas 21.2 percent of their nonimmigrant peers performed at that level. In reading, the difference in the percentages of low performers is smaller between second-generation immigrant students and nonimmigrant students.

Trends in Performance of Immigrant and Nonimmigrant Students.   In many countries the number of immigrant student populations that social, welfare, and education systems have had to integrate has grown over the past decade. Some countries experienced for the first time in their history a large number of immigrants entering their school systems during a time of economic hardship and cuts in public spending brought about by the great economic crisis. PISA can be used to identify the evolution of the performance gap between immigrant and nonimmigrant students between 2006 and 2015 and to assess whether the performance of immigrants improved or declined over that period.

In 2006, 9.4 percent of students across OECD countries had an immigrant background, and they scored, on average, 50 points lower in science than their nonimmigrant peers did. When students with similar socioeconomic status and familiarity with the language of assessment were compared, the performance gap between immigrant and nonimmigrant students was cut by more than half, to 23 score points, a smaller but still significant margin (OECD 2016b).

By 2015, the share of immigrant students across OECD countries had increased to 12.5 percent. The average difference in science performance in favor of nonimmigrant students is 43 score points before accounting for students' socioeconomic status and language spoken at home. However, after we account for these background factors, the gap is reduced to 19 points, a smaller but significant difference. As a result, in 2015, on average across OECD countries, immigrant students continued to perform worse in science than their nonimmigrant peers did, even after accounting for socioeconomic status and language spoken at home, although the performance difference has narrowed slightly since 2006.

However, in a number of countries, notably OECD countries Belgium, Italy, Portugal, Spain, and Switzerland, the differences in performance between immigrant and nonimmigrant students shrank by 20 score points or more over the period, after accounting for socioeconomic status and familiarity with the language of assessment. In Canada and Luxembourg, these differences narrowed by 10 to 20 score points. In some of these countries the difference shrank mainly because of improvements in immigrant students' performance rather than because of poorer performance among their nonimmigrant peers.

For instance, between 2006 and 2015, immigrant students in Portugal improved their science performance by 64 score points while nonimmigrant students improved by 25 points. During the same period, immigrant students in Italy improved their scores in science by 31 points and immigrant students in Spain improved by 23 points, while in both countries the performance of students without an immigrant background remained stable. In none of the three countries can compositional changes in the immigrant population account for these improvements; in both Italy and Spain, for example, the percentage of immigrant students with tertiary-educated parents was about 30 percentage points lower in 2015 than it was in 2006.

Trends in reading and mathematics performance mirror those observed in science, suggesting that across OECD countries performance differences between immigrant and nonimmigrant students decreased modestly between 2006 and 2015 once students' socioeconomic status and familiarity with the language of assessment were taken into account.

Disentangling the Influence of Country of Origin and Country of Destination on Performance.   Previous analyses suggest that although immigrant students tend to score lower than nonimmigrant students, many perform at high levels by international standards, especially those in countries with selective immigration policies, such as Australia, Canada, and New Zealand. Although this finding may seem to support the view that differences in the achievement of immigrant students can mainly be explained by variations in the backgrounds of immigrants across countries and economies, PISA results show that the performance of immigrant students is also strongly related to the characteristics of the education systems in host countries.

In order to identify differences across immigrant populations in different countries that are not captured by language and socioeconomic conditions, it is possible to compare the outcomes of students from the same country of origin and with similar socioeconomic status who migrated to different countries, after also accounting for the socioeconomic composition of the host communities. Although this process does not completely eliminate migrants' self-selection into different countries and the bias this action can create when estimating differences in outcomes, it can increase comparability of immigrant students' outcomes across countries. Since a limited number of countries included a question in the background questionnaire on country of origin and since the sample size of immigrant populations by country of origin is small, reliable estimates can only be obtained by pooling PISA data from multiple cycles (analyses reported here pool data from PISA 2006, 2009, 2012, and 2015).

Figure 16.1 shows, for a selected group of countries with available information, how second- and first-generation immigrant students from the same country of origin and with similar socioeconomic status performed in science across various destination countries, after also accounting for the socioeconomic composition of the host communities. Results indicate that the performance of immigrant students of similar cultural and socioeconomic backgrounds can vary markedly across host-country school systems. For instance, second-generation immigrant students from Arabic-speaking countries living in the Netherlands, traditionally a high-performing country in PISA, scored 77 points higher in science, on average, when compared with those who had settled in Qatar, a country with a significantly lower mean performance in science. They also scored between 50 and 60 points higher than those who had settled in Finland and Denmark, two countries that tend to have a mean performance at or above the OECD average. In addition, both second- and first-generation Albanian immigrant students attending schools in Greece tended to score about 35 points higher in science than compatriot peers attending schools in Switzerland did—despite the higher mean performance of the latter country across PISA assessments.

Figure 16.1 also shows how the performance of students from the same country of origin can vary markedly between first- and second-generation immigrants in a given host country. For example, while students born in mainland China scored above the OECD average across several destination countries, they generally performed better in Hong Kong (China) and Macao (China), where they scored above 550 points in science, than they did in Australia, where their average science score was 502 points. However, among second-generation Chinese immigrant students, this pattern is reversed as students born to Chinese parents who settled in Australia scored 592 points in science on average, outperforming second-generation Chinese immigrant students in both Hong Kong (China) and Macao (China).

These results suggest that it is not only socioeconomic status (and thus the selectivity of immigration policies) and the mean performance of host countries that

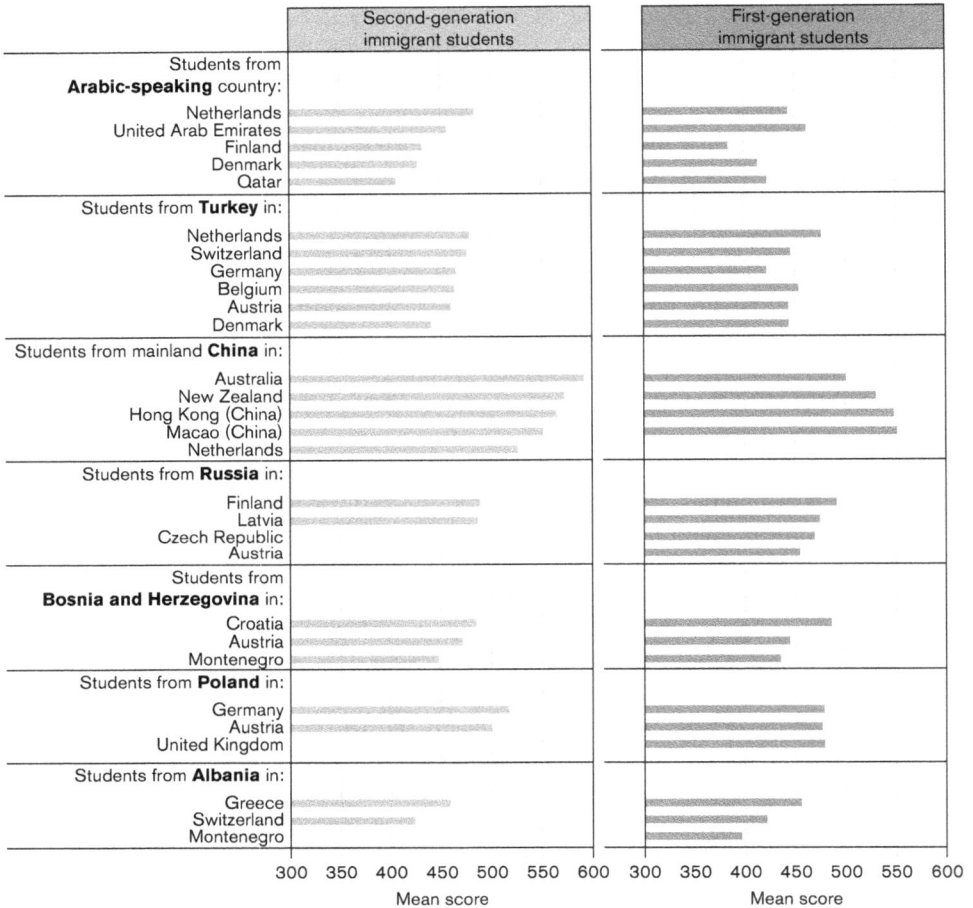

	Second-generation immigrant students	First-generation immigrant students
Students from **Arabic-speaking** country:		
Netherlands		
United Arab Emirates		
Finland		
Denmark		
Qatar		
Students from **Turkey** in:		
Netherlands		
Switzerland		
Germany		
Belgium		
Austria		
Denmark		
Students from mainland **China** in:		
Australia		
New Zealand		
Hong Kong (China)		
Macao (China)		
Netherlands		
Students from **Russia** in:		
Finland		
Latvia		
Czech Republic		
Austria		
Students from **Bosnia and Herzegovina** in:		
Croatia		
Austria		
Montenegro		
Students from **Poland** in:		
Germany		
Austria		
United Kingdom		
Students from **Albania** in:		
Greece		
Switzerland		
Montenegro		

300 350 400 450 500 550 600   300 350 400 450 500 550 600

Mean score   Mean score

FIGURE 16.1. Immigrant students' performance in science, by country of origin and destination. *Notes:* Mainland China excludes Hong Kong (China), Macao (China), and Chinese Taipei. Data from multiple PISA assessments are pooled to reach the minimum number of observations required for the estimation. Results are only shown for pairs of origin and destination countries or economies with data for thirty or more first- or second-generation immigrant students. Results correspond to predicted performance if all the immigrant students from a given country of origin and all the nonimmigrant students across all the destination countries or economies for immigrants of that origin had the same socioeconomic status as the average student across these destination countries or economies did. *Sources:* PISA 2006, 2009, 2012, and 2015 databases.

contribute to differences in the performance of immigrant students who come from the same country of origin but also differences in the destination countries in which they settle. These differences are also related to the capacity of school systems in host countries to nurture the talents of students with different cultural backgrounds and to the overall integration capacities of host societies (in terms of socioeconomic opportunities for immigrant families, social policies, and attitudes toward immigration). Other factors not included in this analysis might also contribute to the differences in the performance of immigrant students from the same national or cultural origin across host countries. These include students' own motivation or the support they receive from their parents (see Crul et al. 2017) and factors not necessarily linked to socioeconomic status that can play a role in immigrant families' decision to settle in a given country, such as personal networks, historical links, or parents' professional aspirations.

Factors Related to Performance Gaps

Language.   In PISA 2015, on average across OECD countries, for 44.7 percent of second-generation and 67 percent of first-generation immigrant students, the main language spoken at home was different from the language of assessment in their host country. Among countries with relatively large immigrant student populations, such as Austria and Luxembourg, more than seven in ten second-generation immigrant students mainly used a language at home that was different from the one of instruction. In Slovenia, Sweden, and the United States, this usage was the case for more than eight in ten first-generation immigrant students. On average across OECD countries, immigrant students who spoke the language of assessment at home scored 31 points lower in science than nonimmigrant students who spoke the language of assessment at home did, but immigrant students who mainly spoke another language in the family context scored 54 points lower than these nonimmigrant students did—that is, more than 20 points lower than immigrant students who had a greater familiarity with the test language did.

This "language penalty" for immigrant students in the science assessment—understood as the difference in performance between students with an immigrant background who speak the language of assessment as their main language at home and those who do not—was greatest in Hong Kong (China) and Luxembourg (between 90 and 100 score points) and in Austria, Belgium, Jordan, Macao (China), Russia, and Switzerland (between 40 and 55 score points). There is a broad similarity in the pattern of association between the language spoken at home and performance in science and reading. Conversely, in mathematics assessments immigrant students who are less familiar with the test language suffer a smaller penalty (15 score points) on average across OECD countries. Analysis of 2012 PISA data also shows that the relative performance of immigrant students is better in the PISA problem-solving assessment—an assessment that uses simple language—than in the reading assessment, suggesting that immigrant students' potential to succeed in school is seriously limited by a lack of language proficiency (OECD 2015b).

Acquiring skills in the language of instruction and assessment as early as possible would help immigrant students to succeed in school and more broadly. However, many education systems struggle to provide the language training necessary for immigrants to flourish in their new communities while ensuring that those immigrants who want to maintain their heritage language also have the opportunity to do so. In 2012, sixteen of the countries and economies participating in PISA administered a special module aimed at capturing students' language training. In this sample of countries, an average of only around 18 percent of students participated in at least two hours of language training per week, although in Singapore as many as 57 percent of immigrant students did (OECD 2015b). Teachers often reported that they did not have the diagnostic skills and tools to assess their immigrant students' linguistic and cognitive capacities (OECD 2010). Thus, practical tools such as assessment kits that are age and culturally appropriate could help teachers to identify the language-support needs of each student.

Concentration of Immigrant Students in Disadvantaged Schools.   Low performance among immigrant students can also be partly linked to the fact that these students are often concentrated in socioeconomically disadvantaged schools. Immigrant students tend to be overrepresented in certain schools because they live in the same neighborhoods or because school systems group them together regardless of their places of residence. The concentration of immigrant students in schools does not automatically have adverse effects on student performance or social integration (Geay, McNally, and Telhaj 2013; Ohinata and van Ours 2013; Schneeweis 2015). However, negative outcomes will likely follow if ethnic agglomerations become enclaves whose residents have little possibility of outward and upward mobility. Therefore, a critical link between the concentration of immigrant students in a school and low performance is the socioeconomic intake of the schools where immigrants tend to be enrolled. Immigrant students' learning will be hindered if they are aggregated in disadvantaged schools that suffer from a shortage or inadequacy of educational resources, including teacher preparedness, or where the concentration of disadvantaged students results in a poorer disciplinary climate.

Measuring the concentration of immigrant students in schools in a reliable and internationally comparable way is challenging in many respects, mainly because of the variation in the percentage of immigrant students across countries but also because of other differences across schools. PISA 2015 relies on two indices to measure the concentration of students with an immigrant background in schools.

The first is the index of current concentration, which represents the percentage of students, both immigrant and nonimmigrant, who would have to be relocated from one school to another so that all schools could have an identical percentage of immigrant and nonimmigrant students. The second measure is the index of maximum potential concentration, which represents the minimum proportion of students who would have to be moved across schools if all immigrant students were allocated to the largest schools. By defining country-specific thresholds for the school-level concentration of immigrant students, these indices address some of the shortcomings of other concentration measures and provide a benchmark that reflects more accurately the relative similarity between the composition of schools and their social contexts.

The difference between the two indices indicates the distance between the current mix of immigrant and nonimmigrant students in schools and the highest possible degree of segregation of immigrant students in a country or economy, given the overall percentage of immigrant students and the size of the country's or economy's schools. The maximum potential concentration is a hypothetical scenario in which all immigrant students attend the largest schools in the country and hence one in which the largest number of immigrant students can be found in the same schools and classrooms. Given this scenario, countries where the difference between the two indices is larger can be seen as having greater success in avoiding the segregation of immigrant students into specific schools.

PISA data reveal that current and potentially maximum levels of concentration of immigrant students differ most—by 30 percentage points or more—in Canada, Hong Kong (China), Luxembourg, Macao (China), Switzerland, and the United Kingdom. In all of these education systems, immigrant students represent a large share of the student population, ranging from 16.7 percent in the United Kingdom to 62.2 percent in Macao (China); however, their current distribution of immigrant students across schools is far below the highest possible level of concentration. By contrast, in Costa Rica, Croatia, Denmark, Estonia, France, Greece, the Netherlands, Norway, Portugal, Russia, Spain, and the United Arab Emirates, the two indices differ by fewer than 15 percentage points, a result that implies that in these countries and economies, current levels of concentration are somewhat closer to their potential ceiling.

Further comparisons can be drawn between countries with similar overall percentages of immigrant students and maximum potential levels of concentration, a measure that indicates comparable circumstances in terms of school size but with different levels of current concentration. For example, in Luxembourg and Qatar, more than five in ten students have an immigrant background, and almost half of the student population would have to change schools if the concentration of immigrant students were to reach its maximum level. Yet in Luxembourg, immigrant students are currently less concentrated in the same schools than they are in Qatar, where the percentage of students who would have to change schools in order for schools to achieve an even distribution is 10 percentage points higher. Similarly, Singapore has a current level of concentration that is 8 percentage points lower than that of the United States, a country with a similar overall percentage of immigrant students and a comparable maximum concentration index.

The main concern behind the concentration of immigrant students in certain schools is its potential association with poorer student outcomes. Before taking into account students' socioeconomic status and immigrant background as well as the socioeconomic intake of their school, a higher concentration of immigrant students in schools is associated with an 18-point lower score in science on average across OECD countries. However, once background factors are accounted for, this negative association with performance disappears entirely. PISA results thus suggest that it is the concentration of disadvantage—and not the concentration of immigrants per se—that has detrimental effects on learning.

The schools where immigrant students concentrate tend to have a level of educational resources similar to that of schools with a lower concentration of such students. PISA 2015 provides two summary measures of the adequacy of educational resources at the school level: the index of shortage of educational material and the index of shortage of education staff. These indices are derived from school principals' responses to questions about whether a shortage or inadequacy of resources hinders their school's capacity to provide instruction. On average across OECD countries, no relationship has been observed between the adequacy of the material and human resources at the school level—as measured by these indices— and the level of concentration of immigrant students in schools, as measured by country-specific concentration thresholds.

Differences in resources between schools with low and high percentages of immigrant students are only found in about a third of the countries and economies with relatively large immigrant student populations, but the associations are not necessarily consistent. In CABA (Argentina), Germany, Macao (China), and Spain, principals in schools with a high concentration of immigrant students tend to perceive that their schools are less well resourced, in terms of both equipment and staff, than principals in schools with a low concentration of students with immigrant backgrounds do. The opposite is true in Estonia and the United Arab Emirates, two countries where few immigrant students come from disadvantaged backgrounds.

Stratification Policies and Practices and Performance Differences.   If immigrant background is related to the likelihood that students are sorted into different programs or schools, educational opportunities will likely differ for immigrant and nonimmigrant students. A common stratification policy is grade repetition— the practice of retaining struggling students at a given grade with the aim of giving them more time to master the curriculum. On average across OECD countries, 19.9 percent of immigrant students had repeated a grade by the time they sat for the PISA 2015 test, compared with 10.9 percent of their nonimmigrant peers. Among countries with relatively large populations of immigrant students, a slightly smaller difference in the incidence of grade repetition between these two groups of students is observed: 19.3 percent of immigrant students and 12.8 percent of nonimmigrant students had repeated a grade in these countries. While the decision to have a student repeat a grade is usually based on his or her performance, in 2015, immigrant students were about 70 percent more likely than their nonimmigrant peers to have repeated a grade, after accounting for students' socioeconomic status and their performance in the science and reading assessments.

Among education systems in which immigrant students represent more than 6.25 percent of the student population, a higher likelihood of grade repetition among immigrant students, relative to nonimmigrant students, is observed in eighteen countries and economies, even when comparing students with similar socioeconomic status and performance in science and reading considered together. After accounting for these factors, immigrant students in Singapore and Sweden are about four times more likely and students in Greece, Slovenia, and the United Kingdom are about two-and-a-half times more likely than nonimmigrant students to have repeated a grade. By contrast, after accounting for students' socioeconomic status and performance in science, there are no significant differences, on average across OECD countries, between immigrant and nonimmigrant students in the likelihood of their being enrolled in vocational rather than academic programs, another common form of sorting students in secondary education. Indeed, in up to thirteen education systems with relatively large populations of immigrant students, these students are less likely to be enrolled in a vocational track, after socioeconomic status and performance in science have been taken into account.

PISA 2015 results suggest that there were no significant differences on average across OECD countries in the amount of science instruction to which immigrant and nonimmigrant students had been exposed at school at the time of the PISA test. This measure is calculated by the percentage of students taking at least one science lesson per week at school and by the average time spent per week on regular science lessons. However, previous analysis of PISA 2012 on the cumulative opportunity students had to learn mathematics by age fifteen showed that immigrant students were much less familiar with the mathematics concepts that they are expected to learn in secondary school (linear equations, exponential functions, divisors, and quadratic functions) than students without an immigrant background were (OECD 2016a). Differences in the quality of instruction and in the depth and coverage of curricula across countries of origin and destination can lead to gaps in students' readiness to learn advanced mathematics material. Immigrant students, and particularly refugees, are also likely to have spent considerable time out of school as they were making their way from their country of origin to their host country. At least one in six immigrant students who attend school in an OECD country has lost more than two months of school at least once in his or her life (OECD 2015b). Apart from these differences, the concentration of immigrant students in disadvantaged schools in host countries might explain why these students are not familiar with certain mathematical concepts.

Nonachievement Outcomes

The Immigrant Gap in Students' Sense of Belonging at School.   Students' well-being is not just about feeling happy and achieving good grades in school but also involves being engaged with life and with other people (Gale et al. 2013). The social aspect of students' well-being captures both the quantity and the quality of students' social networks (Helliwell and Putnam 2004). People with trustworthy connections—a valuable social support network—can be protected from loneliness and mental health problems. The teenage years represent a period of intense social exploration for children. They are discovering their own identity but at the same time are looking for acceptance and validation from their peers and community, with schools being a primary socialization environment. Teenagers place great importance on the relationships they form; thus, the quality and types of relationships are extremely important indicators of their well-being (Armsden and Greenberg 1987; Lippman, Moore, and McIntosh 2011).

Sense of belonging is defined as feeling accepted and liked by the rest of the group, feeling connected to others, and feeling like a member of a community (Baumeister and Leary 1995; Maslow 1943). Human beings in general, and teenagers in particular, desire strong social ties and quality relationships. Fifteen-year-old students spend most of their time at school. Thus, students who feel that they are part of and are accepted by a school community report that their lives have more meaning (Juvonen 2006) than students without such connection do. They are more likely to be healthy (Lippman, Moore, and McIntosh 2011), to perform better academically, and to be more motivated in school (Cohen et al. 2009; Goodenow 1993; Katja et al. 2002; Sánchez, Colón, and Esparza 2005). They are also less likely to engage in risky behaviors such as substance abuse and truancy (Currie et al. 2012; Resnick et al. 1997; Schulenberg et al. 1994).

In many countries fifteen-year-old students participating in PISA are transitioning from lower to upper secondary school. During this transition period, approximately half of these students feel disengaged from school (West, Sweeting, and Young 2010). Those students who feel seriously disengaged are more likely to drop out of school and never return (Lee and Burkam 2003). In PISA 2015 students were asked to report their feelings about belonging to the school community on a 4-point Likert scale ranging from 1 ("strongly agree") to 4 ("strongly disagree").

Students' sense of belonging refers to their belonging to and engagement in their school communities.

Students' sense of belonging in school is a crucial indicator for evaluating how well school systems are able to integrate immigrant students. Students' sense of belonging to the school community is important because it expresses students' affect and schools' ability to promote positive affective states among their students. Students' emotional well-being is not only important in and of itself but is also highly associated with their academic outcomes and ability to overcome difficulties (Borgonovi and Pál 2016). A greater sense of belonging in school stimulates healthy social and psychological development among students and is likely to be associated with lower rates of school dropout. Countries vary widely in the overall percentage of students who agree or strongly agree that they feel like they belong at school and, more specifically, in the extent to which first- and second-generation immigrant students are more or less likely than students without an immigrant background to feel that they belong at school.

Analyses of PISA 2015 data reveal that Belgium, Luxembourg, Malta, Portugal, and Switzerland are the countries in which first-generation immigrant students expressed the most alienation from education systems as compared with responses from students without an immigrant background (OECD 2017). In several countries the process of integration unfolds over time since second-generation immigrant students generally reported a higher sense of belonging as compared with first-generation immigrant students' responses. This result was particularly the case in Belgium, Denmark, Luxembourg, Malta, and Switzerland. On average across OECD countries, 74 percent of nonimmigrant students agreed or strongly agreed that they felt like they belonged at school, and 72 percent of second-generation and 69 percent of first-generation students reported the same feeling. In Australia, Canada, New Zealand, and Qatar, the percentage of both first- and second-generation immigrant students who reported that they felt like they belonged at school was higher than the percentage of nonimmigrant students who reported the same feeling. All four of these countries have adopted highly selective immigration policies.

On average across OECD countries, the gap in the sense of belonging between first-generation immigrant students and students without an immigrant background did not change between 2003 and 2012. However, most countries have experienced a significant drop in the reported sense of belonging for both first-generation immigrant students and students without an immigrant background. In the cases of Germany and Belgium, the reduction for first-generation immigrant students was greater than for nonimmigrant students, resulting in a significant widening of the gap between the two groups. In Australia in 2015, the decline was more pronounced among students without an immigrant background, resulting in lower overall levels of sense of belonging and a smaller gap between first-generation immigrant students and students without an immigrant background.

Figure 16.2 offers a more nuanced comparison by showing the percentage of immigrant students who reported that they felt like they belonged at school by country of origin and country of destination, after controlling for potential selection mechanisms associated with socioeconomic status. Because of sample size issues and the fact that not all countries asked students to report their country of birth or the country of their parents' birth, few groups can be identified. In general, Figure 16.2 suggests that there is a large degree of variability in the percentage of immigrant students from the same country who reported feeling like they belonged at school and who were surveyed in different countries of destination. For example, figure 16.2 indicates that while 57 percent of Polish students who migrated to the United Kingdom reported feeling like they belonged at school, as many as 79 percent of those who migrated to Germany reported such feelings. Similarly, almost 90 percent of students from Turkey who settled in Finland reported feeling like they belonged at school, but only 59 percent of students from Turkey who settled in Denmark reported the same feelings. And while 67 percent of students who migrated from Arabic-speaking countries to Denmark reported feeling as if they belonged at school, 85 percent of those who migrated to Finland reported such feelings. These results suggest that the social integration and emotional well-being of immigrant students are affected not only by cultural differences between the heritage and the host country's cultures but also by the ways in which schools and communities help them feel that they are part of their new communities.

Differences in Perceived Life Satisfaction between Immigrant and Nonimmigrant Students.   Life satisfaction is a subjective aspect of psychological well-being and represents "an evaluation that an individual makes about his or her perceived quality of life overall according to his or her chosen criteria" (Shin and Johnson 1978, quoted in Neto 1993, 126). Adolescents' life satisfaction appears to be particularly influenced by social experiences and social relationships with family, peers, and school (Henry 1994). Among teenagers, high levels of life satisfaction are associated with positive physical and cognitive development, social and coping skills that lead to more positive outcomes in adulthood (Currie et al. 2012). Bullying and victimization (Navarro et al. 2015) and psychosocial problems such as anxiety and depression (Huebner 2004; Huebner, Funk, and Gilman 2000) can cause low levels of life satisfaction and are related to substance abuse, delinquency, and problem behavior (Sun and Shek 2009). Supportive family and peers and strong relationships can help students deal with challenging situations (Currie et al. 2012). Immigrants often experience culture shock and stress while adjusting to their new lives in their host countries, and changes in living conditions and peer influences may affect adolescents more than they do adults. Important mediators of life satisfaction among immigrants include how students perceive their country

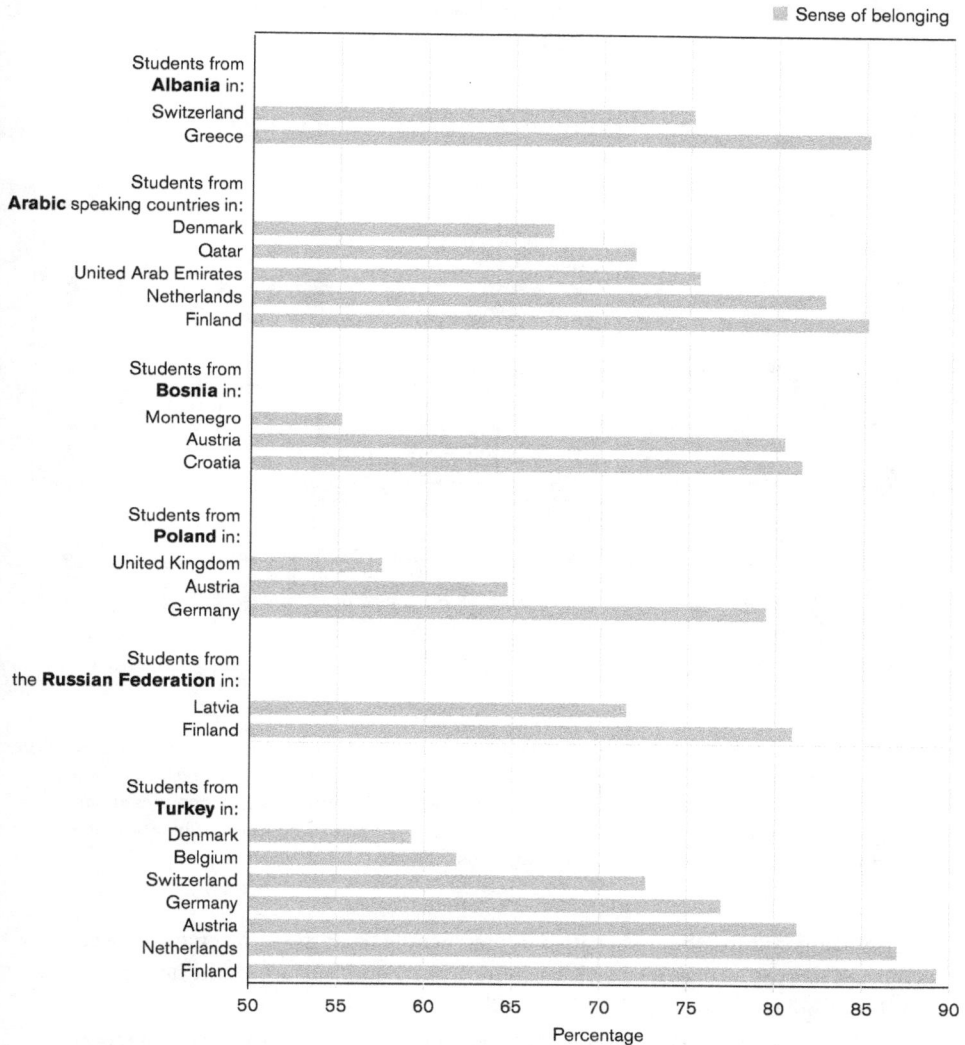

FIGURE 16.2. Immigrant students' sense of belonging at school, by country of origin and destination. *Notes:* The estimates were obtained from data pooled from the PISA 2012 and PISA 2015 databases. The estimates have been adjusted for differences in socioeconomic status by assigning to all students of the same origin group in the different destinations the value of the index of socioeconomic status of the average student in the group. The coverage of destination countries is limited by the fact that only some countries collect detailed information on immigrants' country of birth. Only destination countries with data on at least twenty immigrant students of the same origin are shown. *Sources:* OECD, PISA 2012 and 2015 databases.

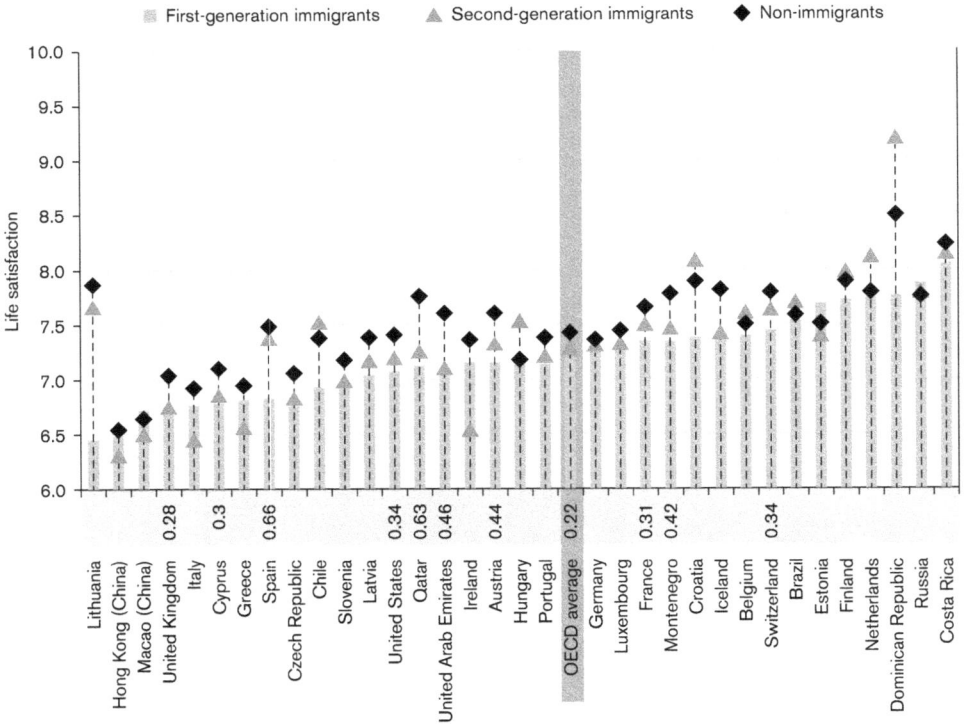

FIGURE 16.3. Life satisfaction, by immigrant background. *Notes:* Statistically significant differences between nonimmigrant students and first-generation immigrant students who reported that they felt as if they belonged at school are shown next to the country or economy name. Countries and economies are ranked in ascending order of the average response of first-generation immigrant students to the question of how satisfied they are with their lives. *Source:* OECD, PISA 2015 database.

of origin and culture, the proximity of young people from the same cultural background, and exposure to open and welcoming peers and teachers in the host country (Liebkind and Jasinskaja-Lahti 2000; Edwards and Lopez 2006).

Figure 16.3 shows that in several countries, and in general at the OECD average level, first-generation immigrant students reported lower levels of life satisfaction when compared with students without an immigrant background. In general, differences in self-reported satisfaction with life between nonimmigrant and first-generation immigrant students are the most pronounced, with second-generation immigrant students reporting levels between the two extreme categories. Differences were widest in Austria, Qatar, Spain, Switzerland, and the United Arab Emirates, where first-generation immigrants reported a considerably lower level of satisfaction when compared with students without an immigrant background.

CONCLUSIONS

The ways in which education systems respond to migration influence whether immigrants are successfully integrated into their host communities as well as the economic and social well-being of all members of the communities they serve, whether those individuals have an immigrant background or not. Since they need to integrate a larger number of school-aged immigrants, some education systems face more pressure than others do because the profile of the immigrants makes them particularly vulnerable (for example, if their native language is very different from the language spoken in their host community) or because immigrant students and their parents are especially socioeconomically disadvantaged (Crul et al. 2017).

Despite the difficulties of integration, data from PISA suggest that migration has not been associated with declining education standards in host communities since the PISA study was first conducted in 2000. In fact, the data show no significant association between the share of immigrant students and the performance of a school system as measured through the mean score on the PISA assessments in science, reading, and mathematics. Furthermore, the performance of school systems seems to be unrelated to the composition of the immigrant population. There is also no clear association between the share of immigrant students who are socioeconomically disadvantaged and a school system's performance as measured by performance on the PISA standardized assessments.

· · ·

This study has shown what existing PISA instruments can reveal about the outcomes of students with immigrant backgrounds and which factors are associated with better outcomes for this target group. However, analyses have also revealed a number of limitations and directions for data collection in the future, both in terms of the information collected through the background questionnaire and through assessment instruments.

Key priorities for research on the integration of immigrant students are to broaden and deepen the available international data on children with immigrant backgrounds; to consider both the academic and nonacademic outcomes of immigrant students and to identify which factors promote the overall well-being of immigrant students; to identify which policies and practices education systems can put in place to promote social cohesion by helping students, both immigrants and nonimmigrants, develop the cognitive and emotional abilities and attitudes to appreciate diversity and interact respectfully in increasingly diverse societies.

The analyses presented in this chapter reveal that as of 2015, only a handful of participating countries in PISA collect information on students' country of birth or, in the case of native-born children of foreign-born parents, on the country of birth of their parents. This lack of information limits the possibility of identifying the ability of different education systems to cater to the needs of diverse student populations and to compare the performance of similar groups in different education systems. Second, the PISA background questionnaire provides some details on living conditions and socioeconomic status through the PISA index of economic, social, and cultural status. However, the measure does not capture important aspects that specifically influence immigrant students' outcomes, such as fluctuations in living conditions or the presence of an extended network to support the household. Finally, although the questionnaire asks students to report whether they predominantly speak a language at home that differs from the language in which the PISA assessment was administered, it does not ask students to report whether they also speak the language of the assessment and/or other languages. The OECD is currently developing plans to address these limitations in future rounds of data collection.

A note of caution on the analyses presented relates to the fact that the migrant populations included in PISA 2015 generally do not include the most recent wave of asylum-seekers. In some of the countries hardest hit by the refugee crisis, such as Jordan, Lebanon, and Turkey, fewer than 3 percent of fifteen-year-old students in the PISA sample were foreign-born. At the same time, the countries' PISA target population (fifteen-year-old students who were enrolled in a regular school at grade 7 or higher) covered only 85 percent, 66 percent, and 69 percent, respectively, of their populations of fifteen-year-olds. The large influx of asylum-seekers in many countries has caused delays in the processing of applications to obtain refugee status and difficulties in the organization of shelter and accommodations for asylum claimants. Consequently, migrants have had difficulty accessing educational facilities and language training in many countries, in particular for older children who would have qualified for inclusion in the PISA age limits.

This limitation means that the results drawn from the analysis presented in this chapter cannot be generalized to the most recent asylum-seekers. Future PISA rounds will be required to fully assess the impact of the most recent migrant flows on the overall performance of educational systems and to identify areas of strength or weakness of specific education systems in supporting the integration of this cohort of students.

New research at the OECD will try to identify the role education systems can play in promoting five key dimensions of immigrant students' well-being—educational, psychological, social, material, and physical well-being—and to identify relationships among different aspects of well-being. A cornerstone of such work will be to move from a deficit model of immigrant students (in which immigrant students are perceived as a liability for host communities) to a model that recognizes the potential of individual students (whereby interventions are designed to recognize and empower the capabilities of all students).

The successful integration of immigrant students will depend, to a great extent, on the attitudes of their host communities. Increasing diversity creates extra demands on individuals (Putnam 2007; Sturgis et al. 2014), and adolescents are exposed, as adults are, to the risk of developing intolerant attitudes and biases. It is possible that education systems, while equipping individuals with subject-specific skills, may not be doing enough to promote the types of skills needed to facilitate the acceptance and integration of immigrants into their countries.

From an educational standpoint, a lot can be gained if the increasing diversity that comes with immigration is seen as a resource (UNESCO 2014). Diversity opens opportunities for self-reflection and reflection on one's own cultural background (OECD 2010). Engaging with people from different cultures and getting to know other languages foster personal development, interpersonal understanding, and connectedness as well as knowledge exchange and innovation (Suedekum, Wolf, and Blien 2014; Niebuhr 2010).

Although schools may seem like ideal places to teach children about tolerance, there is little consensus on how to best reduce negative sentiments and behaviors toward peers of different racial or ethnic backgrounds (Pfeifer, Brown, and Juvonen 2007). Nurturing open and unbiased perspectives about immigrants, and about other cultures more generally, will require radical changes in what students learn about the world and other cultures, in the opportunities they have to practice what they have learned, and in how teachers support this learning by working better with diverse students and experimenting with collaborative learning methods (Van Driel, Darmody, and Kerzil 2016). In terms of knowledge, this effort means enabling a broader and more inclusive understanding of the past, including histories of migration, colonialism, and interethnic conflicts as well as shared histories and cooperation among nations, cultural groups, and communities. It also means providing more opportunities to learn about global drivers of voluntary and forced migration (e.g., the geopolitical and economic background of the Syrian refugee crisis) and about the languages, histories, religions, and cultures of nondominant groups in their own communities and society.

Effective intercultural and global education requires that schools let students engage in experiences that facilitate intercultural relations and foster appreciation for the diversity of peoples, languages, and cultures, encouraging intercultural sensitivity and respect. A broad range of learning activities can have an impact on students' attitudes toward diversity and can involve teachers in all subject areas, although to differing degrees (UNESCO 2007). These may include role-playing activities that promote perspective taking and empathy or involve discussions of prejudice and discrimination. Innovative pedagogic approaches should be pursued to help children and adolescents develop a tolerant, respectful, and appreciative view of all students in their classrooms, no matter what their cultures of origin may be. For example, cooperative learning is a specific kind of pedagogy in which students work together on activities that have specific cooperative principles built into the task's structure. Such practice can lead to improved social skills and conflict-resolution strategies in ethnically diverse classrooms and thus facilitate the integration of students from minoritized groups.

To better understand how schools can facilitate intercultural relations and foster an appreciation of diverse people, languages and cultures, PISA will introduce in 2018 a new assessment of Global Competence. This innovative assessment will provide a comprehensive overview of education systems' success in creating learning environments that invite young people to understand the world beyond their immediate environments, embrace diversity, and support peaceful, sustainable and thriving multicultural communities. This global assessment will represent an important first step toward determining what students learn about the complexity of a globalizing and multicultural world and to what extent they are prepared to collaborate productively across cultural differences in their everyday lives.

NOTES

1. In this chapter, the term *immigrant students* is being used as shorthand for students whose parents are immigrants.

2. See www.oecd.org/pisa to access the PISA databases, questionnaire materials, sample assessment tasks, and technical and data analysis manuals.

3. For details, see OECD (2014) and www.oecd.org/pisa for full documentation on the PISA coverage and technical standards.

REFERENCES

Armsden, Gay C., and Mark T. Greenberg. 1987. "The Inventory of Parent and Peer Attachment: Individual Differences and Their Relationship to Psychological Well-Being in Adolescence." *Journal of Youth and Adolescence* 16 (5): 427–54.

Baumeister, Roy F., and Mark R. Leary. 1995. "The Need to Belong: Desire for Interpersonal Attachments as a Fundamental Human Motivation." *Psychological Bulletin* 117 (3): 497–529.

Berry, John W., Jean S. Phinney, David L. Sam, and Paul Vedder. 2006. "Immigrant Youth: Acculturation, Identity, and Adaptation." *Applied Psychology* 55 (3): 303–32.

Boeri, Tito, Herbert Brücker, Frédéric Docquier, and Hillel Rapoport. 2012. *Brain Gain and Brain Drain: The Global Competition to Attract High-Skilled Migrants.* Oxford: Oxford University Press.

Borgonovi, Francesca, and Judit Pál. 2016. *A Framework for the Analysis of Student Well-Being in the PISA Study: Being 15 in 2015.* OECD Education Working Paper No. 140 Paris: OECD Publishing.

Buchmann, Claudia, and Emilio Parrado. 2006. "Educational Achievement of Immigrant-Origin and Native Students: A Comparative Analysis Informed by Institutional Theory." *International Perspectives on Education and Society* 7: 345–77.

Cebolla-Boado, Héctor, and Luis Garrido Medina. 2011. "The Impact of Immigrant Concentration in Spanish Schools: School, Class, and Composition Effects." *European Sociological Review* 27 (5): 606–23.

Cerna, Lucie. 2016. *Immigration Policies and the Global Competition for Talent.* Basingstoke, UK: Palgrave Macmillan.

Cohen, Jonathan, Elizabeth M. McCabe, Nicholas M. Michelli, and Terry Pickeral. 2009. "School Climate: Research, Policy, Practice, and Teacher Education." *Teachers College Record* 111 (1): 180–213.

Crul, Maurice, Jens Schneider, Elif Keskiner, and Frans Lelie. 2017. "The Multiplier Effect: How the Accumulation of Cultural and Social Capital Explains Steep Upward Mobility of Children of Low-Educated Immigrants." *Ethnic and Racial Studies* 40 (2): 321–38.

Crul, Maurice, Jens Schneider, and Frans Lelie. 2012. *The European Second Generation Compared: Does the Integration Context Matter?* Amsterdam: Amsterdam University Press.

Currie, Candace, Cara Zanotti, Antony Morgan, Dorothy Currie, Margaretha de Looze, Chris Roberts, Oddrun Samdal, Otto R. F. Smith, and Vivian Barnekow, eds. 2012. *Social Determinants of Health and Well-Being among Young People: Health Behavior in School-Aged Children.* Copenhagen, Denmark: World Health Organization Regional Office for Europe.

Deci, Edward L., and Richard M. Ryan. 1991. "A Motivational Approach to Self: Integration in Personality." *Nebraska Symposium on Motivation: Perspectives on Motivation* 38: 237–88.

Edwards, Lisa M., and Shane J. Lopez. 2006. "Perceived Family Support, Acculturation, and Life Satisfaction in Mexican American Youth: A Mixed-Methods Exploration." *Journal of Counseling Psychology* 53 (3): 279–87. doi:10.1037/0022-0167.53.3.279.

EMN (European Migration Network). 2011. *Satisfying Labor Demand through Migration: EMN Synthesis Report.* Brussels: Home Affairs.

Geay, Charlotte, Sandra McNally, and Shqiponja Telhaj. 2013. "Non-Native Speakers of English in the Classroom: What Are the Effects on Pupil Performance?" *Economic Journal* 123 (570): 281–307.

Goodenow, Carol. 1993. "Classroom Belonging among Early Adolescent Students' Relationships to Motivation and Achievement." *Journal of Early Adolescence* 13 (1): 21–43.

Heath, Anthony, and Yaël Brinbaum, eds. 2014. *Unequal Attainments: Ethnic Educational Inequalities in Ten Western Countries.* Oxford: Oxford University Press/Proceedings of the British Academy.

Helliwell, John F., and Robert D. Putnam. 2004. "The Social Context of Well-Being." *Philosophical Transactions of the Royal Society B: Biological Studies* 359: 1435–46.

Henry, Carolyn S. 1994. "Family System Characteristics, Parental Behaviors, and Adolescent Family Life Satisfaction." *Family Relations* 43 (4): 447–55.

Huebner, E. Scott. 2004. "Research on Assessment of Life Satisfaction of Children and Adolescents." *Social Indicators Research* 66 (1–2): 3–33.

Huebner, E. Scott., Benjamin A. Funk III, and Rich Gilman. 2000. "Cross-Sectional and Longitudinal Psychosocial Correlates of Adolescent Life Satisfaction Reports." *Canadian Journal of School Psychology* 16 (1): 53–64.

Huebner, E. Scott, and Rich C. Gilman. 2014. "Adolescent Life Satisfaction Measurement." In *Encyclopedia of Quality of Life and Well-Being Research,* edited by Alex C. Michalos, 37–40. The Netherlands: Springer.

Juvonen, Jaana. 2006. "Sense of Belonging, Social Bonds, and School Functioning." In *Handbook of Educational Psychology*, edited by Patricia A. Alexander and Philip H. Winne, 655–74. Mahwah, NJ: Erlbaum.

Katja, Rask, Åstedt-Kurki Païvi, Tarkka Marja-Terttu, and Laippala Pekka. 2002. "Relationships among Adolescent Subjective Well-Being, Health Behavior, and School Satisfaction." *Journal of School Health* 72 (6): 243–49.

Lee, Valerie E., and David T. Burkam. 2003. "Dropping Out of High School: The Role of School Organization and Structure." *American Educational Research Journal* 40 (2): 353–93.

Levels, Mark, Jaap Dronkers, and Gerbert Kraaykamp. 2008. "Immigrant Children's Educational Achievement in Western Countries: Origin, Destination, and Community Effects on Mathematical Performance." *American Sociological Review* 73 (5): 835–53.

Liebkind, Karmela, and Inga Jasinskaja-Lahti. 2000. "The Influence of Experiences of Discrimination on Psychological Stress: A Comparison of Seven Immigrant Groups." *Journal of Community and Applied Social Psychology* 10 (1): 1–16. doi:10.1002/(SICI)1099–1298.

Lippman, Laura H., Kristin A. Moore, and Hugh McIntosh. 2011. "Positive Indicators of Child Well-Being: A Conceptual Framework, Measures, and Methodological Issues." *Applied Research in Quality of Life* 6 (4): 425–49.

Maslow, Abraham H. 1943. "A Theory of Human Motivation." *Psychological Review* 50 (4): 370–96.

———. 1954. Motivation and Personality. New York: Harper and Row.

Myers, David G., and Ed Diener. 1995. "Who Is Happy?" *Psychological Science* 6 (1): 10–19.

Navarro, Raúl, Roberto Ruiz-Oliva, Elisa Larrañaga, and Santiago Yubero. 2015. "The Impact of Cyberbullying and Social Bullying on Optimism, Global and School-Related Happiness, and Life Satisfaction among 10–12-Year-Old Schoolchildren." *Applied Research in Quality of Life* 10 (1): 15–36.

Neto, Felix. 1993. "The Satisfaction with Life Scale: Psychometrics Properties in an Adolescent Sample." *Journal of Youth and Adolescence* 22 (2): 125–34.

Niebuhr, Annekatrin. 2010. "Migration and Innovation: Does Cultural Diversity Matter for Regional R&D Activity?" *Papers in Regional Science* 89 (3): 563–85.

OECD (Organization for Economic Cooperation and Development). 2010. *Educating Teachers for Diversity: Meeting the Challenge*. Paris: OECD Publishing.

———. 2014. *PISA 2012 Technical Report*. Paris: OECD Publishing.

———. 2015a. *International Migration Outlook 2015*. Paris: OECD Publishing.

———. 2015b. *Immigrant Students at School: Easing the Journey towards Integration*. Paris: OECD Publishing.

———. 2016a. *Equations and Inequalities: Making Mathematics Accessible to All*. Paris: OECD Publishing.

———. 2016b. *PISA 2015 Results (Volume I): Excellence and Equity in Education*. Paris: OECD Publishing.

———. 2017. *PISA 2015 Results (Volume III): Students' Well-Being*. Paris: OECD Publishing.

OECD/EU (European Union). 2014. *Matching Economic Migration with Labour Market Needs.* Paris: OECD Publishing.

———. 2015. *Indicators of Immigrant Integration 2015: Settling In.* Paris: OECD Publishing.

Ohinata, Asako, and Jan C. van Ours. 2013. "How Immigrant Children Affect the Academic Achievement of Native Dutch Children." *Economic Journal* 123 (570): 308–31.

Parrotta, Pierpaolo, Dario Pozzoli, and Mariola Pytlikova. 2012. "The Nexus between Labor Diversity and Firm's Innovation." Institute for the Study of Labor IZA Discussion Paper 6972. Bonn: Institute for the Study of Labor.

Pfeifer, Jennifer H., Christia Spears Brown, and Jaana Juvonen. 2007. "Teaching Tolerance in Schools: Lessons Learned since *Brown v. Board of Education* about the Development and Reduction of Children's Prejudice." *Social Policy Report* 21 (2): 3–23.

Putnam, Robert D. 2007. "*E pluribus unum:* Diversity and Community in the Twenty-First Century: The 2006 Johan Skytte Prize Lecture." *Scandinavian Political Studies* 30 (2): 137–74.

Resnick, Michael D., Peter S. Bearman, Robert Wm Blum, Karl E. Bauman, Kathleen M. Harris, Jo Jones, Joyce Tabor et al. 1997. "Protecting Adolescents from Harm: Findings from the National Longitudinal Study on Adolescent Health." *JAMA* 278 (10): 823–32.

Sánchez, Bernadette, Yarí Colón, and Patricia Esparza. 2005. "The Role of Sense of School Belonging and Gender in the Academic Adjustment of Latino Adolescents." *Journal of Youth and Adolescence* 34 (6): 619–28.

Schneeweis, Nicole. 2015. "Immigrant Concentration in Schools: Consequences for Native and Migrant Students." *Labour Economics* 35: 63–76.

Schulenberg, John, Jerald G. Bachman, Patrick M. O'Malley, and Lloyd D. Johnston. 1994. "High School Educational Success and Subsequent Substance Use: A Panel Analysis Following Adolescents into Young Adulthood." *Journal of Health and Social Behavior* 35 (1): 45–62.

Shin, D. C., and D. M. Johnson. 1978. "Avowed Happiness as an Overall Assessment of the Quality of Life." *Social Indicators Research* 5 (4): 475–92.

Sturgis, Patrick, Ian Brunton-Smith, Jouni Kuha, and Jonathan Jackson. 2014. "Ethnic Diversity, Segregation, and the Social Cohesion of Neighborhoods in London." *Ethnic and Racial Studies* 37 (8): 1286–1309.

Suedekum, Jens, Katja Wolf, and Uwe Blien. 2014. "Cultural Diversity and Local Labour Markets." *Regional Studies* 48 (1): 173–91.

Sun, Rachel C. F., and Daniel T. L. Shek. 2009. "Life Satisfaction, Positive Youth Development, and Problem Behavior among Chinese Adolescents in Hong Kong." *Social Indicators Research* 95 (3): 455–74.

UNESCO (United Nations Educational, Scientific, and Cultural Organization). 2007. *Guidelines on Intercultural Education.* Paris: UNESCO.

———. 2014. *Global Citizenship Education: Preparing Learners for the Challenges of the 21st Century.* Paris: UNESCO.

UNICEF (United Nations Children's Fund). 2015. *Uprooted: The Growing Crisis for Refugee and Migrant Children.* New York: UNICEF.

Vallerand, Robert J. 1997. "Toward a Hierarchical Model of Intrinsic and Extrinsic Motivation." In *Advances in Experimental Social Psychology,* edited by James M. Olson and Mark P. Zanna, 271–360. Cambridge, MA: Academic Press.

Van Driel, Barry, Merike Darmody, and Jennifer Kerzil. 2016. *Education Policies and Practices to Foster Tolerance, Respect for Diversity, and Civic Responsibility in Children and Young People in the EU.* Brussels: European Commission.

West, Patrick, Helen Sweeting, and Robert Young. 2010. "Transition Matters: Pupils' Experiences of the Primary–Secondary School Transition in the West of Scotland and Consequences for Well-Being and Attainment." *Research Papers in Education* 25 (1): 21–50.

EPILOGUE

Pope Francis on Migration

Marcelo Sánchez Sorondo

As this volume suggests, given the causes of this new global phenomenon of migration, the best way to solve it would be to promote sustainable development in the countries of origin, together with a new global distributive justice, so that all the members of the human family can participate with equal dignity in the banquet of life without having to change their place of residence, with the consequent cultural adaptation disorders (linguistic, family related, social, moral, and religious; see Sen 1983 on the causes of famine and Sachs on women and inequality). As John Rawls (1999, 8–9) affirms in *The Law of Peoples*:

> There are numerous causes of immigration. I mention several and suggest that they would disappear in the Society of liberal and decent Peoples. One is the persecution of religious and ethnic minorities, the denial of their human rights. Another is political oppression of various forms, as when the members of the peasant classes are conscripted and hired out by monarchs as mercenaries in their dynastic wars for power and territory. Think of the Hessian troops who deserted the British Army and became citizens of the United States after the American Revolution. Often people are simply fleeing from starvation, as in the Irish famine of the 1840s. Yet famines are often themselves in large part caused by political failures and the absence of decent government. The last cause . . . is population pressure in the home territory, and among its complex of causes is the inequality and subjection of women. Once that inequality and subjection are overcome, and women are granted equal political participation with men and assured education, these problems can be resolved. Thus, religious freedom and liberty of conscience, political freedom and constitutional liberties, and equal justice for women are fundamental aspects of sound social policy for a realistic utopia . . . The problem of immigration is not, then, simply left aside, but is eliminated as a serious problem in a realistic utopia.

This condition also applies to the new tragedy of child migration—a topic carefully examined in this volume (see Bhabha, chapter 3; C. Suárez-Orozco, chapter 4, and others, this volume). Countries of origin lack the capacity to adequately protect their children. A delegation of US bishops found that Guatemala, Honduras, and El Salvador do not have adequate structures in law enforcement, social welfare, child welfare, and education systems to protect children. Unfortunately, gangs and other criminal elements are active in many communities and schools, and governments seem unable to curb their influence because of corruption, lack of political will, or resources. Poorly paid and undertrained law enforcement personnel can be influenced by these criminal elements.

Funds allocated to public education systems are far from sufficient, and many children only reach sixth or seventh grade. Public child welfare services are virtually nonexistent, as are foster care, family reunification, and resettlement. Naturally, if this is the state of things in the countries of migration origin, it would seem to be one further reason to provide these people with documents rather than to deny them. Although the general perception prevalent in the United States is that people want to migrate for economic reasons, the US delegation found that a growing number are fleeing violence in their own countries. The increasing number of asylum applications reveals a more complex picture. For example, many children enter the United States to join their families in search of security. Denying them asylum could mean abandoning them to gang violence and drug traffickers and would ultimately seal their doom. Pope Francis has severely condemned this attitude, which is the worst aspect of the globalization of indifference, numerous times. However, the speech he delivered on the 2017 World Day of Migrants and Refugees is of particular importance (Pope Francis 2017b).

The truth is that despite the commitments made and renewed, the twenty-six most advanced countries allocate only 0.22 percent of their Gross National Product (GDP) to development cooperation policies, instead of the promised 0.7 percent. This situation is truly paradoxical. In the face of rising migratory pressure—as discussed in the previous paragraph—countries in the developed West have responded by reducing development aid instead of increasing it.

The issue of migration thus becomes part of the philosophical reflection, on the one hand, on what our present knowledge of man and woman singularly considered is, and on the other hand, on the larger picture of the political nature of the human being in the new context of a unitary and socially sustainable development of the human family the world over.

THE INALIENABLE RIGHTS OF THE PERSON

As we hope for a new and fairer international society, the continuous growth of migratory flows from the places of origin to the havens of well-being requires a

profound analysis of the reasons that have led to the recognition of the fundamental and inalienable rights of the human persons, men and women, and their relationship to the common good, regardless of their geographical origin.

St. Thomas Aquinas would have said very realistically that what we are addressing is an essential point of human nature, natural law, the law of nations, civil law,
and modern human rights. As well as being inclined to the good, human nature
also possesses a particular light, the ability to discern good from evil. This original
discerning ability to order the acts of each subject and of the entire human society
to the attainment of a goal has been called "natural law," and it comes from man's
participation in the divine light of God: "*Unde . . . lex naturales nihil aliud est quam
participatio legis aeternae in rationali criaturae.*"[1]

Natural law is thus the active principle that informs and directs practical reason
(*ratio practica*), guiding the will and being guided by the will in the choice of the
ends and means in the existential sphere of the life of each person and in the specific order of society or family of persons. Therefore, natural law is determined and
binding as a norm: one must choose good and avoid evil. And this is true not only
for each individual singularly considered but also for the other beings of the same
nature. All human beings participate in the same nature, and each should love her
or his fellow human beings. Therefore, as Pope Benedict reminds us in his Exhortation *Deus Caritas Est*, loving one's neighbor is the direct consequence of God's
love, together with and consequent to the love that each of us has for ourselves:
"both live from the love of God who has loved us first."[2]

Thus, the goods to which the natural law is primarily inclined are individual life
for each person, procreation for the species, and education of one's children. As far
as the higher sphere of the human being, it is the "natural inclination to know the
truth about God, and to live in society: and in this respect, whatever pertains to
this inclination belongs to the natural law; for instance, to shun ignorance, to
avoid offending those among whom one has to live, and other such things regarding the above inclination" ["*inclinatio secundum naturam rationis, quae est sibi
propria: sicut homo habet naturales inclinationem ad hoc quod veritatem cognoscat
de Deo et ad hoc quod in societate vivat*"] (St. Thomas Aquinas).[3]

PRIMARY AND SECONDARY NATURAL LAW

There are many other dispositions that are useful for life as an individual and
within society that are not directly regulated by natural law, hence the need and
opportunity to determine natural law with precise positive laws. For this reason,
St. Thomas distinguishes between primary natural law and secondary natural law.
All that pertains to nature is of primary natural law, whereas the necessary conclusions of the general principles of natural law, deduced by human reason in the
course of a suffered history on the basis of scientific procedures in view of the

common good, pertain to secondary natural law. These conclusions constitute the law of peoples in the ancient world and the human rights of modernity after the last two World Wars. For example, the fact that all human beings have equal freedom of movement and all the other freedoms, together with the common possession of the goods of the earth, pertains to primary natural law "because nature did not bring in the contrary: thus we might say that for man to be naked is of the natural law, because nature did not give him clothes, but art invented them" (St. Thomas Aquinas).[4]

Hence, it is necessary to emphasize above all that freedom of migration, like all other fundamental freedoms, starting with religious freedom, belongs to the inalienable and primary rights of the human being. John XXIII already affirmed this right in his famous Encyclical *Pacem in terris*: "And among man's personal rights, we must include his right to enter a country in which he hopes to be able to provide more fittingly for himself and his dependents. It is therefore the duty of State officials to accept such immigrants and—so far as the good of their own community, rightly understood, permits—to further the aims of those who may wish to become members of a new society."[5]

Now, this primary natural law is followed by the conclusions that reason orders to the common good that are called the law of nations (*ius gentium*) even by some contemporary authors addressing human rights. Thus, private property, social conditions, and clothing were not introduced by nature but by man's reason as useful to human life. If we apply St. Thomas's fruitful distinction between primary and secondary law to the issue of migration, we could say that since fundamental freedoms and the common destination of goods pertain to primary natural law, so does each person's freedom to migrate. Likewise, just as the various social conditions and private property pertain to natural secondary law, so does the legal structuring of the willingness to welcome migrants in the light of the common good. This criterion of the common good for the regulation of migratory flows is one of the indispensable conditions that human reason considers necessary to make sure that migratory settlements are carried out with the necessary guarantee of respect for the dignity of the human person.

In this interpretation, the law of nations and modern human rights belongs to natural law because man is by nature a "social animal," as Aristotle explains in his *Politics*.[6] On the contrary, the provisions derived from the natural law as secondary determinations belong to civil law, which each nation determines according to its needs. With respect to the common good, St. Thomas is also inspired by another principle of the Philosopher, which says, "The whole is greater than the part," hence the "*bonus exercitus est bonus ducis*," which guides a community to its goal.[7] Besides, it is a fundamental principle of the Magisterium of Pope Francis. This principle is extensively explored in EG §§ 234–37 and further examined, in a briefer form, in *Laudato Si'* (§ 141).

THE ROLE OF NATIONAL BORDERS

It can hardly be said that the historical borders of nations pertain to natural law. There is often a certain correspondence between geographical configurations and legal boundaries. For example, it is clear that the peaks of the Andes are a geographical separation that can become a political boundary, and many other examples of this type can be argued, but I do not think it is possible to go much further in this analysis. Therefore, since national borders are historically largely arbitrary, we can conclude that they belong to the law of nations. In the absence of a world state, nations need borders of a certain kind, although when considered in and of themselves, they appear to be arbitrary and somewhat dependent on historical circumstances.

As arbitrary as a nation's borders may seem from a historical and legal point of view, an important function belonging to the government of a nation is to become a representative and effective agent of its nation when it takes on responsibility for a territory and for its environmental integrity as well as for the natural and man-made goods that derive from labor and the size of its population. It can be said that the meaning of the establishment of the territorial limits of a nation is analogous to the establishment of private property within a nation and consists in the fact that if there is no specific agent responsible for the conservation of a source of income or wealth, to whom we can attribute the merit or fault of acting or not in that sense, such wealth will tend to lose value. In our case, the source of income is, on the one hand, the territory where a nation has been established and, on the other, the ability of such a nation to provide the necessary means to guarantee the sustenance of the present and future generations of its citizens. The agent is thus the nation itself, politically organized and responsible for its own territory. However, just as in the case of private property with respect to the universal destination of the goods of the earth, an organized nation must recognize that it cannot compensate for administering its own territory irresponsibly by invading another nation or by migrating to it without reaching a prior consensus or agreement with said nation.

This observation implies that a nation has, through its rulers, on the one hand, the obligation and the right to obtain the common good and the goods necessary for its subsistence. On the other hand, a nation that through its rulers obtains the common good for its citizens also has the right to control migration on its own territory in correspondence with its own natural resources and employment capabilities.

NEED FOR REGULATION

The citizens of a nation intervene in migration issues in different capacities and express different points of view, whether in relation to migrants and their governments, employers who often bring in migrant workers, credit institutions, or trade unions or whether in relation to the rulers of the recipient countries, charities, public opinion, or the media. Hence, there is the need to mediate on behalf of the public and religious authorities in order to reconcile the different points of view and to establish an articulated picture within which each will be able to exercise his or her personal responsibility with respect to the migrants. No one is exempt from exercising her or his own responsibility. This responsibility is exercised at different levels. While individuals should first of all offer migrants a *"cordiale e disinteressata,"* that is, a "cordial and disinterested" welcome, following the wonderful indications of St. John Paul II[8] manifesting the richness of the culture, civilization, and faith of such welcoming people, governors, without falling into overly strict security concerns that are born of selfishness, should promote social peace through ad hoc institutions that assist and aid migrant and indigenous peoples alike to uncover the mutual enrichment that can result from their encounter.

Hence, the need for a regulation of the exercise of the right to migrate by the civil authorities has never been discussed in the numerous documents dealing with the right to migrate. For example, Article 29 (1) of the Universal Declaration of Human Rights mentions "the duties of individuals towards the community in which only the free and full development of their personality is possible." Article 12 of the *International Covenant on Civil and Political Rights,* while fully recognizing the right to freedom of movement, specifies in paragraph 3: "The above-mentioned rights shall not be subject to any restrictions except those which are provided by law, are necessary to protect national security, public order, public health or morals, or the rights and freedoms of others, and are consistent with the other rights recognized in the present Covenant."[9]

A CONFLICT OF DUTIES

With regard to individuals and disadvantaged groups, migration in search of survival is a right that cannot be denied because the preservation of one's life is a primary natural right that the human being shares with all living beings, as we have seen. St. Thomas Aquinas reflects the Christian tradition and guides it when he says, "In cases of necessity all things are common."[10] The goods of the earth, including those in the hands of private property or that are the property of other nations, and land itself, have a common origin and a universal destination, which is to serve for the sustenance of all human beings. For this reason, "it is not theft, properly speaking, to take secretly and use another's property in a case of extreme need . . . because that which he takes for the support of his life becomes his own property by reason of that need."[11] If, in a particular circumstance of extreme need, something were deprived of this common destination, that is, of helping everyone, it would automatically become public or common property because the right to life is higher than the right of ownership.[12] Basically, the European rulers who take in irregular migrants (avoiding the tragedy of casting them into the sea, be it a real ocean or a sea of indifference) landing on their shores (or arriving in other similar circumstances) looking for bread embody this basic need. Likewise, the American nations that are benevolent in welcoming those who are truly disadvantaged act according to these basic rights. This was also the context for John Paul II's appeal in the *Angelus* of November 16, 2003, when he said: "Many see the building of a wall between the Israeli and Palestinian peoples as yet another obstacle on the path to peaceful coexistence. Indeed, *the Holy Land does not need walls, but bridges!* Without the reconciliation of souls, there can be no peace" (italics added).[13] Pope Francis also adopts this dialectic of walls and bridges when he talks about migration. Moreover, as we have seen, St. Thomas (and with him the Magisterium of the Popes) indicates that human beings are social animals and thus also have the primary duty to support their families and educate their children. It is therefore necessary to combine the duty of reception with the obligation of a progressive insertion of the migrant into the economic, social, and cultural fabric of the country where he or she has settled. I would like to add that adequate education for the children of migrants is an essential mediation, as mandated by the recent workshop on education organized by the two Pontifical Academies.

Thus, the citizens of the host country are caught between two opposite needs. On the one hand, they cannot be indifferent to the plight of irregular migrants. In this sense there are already many statements by bishops who adhere to and have commented on Paul VI's maxim for the World Day of Peace in 1971: "Every man is my brother." Of course, this theme is currently being further developed by Pope Francis. An example of this effort can be seen in the four speeches he has delivered, one every year, during the World Day of Migrants and Refugees. The most recent speech he delivered is of particular importance as he addresses the issue of child migrants (Pope Francis 2017b).

On the other hand, the citizens of the receiving country cannot ignore the fact that they belong to a national community and have a consequent duty to respect its laws unless they are manifestly unjust. Laws cannot be judged manifestly unjust when, for reasons pertaining to the common good, they restrict migration. In view of the common good, rulers have the duty to ensure that migration to their countries does not jeopardize the national community made up of its majority population from the economic, social, cultural, political, and even religious points of view. This conflict of duties is clearly reflected in the rights that stem from natural law, the law of nations, the positive laws, and human rights in view of the common good. The question is, what does "common good" mean?

THE COMMON GOOD

The search for the common good is of little importance in ancient Stoicism, in utilitarianism or modern ultraliberalism, or in other contemporary philosophies that propose an overly individualistic and egocentric concept of the human person.

On the other hand, in St. Thomas and in the Magisterium of the Popes, the doctrine of the common good is of capital importance thanks to the concept of man as an eminently social being, as the "political animal" of Aristotelian origin. The human being cannot satisfy his own capabilities and potential, whether material or spiritual, nor can he achieve fulfilment in the cultural and spiritual realm without friendship, justice, collaboration, and solidarity with other human beings. As the Angelic Doctor says, it is also and above all the social and moral capabilities and inclinations that direct the human being toward the common good:

> For men form a group for the purpose of living well together, a thing which the individual man living alone could not attain, and good life is virtuous life. Therefore, virtuous life is the end for which men gather together. The evidence for this lies in the fact that only those who render mutual assistance to one another in living well form a genuine part of an assembled multitude. If men assembled merely to live, then animals and slaves would form a part of the civil community. Or if men assembled only to accrue wealth, then all those who traded together would belong to one city. Yet we see that only such are regarded as forming one multitude as are directed by the same laws and the same government to live well.[14]

Living with other human beings in a social community or state is thus perfectly consistent with human nature and is not simply (as Hobbes affirmed instead) a sort of constraint that must be imposed on it on the basis of recognizing a particular interest. Since human capabilities are manifold and converge only partially or by participation, there arises the need for an institution to orient the multiplicity of the possibilities possessed by human beings toward a single common good.

We can say that Pius XII uses this Thomist notion of the common good in his famous Christmas message of 1942 on the subject of democracy. John XXIII makes more than one reference to the common good in his Encyclical *Pacem in terris*. *Gaudium et spes* and *Dignitatis humanae* also resort to this fecund notion. Pope Francis conveys the doctrine of common good in both of the official documents that he has published: the Apostolic Exhortation *Evangelii Gaudium* and the Encyclical *Laudato Sì*. They, like St. Thomas, consider that the common good corresponds to the search for the external and internal conditions necessary for the development of the good life (ranging from material goods to moral and intellectual virtues, right up to religious virtues) of the people forming a society in order for them to reach the highest possible quality of life compatible with their dignity as human beings.

DETERMINATION OF THE CONTENT OF THE COMMON GOOD

The role of civil authorities, and in part of religious ones, is to achieve what they consider to be the best for all. Thanks to their extensive experience accumulated in the course of history and sufferance, democratic societies are aware that the knowledge that guides action is different from purely theoretical knowledge. Unlike truth, which is a goal pursued theoretically, the goal within the existential sphere of the human being is the pursuit of good and its practical implementation, which means acting well and living well, whether as individuals or as a community. Individual and social life are related to what Sophocles calls *to phronein*, the act of judging wisely. It is the virtue that Aristotle elevates to a high rank with the name of *phronesis*, a term that Latin authors have translated as *prudence*, which we can equate with practical wisdom.

This practical wisdom cannot have the same degree of precision as mathematics or geometry does, as Spinoza claimed for Ethics and Politics. Is consciousness, therefore, reduced to the pure arbitrariness of the ethics of a situation? Absolutely not. Like the doctor and the judge, a prudent person faced with a decision expresses the good and the bad, the better and the worse, often the lesser evil, as it appears at the end of a debate in which what count are the various norms and opinions and the good of the people themselves. The decision is therefore based on wisdom because it arises from a deliberation in the private forum of one's heart or in a public forum by means of a broad debate such as in a senate or council of wise men. Thus, the fact that the various social currents most often gather to defend different ideals forces the authorities to promote the agreement of these social parties with a broad debate, not referring to an abstract perspective as in the theoretical sciences but to a common practical way of thinking, to a similar set of convictions directed to action. Civil authorities must ensure that the various groups of which the population is composed establish a dialogue amongst themselves, on equal footing, in order to reach consensus on the component of the common good that has to be given priority at a particular time. In the absence of a single competent authority recognized by everyone to impose a particular aspect of the common good, the civil authority must encourage the implementation of a general order that can give each person what that individual believes he or she deserves in all fairness.

We can say that this moral-political conception of the common good according to justice leads theologians, philosophers, sociologists, and jurists to analyze its components vis-à-vis the problem of contemporary migration. Thus, they have identified three levels that are the source of three types of rights that clarify the ethical view on the situation of migrants.

Primary rights concern issues related to existence or subsistence and condition other related issues (such as accommodation, food, housing, and security). Pope Francis addressed this issue in Lampedusa (Pope Francis 2013).

Moreover, he further expanded this concept in Lesbos 2016, where he spoke about the good Samaritan and the largest humanitarian catastrophe since World War II (Pope Francis 2016b).

Let us call these rights the rights of peoples, referring to the legal guarantees of immigrants in primary rights, including the founding of institutions favorable to what Paul VI called the "organic participation" of the various social forces in managing a community. More precisely, this pope wrote in the Address to the Assembly of the International Labour Organization: "Your vocation is a freely organized and socially disciplined and organic participation in the responsibilities and in the profits of work" (Pope Paul VI 1969). Without citizenship (or something similar) in today's world, it becomes difficult to develop one's own abilities, especially those directly related to others, such as a profession.

Finally, there are responsibilities related to protecting, examining, and developing the values that underpin the deep, stable unity of a society and, more fundamentally, create a horizon of public peace understood precisely as St. Augustine's "tranquillity in order." The application of these three categories (survival, development of economic and social goods, and communion with deep values, including religious ones) requires a careful look at the various aspects of the issue. Some aspects are of a rather cultural order because not all national traditions ascribe the same importance to practical wisdom, democracy, and dialogue as Western civilization does today, after a long historical journey of configuration of these same values. Other aspects indicate that the structure of social relations, such as job categories, is also evolving despite being basically stable. Such observations are important in judging the attitude to be taken vis-à-vis migratory flows and especially vis-à-vis the degree and timing of social and cultural acceptability by the receiving country. To some extent, this message was established in an interview delivered by Pope Francis during his in-flight press conference from Sweden to Rome in 2016. The pope was asked what his message was to those who fear the arrival of refugees in European countries and what his message was to Sweden, which after a long tradition of welcoming is now starting to close its own borders. I believe his message is of vital importance:

First of all, as an Argentinean and South American, I am deeply grateful to Sweden for its openness because during the period of the military dictatorships many Argentineans, Chileans and Uruguayans found a welcome in Sweden. Sweden has a long tradition of welcoming others. Not only accepting them, but integrating them, finding them housing, schools, employment . . . integrating them into the population. I was told the number—I may be mistaken, I am not certain—[aside] how many inhabitants are there in Sweden? Nine million? Of these nine million—I was told—850,000 would be "new Swedes," that is, immigrants or refugees or their children. That is the first thing. Second, we have to distinguish between migrants and refugees, right? Migrants must be treated according to certain rules because migrating is a right, albeit a right which is highly regulated. On the other hand, being a refugee is the result of situations of war, suffering, hunger, terrible situations, and the refugee's status calls for great attention, greater effort. Here too, Sweden has been exemplary in settling refugees, helping them to learn the language, the culture, and integrating them into its culture. As far as this aspect of integrating into the culture is concerned, we should not be fearful because Europe was formed by a constant integration of cultures, many cultures. . . . I believe that—and here I certainly do not mean to give offense—today in Iceland, Icelanders, with today's Icelandic language, can read their own classics from a thousand years ago without any real difficulty; this shows that it is a country that has experienced little immigration, few of those "waves" that Europe experienced. Europe has been formed by migrations. . . .

Beyond this, what do I think of countries that close their frontiers? I think that, in theory, hearts must not be closed to refugees, but those who govern need prudence. They must be very open to receiving refugees, but they also have to calculate how best to settle them because refugees must not only be accepted but also integrated. Consequently, if a country has, say, the ability to integrate twenty persons, they should do this. Another country that has greater capacity should do more. But always with an open heart: it is not human to close the door, it is not human to close the heart, and in the long run, a price is paid for this. Here, the price is political, just as a political price can be paid for an imprudent judgement, for accepting more than can be integrated. What is the danger when refugees or migrants—and this applies to everybody—are not integrated? They become a ghetto. A culture that does not develop in relationship with another culture, this is dangerous. I think that fear is the worst counsellor of countries that tend to close their borders, while the best counsellor is prudence. I talked with an official of the Swedish government these days, and he told me of some difficulties they are presently facing—and this has to do with your last question—some difficulties because so many are arriving that there is no time to make provision for them so that they can find schools, homes, employment, and learn the language. Prudence has to make this calculation. But Sweden . . . I do not believe that if Sweden lessens its ability to receive, it does so for selfish reasons or because it has lost that capacity. If something of the sort happens, it is for the last reason I mentioned. Today many people look to Sweden because they are aware of its openness, but there is not enough time to settle them all. I don't know if this answers your question. Thank you. (Pope Francis 2016a)

A certain, at least time-related, difference can be found in the practical judgment of each person and of the various groupings in determining the attitude to be taken when faced with the ethical demands of the three categories of the common good and the consequent rights described. While agreements on the essential needs of migrant populations must be reached quickly, divergent views may appear at the other two levels. Participation in cultural goods and other similar ones, which affect the historical structuring of a nation's values, is most often linked to the preliminary achievement of objective conditions of dialogue among social parties. Finally, the mutual recognition and reciprocal valuation that will result from such a dialogue will lead to a more thorough and participatory reexamination of the representation of common goods and values that each nation must be able to give itself.

Hence, against all forms of selfishness of practical reason, the Social Doctrine of the Church recalls that migration, as well as being a primary right for those in need, may also constitute an "aggregate" good for those who receive migrants, not only from the economic and social point of view but also from the cultural and religious one, which is what we have already indicated as "signs of hope." It is necessary, therefore, to encourage orderly migratory flows, whose results can be seen not in the short term but in the long term with historical patience. I cannot fail to mention here the famous political sentence of one of the most considerate presidents of the Argentine Republic, Carlos Pellegrini, who was brave enough to say that "governing means populating." When faced with the "ethical blindness" of practical reason mentioned by Pope Benedict XVI and the globalization of indifference proclaimed by Pope Francis, it is ever more necessary for the Church to be the eschatological energy of God that purifies and elevates. In a world that manifests, whether privately or openly, a certain intolerance, the ecclesial community must be the moral entity that makes possible the will of the God of Love: a world that is friendly and just in the diversity of the human family, the city of love that anticipates as much as possible the heavenly Jerusalem. Nietzsche's nihilistic and relativistic dreams still loom over the transparency of the human environment like threatening shadows. There are still groups and individuals who believe they are called to be supermen, superior to others, to the point of having the right to mediatize or enslave them. For this reason, the words of the Lord of the Last Judgment so masterfully portrayed by Michelangelo in the Sistine Chapel must resound with all their freshness for the good people of the political community and for the life of the Church: "I was a stranger and they welcomed me."[15]

Of course, the growing number of unaccompanied youths reaching the US border through Mexico is a different issue. In recent times, the largest group of such young people have come from El Salvador, Guatemala, Honduras, and Mexico. These youths are detained by the federal immigration authorities for lack of immigration permits and are placed in the custody and care of the Office of Refugee Resettlement (ORR) as well as the Department of Homeland Security (DHS). As discussed by various authors, it is estimated that more than 80,000 unaccompanied minors entered the United States in 2014. This number illustrates a growing trend in child migration (see C. Suárez-Orozco, chapter 4; Bhabha, chapter 3; and Suro, chapter 2, this volume). As these authors have said, it is not about migration but rather about reunification and, above all, about protection. In this case, the protection of these children pertains to primary natural law, and it should be up to the United States to strengthen protection for these unaccompanied migrant children, whom US law refers to as "unaccompanied foreign children" (UAC). These children have primary natural rights and even legal rights that must absolutely be respected. Often, they are frightened and cannot explain their fears or the circumstances that led them to escape their countries, let alone be aware of their rights according to the natural order and even to international and US law.

In short, the novelty of the teachings of Pope Francis regarding refugees is, on one hand, to add climate change as one of the principal causes of migration (this concept was never expressed before by previous Popes) and, on the other hand, to propose assistance to refugees and migrants as one of the main tasks of his pontificate, insisting on the duty that every man has to be "everyone's brother." As can be seen clearly from his first speech and testimony in Lampedusa and subsequently in Lesbos in 2016, this pronouncement does not mean that Pope Francis is neglecting the problem of the "organic participation" of refugees and immigrants in the life, laws, and values of the receiving people. This synthetic vision is well expressed in the last discourse on the subject: "Prudence on the part of public authorities does not mean enacting policies of exclusion vis-à-vis migrants, but it does entail evaluating, with wisdom and foresight, the extent to which their country is in a position, without prejudice to the common good of citizens, to offer a decent life to migrants, especially those truly in need of protection. Above all, the current crisis should not be reduced to a simple matter of numbers" (Pope Francis 2017a).

Balancing security and reception and establishing a ceiling on migration flows should not, however, make one lose sight of the fact that "migrants are persons, with their own names, stories and families. There can never be true peace as long as a single human being is violated in his or her personal identity and reduced to a mere statistic or an object of economic calculation" (Pope Francis 2017a).

Finally, I present an allusion to Italy and Greece, although the Pope did not explicitly mention these two nations in this context: "The issue of migration is not one that can leave some countries indifferent while others are left with the burden of humanitarian assistance, often at the cost of notable strain and great hardship, in the face of an apparently unending emergency. All should feel responsible for jointly pursuing the international common good also through concrete gestures of human solidarity; these are essential building-blocks of that peace and development [that] entire nations and millions of people still await." Finally, the pope expresses his gratitude to the welcoming countries: "So I am grateful to the many countries which offer a generous welcome to those in need, beginning with various European nations, particularly Italy, Germany, Greece and Sweden" (Pope Francis 2017a).

With "a *culture of mercy,*" it "will be possible to build societies that are open and welcoming towards foreigners and at the same time internally secure and at peace" (Pope Francis 2017a, emphasis in original).

NOTES

1. St. Thomas Aquinas, *Summa Theologica,* I–II, q. 91, a. 2.
2. Benedict XVI, *Deus est caritas,* par. 18.
3. St. Thomas Aquinas, *Summa Theologica,* I–II, q. 94, a. 2.
4. Ibid., q. 94, a. 5 ad 3.
5. John XXIII, Encyclical *Pacem in terris,* § 106, AAS 55 (1963) 286.
6. Book I, ch. 1.

7. "Sicut bonum multitudinis est maius quam bonum unius qui est de multitudine, ita est minus quam bonum extrinsecum ad quod multitudo ordinatur: sicut bonum ordinis exercitus est minus quam bonum ducis" (*Summa Theologica,* II–II, q. 39, a. 2 ad 2).

8. John Paul II, *Messaggio per la giornata mondiale dell'emigrazione,* 1989. Cfr. also J.P. II, "Alocución a los participantes de la asamblea plenaria del Consejo Pontificio para la inmigración," *L'Osservatore Romano,* December 3, 2002.

9. This formulation was used again in Article 12.3 of the Covenant of 1990 regarding the limitations that can be applied to the religious freedom of migrant workers.

10. *"In necessitate sunt omnia communia"* (*S. Th.,* II–II, q. 66, a. 7 *sed contra*).

11. "Uti re aliena occulte accepta in casu necessitatis extremae non habet rationem furti, proprie loquendo. Quia per talem necessitatem efficitur suum illud quod quis accipit ad sustentandam propriam vitam" (S. Th., II–II, q. 66, a. 7 ad 2).

12. St. Thomas Aquinas, *Summa Theologica,* II–II, q. 31, a. 3.

13. John Paul II, *Angelus,* November 16, 2003.

14. St. Thomas Aquinas, *De regno ad regem Cypri* [On kingship to the king of Cyprus], ch. 15, §106.

15. *Matthew* 25:35.

REFERENCES

Pope Francis. 2013. "Homily of Holy Father Francis." Arena sports camp, Salina Quarter, Lampedusa. July 8, 2013. http://w2.vatican.va/content/francesco/en/homilies/2013/documents/papa-francesco_20130708_omelia-lampedusa.html.

———. 2016a. "In-Flight Press Conference of His Holiness Pope Francis from Sweden to Rome." November 1, 2016. https://w2.vatican.va/content/francesco/en/speeches/2016/november/documents/papa-francesco_20161101_svezia-conferenza-stampa.html.

———. 2016b. Speech at Mòria Refugee Camp, Lesbos. April 16, 2016. http://w2.vatican.va/content/francesco/en/speeches/2016/april/documents/papa-francesco_20160416_lesvos-rifugiati.html.

———. 2017a. "Message of His Holiness Pope Francis to the Members of the Diplomatic Dorps Accredited to the Holy See for the Traditional Exchange of New Year Greetings." January 9, 2017. https://w2.vatican.va/content/francesco/en/speeches/2017/january/documents/papa-francesco_20170109_corpo-diplomatico.html.

———. 2017b. "Message of His Holiness Pope Francis for the World Day of Migrants and Refugees 2017." January 17, 2017. https://w2.vatican.va/content/francesco/en/messages/migration/documents/papa-francesco_20160908_world-migrants-day-2017.html.

Pope Paul VI. 1969. "Address of His Holiness Paul VI to the Assembly of the International Labor Organization." June 19, 1969.

Rawls, John. 1999. *The Law of Peoples.* Cambridge, MA: Harvard University Press.

Sachs, Jeffrey. 2017. "Economics, Demography, Environment, and Mass Migrations." Paper presented at the workshop "Humanitarianism and Mass Migration." UCLA, Los Angeles, January 18–19.

Sen, Amartya. 1983. *Poverty and Famines: An Essay on Entitlement and Deprivation.* Oxford: Oxford University Press.

LIST OF CONTRIBUTORS

ABDIRAHMAN ABDI is a community organizer for the Shanbaro Community Association in Chelsea, MA. He also serves as a research assistant for the Research Program on Children and Adversity at Boston College School of Social Work. Abdi received an associate's degree in computer science from Northshore Community College in 2012. Abdi was twice awarded an Unsung Heroes Award for Social Justice in the City of Boston and Chelsea for his dedication to improving the health and well-being of his Somali Bantu community.

SAIDA ABDI is a PhD Candidate at Boston University School of Social Work/Sociology. She is also Associate Director for Community Relations at the BCHRTRC. Her research focuses on factors related to resilience among refugee and immigrant children and families and the use of CBPR to promote community engagement in research.

J. LAWRENCE ABER is the Willner Family Professor of Applied Psychology and Public Policy and a University Professor at New York University, as well as co-director of the Global TIES for Children Center. He is a developmental psychologist who conducts rigorous evaluations of innovative programs and policies for children, youth, and families in areas such as promotion of socio-emotional learning, violence prevention, literacy development, social protection, and comprehensive services initiatives. He has co-edited *Neighborhood Poverty: Context and Consequences for Children* (1997), *Assessing the Impact of September 11th, 2001, on Children, Youth, and Parents: Lessons for Applied Developmental Science* (2004), and *Child Development and Social Policy: Knowledge for Action* (2007).

JAMES A. BANKS is the Kerry and Linda Killinger Endowed Chair in Diversity Studies at the University of Washington, Seattle. His research focuses on multicultural education and diversity and citizenship education in a global context. His books include *Cultural Diversity and Education: Foundations, Curriculum, and Teaching* (6th ed., 2016). He is the editor of *Diversity and Citizenship Education: Global Perspectives* (2004), the *Encyclopedia of Diversity in Education* (2012), and *Citizenship Education and Global Migration: Implications for The-ory, Research, and Teaching* (2017).

JENNA BERENT is the program manager for the Refugee Program, part of the Research Pro-gram on Children and Adversity through Boston College School of Social Work. She received her MPH in health policy and management and social and behavioral sciences from Boston University School of Public Health. She has worked domestically and globally in academic, NGO, and clinical settings to improve the health and well-being of refugee, immigrant, and other underserved populations.

THERESA S. BETANCOURT is the inaugural Salem Professor in Global Practice at the Boston College School of Social Work and director of the Research Program on Children and Adversity (RPCA). She is the principal investigator of ongoing mental health services research projects in Sierra Leone, Rwanda, and is engaged in community-based participa-tory research on family-based prevention for refugee children and adolescents resettled in the U.S. She has written on mental health and resilience in children facing adversity, includ-ing articles in *Child Development, Social Science and Medicine, JAMA Psychiatry, BMJ Psychiatry,* and *Pediatrics.*

JACQUELINE BHABHA, JD, MsC, is Professor of the Practice of Health and Human Rights at the Harvard T. H. Chan School of Public Health and director of research at the Harvard FXB Center for Health and Human Rights. She has published extensively on issues of tran-snational child migration and refugee protection, and most recently co-edited the *Research Handbook on Child Migration* (2018). Professor Bhabha currently serves on the board of the Scholars at Risk Network, the World Peace Foundation, the Institute on Statelessness and Inclusion, and the *Journal of Refugee Studies* and is a frequent adviser to UNHCR, UNICEF, IOM, and civil society organizations working on forced migration–related issues.

ÖZGE BINER is an affiliated researcher at the Institut interdisciplinaire d'anthropologie du contemporain, École des Hautes Études en Sciences Sociales. Her research focuses on legal-ization strategies of refugees living in Turkey and their coping mechanisms with "perma-nent temporality" in local and transnational contexts. A book based on her doctoral dis-sertation titled *Refugeehood in Turkey* was published in 2016.

IRINA BOKOVA served two 4-year terms as Director-General of UNESCO (2009–2017). She has been actively engaged in international efforts to advance education for all, gender equality, human rights and cultural dialogue. She was the first woman and the first Eastern European to lead the organization. Before her election, she was Bulgaria's first Secretary of State for European Integration, Minister of Foreign Affairs ad interim twice member of Parliament, ambassador to France and Monaco, and Permanent Delegate to UNESCO, among other distinguished positions, which included contributing to drafting Bulgaria's new constitution in 1991. She graduated from Moscow State Institute of International Rela-tions, was a fellow at the University of Maryland, and pursued an executive program at the John F. Kennedy School of Government.

FRANCESCA BORGONOVI is a Senior Policy Analyst in the Directorate for Education and Skills at the OECD, where she has been responsible for data analysis and analytical work in the Programme for International Student Assessment (PISA) and the Survey of Adult Skills (PIAAC), with a particular focus on gender and socio-economic disparities in academic achievement, engagement, and motivation, and on the outcomes of migrant and language-minority students. Her recent publications include *The Resilience of Students with an Immigrant Background: Factors that Shape Well-being* (2018) and *Immigrant Students at School— Easing the Journey towards Integration* (2015).

MAURICE CRUL is Distinguished Professor of Education and Diversity in the Sociology Department of the Vrije Universiteit Amsterdam. He has coordinated two major international projects: the TIES project (The Integration of the European Second generation) and the ELITES, Pathways to Success project. He is an expert on the school and labor market careers of children of immigrants and refugee children in both Europe and the Transatlantic. In 2017 he was awarded the European Research Council's Advanced Grant for the project Becoming A Minority (BAM) on the integration of people of native descent in majority-minority cities in Europe.

SARAH DRYDEN-PETERSON is an Associate Professor at the Harvard Graduate School of Education. She leads a research program on education in settings of armed conflict, focusing on the role of schools in the creation of peaceful, inclusive communities. Some of her recent work has appeared in the *American Educational Research Journal, Educational Researcher, Comparative Education Review,* and *Curriculum Inquiry.*

FONNA FORMAN is founding director of the Center on Global Justice and Associate Professor of Political Science at the University of California, San Diego. Her work engages issues at the intersection of ethics, public culture, climate justice, and the city. She is vice-chair of *Bending the Curve,* the 2015 University of California report on climate change solutions.

ROCHELLE L. FROUNFELKER is a post-doctoral fellow at the SHERPA Research Center, Department of Psychiatry, McGill University. She received her doctorate in social epidemiology from the Harvard T. H. Chan School of Public Health in 2017. Her research focuses on the psychosocial well-being of war-affected populations, including refugees.

BHUWAN GAUTAM, a former refugee from Bhutan who resettled to the US in 2008, is a co-founder of the Sanitation, Health and Nutrition Study Center, Nepal. He received his MPA from Westfield State University in 2017. He launched a non-profit that aids the social, cultural, educational, and health needs of resettled Bhutanese refugees in western Massachusetts. He also serves as a co-investigator and steering committee member for the Research Program on Children and Adversity at Boston College School of Social Work, and as a co-investigator for the Global Demography of Aging program at Harvard University.

ZAHARA HAJI works as a medical interpreter for the Somali and Maay Maay languages in upstate New York. She formerly worked as a research assistant for the Research Program on Children and Global Adversity at Harvard University and has a degree in Human Rights from a community college in Kenya.

ELIF KESKINER is working as a senior researcher at the Vrije Universiteit Amsterdam in the Becoming A Minority (BAM) project, which investigates the integration processes of native whites to the emerging majority-minority contexts in super-diverse cities. Her research interests cover a wide range of topics such as youth transitions, social mobility, and elite formation among ethnic minority youth. In 2017 she co-edited with Maurice Crul and Frans Lelie a special issue of *Ethnic and Racial Studies* called "The Upcoming New Elite among Children of Immigrants."

FRANS LELIE is working as the project manager of the Becoming A Minority (BAM) project at the Sociology Department of the Vrije Universiteit Amsterdam. She is also a "match-maker" in the project Takecarebnb, matching refugees, who have obtained a status but are still waiting in the Dutch asylum seeker centers for a home, to families willing to host some-one and to contribute in this direct way to the integration of refugees and the host society. She has published on children of immigrants and refugee children both in education and in the labor market.

PIERRE LÉNA is an emeritus astrophysicist at the University Paris–Diderot and Observatoire de Paris, and a member of the French Académie des sciences and the Pontifical Academy of Sciences. Besides his contributions in astrophysics, especially to the European Very Large Telescope in Chile, his involvement in science education, building up the worldwide move-ment *La main à la pâte* since 1995, is detailed in several books, including *L'Enfant et la sci-ence* (2005) and *Enseigner c'est espérer* (2012), and in numerous papers.

ALI MAALIM works for the Refugee and Immigrant Assistance Center (RIAC) in Boston, MA, and for Maine Immigrant and Refugee Services (MEIRS) in Lewiston, ME, as an inter-ventionist and expert consultant for the Research Program on Children and Adversity through Boston College School of Social Work. Ali has a Professional Community Health Worker Certificate and is currently working towards an associate's degree at Bunker Hill Community College. He has been actively engaged in improving the mental health of the Somali Bantu community since 2011.

TEJ MISHRA is a surveillance epidemiologist for the US Navy and Marine Corps Public Health Center in Portsmouth, VA. He received his MPH from Boston University in 2014. He is an active member of the Bhutanese community and has been engaged in improving refugee mental health for five years. He also works as a consultant for the Research Program on Children and Adversity at Boston College School of Social Work and as a researcher studying the mental health of adult Bhutanese refugees at Harvard School of Public Health. He has also served as a board chair, and currently advises the board of directors at The Refugee Center Online.

RICHARD F. MOLLICA, MD, MAR, is Professor of Psychiatry at Harvard Medical School and director of the Harvard Program in Refugee Trauma (HPRT). He is principal investigator in training and research in Lebanon, Liberia, Italy, and the USA. Dr. Mollica established, with his HPRT colleagues, one of the first refugee clinics in December 1981. He is the developer of the Harvard Trauma Questionnaire (HTQ). He has written extensively on refugee mental health. His books include: *Healing Invisible Wounds: Paths to Hope and Recovery in a Vio-lent World* (2009) and *Textbook of Global Mental Health: Trauma and Recovery, A Compan-ion Guide for Field and Clinical Care of Traumatized Persons Worldwide* (2011).

PEDRO A. NOGUERA is Distinguished Professor of Education and the director of the Center for the Transformation of Schools at the Graduate School of Education and Information Studies at UCLA. He is the author of several books, including his most recent, *Race, Equity and Education* (2016), and *The Crisis of Connection* with Niobe Way, Carol Gilligan, and Alisha Ali (2018).

MARIO PIACENTINI is an analyst in the OECD Education and Skills Directorate, where he is responsible for extending the Programme for International Student Assessment (PISA) to new assessment domains. He is the author of several peer-reviewed articles and reports, including the framework for the PISA 2018 Assessment of Global Competence and the PISA report on the well-being of students.

VEERABHADRAN RAMANATHAN is Distinguished Professor of Atmospheric and Climate Sciences, University of California at San Diego. He discovered the greenhouse effect of halocarbons such as CFCs. He represented the Holy See delegation to the UNFCC Paris climate summit as science advisor.

ANDREAS SCHLEICHER is Director for Education and Skills and Special Advisor on Education Policy to the Secretary-General at the Organisation for Economic Co-operation and Development (OECD). In addition to policy and country reviews, he oversees the Programme for International Student Assessment (PISA), the OECD Survey of Adult Skills (PIAAC), the OECD Skills Strategy, the OECD Teaching and Learning International Survey (TALIS), and the development and analysis of benchmarks on the performance of education systems (INES). He is the recipient of numerous honors and awards, including the Theodor Heuss Prize for Exemplary Democratic Engagement. He holds an Honorary Professorship at the University of Heidelberg.

JENS SCHNEIDER is a senior researcher at the Institute for Migration Research and Intercultural Studies (IMIS) of the Universität Osnabrück, Germany. He studied Anthropology and Ethnic Studies in Hamburg and Amsterdam and conducted extensive field research in Chile, Brazil, and Germany. His current research interests are with identity constructions and politics in super-diverse cities, education and social mobility in immigrant families, and—most recently—cultural production in migration societies.

MARCELO SÁNCHEZ SORONDO was born in Buenos Aires and was ordained a priest in 1968. He was Full Professor of the History of Philosophy at the Lateran University in Rome and Dean of the Faculty of Philosophy. He then became Full Professor of the History of Philosophy at the Libera Università Maria SS. Assunta, Rome. In 1998 he was appointed Chancellor of the Pontifical Academies of Sciences and Social Sciences by St. John Paul II, who then consecrated him titular Bishop of Vescovìo.

THEONI STATHOPOULOU is a sociologist and research director at the National Centre for Social Research in Greece. She serves as a member (alternate) of the European Statistical Advisory Committee (ESAC) at the Hellenic Statistical Advisory Board of the Hellenic Statistical Authority; a member of the Sectorial Scientific Council for Social Sciences of the National Council for Research and Innovation, the supreme advisory body for the formulation and implementation of the national policy for research in Greece; and of the Hellenic Foundation of Research and Innovation. Her work has appeared in Ashgate, Cambridge Scholars Publishers, Springer, McGill University Press, and Herbert von Halem Verlag.

CAROLA SUÁREZ-OROZCO is a Professor of Human Development and Psychology at UCLA and is the co-founder of Re-Imagining Migration. Her books include: *Transitions: The Development of the Children of Immigrants* (2016), *Learning a New Land: Immigrant Students in American Society* (2010), *Children of Immigration* (2002), and *Transformations: Migration, Family Life, and Achievement Motivation among Latino Adolescents* (1996).

MARCELO M. SUÁREZ-OROZCO is the Wasserman Dean and Distinguished Professor of Education at the UCLA Graduate School of Education and Information Studies. His research focuses on cultural psychology and psychological anthropology, with an emphasis on migration, globalization, and education. He served as the Thomas Professor of Education and Culture at Harvard and as University Professor at New York University. In January 2018 Pope Francis appointed him to the Pontifical Academy of Social Sciences.

ROBERTO SURO holds a joint appointment as a professor of journalism and public policy at the University of Southern California in Los Angeles. He is also director of the Tomás Rivera Policy Institute, a university research center. Prior to joining the USC faculty in August 2007, he was founding director of the Pew Hispanic Center, a research organization in Washington D.C. Suro worked as senior correspondent for *Time Magazine,* the *New York Times,* and at the *Washington Post.* He is the author of several books and several dozen book chapters, research reports, and other publications related to Latinos and immigration.

MARY C. WATERS is the John L. Loeb Professor of Sociology at Harvard University. She recently led the National Academy of Sciences report, *The Integration of Immigrants into American Society* (2016). Some of her other books include *Inheriting the City: The Children of Immigrants Come of Age* (2009), *Black Identities: West Indian Immigrant Dreams and American Realities* (2008), *The Next Generation: Immigrant Youth in a Comparative Perspective* (2016), and *The Changing Face of Home: The Transnational Lives of the Second Generation* (2006).

ALICE WUERMLI is Associate Director for Low-Income Countries at the Global TIES for Children Center at New York University, and co-founder of the Human Development Intervention Network. She has a PhD in Human Development from the University of California, Davis, and conducts work in both measurement and evaluation of programs for youth and families in low- and middle-income countries. She is currently co-investigator and project director at NYU, leading research and evaluation for the MacArthur Foundation 100&Change partnership between the Sesame Workshop and the International Rescue Committee, which provides early childhood development programming for the Syrian refugee response region in the Middle East.

HIROKAZU YOSHIKAWA is the Courtney Sale Ross University Professor of Globalization and Education at New York University and co-director of the NYU Global TIES for Children Center. His recent books include *Cradle to Kindergarten: A New Plan to Combat Inequality* (2017) and *Immigrants Raising Citizens: Undocumented Parents and Their Young Children* (2012). He is a fellow of the National Academy of Education and the American Academy of Political and Social Sciences.

INDEX

Page references in italic refer to illustrations.

Aadhaar biometric identification system
(India), 196
Aber, J. Lawrence, 22
Abu El-Haj, Thea, 244
academic knowledge: mainstream, 246–47;
transformative, 246, 247–48
Académie des sciences, 256. See also *La main
à la pâte*
Adelman, Elizabeth, 228n6
adolescent girls, migrant: exclusion of, 212;
vulnerability of, 23
adolescents: collective citizenship for, 94; rights
of, 22, 84. *See also* students; youth
Adverse Child Experiences (ACE) study, 134
Affordable Care Act, for immigrant families, 315
Afghanistan: IDPs of, 9; length of exile from, 16;
refugees from, 166, 176
Africa: forced migrations in, 10; human dispersal
from, 30n2; IDPs of, 11; migrant children
from, 85. *See also* children, African
African Americans, civic education for, 232
Aker (refugee), 218, 219
Alberts, Bruce, 255, 265n6
al-Haytham, Ibn: *Kitab Al-Manadhir,* 255,
264n3
American Dream, imperilment of, 295
anomie, mortality rates and, 294

anti-immigrant sentiment, strategies aimed at,
111–12. *See also* nativism; xenophobia
Antiterrorism and Effective Death Penalty Act
(1996), mass deportations under, 319
Apostoli of the Church of Greece (NGO), survey
of unaccompanied minors, 178
Arab Spring, 4
Aras, Bülent, 273, 277
Arbenz, Jacobo, 13
Arctic ice, retreat of, 44
Arendt, Hannah, 227
Aristotle, 360; on *phronesis,* 361; *Politics,* 356
Armenians, expulsion from Ottoman Empire, 3
Arts, Resources, and Curriculum (research
firm), study of school violence, 298
Asia: climate-related displacement in, 47–48, 50;
IDPs in, 9; internal migration in, 1; sea-level
rise in, 48
Asia-Pacific Center of Education for International Understanding, 214
asylum claims: abuse by voluntary migrants, 71;
within EU-28, 166; in Greek law, 165–66;
increases in, 346, 354; for migrant children,
87; nexus with migration, 71; streamlining of,
196; in Turkey, 287n1; for unaccompanied
children, 74, 86; by voluntary migrants, 71;
waiting periods for, 195–96

of, 27; social belonging for, 108; unauthorized, 28, 99; in United States, 26. *See also* education; families, mixed-status; students
children of immigrants (US): crime rates of, 314; education for, 310–12; ethnic discrimination against, 309; family formation patterns of, 314; health of, 313–14; impediments facing, 308, 314–20; inequality facing, 309, 315–16; integration of, 308–22; legal status of, 309; occupations of, 313; parents' education and, 311; targeted policy intervention for, 309; undocumented, 319; undocumented parents of, 209, 315, 318–19; US-born, 308, 319
children of immigrants, second generation, 99, 107; educational attainments of, 311–12, 315; family formation patterns of, 314; health problems of, 310, 313–14; integration of, 308; language attainments of, 335; marital relationships of, 317; Mexican men, 313; obesity rates of, 314; occupational attainments of, 313, 315; in PISA testing, 329, 330–32; racial stratification of, 315
child soldiers, 34n34, 190, 192
China: environmental displacements in, 6, 32n15; internal migration in, 1, 253; "Learning by Doing" project (science education), 253; residency-based registration in, 195
citizenship: conflict with diversity, 24; deculturalization for, 233; definitions of, 194, 195; failed, 24, 222, 223, 228, 244, 244, 293; and global migration, 233; inclusion through, 221–24; loss of, 236; versus national identity, 244; participatory, 244, 245, 246; pathways to, 219; recognized, 221–22, 244, 245, 246; refugees' pathways to, 194–95; socialization for, 244; structural exclusion from, 245; transformative, 24, 222, 244–46; waiting periods for, 195, 222. *See also* human rights cosmopolitan education; multicultural citizenship education; students, citizen
citizenship, global, 23, 209–17; cognitive knowledge for, 213; effect of communication technology on, 209; inclusive societies for, 213; skills for, 213; UNESCO's work for, 209. *See also* global citizenship education (GCE)
Clearing House on Global Citizenship Education, 214
climate change: adaptation to, 49, 51; causes of, 44; civil conflict and, 43; consequences of, 18, 46–48; current effects of, 44; displacement through, 46–48, 50, 262–63; education for,

24; effect on social capital, 48; harm to public health, 46, 56; historical overview of, 49–50; impact on militarization, 50; impact on securitization, 50; and Latin American migration, 75–76; *La main à la pâte* on, 258; models simulating, 55; resilience in, 17, 18; as threat multiplier, 43; urbanization and, 49; vulnerability to, 49
climate justice: global response for, 44, 56; public opinion on, 55; rapid response for, 56
climate migration, 5, 6–8, 43–56, 364–65; adaptation strategies of, 51, 53; agent-based modeling for, 52, 54–55; complex causality models for, 54–55; definitions for, 43, 52; estimates for, 46, 52; ethical response to, 51; global responses to, 7; human stories of, 55; international response to, 50–51; Latin American, 75–76; long-distance, 53; mass, 43–56; methodological challenges for, 51–55; mixed-methods approach to, 51–55; multilevel modeling for, 54; potential solutions for, 54–55; probabilistic approach to, 56; process maps of, 52; quantitative estimates for, 43–44; research on, 49–50, 51–55; short-distance, 53; slow progression factors in, 48; social capital of, 53; sociopolitical factors in, 51; spatial/temporal categories of, 52, 53; stages of, 52; susceptibility of poor for, 56; temporal sequencing of, 53
climate mitigation, international cooperation on, 7
climate refugees: international protocols for, 50; rights of, 18
climate research, disciplines producing, 51
Clinton (Ohio), downward mobility of, 295
Clinton, Hillary R., immigration stance of, 75
CNN, immigration coverage of, 74
coercion. *See* migration, forcible
Cohen, Cathy: *Democracy Remixed,* 245
Cold War: in Central America, 13, 63–64, 66; displacements of, 4; Latin American migration following, 13
common good: civil authorities' role in, 360, 361; cultural goods in, 363; determination of content, 360–65; ethical demands of, 363; and God of Love, 364; human rights and, 359; human solidarity for, 365; international, 365; in Magisterium of Popes, 360; moral-political conception of, 361; natural law and, 359; private property and, 357; in Stoicism, 359; for survival migration, 358–59; Thomas Aquinas on, 356, 358, 366n7

multicultural citizenship education (MCCE), 232–35, 244–46; in civic education, 232–34

Murphy, Kate, 197

Myanmar, Rohingya exodus from, 10

Myrdal, Gunnar, 321

Nairobi, New Eastleigh School, 225–26

Nansen Initiative (Norway and Sweden): Platform on Disaster Displacement, 51; Protection Agenda of, 50

narratives: of belonging, 29–30; of character, 111; family, 149–50, 152, 153; of refugee camps, 127; therapeutic, 168. *See also* trauma stories

National Academy of Sciences (NAS): on integration of immigrants, 308, 310, 314–15; on race, 317; on second-generation immigrants, 312

National Center for Social Solidarity (EKKA, Greece), unaccompanied minors under, 177

National Centre for Social Research, REHEAL survey of, 21. *See also* Refugees' Healing (REHEAL)

Norwegian University of Science and Technology, REHEAL project of, 181n1

National Registry of Effective Programs and Practices, 148

nation-states: cultural order of, 362; environmental integrity of, 357; hosting refugee education, 253; legality of, 244; legal minorities of, 238; migrants' commitment to, 24; private property in, 357; refugees' integration into, 221–22

native citizens: contact with immigrants, 115; improved perceptions for, 114–15

nativism: in European Union, 4; following September 11 attacks, 107; global, 23–24; in migration policies, 95. *See also* xenophobia

natural disasters: Central American surge and, 68–69; fatalities from, 46; human impact of, 262–63. *See also* catastrophes

natural law: common good and, 359; divine law and, 355; inalienable rights in, 355; and modern human rights, 356; primary, 355–56; protection of children under, 364; reason and, 356; secondary, 355–56; Thomas Aquinas on, 355–56; unaccompanied children under, 364

natural resources, global conflict over, 50

Nayyar, A. H., 223

neighborhoods, immigrant: educational achievement in, 28

Nepal: child soldiers of, 192; environmental displacement in, 7, 32n17; literacy rate of, 222

Newton, Isaac, 254–55

New World, displacement in, 31n5

New York Declaration for Refugees and Migrants (United Nations, 2016), 90, 210; child protection in, 92; on education, 93; education in, 95; employment opportunities in, 95

NGOs, humanitarian assistance model of, 123

Nguyen, Diem, 244, 245

Nicaragua, exodus from, 13

Nietzsche, Friedrich, 364

Nogent-sur-Oise (France), *La main à la pâte* in, 261–62, 262

Noguera, Pedro, 25–26

noncitizens: identity as citizens, 236; length of residence of, 235–36; marginalization of, 240; rights of, 236. *See also* students, noncitizen

non-refoulement (right not be returned), 16

North Africa, displacements through war, 8

Northern Triangle (El Salvador, Honduras, Guatemala): asylum claims from, 65–66; criminal gangs of, 66, 70; lawlessness in, 354; length of journey from, 73; mothers and children from, 18–19, 65, 66–67; remittances to, 63; unaccompanied children from, 65, 85; unauthorized migrants from, 63; volatility of, 73; vulnerable populations of, 68. *See also* Central America; El Salvador; Guatemala; Honduras

Norwegian University of Science and Technology, REHEAL project of, 181n1

Nussbaum, Martha, 237

Obama, Barack: DACA program of, 115n2, 235, 320; deportations under, 33n21; response to immigration surges, 60, 74

Office of Refugee Resettlement (ORR), 364

Oppenheimer, Frank, 255, 265n5

Organization for Economic Cooperation and Development (OECD), 269; children of immigrants and, 27; new research at, 346

Organization for Economic Cooperation and Development (OECD) countries: alienation of students in, 341; attitudes toward immigrants, 347; educational system characteristics of, 332–35; immigrants in disadvantaged schools, 336–38, 340; immigrant student performance in, 264; increased immigration to, 325–26; mathematics attainments in, 331, 332, 335, 339;

refugees (Greece), 165–81, 220, 365; asylum-seeker cards for, 169; deaths of family, 175; discrimination against, 175; ethnicities of, 166, 169, 174; health care services for, 176; relocation emergency plan for, 167; social media usage, 176; traumatic experience by nationality, 175–76; unaccompanied children, 176–80

refugees, Lhotshampa Bhutanese: breathing exercises of, 154; CBPR research assistants work with, 141–55; community advisory boards (CABs) for, 144, 148–49; community-based participatory partnership for, 142; expulsion from Bhutan, 140; Family-Based Preventive Intervention (FBPI) for, 148; key informant (KI) interviews with, 148; problems and protective resources for, 159–60; psychosocial needs of, 156; qualitative data for, 147–48; resettlement in New England, 21, 139–40; suicide rates of, 140, 152. *See also* children, Lhotshampa Bhutanese

refugees, Somali: resettlement in US, 226

refugees, Somali Bantu: *aasiwaalidin* behavior of, 143; advocacy groups for, 141; alcohol prohibition of, 152; CBPR intervention for, 141–55; CBPR study of, 138, 142–43; community advisory boards (CABs) for, 138, 144, 148–49; community-based participatory partnership for, 142; community support for, 144, 155; Family-Based Preventive Intervention (FBPI) for, 148; key informant (KI) interviews with, 143, 148; problems and protective resources for, 159; psychosocial needs of, 156; qualitative data for, 147–48; resettlement in New England, 21, 139–42; use of prayer, 154. *See also* children, Somali Bantu

refugees, Syrian: in Egyptian schools, 224; in Greece, 166; nonformal schooling of, 225; in Turkey, 272, 273–77, 287n2. *See also* children, Syrian; Syria

Refugees' Healing (REHEAL): founders of, 181n1; insights from field, 170

Refugees' Healing (REHEAL) survey, 167–76; bureaucratic hindrances to, 170; constraints on, 169; cultural challenges for, 168; data collection for, 169; ethical challenge for, 167–68; fieldwork in, 182n5; main findings of, 173–76; methodology of, 167–68; paradata from, 170; population for, 168; questionnaire development, 168–69; refugee camps visited, 170–73; sample selection for, 168

Refugees' Healing-Unaccompanied Minors (REHEAL-UAM) survey, 176–79; interviews of, 177–78

religion, racialization and, 108

resettlement: children's eligibility for, 226; of families, 138; of Lhotshampa Bhutanese, 21, 139–40; of Somali Bantu, 21, 139–42; stressors of, 138, 140

Richmond, Anthony, 70

Richmond High School (San Francisco Bay Area), interracial violence in, 298, 299

right to life, priority over ownership, 358

Rohingya: in Bangladeshi refugee camps, 29; exodus from Myanmar, 10

Rumbaut, Ruben G., 100

Russian Empire, minorities in, 2–3

Russian Federation, refugees to, 12

Rwanda: community-level intervention for, 198; HIV in, 148, 156

Sachs, Jeffrey, 17; on Africa, 33n20; on environmental disruptions, 75; on migration demography, 7

Sacks, Oliver, 255

Sahel Belt (Western Africa), sea-level rise in, 48

Saltarelli, Diana, 223

Samos Refugee Camp (Northeastern Aegean): living conditions in, 173; local population and, 173

Sánchez Terán, Gonzalo: on confinement crises, 8, 219; on migration instinct, 83

Save the Children (organization), 87

Schisto Refugee Camp (Attica), living conditions at, 172

Schleicher, Andreas, 26

science: language penalty for, 335; PISA findings on, 264, 330–32, 334; universal interest in, 260–63, 264. *See also* Inquiry-Based Science Education

science education, 24–25; across cultural boundaries, 254–57; big ideas in, 257–58; for children, 252–64; cognitive skills in, 253, 261; curricula for, 257–58; in difficult situations, 261; discovery in, 256; evidence-building in, 259; experimental material for, 263; experimental process in, 255, 261; goals of, 257; for handicapped children, 264; for IDPs, 253; during migration surges, 263; multicultural, 254, 263–64; in natural disaster areas, 263; natural phenomena in, 256; natural skills in, 264; partnerships in, 263; phase transition study, 262; pilot projects for, 252, 253; in

primary school, 259, 261, 262; reasoning in, 256, 261; as reference system, 258; at refugee camps, 263; scientific investigation in, 259; sustainability of programs, 263; teacher training for, 259–60, 263
sea levels, rise in, 48
self-respect, loss though humiliation, 128
September 11 attacks, nativism following, 107
Shanbaro Community Association (Boston), advocacy for Somali Bantu, 141
Sierra Leone, 199; child soldiers of, 190, 192; educational inequalities in, 222
Skaramagas Refugee Camp (Attica): aggressive behavior at, 173; living conditions at, 173
Skyline High School (Oakland): ethnic studies at, 298; interracial violence in, 298
social capital, benefits of, 294
societies: deep values of, 362; mythologized pasts of, 210; survival of, 362
solidarity, global: crisis of, 209–10
Somalia: IDPs of, 9; length of exile from, 16
Somali Bantu, enslavement in Africa, 140. See also children, Somali Bantu; refugees, Somali Bantu
South, US: immigrant population of, 316
South Sudan, 86; children from, 86; environmental collapse in, 10; IDPs of, 9; refugees from, 10, 33n24
Soviet Union, refugees from, 4
Spinoza, Baruch, 361
Spring, Joel, 233
Stages of Cultural Identity Typology, 240–45; Biculturalism, 242, 243; Cultural Encapsulation, 242, 243; Cultural Identity Clarification, 242; Cultural Psychological Captivity, 242, 243; Globalism and Global Competency, 242; Multiculturalism and Reflective Nationalism, 242, 243
Starkey, Hugh, 237
Stathopoulou, Theoni, 21; on no-man zones, 29; refugee displacement studies, 138
STEM subjects (science, technology, engineering, and mathematics), teaching of, 252–53
stereotypes, combatting, 115
St. Louis (Missouri), homicide rate of, 33n31
Stoicism, common good in, 359
stress: acculturative, 138; among Syrian children, 85; displaced children's, 28, 104, 138, 187, 320; duration of exposure to, 191; family, 137, 138, 152; holistic intervention for, 150; parental, 139, 191, 197; research on, 198; of resettlement, 138, 140. See also mental health; trauma

students, citizen: civic education for, 232–47; failed citizenship of, 244, 245; internalization of values, 235; marginalization of, 245; multicultural citizenship education for, 244–46; structural inclusion for, 244. See also children of immigrants; education
students, immigrant: academic outcomes of, 326; alienation of, 341; attitudes toward diversity, 347; background characteristics of, 327; at Boston schools, 300–303; cognitive development of, 342; collaborative learning for, 347, 348; connection with shool environment, 328; country of origin, 345; in disadvantaged schools, 336–38, 340; dropout rates of, 330–31; educational delays, 327; as educational liability, 327; effect of education system characteristics on, 332–35, 345; emotional well-being of, 328, 341; family relationships of, 342; geographical differences affecting, 327; grade repetition by, 338–39; integration of, 325–48; language proficiency of, 327, 331, 332, 335, 336, 345; life satisfaction among, 342, 344; mathematics attainments of, 331, 332, 335, 339, 345; mix with nonimmigrants, 336–38; negative sentiments toward, 347; nonachievements of, 340–42; performance differences for, 330–33, 335–36, 338–40; performance in OECD countries, 264; from poor households, 327; psychological development of, 341; readiness to learn, 339; reading performances, 330, 336, 345; relocation of, 337; resilience of, 327; school resources for, 338; science attainments, 264, 330–32, 333, 335, 339, 345; sense of belonging, 330, 340–42, 343; social development of, 341; social well-being of, 328, 340–41; socioeconomic status of, 331, 333–34, 342, 346; stratification of, 338–40; time missed from school, 339–40; in US education, 293–305. See also children, migrant; education, immigrant
students, noncitizen: acceptance for, 240; civic education for, 232–47; cosmopolitanism and, 236, 244; development of cultural identity, 241; discrimination against, 241; human rights and, 236; integration of, 299, 302; knowledge of victimization, 241; marginalization of, 299; self-acceptance among, 240. See also children, migrant; education, immigrant; education, refugee

www.ingramcontent.com/pod-product-compliance
Lightning Source LLC
Chambersburg PA
CBHW020451270326
41926CB00008B/562